THE CIVILIZATION OF GREECE

THE CIVILIZATION OF ROME
by Pierre Grimal
Translated by W. S. Maguinness

FRANÇOIS CHAMOUX

THE CIVILIZATION OF GREECE

TRANSLATED BY PROFESSOR W. S. MAGUINNESS
King's College, London

ILLUSTRATED

SIMON AND SCHUSTER · NEW YORK · 1965

*Published by Simon and Schuster, Inc.
Rockefeller Center, 630 Fifth Avenue, New York 20, N.Y.*

First Printing

Library of Congress Catalog Card Number: 65-23245

*Lord Phoebus, who hast fenced our citadel
with walls, ward off the threat of Persian
attack from my native city. Then the
people will come to honour thee in the
first days of spring, bringing thee
splendid hecatombs in glad revelry, en-
joying the merry festival with the music
of lutes, hymns, dances, and cries of
rapture around thy altar. How dark
the future seems to me when I see the
Greeks ready to ruin themselves with
their senseless discord! But be thou
gracious unto us, Phoebus, and guard this
native city of mine.*

INVOCATION TO PHOEBUS APOLLO
Elegy surviving under the name
of Theognis of Megara, lines 773 ff.

PREFACE

The Civilization of Greece in the Archaic and Classical Age, by François Chamoux, is the second volume in a series brilliantly inaugurated by Pierre Grimal's *The Civilization of Rome*. The two books form a pair, and each of them will enrich our knowledge of the ancient world.

As for the division at the beginning of the Hellenistic Age, it is to be explained by the difference of the subjects and the facts of the case. In spite of the vast sweep of Rome's historical career both in time and in space, her civilization retains a character of real and deep-seated unity. This is not so in the case of Greek civilization. In it there is a line of profound division, coinciding with Alexander's conquests. At this point we witness a complete transformation in Greek life. The small cities of Greece proper, with their diminutive territories, were thenceforth dominated by huge states with large populations and great wealth, mainly Oriental in situation and character. The position and rôle of the individual, which had been outstanding and fundamental in the framework of the Greek city-state, diminished and disappeared. The individual ceased to be a citizen and became a subject in monarchical states in which all powers and rights were concentrated in the person of a sovereign. This development was accompanied by a shift in the centre of gravity of religion; king-worship now united the multitudes in a devotion absolutely foreign to the mentality of Greece in earlier times. There was a change in the course of history, so that the Hellenistic world has to be examined separately.

At the beginning of the work François Chamoux explains his purpose, which is to offer the reader a sort of meditation on the main aspects of archaic and classical Hellenism. And indeed long intimacy with the land and people of Greece and deep love of a civilization to which we are united by so many ties find expression from beginning to end of a presentation whose sobriety and elegance are fully worthy of the people with which it deals. An extensive and authoritative fund of literary, epigraphical, and archaeological knowledge, the result of personal research and discoveries, sustains and strengthens the texture of the work throughout, giving it a quality of richness, concreteness, and precision. This explains the most striking thing about the book, the way in which, as if by a kind of natural necessity, general considerations and ideas arise out of direct acquaintance with places, persons, and things.

The impression which emerges from the course of events is that Greece, a country split up to an extreme degree, was the scene of incessant wars and conflicts. Political particularism brought about disorder, enfeeblement, and finally loss of liberty. The fact is that the Greek had, as the basic framework of his life, the city, a city whose population and territory were small, but which nevertheless dominated his whole existence. He fought for it, worshipped its gods, whose immediate presence he felt and with whom he kept up a daily dialogue, and took a direct part in its administration and government. As a result the Greek could define with brilliant clarity the relationship between the state and the individual and set forth the ideal of all political life: harmony among citizens united in their respect for the laws.

Nevertheless, beyond the frontiers of the city-states, too jealously closed against one another, feelings of fellowship did on several occasions succeed in rousing the Greek people against an invader. These feelings were based upon the possession of a common language and religion. But, as Francois Chamoux rightly states, the Greek people, more than any other, needed its literature and art in order to achieve full self-awareness. Their spiritual unity was soon asserted by their exceptional gifts and constant success in these two domains. The extreme beauty of the country and the limpidity of its light were matched by brilliance of intellectual productions and artistic creations.

Thus there takes shape before our eyes the living picture sketched by François Chamoux of an epoch in the history of humanity towards which our memories and our affection most often turn. His book seems to me destined to render great service and to endure. It entitles him to our highest gratitude.

RAYMOND BLOCH

TRANSLATOR'S ACKNOWLEDGMENT

The translator acknowledges with gratitude help and advice on various points given by Professors J. M. Cocking and P. E. Corbett of the University of London. Also Mrs A. M. Cameron, who produced the index for this volume.

Photographs which are reproduced in this volume were provided as follows:

A. Abegg, 6. Acropolis Museum, Athens, 49. Alinari, 89, 90, 153, 158, 159, 171. Alinari-Giraudon, 82. Alinari-Viollet, 86, 225. American School, Athens, 113, 114. Anderson, 164, 166. Anderson-Viollet, 68. Archaeological Museum, Ferrara, 198. B. Arthaud, 11, 12, 33, 34, 39, 51, 69, 70, 73, 77, 78, 79, 95, 96, 115, 120, 127, 130–3, 136–40, 178, 194, 196, 201, 202–4, 206–9, 220, 222, colour plates II to VI. Ashmolean Museum, Oxford, 152. Bibliothèque Nationale, 35, 205. Boudot Lamotte, 10, 22, 25, 53, 65, 87, 88, 102–4, 172, 181–2, 218. British Museum, 44–7, 50, 134–5, 155, 200, 229. M. Chuzeville, 19. R. Descharnes, 37, 58, 80, 81, 185–8, 221, 223–4, 226–7, colour plate VIII. Ecole française d'Athènes, 17, 38, 57, 64, 105, 118, 191. Fotonews, Ravenna, 42. German Archaeological Institute, Athens, 21, 23, 59, 83, 84, 228. Giraudon, 28, 48, 54, 74, 123–5, 199, 217. Glyptothek Antiker Kleinkunst, Munich, 111. Glyptotheque Ny Carlsberg, Copenhagen, 157, 160, 165, 170. Greek Royal Air Force, 1, 2, 3, 8, 40, 66, 67, 116, 119. Hirmer, Munich, 72, 91–3, 156. K. Konstantopoulos, 94, 108, 110. Kunsthistorisches Museum, Vienna, 60–2. J. Lacarriere, 4. Leonard von Matt, 175. L. Y. Loirat, 99, 117, 173–4, 179. Louis-Frederic (Agence Rapho), 16, 26, 101, 107, 112, 183, 184, 216. Metropolitan Museum of Art, 142–3, 150–1. S. Moulinier, 176–7, 180, 215. Museum of Fine Arts, Boston, 29, 31, 36, 63, 76, 121, 122, 126, 144–9, 154, 167, 169, 193, 197, 210–14. Nationalmuseet, Copenhagen, 24. National Museum, Athens, 13. Nicosia Museum, 15, 20. R. Obligi, 75, 85, 97, 98. Roger-Viollet, 5, 7, 9, 55, 56, 100, 106. Samivel, 219. Scavi, Cyrene, 190. Soprintendenza alle antichita, Naples, 161–2. Soprintendenza alle antichita, Ostia, 43. Soprintendenza alle antichita, Rome, 163. Soprintendenza alle antichita, Tarento, 141. Staaliche Museum, Berlin, 52, 71, 128–9, 168, 189. J. P. Sudre, colour plates I and VII. Tel, 32, 195. O. Vaering Naisjona Galleriet, Oslo, 41. G. Vehrheim, Antiksammlungen, Munich, 27. G. Viollon, 30. H. & J. B. Wace, 18.

CONTENTS

B

ILLUSTRATIONS

MAPS AND PLANS

INTRODUCTION

Object and method of the book

The debt owed by the modern world to the Greek people is an immense one. It was the Greeks who first defined the categories of thought that we still employ. We owe to them not only the main part of our intellectual tools, but also the principles of our morality. Even the teaching of Christianity, which still inspires all Western civilization, reached us through the agency of Greek thought, which elaborated and systematized its basic doctrines. It made the universal character of Christianity perceptible to all and acted as its swift and effective medium of transmission: we must not forget that Greek was the language of the early Church. Here, as elsewhere, Rome at first played only a secondary part, before taking over the task and finally emerging, thanks to the contribution of her own genius, as the mistress and guide of the West. Everyone admits the prime importance of the contribution made by Hellenism to the common heritage brought to fruition with varying success by our thinkers and artists during the last fifteen centuries.

The people of today have therefore a lively curiosity about a nation and civilization to which we feel so largely indebted. This curiosity can find abundant satisfaction, since the sources of our knowledge of ancient Greece are exceptionally rich and varied. The Greek language is represented by an uninterrupted series of literary texts from the eighth century B.C. down to the present. The recent decipherment of the Mycenaean tablets even makes it possible to go back at least as far as the fifteenth century B.C., though the documents in question are purely administrative and difficult to interpret. No other language offers for study so rich a literature extending over so long a period of history, nearly three thousand five hundred years. Side by side with these literary sources, archaeology provides us with information about Greece that is extremely copious and, on the whole, very well classified. The monuments brought to light and studied by archaeology are not only of interest in informing us about the civilization to which they bear witness; they often possess an aesthetic value as well, to which we are still responsive, independently of their remoteness in time. Finally (and this is by no means the least favourable factor), the country in which the Greeks lived, in which they evolved their conception of the world and their moral philosophy, is easily accessible to us. Nothing is easier nowadays than to visit Greece, and we have (and shall still have for some time to come) the privilege of discovering at small expense the same landscapes that Homer, Sophocles, and Plato once beheld, still preserving their genuine appearance, largely unspoilt by the uniformity of modern life.

Such are the means at the disposal of a modern man who desires a better knowledge of the distant origins of his own thought. The material is certainly abundant enough to astonish the layman; the professional Hellenist, conscious of the precariousness of his learning and the weakness of his powers, obviously unequal to such an extensive task, might reasonably shrink from the attempt. Yet this is hardly a reason for continuing to put off an attempt at synthesis, difficult no doubt, but of an urgency clear to anyone who senses the need our fellow-countrymen have in the present age to establish clear contact with their own history. Their need is to safeguard against the perils that assail it the vigour and continuity of a civilization that has made us what we are, but whose universal value and originality we are too often in danger of failing to appreciate. Let his keen awareness of such a necessity in our time provide the author of this book with the excuse he needs for having undertaken it!

In any case his object is not and could not have been to contribute an epitome, reduced to the dimensions of a single volume, of all the knowledge of ancient Greece that we owe to the labours of Hellenists, archaeologists, philologists, and historians. Such a claim would be laughable, and he explicitly renounces it. The toil of a lifetime would be insufficient for it and, whatever pains one could bring to the task, such a work would always suffer from some serious gaps or some major defect of proportion. The purpose is rather to offer the reader, in an accessible and relaxed form, a kind of meditation on the main aspects of Archaic and Classical Hellenism as they appear today to a man who has made the study of them his profession for the last twenty-five years. The subject-matter of these reflections, the ground covered and the direction taken, will depend to a considerable degree on the subjects of research that have been offered to the author by the accidents of his career. That is why certain aspects may seem to have been expatiated on to a surprising extent, at the expense of other subjects, which will

I. GREECE AND THE ISLANDS IN THE AEGEAN SEA

perhaps seem to have been unjustly neglected. Still it was better to admit this risk frankly than to introduce at all costs a deceptive and studied equilibrium. Even if every human task is liable to imperfection, at least this book would wish, kind reader, to be an 'honest' book.

The natural setting

We no longer think, as Taine did, that everything, or nearly everything, can be accounted for by the influence of natural setting and climate. It is men who make history, and they take advantage of geographical conditions in proportion to their perseverance and ingenuity. But it is true that these conditions render their task harder or easier and that inversely they play a part in moulding the characters of peoples. Anyone who has visited Greece and the surrounding regions cannot doubt that this area of the Mediterranean exercised the most beneficent influence on its ancient inhabitants. If for the modern, equipped with so many different means of escaping from the exigencies of the soil and the vagaries of climate, the Aegean world still holds such strong attraction, how must it have been in an age when man's dependence upon natural conditions was much more pronounced than it is today? Let us then recall in broad outline the nature of this privileged country.

Greece proper forms the southern extremity of the Balkan peninsula. It is a land of moderate dimensions: it is hardly more than 400 kilometres from the mountain mass of Olympus, which marks the northern boundary of Thessaly, to Cape Taenarus (or Cape Matapan), the most southern point of the Peloponnesus. But this little country is extremely split up on account of its mountainous nature and its extremely indented coasts. Thus even now one who travels through the country gets the impression that it is much larger than its dimensions on the map would lead him to believe. The variety of the landscape, nearly always characterized by mountains soaring upwards, often combined with views of the sea, still further intensifies this impression of breadth and volume that excites the spectator.

Continental Greece, continued beyond the Gulf of Corinth by the peninsula of the Peloponnesus (or Morea), is in fact covered nearly everywhere by mountains which, if not very lofty (none reaches 3,000 metres), are at least very steep. The only two plains of any importance are the plain of Boeotia, a large part of which was occupied in ancient times by Lake Copais, now drained, and, further

to the north, the plain of Thessaly, the only one in which it is often possible not
to see a mountain barrier on the horizon. Everywhere else all that can be found is
small inland basins between the mountains and hills, or terraced stretches on the
hillsides rarely more than twenty kilometres long. Between these basins the
relief is usually broken up in such a way as to permit the use of narrow passes,
traversed by hill tracks or precipitous and winding valleys. It may also happen
that the sea, gliding deeply between the mountains, offers a convenient line of
communication: no point in Greece proper is more than 90 kilometres from the
coast.

The Greece of the islands is the natural complement of mainland Greece.
More important than the Ionian Islands, somewhat isolated on the edge of the
lonely stretches of the central Mediterranean, are the islands of the Aegean Sea.
Closed towards the south by the long, narrow, and lofty barrier of Crete, which
reaches a height of 2,500 metres with Mount Ida, and to the north by the coasts
of Macedonia and Thrace, this sea is so dotted with islands that a ship rarely
passes out of sight of land. From Euboea to Rhodes, the Cyclades and the southern Sporades (or Dodecanese) form a continuous chain of land rising from the
sea. Thanks to these mountainous islands, which provide a refuge or a shelter for
the seafarer, the whole Aegean basin has always been virtually a dependency of
Greece.

Most of these islands have a stony soil, lacking in fresh water, not at all favourable to vegetation. Only the largest of the Cyclades—Andros, Tenos, Naxos,
Paros and Melos—provide better conditions. The volcanic island of Santorin
(Thera in antiquity) is particularly fertile, owing to its pumice-stone soil, but
lack of a natural harbour has proved an obstacle to its development. The large
islands of the Asia Minor coast, Lesbos, Chios, and Samos, barely separated
from the mainland by narrow channels, are richer: they naturally participate in
the life of the Anatolian seaboard. Rhodes, to the south, occupies a place apart,
rather far from the centre. To the north, Samothrace, Thasos, and the three
prongs of Chalcidice form the advance posts of Thrace and Macedonia. Between
them and the Cyclades, Lemnos, Scyros, and the archipelago of the Sporades
provide useful landmarks throughout the southern half of the Aegean Sea.

There are certainly considerable differences between the regions of such a
varied country: while the summits of Pindus are covered with Alpine forests,
Delos and Cythera are just bare rocks, and in summer the smiling countryside of

C

Elis, with horizons always green, is in striking contrast with the dusty, sun-scorched plain of Thessaly. But these variations, apart from extreme cases, play a part only within a geographical whole which derives a basic unity from its Mediterranean climate. In ancient times the climate was already regarded as particularly favourable. According to Herodotus, 'Greece is blessed with by far the most temperate seasons' (III, 106). Sea and mountain, and still more the action of the etesian winds (now known in the Cyclades as the *meltem*), render the heat of the long summer tolerable. The winter, generally mild, is the rainy season, but also has fine sunny days. Frost is certainly not unknown, and some-times there is snow, even in Attica, but these rigours of the weather, like the rare but impressive storms, do not last long. In short, it is a healthy and bracing clim-ate, favourable to outdoor life. The purity of the air is justly famous: Euripides praises the atmosphere of Athens, 'the clearest and brightest of all' (*Medea*, 829–830). Real rivers, like the Achelous and Arachthus in Acarnania and Epirus, the Peneus in Thessaly, and the Alpheus in Arcadia and Elis, are rare, but there is no lack of springs, except in the Cyclades, where tanks are generally used.

The soil lends itself to various forms of cultivation: cereals (barley and wheat), vines, olives, and figs. Heavy cattle can find grazing only in the mountains or in the plain of Thessaly, whose horses were renowned. On the other hand, sheep, goats, and pigs can easily find food in the brush. Game was found in pro-fusion in ancient times: rabbits and hares, wild birds, boars, stags, and fallow-deer. There were also savage beasts: bears, wolves, and even lions, which were still being hunted in the mountains of the north during the Classical period. The lakes provided plenty of fish, for example, the eels of Lake Copais in Boeotia, which were exported to Athens. Sea fishing was actively pursued, the catch ranging from anchovies and sardines to large fish such as tunny. The Greeks also knew the art of bee-keeping at a very early date. Both soil and subsoil provided a variety of resources: excellent building stone, such as the freestone (or *poros*) of Sicyon, the blue-grey limestone of Parnassus and the marbles of the Cyclades, Thasos or Attica; clay, from which unbaked bricks could be made and which also enabled the potter's craft to develop so successfully, especially when this clay was, as in Attica, of exceptional quality; useful and precious metals. There is copper in Euboea; silver in Thasos, in Siphnos (in the Cyclades), and above all in the hills of Laurion, at the tip of Attica; gold in Thasos and on the neighbour-ing mainland in Thrace. The iron ore, although of mediocre quality, is at least very widely found. Even obsidian, a black stone as hard and sharp as glass, so rare and so highly valued in neolithic times, is found in abundance in Melos.

Greece thus offers conditions favourable to those who inhabit it; yet man must prove himself worthy of it and make the effort necessary to profit from it. For, side by side with the advantages bestowed by nature, there are some serious disadvantages. The threat of earthquakes is very real: Corinth, Santorin, and Cephallenia have suffered cruelly from them in our own times. Excellent though the arable land may be, it only amounts to 18 per cent of the area, and the farmer had constantly to protect it against erosion or to irrigate to combat drought. The extreme partitioning of the soil, because of the mountainous nature of the country, promoted the growth of political units on a small scale but was unfavourable to the establishing of a major state. While the sea, penetrating at all points, facilitated communication with the outside world, export and import could only be established by dint of hard work and ingenuity; Greece could only export products fashioned by means of complicated techniques, wine, oil, perfumes, and terracotta or metal objects, while she stood in need of certain raw materials and especially of wheat. Her inadequate production of cereals placed her under a constant threat of shortage of food: the moment there was an increase in population, she would immediately suffer from 'lack of land', the *stenochoria* which was one of the main causes of Greek emigration to foreign lands. The Greek people was therefore committed to a programme of activity, intelligence, and expansion in order to avoid decline. This was a stimulating, if uncomfortable, situation, and their history shows that they managed to turn it to good account in a spirited way.

CHAPTER I

MYCENAEAN CIVILIZATION

The Mycenaeans were Greeks

RECENT years have witnessed an event of great importance for Greek history: a form of writing known as *Linear B,* which had until then remained a mystery, was deciphered in 1953 by the Englishmen Ventris and Chadwick, and the progress made since then has confirmed what the two British scholars had recognized at once, that the language thus transcribed was Greek. This discovery is of supreme importance, not so much perhaps for the actual contents of the texts that we can now understand as for the new light it has begun to shed on the origins of Hellenic civilization. It was, indeed, well known from the legendary traditions assembled in the Homeric poems, the historians and the mythographers, that Indo-European peoples, precursors of the Greeks of the Heroic Age and closely akin to them, had made their way into the peninsula in the course of the second millennium B.C. According to Homer they were called Achaeans, and their name was thought to be recognized in certain Egyptian and Hittite documents. They were assumed to have played a decisive part in the development of the so-called Mycenaean civilization, which had been revealed by excavations on the Greek mainland and at numerous other sites in the Mediterranean basin. But the tendency was to accentuate the kinship between this civilization and Cretan civilization, brought to light by Sir Arthur Evans at the beginning of the century from the ruins of Cnossus in Crete, and the conviction persisted that there was a complete break between the blossoming of Mycenaean culture, during the fourteenth and thirteenth centuries B.C., and the beginnings of Archaic Greece in the eighth. The obscure period known as the Middle Ages of Greece, with the profound disorders it experienced, of which we can catch glimpses, but of which we know little, was regarded as dividing two worlds, the pre-Hellenic world of the second millennium, assumed to have ended in the twelfth century in the disturbances resulting from the Dorian invasion, and the Greek world properly so called, beginning with Homer. It is true that, for twenty years before, the work of archaeologists, relying on numerous vases discovered mainly in Attic cemeteries, had enabled these views to be somewhat modified; a certain continuity began to appear between Mycenaean art and Geometric art, from the twelfth to the eighth century. To designate the stages of this transition, the terms *sub-Mycenaean* and *protogeometric* had been adopted, and a relative chronology for pottery was being gradually established. But there was still hesitation about proceeding to firm conclusions on the historical plane, and the Mycenaeans were still regarded as a pre-Hellenic people.

It is this opinion, so generally accepted, that must henceforth be abandoned. When they read for the first time the documents written in Linear B, Ventris and Chadwick established the fact that the Mycenaeans were Greeks, or at least that they spoke Greek, which for us is the main point, since entitlement to the description 'Hellenic' is primarily shown by possession of the language. Since then we have been obliged to admit that Greek history and civilization do not begin in the eighth century, but at the moment when the first decipherable texts appear, that is to say in the middle of the second millennium, about the end of the fifteenth century, perhaps even earlier. The whole Mycenaean civilization henceforth forms a part of Hellenism, no longer as a foreword, but as the opening chapter of its history, which thus begins at least six hundred years earlier than had been thought. Henceforth we know the Greek language from texts extending from the fifteenth century B.C. to our own times, a period of over three thousand years: this is a unique phenomenon, of supreme interest for linguists. Looking at it from another point of view, we no longer see the early stages of Archaic Greece as a beginning, but as a continuation or a rebirth, and this new view of the past warrants our emphasizing, not a break between the two ages, but their continuity. The Mycenaean Age emerges from pre-Hellenic times and passes into history; the heroes of epic become men again for us.

Linear B and the Mycenaean tablets

What is this Linear B, whose decipherment brought such consequences in its train? From 1900 to 1904, Sir Arthur Evans was bringing to light in his excavations at Cnossus, among other surprising objects, clay tablets that bore what looked like writing, clearly of a non-alphabetical kind. A preliminary sorting out made it possible to distinguish between two fairly similar, yet different, systems of symbols of simplified design, to which the names *Linear A* and *Linear B* were given. The number of Linear B documents from Cnossus is about three thousand. Shortly before the Second World War, in 1939, the American Carl Blegen, who was exploring the site of a Mycenaean palace at Pylus in Messenia, found a set of 600 tablets inscribed in Linear B, to which others were added in the course of excavations resumed after the war; there are now about a thousand of them. Finally, in the years following 1950, the English archaeologist A. J. B. Wace and his fellow-workers, who had now begun new investigations at Mycenae, found about fifty new tablets in the ruins of houses near the citadel. The material for study is increasing every year as a result of new discoveries.

From the beginning scholars had made a great effort to interpret these documents. They had carefully compared and classified them, but without succeeding in understanding them, since they had not at their disposal any bilingual document capable of helping them as the Rosetta Stone helped Champollion. So they were reduced to groping in the dark until the young English architect Michael Ventris, starting from the hypothesis that the language written in Linear B was Greek, established, with the help of his fellow-countryman John Chadwick, satisfactory equivalences and a coherent process of transcription. In an article which appeared in 1953 in the *Journal of Hellenic Studies* and excited widespread interest they communicated their initial findings and offered an interpretation of sixty-five out of the some ninety symbols known in Linear B. Since then, in spite of Ventris's death in a motor accident in 1956, the work of decipherment has been continued with enthusiasm and tenacity, essentially confirming the discovery by the young scholar whom an untimely death had removed.

Linear B is a graphic system whose symbols mostly represent syllables. In addition to the signs with a syllabic value there are certain ideograms that represent words as a whole (man, woman, wheat, chariot, cup, bronze, etc.), other symbols representing units of calculation or measure, and finally numerals. These signs were cut by means of a stylet on tablets of soft clay, which were sometimes in the shape of a rectangular slab like a page of a notebook, on which the lines of writing go from left to right and are usually separated by a horizontal line, and were sometimes of a narrow oblong form, only providing enough space for one or two lines of writing. The signs consist of a few lines forming a simple shape. Only the ideograms sometimes suggest a concrete image with some degree of precision. The numerals are in accordance with the decimal system; there are in addition special signs for fractions.

It is fairly clear that this system of transcription, which the Greeks borrowed from the Cretans, had not originally been devised for the Greek language. In fact it is established that the values ascribed to the different signs in the syllabary require to be treated with a certain freedom in order to achieve a coherent transcription into a Greek dialect, even of a very archaic type. Most of the diphthongs are not indicated as such and no distinction is made between long and short vowels, between voiced, unvoiced, and aspirated consonants, or between the liquids *l* and *r*. For example, the same sign can be read as *pe* or *phe*; another will represent either *lo* or *ro*. Moreover the final consonant in a syllable, if there is one, is generally not indicated. Thus the Greek word *elephantei*, meaning 'ivory' (dative case), is written *e-re-pa-te* in Linear B, while *doulos*, meaning 'slave' (nominative case), is written *do-e-ro*.

These brief indications show the difficulties involved in the reading of these texts: but, due allowance being made for some signs that are still puzzling and some uncertain transcriptions, the progress achieved since 1953 has been continuous and the principles of Ventris's decipherment are no longer seriously contested; from now on eminent linguists will devote themselves to the task of defining the original features of 'Mycenaean philology' with these texts as their starting-point. But it is already possible to indicate some details of the information which they give us.

The Mycenaean tablets have not yet given us any literary texts, contracts, or correspondence, or treaties between rulers. As yet we have only documents for record purposes from the administrative departments attached to the palaces of Cnossus, Pylus, and Mycenae. They contain inventories of property, stores, livestock, pieces of furniture; lists of officials, workmen, and soldiers; statements of dues owed to the sovereign or offerings made to divinities. These documents were clearly not made to last: they served a purely practical purpose, the keeping of the palace accounts. For precisely this reason they put us in direct contact with the

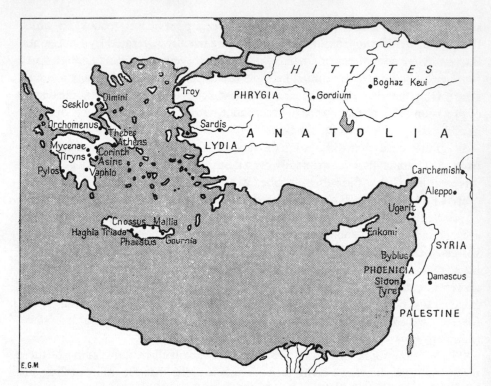

2. THE NEAR EAST AT THE END OF THE SECOND MILLENNIUM B.C.

daily life of the first Greek people that we meet in history. We not only learn
what language it spoke but also see something of its social organization. The
sovereign governed his subjects and his domain with the aid of officials whose
duty it was to keep his records up to date. His stores were kept supplied by
compulsory contributions in kind: wheat, oil, wine, honey, and also aromatic
herbs and spices, mint, fennel, sesame, coriander, and cumin. A census was kept
of herds grazing far from the palace. Artisans (some free, some slaves) worked
for the master; smiths were supplied with bronze ingots as their raw material:
potters fashioned various kinds of vases; carpenters and wheelwrights made
furniture, chariots, and wheels. Some texts allude to troop movements or naval
operations. Lastly, others mention the names of deities to whom offerings were
made.

Birth, growth, and culmination of Mycenaean civilization

Thus the first Greek civilization in history comes to life again before our eyes, not in the details of political events, but at least in certain aspects of its religious and social organization. At the time at which it is revealed to us by the Mycenaean tablets, it had already been established in the Aegean basin for several centuries. It was apparently at the beginning of the second millennium B.C. that the first Hellenes spread over Greece proper, starting from the northern regions, Macedonia and Thessaly, into which they had made their way earlier. They mingled with a population already settled in Greece of whose industrial activities we have knowledge from neolithic times (as far back as about the middle of the third millennium), and later in the so-called *Early Bronze Age* (about 2500 to 1900 B.C.). The newcomers imposed their language on these earlier inhabitants, an Indo-European language, which was to become Mycenaean Greek. The civilization known as *Middle Bronze*, stretching roughly from 1900 to 1600, was the result of fusion between these invaders and the existing population; while the new type of house, with a *megaron*, became common, a kind of pottery made on the wheel, the so-called *Minyan ware*, with shapes imitated from metalwork, began to appear side by side with the traditional unglazed pottery.

From the beginning of the *Late Bronze Age* (about 1600–1100 B.C.), the mainland Greeks, whose relations had until then been chiefly with the northeastern part of the Aegean Sea and the Cyclades, entered into frequent contact with Minoan Crete. This contact proved of decisive importance. From now onwards the warlike Greeks found themselves in touch with an ancient, brilliant, and refined civilization. At this period Crete was a centralized state, with a capital, Cnossus, with a population of more than 50,000. Here a rich and powerful monarch reigned, surrounded by an aristocracy with a taste for court life, palaces adorned with frescos, comfortable manor-houses, festivals and games. Thanks to a thriving sea trade, Cretan commerce flourished and spread abroad the products of an original and delicate art. The Greeks very soon came under the influence of these southern neighbours. They were then tempted to go and take a closer look at the country from which such riches reached them; they had developed a taste for navigation and soon they became past masters of the art. If we stick to the interpretation of the archaeological facts which has been traditional since the time of Evans (but which has recently been questioned), they landed in Crete about 1450 B.C. and overthrew the Minoan state, establishing themselves in its place. Then followed the period, from the middle of the fifteenth century to about the twelfth, when the Mycenaean Greeks were overlords of the Aegean basin and distributed their manufactured products over a very wide area, from Syria and Egypt to southern Italy and Sicily. The international situation favoured them, since the two great empires of the Hittites and the Egyptians had established a certain mutual equilibrium and the states of Palestine and Syria, which lay between them and were nominally dependent on one or other of them, nevertheless enjoyed great liberty in their economic relationships. The Greeks took advantage of this to develop their commerce in these intervening regions, in Cyprus, where they seem to have settled as early as this period, at Ugarit (Ras Shamra) on the Syrian coast and in the Syro-Palestinian hinterland. The Trojan War, which, as the recently published American excavations have shown, really took place about the end of the twelfth century, was one of the latest episodes in this expansion, which was to be succeeded immediately afterwards, during the twelfth century, by a profound and lasting decline.

Schliemann. Tombs and palaces at Mycenae. Tiryns. Pylus
It is, therefore, during this brilliant period, from the end of the fifteenth to the end of the thirteenth century B.C., that we have to consider the first Greek civilization, then at its height. It owes the name *Mycenaean*, by which it is generally known, to the importance of Mycenae, in Argolis, the site which the German Schliemann investigated in 1876 with extraordinary results. The intrepid excavator was impelled by his desire to discover the grave of Agamemnon. If Fortune had not this joy in store for him, it gave him much more, since it was the whole Greek civilization of the second millennium, theretofore entirely forgotten, which rose from the soil of Mycenae. A royal cemetery, with rudely sculptured stelae, surrendered the secrets of its grave-tombs, in which the remains of the entombed were found along with weapons and magnificent pieces of jewellery: diadems, necklaces, rings, bracelets, gold plaques sewn onto garments, gold belts and baldricks, gold face masks that preserved the features of the dead, cups and vases of precious metal, inlaid swords and daggers with sheaths decorated with gold studs; all these brilliant ornaments are now assembled in the great Mycenaean gallery of the National Museum at Athens and bear witness to the splendour of the Greek dynasty that ruled Argolis in the sixteenth century B.C. This is the date ascribed to this cemetery on the basis of the archaeological

material (pottery and ivory and metal objects) found there by the excavators.

The successors of this dynasty, in the following century, were buried in tombs of a completely different shape, which are among the most extraordinary creations of antiquity. Such a tomb is called *tholos*, from the name given by the Greeks to buildings of rotunda type. They are round chambers hollowed in the ground, with corbelled conical ceilings made with successive courses of large stone blocks carefully bonded. Access is by an open trench or *dromos*, leading to an enormous and richly decorated doorway. The most noteworthy of these tombs is the one traditionally called the *Treasury of Atreus*; it is in the side of a hill facing the acropolis of Mycenae, and was built in the second half of the fourteenth century. Its vault remains intact, but the architectural decoration of the entrance has disappeared. The spacious dimensions of the interior (more than 13 metres high with a diameter of 14·5 metres), the enormous blocks serving as a lintel above the doorway (one of them weighs almost a hundred metric tons), and the quality of the bonding still make a deep impression on the visitor.

The same admirable qualities of construction are to be seen, a short distance away, in the fortifications of the great walls that surround the citadel area. The famous *Lion Gate*, with the wall and bastion flanking it, dates from the middle of the fourteenth century. Made of enormous blocks, which have resisted both earthquakes and the destructive endeavours of man, it still presents an imposing appearance. The relieving triangle above the lintel is filled by a monolithic relief of grey stone, representing a heraldic emblem, two lions facing each other with their forepaws resting on the pedestal of a sacred pillar. This sculptural scheme is borrowed from the Cretan decorative tradition, but the technique of the monumental sculpture is unexampled in Crete and must be peculiar to the Greeks of the mainland.

Mycenae is in the heart of a mountainous region, on a wild site which fully suggests to modern eyes the sombre tragedies ascribed by the imagination of the classical Greeks to the family of the Atridae. In the plain of Argolis, fifteen kilometres to the south, and barely two kilometres from the sea, there is a small isolated piece of rising ground that bears other Cyclopean ruins, those of the palace of Tiryns. The strength of the surrounding walls, the gigantic dimensions of the stone blocks of which they are composed (these reach three metres in length) are still more tremendous here than at Mycenae. At Tiryns, as at Mycenae, the fortress sheltered a palace, the plan of which is still better preserved.

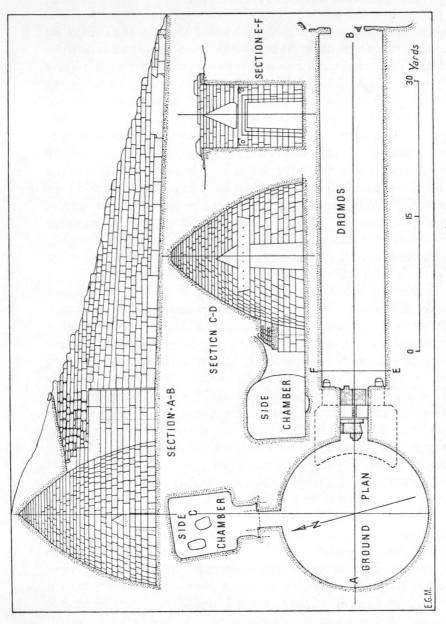

SECTION E-F

SECTION C-D

SECTION A-B

SIDE CHAMBER

SIDE CHAMBER

DROMOS

GROUND PLAN

A

B

E

F

N

0   15   30 Yards

E.G.M.

3. PLAN OF THE 'TREASURY OF ATREUS' AT MYCENAE

(*After A. J. B. Wace*). This magnificent tomb, formerly known as the Treasury of Atreus, dates from about 1325 B.C. The underground funeral chamber is approached by a long unroofed passage-way (*dromos*) flanked by side walls of masonry. The doorway is surmounted by two enormous monolithic lintels above which there is a relieving triangle. The interior is a vaulted bee-hive formation. There was a side chamber, hewn straight into the rock.

It is here that we see the first appearance of a form of architecture to which the Greeks were to remain devoted: the *propylaea*, that is to say a monumental gateway in which the gate piercing a wall was fronted on each side of the wall by a porch with columns. This arrangement was employed in the two successive courtyards of the palace at Tiryns. In the far wall of the second courtyard, which was surrounded by porticos on its other three sides, there was a door with a still larger porch, leading through an antechamber into the great hall. This great hall, or *megaron*, finely proportioned (nearly 12 metres by nearly 10), with four columns supporting the roof, around the central hearth, was properly the royal abode, where the prince had his throne and presided over meetings and banquets. This type of building, with a columned porch between the extremities of the lateral walls, an antechamber and a great hall, foreshadows the plan of the Greek temple: the king's palace was to become the god's temple.

The best preserved of all the Mycenaean palaces whose remains have been unearthed is that of Pylus in Messenia, not far from the famous roadstead of Navarino. It has been excavated since 1952 by an American team. It is ascribed to the dynasty of the wise Nestor, glorified by Homer in the *Iliad*. The main part, where the groundwork of the walls is still quite visible, occupies a rectangle of 55 by 30 metres, at the centre of which we find the *megaron*, with its four columns around the central hearth, preceded by its antechamber and its porch opening on a small inner courtyard. All around this main suite there are a large number of smaller rooms: bedrooms, bathrooms, offices, and different kinds of storerooms, in which the large earthenware jars that contained reserves of provisions still stand in rows on the benches in the hollows made to receive them. It was in a room to the left of the entrance that the Linear B records which have made this excavation renowned were discovered. The tablets of soft clay had been baked in the conflagration that destroyed the palace; hence their miraculous preservation.

As at Tiryns and Mycenae, there was an exquisite scheme of decoration: the ground was paved with gypsum flagstones and the walls were covered with frescos which attentive study has made it possible to reconstruct with reasonable certainty. On each side of the king's throne were griffins facing one another, each accompanied by a lion. Some distance further on there was a lyre-player sitting on a rock, while a great white bird took wing in front of him. In other rooms there were hunting scenes. At Mycenae the *megaron* was decorated with battle scenes.

There is no doubt that the building technique, with the lower part of the walls in stonework and the rest in unfired brick, the main lines of the architectural plan, with a large number of rooms placed around a central courtyard, and lastly the main motifs of the decorative scheme, are strongly marked by Cretan influence: the 'Minoan' palaces of Cnossus, Mallia, and Phaestus provided the models from which the Mycenaean palaces are derived. But, although the relationship is self-evident, the Mycenaean palaces nevertheless show individual characteristics, of which the *megaron* is the most noteworthy one. This great central hall, with its antechamber and its porch, is unknown in Minoan architecture. The Mycenaeans, whether they borrowed it from Anatolian Asia or invented it themselves, introduced it into the complex plan of the Cretan palace, but at the same time they also introduced a quest for symmetry, an absorbed interest in the median axis entirely foreign to the island architects. Similarly, while borrowing the technique of the fresco from Crete, they used it when the opportunity offered to paint subjects—e.g. war scenes—quite different from those that attracted the Cretans. In their normal dwelling-places, as in their

---

4. THE PALACE OF PYLOS

(*After Blegen*). This plan shows the main buildings of the palace, which was surrounded by more modest buildings. We see the main entrance (1), whose gateway has on its outer and inner sides roofed porches with one central column: here we have already the lay-out of the propylaea, later extensively developed in Greek architecture. From here one enters an inner courtyard (2) lined by two porticos with two columns each. The portico in the axis of the palace leads, through an antechamber, to the great hall or megaron (3), in the middle of which is the circular hearth, surrounded by four columns which supported the roof with a lantern for ventilation. The floor is stuccoed and decorated with incised lines. The king's throne, on the right, was flanked by griffins painted in fresco on the wall. To the right of the courtyard, one reached a separate appartment (for the queen? or for distinguished guests?) whose main room (4) had a central hearth. An adjacent room (5) was a bathroom with the bathtub still in position. The other rooms in the palace were service quarters: (6) and (7) were store-rooms, where there are large earthenware jars set in ledges of plaster.

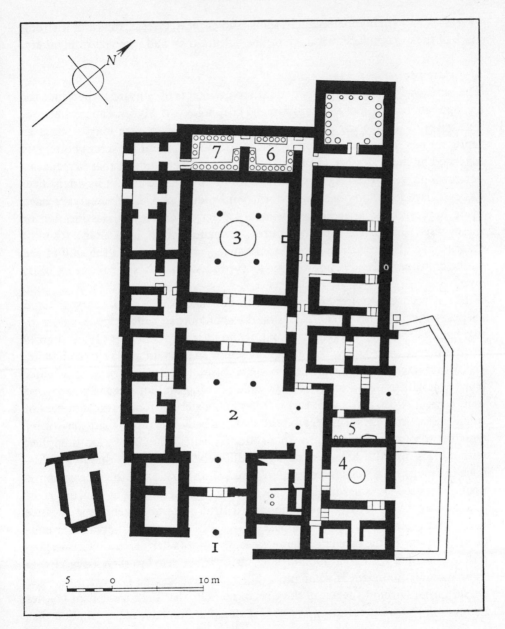

fortresses and their monumental tombs, the earliest Greeks thus left a strong mark of their original contribution on the culture they had received from others.

Mycenaean pottery

The same was true in the domain of pottery, which is of extreme importance for a proper appreciation of the diffusion and chronology of Mycenaean civilization. The vases of the closing period of the Late Bronze Age were long thought to represent merely a final stage of decline in the development of Cretan pottery as inherited by the craftsmen of the mainland. The present view is that Mycenaean pottery is in itself deserving of study both for its abundance and for its originality. Experts have listed the decorative forms and motifs and these researches have made it possible to arrive at a reasonably exact chronological classification of these vases. There were many centres of manufacture: in Argolis, Rhodes, Cyprus, and also in Attica; here the fine quality of the clay and the skill of the native craftsmen already endowed the local products with a special quality of its own.

The Mycenaean potters fashioned with deft skill vases with clearly defined shapes: large jars with three handles on the shoulder; so-called *stirrup-jars*, with two handles meeting at a false opening, while the real opening is placed slightly further down; wine-jugs with a gracefully lengthened spout and a ribbed handle, visibly imitated from metalwork models; vases for mixing wine and water (*crateres*), with a broad bulge, a very wide opening and an elegantly narrowed foot; cups of *calyx* shape with two handles and a slender foot; great numbers of small vases, smaller specimens of those described, the most characteristic of which is the small stirrup-cup with a rounded belly. The decoration is applied with a black or reddish-brown glaze (the difference in colour is due to a difference in firing) on a polished cream-coloured slip. Very often this decoration is mainly reduced to horizontal lines of varying thickness, grouped in the right places to lay stress on the shape of the vase, with an admirable feeling for elegance and rhythm. Simple motifs also appear on the shoulder: shells, network, or concentric curves. In the case of the large vases, the motifs derived from Cretan pottery are handled with great soundness of taste, but stylized to such a degree that their naturalistic origin is sometimes difficult to recognize. For example, who would guess, without the aid of the Cretan models, that the three pliant volutes painted on the bulge of a jug are in fact derived from the representation of a nautilus, raising three of its tentacles above its shell to serve as a sail? So it is described by the Elder Pliny, with his characteristic curiosity about the wonders of nature, and by Callimachus in an attractive epigram: '. . . Once I used to sail upon the waves, spreading my sail to the winds. . . .' The Mycenaean painter has transformed the charming fantasy into a purely diagrammatic representation adapted with masterly elegance to the curve of the vase.

We find the same simplification in the decorative use of the octopus and murex motifs, and also in the case of plant models, all similarly inherited from Crete, all similarly transformed by the genius of the Mycenaean Greeks with its vigorous capacity for simplification. Moreover they call upon sources of inspiration which had been neglected by their Cretan predecessors: birds and quadrupeds provide a theme for the decoration of large vases; also the human figure, which had previously been restricted to frescos. Mixing-bowls were the vases that better than any others offered convenient room for scenes in which, for example, we see a bull whose neck is being pecked by a bird, or a two-horse chariot with two men riding in it. In these works of bold innovation the drawing is often very clumsy, but more than any other type of work they give us direct entry to the world of history, as does the famous vase of the warriors from Mycenae, or of legend, as does the mixing-bowl from Enkomi, in Cyprus, in which certain theorists identify a mythological scene re-echoed in the *Iliad*.

Another class of document valuable for the study of Mycenaean civilization is carved ivories. The Linear B inventories on several occasions mention pieces of furniture decorated with ivory reliefs representing men or animals. Excavations have brought to light ivory plaques which may have formed part of such units: the tradition of their use persisted in the Greek world down to Byzantine times. Thus the warrior carved in ivory or the animal groups discovered at Delos are works characteristic of the thirteenth century B.C. Side by side with these there are numerous ivory caskets and boxes that attest the popularity of a technique of eastern origin, but employed with deliberate preference by the Mycenaean artists. They also carved figurines in the round, like the ivory group found at Mycenae, consisting of two seated women with their arms around each other, accompanied by a little boy. Are they divinities or mortal women? In truth we do not know, and our doubt betrays a profound ambiguity. The vigorous realism expressed in these works is decidedly akin to that revealed to us by the lion relief at the fortress of Mycenae or the vases painted with living forms. In this dawn of

D

Greek art, even when it is borrowing monsters like griffins from an Oriental tradition, we already find them represented with remarkable sharpness of vision and brought within the compass of human experience.

Mycenaean society

Linear B tablets, tombs, fortresses and palaces, pottery and ivory, such are our sources of evidence for a still very provisional picture in outline of Mycenaean civilization. They show us a warlike people, strongly organized in independent kingdoms. The king, who had the Homeric title *anax*, lived in a rich and mighty palace and, through the agency of specialized officials, supervised all the activities of the social group whose leader he was: he administered the state lands, gave work to craftsmen and labourers, and provided for the maintenance of religious cults. The troops at his disposal were well provided with bronze weapons: spear and sword, helmets sometimes decorated with boars' teeth or many-coloured plumes, and a leather breastplate with thin plates of bronze. Cavalry was not yet known, but two-horse chariots bore the élite of the army to the scene of action. A navy protected merchant shipping and carried out profitable raids on foreign territory. Piracy, regarded as a noble calling, and trade brought these little states into contact with the whole Aegean world, from Troy to Crete, by way of the Cyclades and the coast of Asia Minor. A strong tide of barter, as we have seen, was flowing towards the Eastern world, via Rhodes and Cyprus, where Mycenaean colonies had made a lasting settlement. The Syrian coast, Palestine, and Egypt welcomed Greek products. In exchange, they provided textiles, gold, ivory, and spices. At a still farther distance, Mycenaean trade reached Sicily, the Lipari Islands, Ischia and (most important of all) Tarentum, where a colonial banking establishment seems to have been founded about 1400 B.C. by Greeks from Rhodes. Thus an early Hellenic expansion, starting from the Peloponnesus and from Greece north of the Corinthian Gulf, was already spreading over the whole eastern basin of the Mediterranean in the fourteenth and thirteenth centuries and making itself felt even in the western approaches.

This Greek people which we have thus seen engaged in commercial and military action shows a remarkable taste for art. It entered into the rich and perennial inheritance of Crete, which provided it with models and technical traditions. But it made this inheritance bear fruit and transformed it by setting its mark upon it: the sense of grandeur and power, and the twofold and seemingly contradictory quality which from the beginning never ceased to be a characteristic of Greek art, namely realistic observation and a capacity for abstraction. Hence comes the architectural nobility of its walls and its tombs, the formal perfection of its vases, the vigorous pattern of its reliefs, in which even the clumsiness of craftsmen not yet skilful enough fully to master natural forms expresses with inspired artlessness the elementary forces of life. From this the best works acquire a kind of inner tension which still moves us today and which we should not be surprised to find again, at the other end of the chain, in the masterpieces of Byzantine art.

The Greeks of this early period already worshipped the same gods as their remote descendants. The decipherment of Linear B has given us the names of numerous deities to whom the Mycenaeans brought offerings and has also revealed, to our great surprise, the fact that the majority of the Olympians of the classical pantheon were already worshipped during the second millennium B.C. There could be no better proof of the Hellenic character of the peoples of Pylus, Cnossus, and Mycenae than the fact that we find in their tablets the names of Zeus and Hera, Poseidon, Athena, Hermes, Artemis, Ares, and even Dionysus, who was assumed to have been introduced much later into the company of the Greek gods. We already see Hellenic polytheism, in all its rich complexity, established in the same places in which temples and sanctuaries were later to be erected. We even find dedications to *all the gods*, which embrace in a collective reverence all the major divinities (or those whom we assume to be such) and others later to be more or less absorbed or eclipsed by more important divine figures: for example, Enyalios, the god of war, whose name later became an epithet of Ares; Paeon, the god of healing, later to be identified with Apollo; Ilithyia, goddess of childbirth, daughter of Zeus and Hera and closely associated with her mother; and the heroine Iphimedia, the beloved of Poseidon. These various gods were served by priests and priestesses who sometimes bore the same titles—*Key-holder*, for example—later given to them by the Greeks of the Classical Age.

It has not been incontrovertibly proved that these divinities, particularized by names which have become familiar to us, were already envisaged by the Mycenaeans in an anthropomorphic form, yet it is extremely probable. The famous sarcophagus of Hagia Triada, dating from the beginning of the fourteenth century B.C., in which 'Minoan' recollections and 'Mycenaean' scenes are closely mingled, shows us a divine effigy in human form, to which offerings are being made. If the ivory group from Mycenae with the two women and the child is not certainly a religious representation, at least we are entitled to recognize Apollo *Alasiotas*, the god of Alasia (the ancient name of Cyprus), in the curious bronze statuette wearing a helmet with long horns recently discovered at Enkomi in Cyprus in a sanctuary attached to a great mansion. It represents the prototype of all later Greek statuary.

Disappearance of the Mycenaean states. The Dorian invasion
How did this civilization which had lasted so long, this enterprising people, this society that seemed so firmly established, collapse so quickly during the twelfth century? Until recently, the ruin of the Mycenaean world and the profound decline which, between the twelfth and tenth centuries, marks the period known as the Greek Middle Ages, were wholly attributed to the Dorian invasion. The Dorians were Greeks at a less advanced stage of development who, starting from the mountainous regions of the northwest, gradually occupied central Greece, the great part of the Peloponnesus, and finally the islands in the south of the Aegean Sea and Crete itself, in the course of a long and slow advance which extended over the whole of the eleventh century and a part of the tenth. Since this penetration was accompanied with a great change in the way of life, following upon the adoption of iron, there was naturally an inclination to attribute the upheaval which destroyed Mycenaean civilization to the arrival of the more primitive and better armed invaders from the north.

These long accepted views are now the subject of much debate. A more careful study of the Mycenaean sites shows little sign of massive and radical destruction, of the total break with the past which the first investigators thought they had seen. The decline seems to have developed in successive stages and the loss of security was gradual, leading to gradual abandonment of less well-defended districts. The appearance of iron and of the new funerary rite of cremation, which now tended to replace burial, are no doubt earlier than the arrival of the Dorian tribes. We are therefore impelled to attribute less importance to the Dorians as the direct cause of a phenomenon which must have begun before their invasion.

An explanation recently put forward seems to account satisfactorily for the facts as we know them. During the thirteenth and twelfth centuries B.C., very complicated migrations affected the Near East as a whole, throughout the eastern

Mediterranean. They are known to us from Egyptian documents which frequently refer to attacks by the *Peoples from the Sea*, a heterogeneous coalition which certainly contained Greek contingents. These invasions, which were at first repulsed and then partly successful, gravely affected the political equilibrium of the Near East. The Hittite empire collapsed. Egypt fell back upon the Delta, abandoning its possessions in Asia. The conditions favourable to trade in the eastern Mediterranean basin disappeared as piracy became more widespread. The Mycenaeans, who had an immediate interest in this commerce, suffered cruelly from its interruption. They were soon cut off from their eastern partners and reduced to dependence upon the resources of their own soil. But their soil, which had never been rich, could not maintain a population which was large and accustomed to opulence. The Mycenaean kingdoms seem then to have turned against one another, under pressure of necessity, in a series of intestine struggles which brought about first partial destruction, and then ruin for most of them. Hence came the swift decline of a culture which in the end forgot its sources of inspiration and its former riches, including the use of Linear B writing, and, by dint of repetition of now barren formulas, lost all capacity for new creation. Thus the Dorians, when they spread over a great part of the Greek world, must have found, not a civilization at the height of its glory which they brutally destroyed, but a moribund civilization in a declining community. Their coming must have speeded up the general deterioration of physical conditions in Greece, thus bringing about emigration to the richer lands of the Anatolian coast, where Hellenism was destined to recover its strength and its brilliance. It was only at about the beginning of the ninth century B.C. that foreign trade was able to start up again and that Greece proper, once more in a position to enrich herself by contact with the east, began little by little to come to life again.

CHAPTER II

GEOMETRIC CIVILIZATION
OR THE HOMERIC AGE

The colonization of Ionia

WHEN in the ninth century B.C., after a long period of obscurity and misery, the Hellenic world has recovered its vitality, it appears to us in a new form, very different from what it had been in the Mycenaean Age. The decline of the Achaean states and the invasion of the Dorian tribes had during three centuries brought about movements of population which had profoundly altered the distribution of the Greek people in the basin of the Aegean Sea. While the newcomers were progressively occupying the greater part of the Greek mainland and the Peloponnesus, the former inhabitants, if they wished to escape from Dorian domination, left their homes to seek a more welcoming land elsewhere. Little is known about the details of these migrations, which continued for several centuries and the memory of which remained with the Greeks only in the form of legends whose historical substratum is very difficult to discern at all clearly. But it is certain that the movement was in an eastward direction, towards the Cyclades and the Anatolian coast, and that it reached its fulfilment in the permanent establishment of a series of populous and prosperous Greek colonies all along the western fringe of Asia Minor. Since the most important of these colonies spoke the Ionian dialect, the historical phenomenon which led to their foundation is usually referred to as *the Ionian migration*. The contrasting expression is *the Dorian invasion*, and the two form a diptych that gives a certain mental satisfaction. But neither the Dorian invasion nor the Ionian migration should be regarded as an uncomplicated operation. On the contrary, recent work has revealed the extreme complexity of the latter.

The time has not yet come for a detailed reconstruction of such a complicated movement of populations. Archaeological excavations will do more than critical examination of the legendary tradition to enable us to determine the precise date of the arrival of Greek settlers at the various points on the coast of Asia Minor. This form of investigation, which already shows promising results, as has been seen at Smyrna and Phocaea, is still in its initial stage. It is at present thought that the first Hellenic settlements on the Anatolian mainland were prior to the end of the Mycenaean period: at Miletus and at Clarus, so it seems, the Greeks may have arrived as early as the fourteenth century, perhaps in the wake of the Cretans already settled there. Afterwards colonization spread in successive waves. The origin and importance of these movements varied greatly, corresponding to the gradual withdrawal of the Achaean populations as the Dorian invasion developed. Sometimes they occupied new sites, from which they expelled the natives, sometimes they came and strengthened a previously existing colony. The Dorians also followed the movement by conquering the southern islands, Crete and Rhodes, and various points on the coast of Asia Minor. In the ninth century these migrations were virtually complete. The appearance in the heart of Anatolia of a new power, the kingdom of Lydia, set a limit to Greek expansion towards the interior. From this date onwards the distribution of the Hellenic peoples around the Aegean Sea, which had become a Greek lake, was almost finally settled, apart from the northern coast, which was not occupied until later.

Distribution of Greek dialects

The ancients distinguished the various Greek groups in terms of broad linguistic divisions, based on dialects, which they regarded as corresponding to divisions of race. Even if the moderns no longer consider this correspondence as valid in all cases, they nevertheless acknowledge that language often agrees with institutions in characterizing the predominant element in a given region. Stated in these terms, the occupation of the Aegean world at the end of the great migrations that marked the Greek Middle Ages, was as follows:

Aeolian dialects were spoken in the northern section of the coastal strip colonized by the Greeks, from the lower valley of the Hermus, north of Smyrna to the part facing the island of Lesbos, and also in this island itself. The Aeolian settlers

1. CAPE SUNIUM (AIR PHOTOGRAPH)
At the southeastern tip of Attica, the steep promontory of Sunium is dominated by the temple of Poseidon, with its Doric colonnade still partly standing. A rocky and very indented coast and sparse vegetation.

2. THE PENINSULA OF ACTE AND MOUNT ATHOS (AIR PHOTOGRAPH)
In the foreground, the isthmus through which Xerxes cut a canal so that his fleet should not have to round the dangerous promontory of Mount Athos (altitude, 2,000 metres), whose outline is visible on the horizon.

3. THE VALE OF TEMPE (AIR PHOTOGRAPH)
After watering the plain of Thessaly, the River Peneüs makes its way into the sea through a deep gorge between the foothills of Mount Ossa, to the south (to the right on the photograph), and the mountain mass of Olympus. The poets extolled the coolness of this shady valley, in contrast to the bare mountains surrounding it.

4. VIEW OF THE ISLE OF PATMOS
A landscape characteristic of the islands of the Aegean Sea: hilly ground, deep indentations in the coast, hardly any trees, cultivation on terraces, walls of dry stones.

5. LANDSCAPE OF EPIDAURUS
A small enclosed plain in Argolis. Fertile and well-cultivated soil. Olives and pines. Background of snow-capped mountains, towards the interior of the Peloponnesus. The sanctuary of Asclepius stretched beneath the slope of the theatre, from which this photograph is taken.

6. THE VALLEY OF THE PLISTUS, NEAR DELPHI
A deep gorge, planted with olives, between steep slopes. On the left, Mount Cirphis. On the right, the first slopes of Parnassus. The Mycenaean city of Crisa stood on the rock that juts forward at the opening of the gorge. The sanctuary of Delphi was a little higher up, towards the right. In the background, the Gulf of Itea and the mountains of western Locris.

7. THE BEACH OF TOLON
Beside Nauplia, on the Argolic Gulf, the picturesque Bay of Tolon was dominated in the Mycenaean Age by the acropolis of Asine. Sand and pebbles. The eucalyptus, in the middle ground, fairly wide spread in modern Greece, was only recently introduced into Mediterranean lands.

came from Thessaly and Boeotia, where, after their departure, the Aeolian dialect became strongly coloured by northwestern influences. Populations speaking the *Ionian* language were settled in Attica and Euboea, in the Cyclades (apart from the most southern islands), on the Anatolian coastline from Smyrna to a point just north of Halicarnassus, and also in the large islands of Chios and Samos. *Dorian* tribes subdued and imposed their language upon Megara, Corinth, the Argolid, Laconia, the southern Cyclades (including Melos and Thera), Crete, Rhodes and the Dodecanese, and lastly, on the Asiatic coast, Halicarnassus and Cnidus in Carian territory. In the northwestern region of the Greek mainland, and in the Peloponnesian states of Achaea and Elis, dialects known as *northwestern* were spoken; these dialects, which were very close to Dorian, exercised a marked influence on those of Thessaly and Boeotia. Lastly, in two regions very distant from one another, Arcadia and the island of Cyprus, a dialect was preserved which is known as *Arcado-Cyprian* and which seems to have kept the greatest affinities with Mycenaean Greek.

This distribution was lasting, and it produced its own effects both on political history and on civilization. The possession of the same or of a related dialect was, in the Greek world so easily torn by rivalries between Greek cities, a factor promoting unity or at least feelings of brotherhood between individual states. This was evident enough during the wars of the fifth century, in which Athens and Sparta, with varying degrees of success, drew Ionian and Dorian cities into their respective camps. It was also evident at an earlier date, when the Ionian cities of Asia joined in a league during the tenth and ninth centuries B.C. It is true that community of religious traditions, which, for the Ionians as for the Dorians, was additional to the possession of a common language, must have done much to maintain their sentiment of original kinship. In the case of the Ionians, the citizen body was usually divided into *four* tribes with traditional names and the festival celebrated was that of the Apaturia. Among the Dorians we usually find a similar division, but into *three* tribes, and common cults such as that of Apollo Carneios. These points of similarity certainly do not preclude profound differences between one city and another, and, on occasion, open hostilities within one of these groups: so it would be wrong to attribute exclusive importance to the distinction between Dorians and Ionians in attempting to explain Greek history. Nevertheless, even if this distinction has little validity on the ethnical plane, in view of race admixtures, yet it played an important psychological part in the

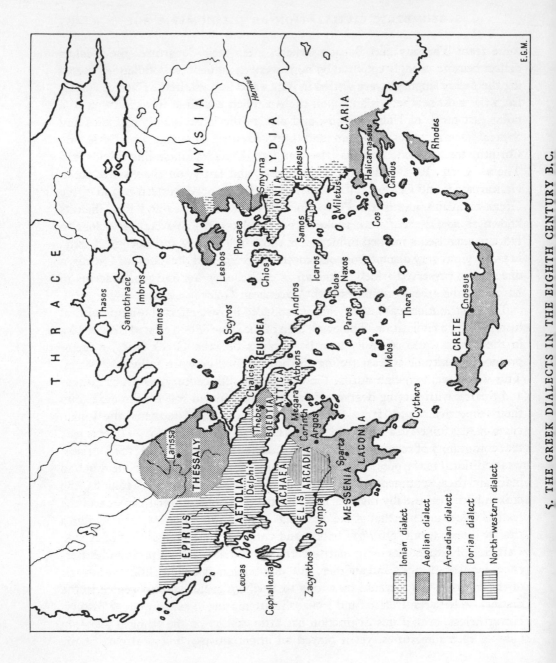

MYSIA

Hermus

CARIA

LYDIA

Smyrna

Rhodes

Ephesus

IONIA

Halicarnassus

Miletus

Cnidus

Cos

Phocaea

Samos

Lesbos

Icaros

Chios

Naxos

Delos

THRACE

Andros

Paros

Thasos

Samothrace

Imbros

Thera

Melos

Lemnos

CRETE

Cnossus

Scyros

EUBOEA

Chalcis

Cythera

ATTICA

Thebes

BOEOTIA

Athens

Megara

Corinth

Larissa

Argos

THESSALY

ACHAEA

Sparta

AETOLIA

Delphi

LACONIA

ARCADIA

EPIRUS

ELIS

MESSENIA

Olympia

Leucas

Cephallenia

Zacynthos

Ionian dialect

Aeolian dialect

Arcadian dialect

Dorian dialect

North-western dialect

5. THE GREEK DIALECTS IN THE EIGHTH CENTURY B.C.

opposition between Sparta and Athens, since they found a convenient justification for their rivalry in their connection with two different sections of the Greek nation.

On the cultural plane, diversity of dialects long remained an essential feature of Hellenism. The Greeks felt in a profound way that their kinship was based on possession of a common speech: the use of the Greek language was what distinguished them from the Barbarians and established in their own eyes their unity in relation to the rest of the world. Even if varieties of speech promoted particularism within this larger unit, they were also a source of verbal richness from which poets and other writers, as conscious artists, managed to derive many effects. Thus, at a very early stage, several literary languages were formed, which borrowed their individual colour and tone from one dialect or another, or from a combination of several dialects, while remaining within the grasp of any educated Greek. The most striking as well as the earliest example is the epic dialect, which unites in a synthesis as complicated as it is harmonious Ionian and Aeolian elements subjected to the requirements of a subtle metrical system. This artificial language, strictly confined to epic diction in hexameters and never anywhere *spoken*, enjoyed extraordinary popularity, since it never passed out of use until the end of antiquity, and even persisted later in Byzantine learned circles. Thus in the fortuitous development of literary forms, according as the genius of a given author had set its mark on a given genre, the dialect which he had used was held to be suitable for any compositions in the same style and led to imitations, though indeed transpositions into other dialects were still regarded as permissible. Even mixtures were accepted: the choral odes in Attic tragedy are not composed in the Attic dialect like the rest of the play, but in a Dorian dialect (subject, however, to rules of its own), regarded as more suitable for choral lyricism. In comedy, Aristophanes achieved picturesque effects by the use of dialects in the mouths of foreign Greeks.

It is also worth while to remember that the ancients themselves gave the names *Doric* and *Ionic* to their two main 'orders' of architecture. In fact the use of one or the other became predominant as early as the sixth century B.C., by which time they appear in perfectly defined forms, in different regions of the Hellenic world: Doric in the Greek mainland, Ionic in hellenized Asia Minor. But these distinctions were never rigorously observed, and soon certain architects thought of combining the two orders, to create particular effects, in a given collection of buildings, for example on the Acropolis at Athens, and even in the same buildings, for example in Mnesicles' Propylaea. Here, as in the case of literature, the varying tastes and different traditions of the diverse branches of the Greek people contributed to the enrichment of a culture which had become their common possession.

Geometric pottery. Primacy of Athens

The ninth and eighth centuries B.C. are usually described as the *Geometric Age*, because of the individual character of the pottery of this period. On sites occupied in this age we find vases or at least potsherds whose decoration consists essentially of straight lines or simple geometric motifs. The first appearance of this style was long associated with the Dorian invasion: it was thought to show the influence of a new spirit, introduced by the invaders from the north. This interpretation of the facts has now been almost entirely discarded: the progress made in excavation has shown that the geometric style, far from being due to a revolution in taste following upon a sudden transformation in the ethnical sphere, had slowly and progressively emerged from the Mycenaean tradition. It is particularly worthy of note that this continuity has been recognized in Attica, where the Dorian element never penetrated and where, nevertheless, geometric pottery attained unequalled perfection. But the same slow evolution appears elsewhere as well. For convenient designation of its stages, archaeologists have invented the terms *sub-Mycenaean* and *protogeometric*, which, in the absence of any certain historical data, make it possible to establish at least a relative chronology of the 'Dark Ages'. The sub-Mycenaean is acknowledged to extend approximately from the end of the twelfth century to the middle of the eleventh ($\pm$1100–1050 B.C.) and the protogeometric from the middle of the eleventh century to the beginning of the ninth ($\pm$1050–900 B.C.). Within the geometric properly so called, authorities on pottery distinguish between three separate styles: a pure geometric style (*early geometric*), which lasted from about 900 B.C. to a little before the middle of the eighth century; a more elaborate geometric style (*mature geometric*) at the middle of the eighth century, which produced magnificent masterpieces in which the human figure, in a stylized form, already occupies a place in the midst of geometric motifs; and lastly a *late geometric* style, belonging to the later part of the eighth century, in which pictorial designs acquire more and more importance and thus bring about a speedy dissolution of the geometric style properly so called.

It must be made clear that these divisions are essentially based upon study of Attic pottery, which is by far the best known. In other parts of the Greek world we often find evidence of backwardness in comparison with Attica: the difficulties of communication during the Hellenic Middle Ages made for conservatism in remote regions. But on the whole the lines of development were the same everywhere.

We need not be surprised at the importance ascribed to pottery in the establishment of a chronology for this period of Greek history. The political events of the Dark Ages are hidden from our view, and archaeological research, which alone can give us information, has to be based upon the pieces of evidence most commonly found in excavations, that is to say, fragments of earthenware: these have the threefold advantage of coming from objects in common use and therefore universally distributed, of being comparatively easy to classify because of their painted decoration, whose style was constantly developing, and lastly of being generally well preserved, since, even if vases of painted earthenware are easily broken, at least their fragments resist the corrosion of centuries without appreciable damage. One could therefore say, parodying the poet's phrase: *the potsherd alone has eternity*.

This geometric pottery has been found in many places in the Greek world: at Corinth and Argos, in Boeotia, in the Cyclades and more especially in Thera, in Rhodes and Cyprus, and even in Italy. But it is in Attica that its development from the sub-Mycenaean period can best be traced, thanks to the excavation of such a necropolis as that of the Ceramicus, situated close to a district of Athens later occupied by numerous potters, whence its name. Outside the city wall, near the Dipylon Gate, stretched a cemetery still used for burials in the Classical Age. The discoveries made in the most ancient of these tombs, in the course of work carried out between the two world wars, have revealed the arrangements characteristic of these cremation-burials, which first appear as early as the sub-Mycenaean Age, became general in the tenth century, and continued to be practised during the succeeding centuries, although entombment, a less expensive method than cremation, reappeared during this period. At the bottom of a simple pit dug in the ground there was placed the urn containing the ashes and some vases as an offering to the dead person. This pit was half-filled with earth, on the surface of which was erected a tombstone that served as a stele, often accompanied with a capacious vase for the libations which were an essential element in the funeral ceremonies. Naturally this cemetery and others like it, such as the one at Eleusis, have proved particularly rich in poetry.

The various forms of vases (amphoras, mixing-bowls, jugs, cups, goblets, boxes with a lid, called *pyxides*) evolved in a very positive direction: the several parts of the vase (in the case of amphoras, for example, the belly and the neck) became more and more clearly marked by separations, instead of the transitions by imperceptible curves beloved by the Mycenaean potters. A more and more exacting architectural sense seems to have been making itself felt, leading the craftsmen to construct the vase as a combination of clearly differentiated elements. The boldness of the potters increased along with their technical mastery: it eventually led them to fashion veritable monuments in earthenware, like the funerary amphoras and mixing-bowls from the Dipylon Gate, which rise to a man's height and represent extraordinary technical achievements.

At the earliest stage the black varnish decoration was applied to the light-coloured clay; later, in the protogeometric period, the practice was introduced of covering the vase with black varnish, but with a rectangular area set aside, on the neck or the shoulder, for a geometric decorative pattern, concentric circles or semicircles, wavy lines, strips of triangles or lozenges, rectangular or chequer-board patterns. The plastic beauty of these vases, with the lively contrast of dark and light shades and the sober elegance of the decoration, is incomparably impressive. It is at this period that we first find the 'meander', already known in Egypt and in Crete, but which Hellenic art was to use so extensively that it is now known as the *Greek* key pattern (or Greek braid). Always becoming richer as time went on, the ornament repertoire kept turning towards the living world: but the inspiration which it derived therefrom remained subject to a vigorous abstract interpretation. Friezes that differed little from those consisting of purely geometric patterns were composed of animals represented in black silhouette, decidedly schematic in form: birds or quadrupeds were figures rather than animated forms, multiplied tirelessly like shapes in a tapestry. This enlargement of the stock of themes encouraged the potter to devote more space to the decoration, which eventually occupied almost the entire surface of the vase.

The colossal amphoras and mixing-bowls from the Dipylon Gate belong to this period of mature geometric or to late geometric. In the presence of these mon uments, one is amazed by the refined taste which dictated the division into orna mental zones: the pattern chosen is always perfectly adapted to the area assigned to it, and in addition correspondences and recurrences are subtly contrived within a general arrangement planned in the smallest detail. By an innovation of the greatest importance, the potter finally drew upon the human form, treated in as conventional a manner as animals had been. At the same time, as soon as human beings were represented, there was a great temptation to bring them into a composed scene. This is what we find in the great Dipylon amphora, where the rectangle reserved for decoration between the two handles contains a picture of the mourning for the deceased, who is laid upon the bier surrounded by seated and standing mourners. It must be admitted that these diagrammatic figures are all alike; they show no distinctions of clothing or of sex. But the gesture of the two arms holding the head is already expressive of a certain sentiment: the human element introduced by their presence into an otherwise purely abstract representation was destined to act as a disintegrating agent that would very soon alter its character. If the swift development of scenes with human figures is a feature characteristic of Attic geometric painting, it thereby emphasizes the exceptional gifts of a nation of artists already far ahead of the other Greeks in this field of art.

Adoption of alphabetical writing. Homer and Greek civilization in the eighth century
Athenian superiority in geometric pottery eclipses all other manifestations of civilization on the material plane during this period. We know hardly anything of architecture, except from some few plans of temples or houses that have been reconstructed on the evidence of their foundations, which alone have survived. A considerable number of solid-cast bronze statuettes go back as far as the eighth century: they represent animals or human figures in stylized form, fairly similar to the painted silhouettes of the latest geometric period. Some are attached to a base which served as a seal. Some were mounted on vases or large tripods of bronze of which some mutilated specimens have been found. Others served as offerings in shrines. Bronze fibulas, necessary for the fastening of Dorian garments, which were draped, not sewn, bear geometric designs. Earthenware statuettes reproduce the same diagrammatic models as those of bronze, apart from the curious 'bell-shaped' figurines from Boeotia, with detachable legs and bodies sometimes decorated with painted geometric patterns. All this, however, counts for very little compared with the great Attic vases. But Geometric Greece did much more for civilization: she gave it the alphabet and Homer.

8. THE ACROPOLIS OF MYCENAE (AIR PHOTOGRAPH)
The triangular shape of the acropolis is clearly discernible. In the foreground, on the left, the main entry (Lion Gate), with its strong walls. Just behind, the 'grave circle'. Above, the terrace on which the palace stands.

9. TIRYNS: THE MYCENAEAN PALACE
At a height of 20 metres above the Argive plain (which can be seen in the middle ground), the hillock of Tiryns was surmounted by a palace dating from the end of the thirteenth century B.C. On the northern side of the inner courtyard floored with concrete stood the porch leading to the antechamber of the megaron. Only the foundations of the walls are now standing. Two large quadrangular blocks supported the extremities (antae) of the side walls. Between the antae can be seen on the ground the site of the two round wooden columns which supported the architrave. The wall composed of irregular blocks which can be seen level with the second column has been thought to belong to a temple of Hera erected in the seventh century on the site of the megaron.

10. TIRYNS: THE SLOPE LEADING TO THE PALACE
Strong walls of crude masonry line the passageway which, crossing the fortress, gives access to the upper level of the hillock.

11. MYCENAE: INTERIOR OF THE 'TREASURY OF ATREUS'
We can see the level where the corbelled vault begins. The massive monolithic lintel (above the doorway) has a discharging triangle above it. The walls of the vaulted structure are made of regular courses of large blocks.

12. MYCENAE: THE LION GATE
In the encircling wall, with regular courses of stones (called Cyclopean, because of the enormous size of the blocks of breccia of which it is composed), there is a gateway wide enough for chariots, framed by four gigantic monoliths (the lintel is 4.5 metres long, 1 metre high, and 2 metres thick). The lion relief fills the discharging triangle. The heads of the two beasts were made separately and have disappeared. As guardians of the gateway, the lions face each other and have their front paws on an altar, on each side of a pillar that stands between them.

10

11

The adoption of the Phoenician alphabet by the Greeks probably took place in the ninth century B.C. or at the beginning of the eighth. The oldest alphabetic inscriptions are from the second half of the eighth century. When adapting for their use the ingenious phonetic notation devised by the Phoenicians, the Greeks introduced an innovation of supreme importance, the indication of vowels, which had not been practised by the Semites. Perhaps a memory of the ancient Mycenaean syllabary, which distinguished clearly between syllables of different vowel constitution, contributed to this enrichment of the alphabetical system which was destined to endow it with universal value. This new technique of writing had immediate success and, with certain variations of detail, spread right through the Hellenic world. It was later to give birth to the Latin alphabet and most of the alphabets used today.

It is surely no accident that the first two literary works of considerable length, the *Iliad* and the *Odyssey*, are now attributed by the majority of scholars to the ninth or, more frequently, to the eighth century, that is to say to the period when the Greeks were beginning to employ alphabetical writing. In spite of the extreme complexity of the Homeric question, many modern readers feel acutely aware of a rigorous strictness of construction apparent in both poems to anyone who studies them without preconceptions. The ancients, whose familiarity with the Homeric texts was infinitely greater than ours, had no doubt of the fundamental unity of each of the two epics; few of them even entertained the hypothesis that the *Iliad* and the *Odyssey* were not the work of a single author, and Aristarchus, the best literary critic of ancient times, clever though he was at detecting late interpolations in the traditional text, fought very vigorously against the 'separatists' or *chorizontes*, as they were called. For my part, I am inclined to follow such an authoritative opinion, which is being confirmed by the analyses made by certain modern scholars, who show correspondences between various parts of the poems which indicate an architectural construction consciously organized by a single creative intelligence.

However well practised the memory of poets dedicated to epic recitations may have been, it is scarcely possible to imagine that effects of this kind can have been achieved without the aid of writing. Even if the epic style, by virtue of its formulary character, still preserves the features of an oral style, it must be admitted that the author of the *Iliad* and the *Odyssey*, though a late tradition represented him as blind, wrote out his great compositions from the beginning. Moreover, the

E

earliest Greek inscriptions that we possess, such as the one which promises as a prize to the best dancer the Attic vase on which it is inscribed, or the recently deciphered one on *Nestor's Cup*, which was found in Ischia (both go back to the second half of the eighth century B.C.), prove that the epic language and versification were at this period already in current use not only in Athens but also in the distant western Mediterranean colonies.

The very perfection of the two epics proves that they were the culmination of a long tradition. The ancients were conscious of this. Aristotle says in his *Poetics*: 'We have no knowledge of any comparable poem composed by Homer's predecessors, and yet everything suggests that there were many.' The disappearance of any earlier literature must be due to the absence of a convenient means of recording it in writing: the Mycenaean syllabary, if it did remain in use (which is by no means certain), was too undeveloped to ensure the preservation of a literary work of substantial length. On the other hand, Homer must have benefited by the use of the alphabet, and his work drove into oblivion all those which had come before it.

Many cities competed for the honour of having given birth to Homer. But, whether he was born in Chios, or at Smyrna, Colophon, Ios, or Cyme, it is certain that the poet composed his works in the world of the Ionian cities of Asia Minor. In the eighth century B.C. these cities were prospering after their difficult beginnings. Joined in a league of twelve cities, united by affinities of language and religion, such as the common worship of Poseidon in the Panionian sanctuary at Cape Mycale, bound to Athens by ties of sentiment and historical memories, they had a strong social organization, whose essential element was an aristocracy consisting of great landowners who wielded the real power, whether or not they had a monarch at their head. It was in the palaces of the Ionian lords that the *Iliad* and the *Odyssey* were first recited. The *Iliad* recalled the tradition, stretching far back in time, of a glorious expedition whose memory was dear to the Hellenes settled in Asian territory: not without reason they saw in the Achaean expedition to Troy a foreshadowing of Ionian colonization in Asia Minor, and the accounts of outstanding warlike exploits pleased this noble audience, for they were themselves ardent devotees of hunting and of military exercises. The *Odyssey* charmed their imagination by its account of adventures in the distant regions of the western seas, such as the seamen of Euboea and the mainland, following in the wake of the Phoenicians, were beginning to experience anew. The two activities of war and seafaring provided fine subject-matter for epic. The memory of the Achaean world had been preserved throughout the Dark Ages, thanks to the poetic compositions implied by Homer's work but later eclipsed by it.

Since the discoveries made by Mycenaean archaeology, and still more since the decipherment of Linear B, modern commentators make a point of emphasizing everything in the Homeric poems that can be related to the Mycenaean tradition, and it must be admitted that this legacy from the second millennium B.C. is of considerable importance. Yet it would be wrong to forget the fact that Homer, who lived in the Geometric period, also owed much to his own age. One thing he specially owed to it is an essential element in his poetry, the often highly developed comparisons between a heroic event and some fact of daily life, a proceeding which enabled him to make the epic world intelligible to his hearers by an appeal to the daily experiences that they all shared. He owed to it the direct and personal knowledge of nature and of man which, both in the *Iliad* and in the *Odyssey*, puts us in immediate sympathy with the feelings of the characters and re-creates for us with the most effective simplicity the natural setting in which their adventures took place. Hence the impression of unpretentious truthfulness which we still derive, through the magic of the style, when we read the works of Homer, and which endows them with eternal youth.

So it is not without reason that, for some years past, repeated emphasis has been laid upon the affinities between Homer's art and that of the finest geometric vases. They show the same feeling for composition in fashioning large artistic units with subtle combination of their constituent parts, a clear conception of relative dignities in the aesthetic as well as the religious and social domains, the unremitting action of a clear intelligence that interprets the world in terms of man and constructs the work in terms of intellectual requirements: all this we find in the two great Ionian epics, and likewise in the masterpieces of the Attic potters of the eighth century. But there are still more precise resemblances. When, during the second half of this century, Athenian vase-painters enlarged the space devoted to the representation of living forms, they decorated large mixing-bowls with paintings of battles on land and sea whose connection with similar scenes in the *Iliad* has often been stressed. These works, though often preserved only in a fragmentary condition, are nevertheless very significant. While maintaining contact with the tradition which provided him with his little diagrammatic figures, the vase-painter brings them to life by exact rendering of an attitude or a gesture that gives them a unique truthfulness. How remarkable it is that Homer adopts exactly the same method in his descriptions, choosing out the essential or characteristic detail in a complex of factual tradition and retaining it alone to fix it permanently in our memory! Both the poet's and the painter's art are based upon complete mastery of a craft that provided them with formulas or conventional patterns fashioned by the labours of their predecessors, but their own creative genius endowed these traditional elements with a new breath of life by virtue of the keenness and accuracy of their individual vision of the world. The expressive power of the works and the impression of fullness and perfection that they make upon us lie just in this equipoise between the legacy of the past, consciously accepted by the artists, and the original contribution of an intelligence that goes straight to essentials. This connection between two forms of art, belonging to such different provinces yet so clearly inspired by the same spirit, is an instructive fact of civilization.

Rural Greece in the time of Hesiod

In Homer, as in Attic geometric pottery, we see Greek society in the eighth century B.C. in its most favourable aspect. The other side is presented to us by another poet, harsher and less attractive, Hesiod, who probably lived in the second half of the century, or perhaps a little later. He knew the works of Homer, whom he sometimes imitates pretty closely and with whom a legend of later date represents him as having engaged in rivalry. Unlike the Ionian poet, he did not frequent the mansions of powerful lords: he was a countryman of Boeotia, the owner of a small property near the little market-town of Ascra, at the foot of Helicon, not far from a small valley sacred to the Muses. Two of his poems have survived, both composed in the epic dialect, the *Theogony*, or genealogy of the gods and the *Works and Days*, a didactic poem dealing with agriculture. In the latter he often refers to himself, telling us about his reflections and his anxieties. While Homer's personality is never revealed in his work, Hesiod's work, in spite of the formulary style and, at times, a certain awkwardness of expression, has a very individual tone and gives us exact information about the lot of humble countryfolk in Greece during the Geometric Age.

Their lot was certainly not enviable. The peasant toiled hard on his bit of land, exposed to the successive trials of the seasons. Work was the law that governed his life. If successful, he might achieve wealth, which alone won respect. But quarrels with relatives or neighbours gave rise to lawsuits which the 'kings', that is to say the great and powerful, too often decided by crooked judgments, having allowed themselves to be corrupted by bribes. Hesiod passionately invokes the name of Justice and proclaims his trust in the even-handedness of Zeus, the supreme deity: but just by doing so he shows how rarely, in his opinion, this justice was observed. At least his constant appeals to this deified abstraction show the strength of demands based on moral grounds that were making themselves heard among the needy citizens, ill-satisfied with their condition and conscious of deserving a better lot. In this condition of affairs in the Greek states lay the source of social conflicts which were destined to culminate, during the succeeding period in the great enterprise of colonization in distant lands and in profound political disruption.

CHAPTER III

THE ARCHAIC AGE (FROM THE EIGHTH TO THE SIXTH CENTURY)

The social crisis and colonization. Thera as an example: foundation of Cyrene. Phalanthus and the foundation of Tarentum. The founders as Heroes

THE account in the preceding chapter has set forth the main facts relative to civilization which make the Geometric Age one of decisive importance in the history of the West. Our present task is to recall in general outline the main events that marked the development of the Greek people from the eighth to the sixth century B.C., from the moment when we begin to discern it again after the Dark Ages down to the period of the Persian Wars, when the very future of Hellenism was threatened. During this period documents are but rarely found that enable us to retrace in detail a history which, especially in the earlier stages, contains a great admixture of legendary elements. Yet, in contrast to the Greek Middle Ages, the Archaic Age does not vanish into utter darkness. The adoption of alphabetical writing now made it possible to preserve documents containing records: lists of magistrates, lists of victors in the Games, oracular responses, and later the text of laws, decrees, and treaties. The list of victors in the Olympian Games, which much later served the purposes of a universal chronology, began in 776 B.C., when this Panhellenic festival was established. A kind of historiography, still rather involved with epic traditions, made a half-hearted appearance at the end of the eighth century in the writings of the poet Eumelos of Corinth. The great historians of the fifth century, Herodotus and Thucydides, both made use of these sources to the moderate extent to which they needed to do so for their purpose. Thanks to these texts, sometimes supplemented or confirmed by archaeology, we can sketch in its main outlines the history of this complicated period during which classical Hellenism slowly took shape.

Rather than attempting to follow the details, which are too often uncertain and incomplete, in the setting of individual cities, it is preferable to present some general views which will make it easier to discern the general direction in which the Archaic Greek world was evolving, without lingering over local problems whose complexity defies analysis. The following are the main phenomena: a very widespread social crisis, springing from a bad distribution of property in land, led to emigration on a large scale, as a result of which Greek colonies swarmed far beyond the limits of the Aegean world, from the Black Sea to Spain; this emigration not having sufficed to resolve the problem, the internal evolution of the city-states speeded up, often leading to violent counter-currents and the setting up of new forms of government such as 'tyranny'; and, concurrently with these political events, the whole period is characterized by a fact of great importance to civilization, the renewal of close contacts with the East. Let us examine these separate points one by one.

The social crisis is revealed no less by its effects than by the witness of Hesiod, which, after all, is valid mainly for one region, Boeotia, and for one period, the end of the eighth century. Within the narrow limits of the individual city-states, established from one end of the Greek world to the other along the two shores of the Aegean Sea, each autonomous region would have a population of several thousands, sharing the resources of a territory of modest size. Each of these political units, whether it was composed of scattered country towns and villages or ruled from an important leading city, had once had a monarchical system of government, as described in the Homeric poems; a hereditary ruler, attended by the heads of the great families, directed the affairs of the little state. Ties of kinship or religion, 'clans' based on family connection (gene), or groups united by a common worship (phratries), increased the cohesion of the whole body. Within the city-state, the power was in the hands of the main landowners (land being the essential source of wealth), who alone possessed the means of maintaining the horses necessary for their war-chariots and providing themselves with expensive heavy armour. This landed aristocracy often reduced the monarch to the position of primus inter pares: the royal function then became no more than a

LIGURIANS

ETRUSCANS

ITALIC
PEOPLES

IBERIANS

Agde
Marseilles
Nice
Antibes
Olbia

Ampurias

Alalia

Cumae
Ischia
Posidonia
(Paestum)
Tare

Velia
Metap
Sy

Hemeroscopium

SICULI

Zancle
Loc
Himera
Rhe
Selinus
Naxos
Acra
Agrigentum
Catana
Gela
Leont
Camarina
Mega
Syra

Tartessus
Malaga

Carthage

Cinyps

Principal mother—cities and their colonies

CHALCIS ■   Rhegium ▪
CORINTH +   Leucas +
MEGARA ★   Heraclea ✳
MILETUS ▲   Sinope ▲
PHOCAEA ●   Marseilles •
            ○ Other mother—cities and colonies

S C Y T H I A N S

Tanais ▲

Olbia
▲

Panticapeum ▲

Theodosia ▲

*Chersonesus

BLACK SEA

Dioscurias ▲

Phasis ▲

Istrus ▲

Odessus ▲
*Mesembria
Apollonia ▲

THRACIANS

Byzantium ▲
*Chalcedon
*Heraclea

Sinope ▲

Amisus ▲

Trebizond ▲

idamnus

Abdera

Maroneia

Aenus ▲ Perinthus
Cyzicus ▲

ollonia Stagira

Acanthus

Methone
cyra Potidaea
Torone
Mende

Lampsacus

Abydus

PHRYGIANS

Ambracia
Anactorium
s
MEGARA
CORINTH
Sparta

Lesbos

CHALCIS
Chios

Andros

PHOCAEA ●

Teos
Samos
MILETUS ▲

Thera

Cyrene
ceo
Euesperidae

Naucratis Daphne

YANS

EGYPTIANS

S E M I T E S

E.G.M

ONIES

title, one magistracy among others, retaining a mainly religious character. But at the same time, by an inevitable development, the economic foundations of the social order were in process of change. The system with regard to inheritance seems to have been as a rule equal division of property among the direct heirs. As a result, if a landowner had more than one son, his patrimony would be divided at his death into portions, which continued to dwindle in size with each generation: before long, the owner of each patch of land was in a wretched condition and his impoverishment would compel him either to go into debt or to mortgage his land to a rich man, who would, sooner or later, take advantage of the opportunity to get the little property into his own hands. Hence arose a general tendency towards concentration of land ownership to the advantage of a privileged few, while an increasing mass of the population would be toiling under difficult conditions, always in danger of losing their economic independence, and even, as a result of debts and the system of enslavement for debt, their very freedom. This is merely a somewhat extreme and perhaps overrationalized description of a phenomenon which must have existed almost everywhere in the Greek world at the beginning of the Archaic Age, and which, added to the steady increase in population, involved the Greeks in the enterprise of colonization.

The ancients somewhat summarily defined this vital cause of emigration as 'lack of land' (*stenochoria*). In practice, the circumstances that caused the departure of colonists to foreign countries varied greatly. Sometimes it was a case of rivalries between political leaders, sometimes a taste for adventure, sometimes a decree of banishment against a section of the community; later, expansionist aspirations prompted by political or commercial imperialism. But there was nearly always an underlying need to find a radical solution of an overpopulation problem or a land crisis.

The circumstances accompanying the foundation of colonies made such an impression on the imagination both of contemporaries and of the colonists themselves and their successors that legends perhaps tended to proliferate more in this sphere than in any other. Yet for some colonies we have precise accounts which enable us to form a good enough picture of the normal course of operations. Let us take as an example the small volcanic island of Thera (now Santorin), in the Cyclades, from which an expedition set out to Africa shortly after the middle of the seventh century. The vicissitudes of this adventure are related in great detail by Herodotus (IV, 150 ff.), whose account is interestingly corroborated in the main by an inscription at Cyrene, dating from the fourth century B.C. but reflecting an earlier tradition which is certainly not the text of Herodotus. The agreement between the two sources is therefore all the more significant.

From these two texts it appears that, about the middle of the seventh century, the island of Thera experienced a period of disorder resulting from bad harvests. The oracle of Delphi, being consulted by the king who ruled the island, counselled him to send an expedition to Libya to found a colony. The Theraeans complied in a half-hearted manner: the citizen assembly, convened by the king, decided to put the expedition under the command of a certain Battos. The future colonists were to be recruited in the ratio of one son from each family. Those drafted would be obliged on pain of death to embark and to settle in the new colony. They would not be entitled to return to Thera unless the enterprise proved a complete failure after five years of persistent effort. The contingent thus formed embarked in two *pentekonteroi* (ships with fifty oars); there must therefore have been at the most two hundred men. The two ships made their way to Itanos, in Crete, where they procured the services of a Cretan pilot and had themselves steered to Libya, where they landed off the eastern coast of Cyrenaica, on an uncomfortable islet which gave them a safe base from which to explore the mainland. Starting from this outpost, they ventured inland, established contact with the natives, who gave them a friendly welcome, and, after a temporary settlement of six years in eastern Cyrenaica, they settled finally in the centre of the country on the edge of an elevated plateau, in a most favourable position, which provided a plentiful supply of spring water and well watered land ideally suited for agricultural colonization. The city of Cyrene was founded in 631 B.C., according to the traditional chronology, and it was destined to enjoy brilliant prosperity for thirteen centuries, until the coming of the Arabs in A.D. 642.

The history of this colonization, on which we have the good fortune to be particularly well informed, is very characteristic. Here we find the essential elements that reappear in most accounts of such a foundation: the economic and social crisis which brings about the decision to emigrate; the consultation of the oracle at Delphi, which is to endow the enterprise with the safeguard of an unquestioned religious authority and perhaps also, in view of the numerous problems of this kind submitted to the oracle, with useful advice about the right direction to take in order to avoid coming into collision with other colonists; authoritative intervention by the state, in the form of a decree of the assembly, to organize the expedition, nominate its leader and the participants, compelled to leave their country on pain of the severest penalties; the departure of a small company, since the small size of a Greek city-state enabled a serious social problem to be solved by the emigration of merely a few hundred men; their settlement in an island off the shore, close to an unknown mainland, in order to provide themselves with a place of refuge before penetrating into the interior; and lastly the firm establishment of an agricultural colony on a favourable site, offering water and land good for tillage. All this we find again and again, with some modifications depending on circumstances, in the history of other colonies founded under pressure of the same necessities and experiencing vicissitudes of the same kind.

At Cyrene and many other places the Greeks did not, at least in the early stages, encounter hostility from the natives: their dealings were with nomadic tribes, which took no offence at the establishment of permanent foreign settlements on their territory. But this peaceful colonization was not successfully achieved everywhere. In certain places, such as the south of Italy, long and violent warfare was necessary to overcome the resistance of the Barbarians. The most striking example is undoubtedly that of Tarentum, as related to us by the Greek traveller Pausanias, who wrote during the second century A.D. but used early sources:

'It was the Lacedaemonians who colonized Tarentum, and the founder of the city was the Spartan Phalanthus. When appointed to command the colonizing expedition, Phalanthus received from Delphi an oracle saying that, when he felt rain under a cloudless sky (aethra), he would then gain possession of a territory and a city. For the moment he did not examine the meaning of the oracle himself and neglected to have it expounded by one of his professional interpreters. So he landed in Italy with his ships. There he won several victories over the natives, but could not succeed in capturing a city or making himself master of a territory. Then he remembered the oracle and said to himself that the god had predicted an impossibility, since rain could never fall from a clear and cloudless sky. When he was giving way to despair, his wife, who had accompanied him on his expedition, tried to cheer him up: she placed his head on her knees and began to pick out the lice in his hair. While she was thus occupied, thinking of her husband's hopeless situation, her affection for him made her burst into tears. Her tears falling in showers wet Phalanthus's head, and suddenly he understood the meaning of the prophecy; for his wife's name was Aethra which also means cloudless sky. So on the following night he attacked Tarentum, the largest and most prosperous of the cities on the coast, and took it from the Barbarians.'

In spite of its anecdotal and legendary character, this account shows what difficulties the Greek colonists encountered in attempting to settle in this region of Apulia, where the Messapians opposed them vigorously at the time of the foundation of the colony, at the end of the eighth century, and hardly ever ceased to worry them afterwards. It also shows the vital rôle played in the foundation of every colony by the leader appointed to direct the operation, who bore the title of founder (*oikistes*), and who, under the protection of the deity, enabled the emigrants to surmount their difficulties. We can well understand that these men, who bore the burden of exceptional responsibility, had exceptional honours bestowed upon them: after their death, they were generally regarded as heroes and a hero-cult was established at their tomb.

One would like to be able to examine this amazing expansion of the Greek people in detail but reliable documents are too often lacking, especially for the earlier periods, and the foundations were also too numerous for anything but a selective account. Moreover some colonies, after becoming firmly established in their own territory, splintered in their turn, themselves sending colonies into neighbouring regions. Finally, it is difficult to distinguish clearly between the successive phases of a movement which pursued its course in very different directions through nearly three centuries. It is certain enough that the earliest colonies, down to about the middle of the seventh century, were mainly agricultural settlements, because of the social crisis described above, while commercial motives must have played a greater part in the later period, but this development, real though it was, did not advance along strict lines, and it hardly enables us to set up chronological limits valid for colonization as a whole. We must therefore confine ourselves to presenting it, as is usually done, in terms of wide geographical divisions.

Colonization north of the Aegean Sea. Chalcidice and Thrace. Propontis and Euxine. Milesians and Megarians in the Black Sea area
At the beginning of the eighth century B.C., the eastern basin of the Mediter-

ranean presented the Greeks with a free sector only towards the north. The interior of Anatolia, being mountainous and difficult of access, had few attractions
for a people who did not like to be far from the sea. The Assyrians and Phoenicians prevented any penetration in Cilicia or Syria. They had in fact even secured
a foothold in Cyprus, where the Greeks had to reckon with them later. In the
south, though Egypt was now weakened and divided, it was too densely populated
to present an easy conquest. The northern shore of the Aegean was the only one
not occupied by large and well-organized populations. As early as the first half of
the eighth century it attracted colonists from Euboea, where two neighbouring
cities, Chalcis and Eretria, took the first step in colonization. Very little is known
of the detailed chronology of the movement, but colonies were founded in rapid
succession in this region, which because of the large number of colonies from
Chalcis (some thirty or more) received the name of Chalcidice. The three penin-
sulas projecting from it, Pallene, Sithonia, and Acte, were occupied in force, the
most important cities being Mende in Pallene and Torone in Sithonia. Shortly
afterwards Methone was founded on the Macedonian coast, midway between
Mount Olympus and the upper end of the Thermaic Gulf. Most of these cities
remained comparatively small and attracted little notice, except for the quality of
their wine. The most powerful of them, Potidaea, on the isthmus of Pallene, was
not founded until the end of the eighth century, by colonists from Corinth, not
Euboea.

Eastwards the coast of Thrace, where warlike tribes were established, attracted
Ionians from the Cyclades. In the first half of the seventh century, colonists
from Paros founded a city on the island of Thasos, which lies near the mouth of
the River Nestus and not far from the mountain range of Pangaeum. Important
gold mines, both on the island itself and on the mainland, were later to enrich the
colony. But this enterprise, in which the poet Archilochus took part, did not
succeed without violent warfare with the Thracians: as a result of this the Thasians
occupied a large part of the territory stretching between the mouth of the Nestus
to the east and that of the Strymon to the west, thus securing the foundations of
their future prosperity. West of the Strymon, on the eastern shore of Chalcidice,
Greeks from the island of Andros founded Acanthus and Stagira in the middle of
the seventh century. On the eastern side of the Nestus, Ionians from Chios
settled about the same period at Maronea, while others, from Clazomenae, vainly
attempted to hold their ground at Abdera against the neighbouring Thracian

tribes; a century later, other Ionians, driven from Teos by the Persians, made a second attempt to colonize Abdera, this time with success. Lastly, still farther to the east, at the mouth of the River Hebrus, the town of Aenus was founded by Aeolian settlers, while other Aeolians occupied Samothrace at the beginning of the seventh century. The whole coastline from Mount Olympus to the Thracian Chersonese, with the adjacent islands, was henceforth under Greek control.

A colonizing movement into the Black Sea through the straits and the Propontis (Sea of Marmara) may have begun as early as the closing years of the eighth century, but the first settlements were swept away by the Cimmerian tribes and Greek colonization was thus delayed by half a century. Cyzicus, a city on the southern shore of the Propontis, had been founded some time in the eighth century by the people of Miletus; it had to be refounded in 676, after a Cimmerian raid. Several other Milesian settlements came into existence not long afterwards, e.g. Abydus, on the Asiatic shore of the Hellespont (Dardanelles). Between Abydus and Cyzicus, the Phocaeans settled at Lampsacus. The European coast soon provided a home at Sestus, on the Hellespont, to Aeolians from Lesbos, and later (about 600 B.C.), at Perinthus, to Ionians from Samos. But Megara, a city of Greece proper, competed in this region with the Greek cities of Asia: in 676 she sent a colonial expedition to Chalcedon, on the Asiatic shore of the Bosporus, and sixteen years later (660) she founded on the opposite shore the city of Byzantium, which was to have a most glorious future. According to Herodotus, the fact that the Megarians waited sixteen years before settling on the site of Byzantium led a Persian general in the Age of Darius to express disapproving astonishment. At least the Megarian colonies on the Bosporus thereafter controlled the approach to the Black Sea.

The Greeks called it *Pontos Euxeinos*, 'the Hospitable Sea', by an antiphrasis, because of the terrible storms that swoop down upon this islandless sea, the fogs and the currents which make it dangerous for navigation. But all this did not stop them from exploring its coasts from the Bosporus eastwards, in the direction of the Caucasus and Colchis, the mythical land of the Golden Fleece, and northwards, beyond the mouths of the Danube as far as the Crimea. Miletus here played the leading part, as in the Propontis, supported, as in the Propontis, by Megara. It was about 630 B.C. that the Milesians made a permanent settlement at Sinope, midway along the northern coast of Anatolia. Later, in the sixth century, they founded Amisus, some distance east of Sinope. Sinope itself sent colonists

13. LINEAR B TABLET

This baked clay tablet (No. AN 1) was the first one to be discovered in the excavations at Pylos. It gives the distribution of rowers sent to Pleuron, in Aetolia. Lines 2 to 6 each show (1) the place of origin of a group of rowers, (2) the number in each group, by means of a vertical stroke per man, preceded in each case by an ideogram (meaning 'man'), in the form of an outline of the human form. National Museum, Athens.

14. MYCENAEAN AMPHORA

This fourteenth century amphora is decorated, in the traditional manner, with a large octopus (three of whose long tentacles can be seen hanging down on the left), and also with a more original scene containing living figures, two men in a chariot with a third figure in front carrying a pair of scales. Some commentators see in it a Homeric scene (Zeus weighing the fates of the fighters at Troy). These scenes with living figures call to mind palace frescos. Cyprus Museum.

15. MYCENAEAN CRATER

This thirteenth century vase is decorated with bulls and goats. It was found in the excavations at Enkomi. Cyprus Museum.

16. THE WARRIOR VASE (DETAIL)

This crater, found on the acropolis of Mycenae, dates from the close of the thirteenth century, the period just before the Trojan War. It gives us a lively image of the Achaean warriors setting out for battle, in serried formation, wearing their helmets, with indented shields on their left arms and pikes in their right hands. Vigorous drawing with a touch of caricature. Impression of discipline and rugged determination. National Museum, Athens.

17. MYCENAEAN IVORY OF A WARRIOR

This thirteenth-century relief, found in the votive deposit under the sanctuary of Artemis at Delos dug up in 1946, represents an almost nude warrior (wearing only a loin-cloth), carrying a large figure-of-eight shield and a spear. He wears a helmet decorated with boar's tusks, of a type known from archaeological and textual evidence. Museum of Delos.

18. IVORY GROUP FROM MYCENAE

Discovered near the palace at Mycenae, this group of statuettes (thirteenth century) modelled in the round represents two seated women with their arms round one another, accompanied by a child. Some commentators see them as divine figures (Demeter, Kore, and Triptolemus), but this interpretation is not certain. National Museum, Athens.

14

15   16

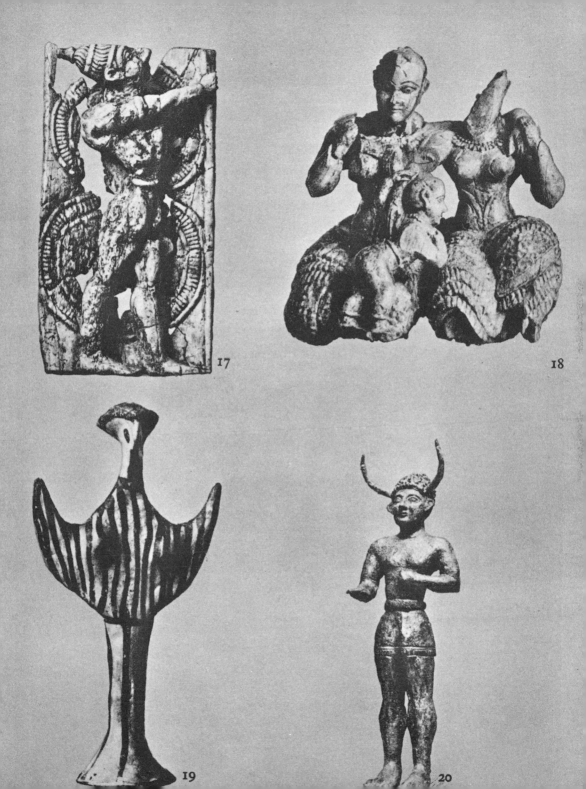

17

18

19

20

21

22

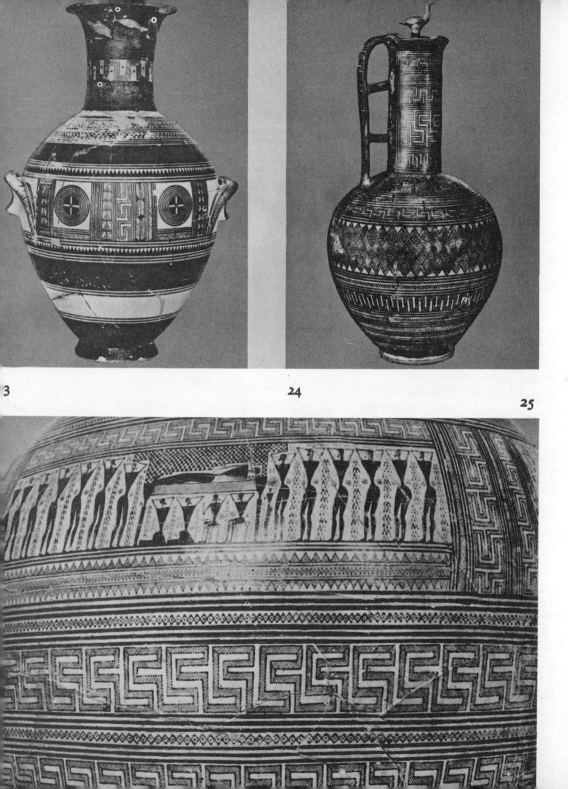

23

24

25

26

19. TERRACOTTA FIGURINE

Mycenaean statuette of a very widespread type, known as 'crescent-shaped', from Tiryns (thirteenth–twelfth centuries). It is a highly stylized image of a female deity whose breasts are conspicuous beneath the ample drapery. The head, greatly simplified ('bird profile'), is covered with a broad bonnet. A plait hangs down on the nape of the neck. It has its arms raised (others have them hanging down beside the body). Louvre.

20. APOLLO ALASIOTAS

A bronze statuette found at Enkomi in 1948, .55 metres high, representing a young male figure wearing a loin-cloth and a conical helmet adorned with large bull's horns. The circumstances of its discovery enable it to be dated in the twelfth century and make it probable that it represents the Cyprian Apollo, who had a cult here. Cyprus Museum.

21. GOLD CUP FROM DENDRA

Found on an important Mycenaean site, on the eastern edge of the plain of Argos, this fine piece of thirteenth-century gold plate is decorated with a characteristic motif originating in Cretan art and very popular in the Mycenaean Age. National Museum, Athens.

22. GOLDEN MASK FROM MYCENAE

One of the masks, done in repoussé work, which covered the faces of the bodies buried in the grave-tombs at Mycenae (sixteenth century). The face, with stylized features, closed eyes, and set lips and with the chin partly shaven, between the well-groomed moustache and beard, still bears the impress of ruggedness and majesty. National Museum, Athens.

23. GEOMETRIC AMPHORA

This Attic vase belongs to what is called *early Geometric* (ninth century). The decorated zones are still divided by wide black strips. Between the handles there is a design arranged in 'metope' form; concentric circles, a common pattern in the preceding period, known as *Protogeometric*. But the new design of the Meander or 'key pattern' appears on the neck and, employed vertically, between the two 'metopes' on the belly. The total effect, with its lively contrast between black strips and decorated areas, shows unerring taste. Museum of the Ceramicus, Athens.

24. ATTIC GEOMETRIC JUG

A fine specimen of 'mature' Geometric (eighth century): the whole body of the vase is covered with linear patterns arranged in bands with a perfect feeling for the adaptation of each pattern to the place assigned to it. The key pattern is extensively used in different forms. The swastika appears on the shoulder of the vase. The globular belly and the cylindrical neck are in marked contrast. There is no naturalistic element, except for the little bird that serves as a handle for the lid. National Museum of Copenhagen.

F

25. THE GREAT DIPYLON AMPHORA (DETAIL)

This monumental vase, more than 1·5 metres high, is justly regarded as the master-piece of the Attic 'Dipylon workshop'. In addition to abstract Geometric designs, this eighth-century painter made use of two animal friezes (on the neck) and, between the handles, a representational scene containing human figures: a body lying in state, surrounded by mourners either standing or kneeling near the bed. These vases were placed on tombs. National Museum, Athens.

26. DETAIL OF A LARGE GEOMETRIC CRATER

On another, slightly later, Dipylon funerary vase, a procession of chariots (whose two wheels are represented as one in front of the other) occupies a zone beneath the lying-in-state scene, which is placed between the handles. We can recognize the file of female mourners, with their arms raised in token of lamentation. National Museum, Athens.

farther east to Trebizond. The prosperity of these Greek cities did not entirely depend on stock-raising, fisheries, and agriculture: maritime trade in these waters also profited from an attractive outlet, since certain forms of merchandise were conveyed from Sinope or Amisus by a land route over the upland plateaux of Anatolia down to Cilicia, facing the island of Cyprus.

Sailing along the European shore of the Black Sea, the Milesians soon reached the Danube: they had already founded Istrus, a little south of the river, by the middle of the seventh century. Ten years later they settled at Olbia, at the mouth of the Bug and the Dnieper, which they called the Borysthenes. Before the end of the seventh century, they were fitting out a port of call at Apollonia on the Thracian shore, and then one farther north, at Odessus (Varna). It was during the first half of the sixth century that they reached the Crimea (or Tauric Chersonese), where they founded Panticapaeum (Kerch) and Theodosia, before penetrating, towards the end of the century, to the far end of the Sea of Azov, there to found the city of Tanais at the mouth of the Don. Smaller trading-posts were eventually set up even on the Caucasian shore of the Black Sea, e.g. Phasis and Dioscurias. The Megarians were less active than the Milesians, but by about 560 B.C. they had founded Heraclea Pontica, between the Bosporus and Sinope, and in 510 Mesembria, between Apollonia and Odessus. It was not until 422 that the inhabitants of Heraclea Pontica set up a new colony, at the southern point of the Crimea.

This Milesian and, to a lesser degree, Megarian colonization in the Black Sea area had a special characteristic of its own: the majority of the towns with which it dotted this vast area were commercial establishments, very isolated amid barbarous peoples, with whom it was often necessary to come to terms by agreeing to pay them tribute. But the resources of these distant lands provided the means of profitable trading, to the advantage of Greece proper; iron, lead, and copper from the Thracian mines, wood from the Balkans, dried or smoked fish from the fisheries in the large estuaries, Thracian and Scythian slaves, and, last and most important of all, the wheat from southern Russia—such were the main products which the Greek ships came to seek in the trading stations of the Euxine. They brought in exchange articles manufactured by Greek craftsmen, gold and silver jewels and vases, pottery, wines, oil, and perfumes, which had a great appeal for the barbarians. Native tombs of Thrace and southern Russia have yielded many treasures that show the extent of this trade: a certain class of Attic vases of the fourth century B.C. is so abundantly represented in the funerary offerings found in the Crimea that it has been given the name 'Kerch style'.

Colonization in Italy and Sicily. Establishments on the Adriatic
Colonization in Italy and Sicily bears a very different aspect: here we find not only trading stations but powerful settlements for habitation, which prospered and led an independent existence, contributing richly to the brilliance of Greek civilization. The adventure of Hellenic colonization in the west is a brilliant chapter in Greek history.

It begins at a very early period with the foundation of Cumae, in Campania, in 757 B.C., according to the traditional chronology, which archaeology seems fully to confirm. About twenty years earlier, the Euboeans had already seized the island of Ischia (Pithecusae), before crossing over to the mainland. Cumae, a colony of Chalcis, was thus from the very beginning the northernmost of the Greek cities in Italy, on the edge of the rich Campanian plain, well placed for seagoing trade with the Etruscans, who held sway in the northern part of the peninsula. About the same time other Chalcidians were settling at Naxus, near Taormina in Sicily, from which they almost immediately established other settlements, farther to the south, at Catana and Leontini. Round about 740–730 other Chalcidians were founding Zancle (Messana), then Rhegium, on the Calabrian coast, on the opposite side of the straits: like the Megarians on the Bosporus, the Chalcidians were thenceforth in control of the indispensable passageway towards the north. We also find the Megarians in the west, no less active than in the direction of the Black Sea; their colony of Megara Hyblaea was established at this period to the south of Leontini. Finally it was a Corinthian, Archias, who in 733 chose for his settlement the advantageous site of Syracuse, from which he drove out the native Sicels: it was soon to be the most prosperous among the Greek cities in Sicily. The Syracusans extended their territory towards the interior, where they founded Acrae, and as far as the southernmost point of the island. Then, advancing westwards along the south coast, they founded the colony of Camarina early in the sixth century.

But other Greeks had already been before them in this movement towards the west. A joint expedition of Rhodians and Cretans had settled at Gela in a fertile plain, during the opening years of the seventh century; a century later the inhabitants of Gela sent colonists to Agrigentum (about 580 B.C.). The Megarians of Megara Hyblaea had already founded Selinus, still farther to the west, about the middle of the seventh century. The only Greek city of any importance on the northern coast was Himera, a colony of Zancle, whose foundation was contemporary with that of Selinus. The western corner of Sicily remained in the hands of the native Elymi and the Phoenicians, who, coming from Carthage, had established themselves firmly there. They were frequently at war with the Greeks, who never succeeded in dislodging them and eventually even lost such an important place as Selinus, towards the end of the fifth century.

The occupation of southern Italy progressed concurrently with that of Sicily. About 720 B.C., colonists from Achaea, in the Peloponnesus, landed at Sybaris, at the western angle of the Gulf of Tarentum, in a plain which they proceeded to cultivate to good purpose. A land route across the mountains of 'Bruttium' (now Calabria) made it possible to reach the Tyrrhenian Sea without making the roundabout journey by way of Messana. Farther south, other Achaeans founded Croton, which was later to rival Sybaris, and finally, in 511–510, to destroy it. But in the meantime the Sybarites had established colonies at Metapontum, on the western shore of the Gulf of Tarentum, and at Posidonia, better known by its Latin name Paestum, in Lucania, on the Tyrrhenian Sea. Meanwhile Tarentum, the most powerful city in all this district, had been founded by the Spartans towards the end of the eighth century under the conditions described above; an excellent harbour and a fertile hinterland brought it immediate prosperity. Lastly Locrians founded Epizephyrian Locri, not far from the toe of Italy, in the first quarter of the seventh century. Fringed with populous and active Greek cities, southern Italy well deserved the name of Magna Graecia, by which it came to be called.

The route leading thither from 'old Greece' crossed the Strait of Otranto after a journey along the coasts of Acarnania and Epirus. As was natural, this route was also marked out with Greek colonies. The earliest was Corcyra (Corfu), first occupied by Eretria early in the eighth century but later taken by the Corinthians about 733, when on their way to found Syracuse. Later on, Corinth strengthened her control of the outlets from the Gulf of Corinth towards the west and the north by settling colonists at Leucas, Ambracia, and Anactorium, and afterwards farther to the north, at Apollonia in Illyria. The Corcyreans had already been ahead of them by founding Epidamnus (Durazzo), on the Adriatic shore. When, towards the end of the sixth century, Athenian ships pushed on as far as the mouths of the Po, bringing the fine vases which have recently been discovered in the Etruscan cemetery at Spina, they could put into harbour in Greek ports all the way until they were well beyond the Strait of Otranto.

Colonization in the far west. Spain, Provence, Corsica

It was Ionians who ventured farthest to westward. Herodotus tells us the story of a Samian trader who, while sailing to Egypt in 639 B.C., was blown out of his course to the coast of Cyrenaica and then driven by storms right to the Pillars of Hercules (Straits of Gibraltar), through which the ship passed before touching land in Spain at the mouth of the Guadalquivir, near Cadiz, in a region until then unknown to the Greeks and to which they gave the name Tartessus. The Samian made a fortune with the cargo which he brought back, for which he expressed his thanks to the gods by dedicating a huge bronze vase, seen and described by Herodotus, in the shrine of Hera at Samos. Silver and copper seem to have been the chief commodities found in Spain. The Ionian seamen of Phocaea specialized in this branch of trading, in which the natives seem to have played their part quite willingly from the first half of the sixth century. In spite of rivalry from the seamen of Carthage, who frequented the shores of the western Mediterranean and had trading stations in Spain, in the west of Sicily, in Sardinia, and in the Balearic Isles, the Phocaeans reached Spanish ports by the northern route. In this way they established themselves about 600 B.C. at Massilia (Marseilles), where one of them, Protis, married Gyptis, a daughter of the king of the country. The city was a centre for trading with the hinterland rather than an agricultural colony. Massilia set up a number of trading-posts on the French coast, Agathe (Agde) to the west, Olbia (Hyères), Antipolis (Antibes), and Nicaea (Nice) to the east. Other Phocaeans established commercial ports on the Spanish coast: Emporium (Ampurias), Hemeroscopium (near Cape Nao) and even Maenace (Malaga). When the mother-city, Phocaea, was taken by the Persians in 545, some of its inhabitants reached Marseilles and later settled at Alalia, on the eastern shore of Corsica.

This Greek movement into the western Mediterranean came up against joint opposition by the Carthaginians and the Etruscans. In 540, their united fleets clashed with that of the Phocaeans of Alalia in a great sea-fight off Sardinia. Though the battle ended indecisively, the Greeks lost so many vessels (two-

thirds of their whole fleet) that they had to give up Corsica and retire to southern
Italy, where they founded Elea (Velia) in Lucania, south of Paestum. In Spain,
Carthaginian pressure similarly compelled the Phocaeans to abandon Maenace.
But their positions in Gaul and in Catalonia were maintained.

Colonization in Africa: Cyrene. The Greeks in Egypt. Hellenism in Cyprus
In Africa, the presence of the Carthaginians prevented any attempt to colonize
the Magrab. But Cyrenaica, a verdant plateau surrounded by deserts, attracted
Greek settlers during the second half of the seventh century. We have seen in
what circumstances the Theraeans led by Battus founded Cyrene in 631. The
new city fairly soon became prosperous and developed a rich agricultural colonization, with the aid of immigrants from the Peloponnesus, the Cyclades, and
Rhodes. She repulsed the attacks of the neighbouring Libyans, who at one stage
were supported by the Pharaoh Apries, and herself founded daughter-colonies in
the district: Barca, about one hundred kilometres west of Cyrene, and Euesperides (Benghazi) on the western coast, facing the desolate expanse of the
Greater Syrtis. A characteristic of Cyrene and Barca is that each occupies an inland position on high ground. The two cities had of course ports at their disposal
that served as seaward outlets, but for the Greek colonists in Libya the essential
thing was the possession and exploitation of arable land. To this they applied
themselves with complete success and Cyrenaica soon became one of the gran-
aries of the ancient world.

On the eastward side the rich and populous land of Egypt, a country with an
ancient civilization, did not lend itself to the establishment of colonies. In the
Mycenaean period, the Greeks had formed close relationships with Egypt, but
these relationships had become very much less close, even if they had not completely ceased, during the Dark Ages, and the Assyrian conquest of Egypt did
not encourage their resumption. It was not until Psammetichus I freed Egypt
from foreign domination in the years following 663 B.C., and re-established a
unified state, that the Greeks again had access to the country. The Saitic Pharaoh
and his successors in fact called in Ionian and Carian mercenaries, the very men
whose names survive in the graffiti in Abu Simbel, in the upper valley of the
Nile. The Greek soldiers in the service of the Egyptian monarch drew traders
in their wake and commerce between the Aegean world and Egypt flourished
once more. But the permanent establishment of trading stations was not left to

the unfettered initiative of the Greeks. The soldiers, naturally enough, had their abode in camps, such as the one at Daphnae, at the eastern frontier of the Delta, on the Pelusiac branch of the Nile. As for the traders, they had a place assigned to them for their business and their wares at Naucratis, in the western part of the Delta, near the Canopic branch of the river. Archaeological evidence reveals that the Greeks were already in occupation of this site in the first quarter of the seventh century. But it was not until the reign of the philhellenic Pharaoh Amasis (568–526) that the status of Naucratis was precisely defined. The Greeks here enjoyed administrative autonomy and freedom to practise their native worship. Twelve Greek states had a share in the activities of this privileged trading centre: they were nearly all cities of Asia Minor, such as Miletus, Phocaea, Cnidus, and Halicarnassus, or large islands, such as Samos, Chios, and Rhodes. Greece proper was represented by Aegina alone. The settlement was astonishingly prosperous until the conquest of Egypt by Cambyses in 525: the Greek ships brought to it silver mined in Siphnos or Thrace and took on board the cereals of the Delta. Everyone benefited by such profitable trading.

A similar attempt may have been made in Syria, at Poseidium (Al Mina), near the mouth of the Orontes. Mycenaean pottery has been found there in recent excavations, and also potsherds of Archaic Greek ware, proving importation of Greek products between the middle of the eighth century and the end of the seventh. But we do not know whether there really was a permanent station here: the Phoenicians and Assyrians seem to have made it their regular policy to keep the Greeks away from the shores of Syria and Palestine. Cyprus was shared between Greeks and Semites, the former holding the greater part of it with Salamis, Soli, and Paphus, while the latter occupied the south-eastern region with Amathus and Citium. Cypriot Hellenism was a vigorous plant, as is shown by the *Cypria*, an epic poem in the Homeric tradition by Stasinus, but here more than anywhere else Hellenism was susceptible to eastern influences, to which the Archaic sculptures found in the island owe their very individual character.

Archaic civilization in Greece proper and in Ionia; the Greek cities
Let us consider what was happening in Greece proper and in Ionia while the Greeks were thus spreading over the world from Spain to the Caucasus. As we have seen, colonization was the result of a very widespread social crisis in the Aegean world. Political developments within the city-states and the conflicts

between them reveal other aspects of this crisis, while Greek civilization was developing and became richer as a result of its contacts with the east.

It is in the eighth and seventh centuries B.C. that the unique political creation represented by the city-state comes within our range of vision; it was a state of very modest dimensions, with a small urban centre that was the seat of its communal institutions and its religious cults. Wherever a city had been formed, often by the union, or *synoecism*, of several rural towns or villages, we see this political unity spring into existence: it provided the framework within which classical civilization developed. The multiplication of Greek city-states is as surprising a phenomenon as the extension of their colonies: there were hundreds of them, most of which had no history as far as we know, but showed a no less lasting vitality because of that. The territory attached to each of these cities was diminutive: in Phocis, for example, with a total area of 1,650 square kilometres, there were as many as twenty-two independent city-states. Crete, whose surface comprises 8,500 square kilometres, was divided between some hundred little states: Homer already calls it the island 'with a hundred cities'. Corinth, with its 880 square kilometres, and Argos with 1,400, counted as important states. As for Athens (2,500 square kilometres) and Sparta (8,400, counting Messenia), these were states of quite exceptional area. As we have seen, even when the colonial cities sought to extend their territory inland, they scarcely exceeded these dimensions. Cyrene and Syracuse, which were the most powerful, were in control of a territory that was smaller than a French *département*. It is impossible to understand Greek history without taking into account this extreme political fragmentation, which was mitigated only to a very limited degree by the formation of leagues and confederacies. The sense of unity among the Greeks, of which the Olympic Games were, from 776 B.C. onwards, both a manifestation and a symbol, did not stop either rivalries or wars. Local patriotism, glorified by the poets, maintained and aggravated the conflicts. The needs of warfare led to an increase in the number of soldiers, and produced modifications in equipment and tactics: by an inevitable repercussion, the equilibrium of society was affected. Internal crises and wars with other states, such is our picture of Archaic Greece, allowing for the simplification and exaggeration imposed by historical remoteness.

As for its development, which is extremely complicated in its details, some main facts stand out: on the plane of domestic policy, many cities underwent political and social changes resulting in enlargement of the civic body and the granting of a larger share of civil rights to the poorest of the citizens. On the plane of relations between cities, some states played the most important rôles, whether they shone by virtue of their commercial activity, like the cities of Euboea and above all Corinth, or commanded respect by their military valour, like Argos and above all Sparta. From the sixth century onwards, the growing importance of Athens became the most important factor of all. At the same time, on the opposite shore of the Aegean, Anatolian Hellenism, with all its prosperity, first experienced vassalage under the pressure of Lydia, and then servitude after the Persian conquest. An external threat was now looming up against Greece: it culminated in the Persian Wars. These various aspects of Archaic Greek history will now claim our attention, each in its turn.

Social evolution. The land problem. Nobles and people. Lawgivers and their reforms. Tyranny and the tyrant
The Greek cities of the eighth century B.C. had mostly an aristocratic form of government based on the ascendancy of the big landowners. Even when hereditary kingship continued to exist, these noblemen wielded the real power. They possessed the land, hence their title 'landowners', *geomoroi* in Samos, *gamoroi* at Syracuse. They had horses, needed to draw the chariots in which, in accordance with the Achaean custom still illustrated on the Dipylon vases, rode the heavily armed warriors, who were alone capable of deciding the issue of a battle: hence the title 'horsebreeders', *hippobotai*, proudly borne by the nobility of Chalcis in Euboea. The laws of inheritance, the practice of borrowing and lending in kind, and the rule of enslavement for debt resulted in a concentration of wealth in terms of land and impoverishment of the small peasants and yeomen, who tried to resist. But an unexpected remedy now came within their grasp. Military tactics were altering to their advantage: in place of single combat between the nobles of the opposing forces, riding to the battlefield in their chariots, an innovation of far-reaching consequences was introducing a more effective way of fighting: manoeuvres on foot by a battalion in close formation, known as a *phalanx*. With his large round shield, his helmet, his breastplate, and his greaves, the heavily-armed warrior, or *hoplite*, wielding spear and sword, formed with his companions a compact and formidable mass against which solitary champions borne in a chariot were helpless. Soon every army needed to possess a fighting

force consisting of these well-equipped infantrymen, who had no need of a chariot but only of an armour-bearer to help them carry their equipment. The hoplites were recruited from the yeoman class, who were rich enough to provide themselves with an outfit of armour and an orderly but who could not have afforded to buy a horse. Indispensable for warfare, these men were soon able to claim their share of political responsibility. Herein lies the foundation of many subsequent reforms. Later we shall see the same causes producing similar effects when the development of a war fleet makes it necessary to recruit a large number of oarsmen for the squadrons: these oarsmen, people of humble rank, whose only wealth was their hands, would soon also wish to play their part in the city-state and thus hasten the political development of several maritime states.

The struggle against the privileges of the aristocracy—political and judicial privileges and those arising from the ownership of land—often resulted in a concentration of power in the hands of one man. When it was a question of an arbiter appointed by the conflicting social groups, this man endowed with exceptional authority would give the city laws, which the parties undertook to respect. The Archaic Age in Greece was the golden age of legislators. It might be a foreigner, to whom the citizens appealed because of his reputation for wisdom or because it was hoped that he would be more able to show himself impartial if he was not involved by birth in the local disputes. Thus the Cyrenaeans, wishing to reform their institutions in the middle of the sixth century, summoned to Libya a sage from Mantinea. Ephesus appealed to an Athenian, Thebes to a legislator from Corinth. Elsewhere it was one of their fellow-citizens to whom the inhabitants entrusted the task of restoring order and law. Zaleucus, at Epizephyrian Locri in the first half of the seventh century, was the earliest of these half-legendary figures. Draco at Athens, about 625–620 B.C., was a member of the Attic nobility, as was Solon early in the sixth century. At Mytilene, on the island of Lesbos, the legislator Pittacus restored civil concord by holding supreme power for ten years: by his firmness, justness, and moderation he gained a place among the Seven Sages, in spite of the fact that he sent the poets Alcaeus and Sappho into exile.

Most of these legislators concerned themselves with the same essential problems. First of all they had to codify the law of property, especially for estates of land, since political privilege was linked with possession of a certain degree of wealth, mainly represented by a portion of land: hence the importance which they attributed to regulations concerning inheritance, with the object of preventing either excessive breaking up or undue concentration of landed property. Regulations forbidding luxury were linked with the same considerations, whether they dealt with female finery or funeral ceremonies, the purpose being to remove a serious cause of squandering of inherited wealth. Their next care was to set up more equitable rules in the judicial field, in order to reform the abuses and 'crooked verdicts' of the aristocratic judges against which Hesiod raised his protest: by drawing up codes which, like that of Draco, were often very severe, but which applied to everyone, they tried to satisfy a primary demand of the humbler members of the community. Lastly, they tackled the problem of homicide: in place of the custom of private vengeance, which, in cases of murder, perpetuated a vendetta between one family or one clan and another, they introduced a system of public justice, in which religious considerations had a place, and which, in spite of its extreme severity, in one respect delivered the individual from subjection to the ancestral clan or *genos*.

These reforms do not appear to have been inspired by revolutionary intentions; on the contrary, the desire of those who introduced them was to preserve the equilibrium of the traditional social order, which in their eyes stood for virtue. But their conservative tendencies did not prevent them from perceiving the need to satisfy the reasonable aspirations of the multitude. Wherever they succeeded in this, that is to say in the great majority of the Greek cities, internal political evolution proceeded peacefully, within the limits of an aristocratic régime based on property, capable of opening its ranks as occasion demanded.

On the other hand, when the lawgiver failed or the city neglected to call upon his services, recourse had to be had to force. Here again the part played by individuals was of primary importance: the Archaic Age of Greece was also the age of the first tyrants.

The term 'tyrant', *tyrannos*, whose probably foreign origin is still a matter under discussion, was first applied to any individual invested with supreme power: originally there was no difference between a tyrant and a king, *basileus*. Later the title was confined to usurpers who had seized power and held it by force. The word then acquired an unfavourable sense, which we can already perceive in Herodotus and which became accentuated in Plato and the other fourth-century philosophers. But the phenomenon of tyranny does not interest us so much because of the moral considerations which it aroused in writers as for the rôle it played in the Archaic Greek city. Thucydides, with his usual lucidity, was fully aware of it when he wrote: 'Tyranny was usually set up in a city when incomes increased.' By this he means that increase in the wealth acquired by manual and skilled labour and trade, by creating a new source of social unbalance in the state, promoted political upheavals. In face of the opposition of the landed aristocracy to the claims of the other social classes, these last eventually put their trust in some energetic and unscrupulous man, who, by violence or cunning, seized power and broke the resistance of the nobles. Often this man was himself a noble who already held some important office in the state. Cypselus, the first tyrant of Corinth, belonged to the ruling family and was perhaps in command of the citizen army at the time when he set up the tyranny. Arcesilas III of Cyrene was a dethroned monarch who recovered possession of his kingdom by the methods of a tyrant and then continued to act in the manner of one. Others were of humble origin: Orthagoras, the first tyrant of Sicyon, was a butcher's son. But all of them made clever and resolute use of local conditions to achieve their ends.

They put themselves at the head of the malcontents: either of the poor, as did Theagenes of Megara, who gained popularity by having the rich men's herds slaughtered; or of the small rural landowners, as did Pisistratus at Athens; or of a certain racial section in the population which considered itself oppressed, as did Clisthenes of Sicyon, who pursued a policy hostile to the Dorians, formerly the ruling element in the city. The tyrant formed or had himself allotted a bodyguard, the *doryphoroi* or spearmen, which brought him security and respect. He often recruited it from the mercenaries who at this period were already available in the Greek world to anyone who would pay for their services. He employed this force to reduce the aristocracy when it refused to recognize him: thus Pisistratus exiled the family of the Alcmaeonidae, Arcesilas III confiscated the estates of the Cyrenaean nobles, giving their lands to his followers, and Thrasybulus of Miletus advised Periander of Corinth (unless it was the other way round, since both versions of the anecdote are attested) to cut off the heads which rose above the others, as he did with his cane to the tallest heads of corn. At the same time he offered certain satisfactions to the middle and working classes: at Athens, Pisistratus reached a practical solution of the problem of debt and of peasant property which Solon had tackled earlier. He initiated many large public works, largely for the sake of his own prestige but also to provide employment for the workers and to promote the material welfare of his subjects. At Samos, Polycrates had a subterranean aqueduct (which, a century later, aroused the admiration of Herodotus) constructed by the engineer Eupalinus of Megara, and also a mole in deep water. He rebuilt the colossal temple of Hera, 'the largest temple I have ever seen', the historian tells us. Pisistratus and his sons acted similarly by leading the waters of Mount Hymettus into the centre of Athens, to the *Well with Nine Spouts*, whose site is still disputed, and by undertaking the construction of the temple of Olympian Zeus, which they had not time to finish. Battus IV, the successor of Arcesilas III, a tyrant-king like his father, erected a temple of Zeus at Cyrene, which remained the largest Greek temple in Africa.

The tyrants also patronized the plastic arts and literature because of their taste for splendour and their desire to strike the public imagination. They made magnificent offerings in the great panhellenic sanctuaries. Cypselus built a treasury at Delphi and dedicated such a splendid ivory chest in the *Heraeum* at Olympia that Pausanias was glad to describe it in minute detail in the second century A.D. Clisthenes of Sicyon had a building erected at Delphi, whose sculptured metopes, happily discovered in our own times, illustrate legends carefully chosen by him in keeping with his anti-Dorian policy. Periander welcomed and honoured at Corinth the poet Arion who, according to the legend, was saved by a dolphin from the cruelty of pirates. Polycrates received at his court the poets Ibycus of Rhegium and Anacreon of Teos, while he had his famous ring engraved by Theodorus of Samos, the most illustrious artist of the age. Pisistratus and his sons encouraged the wonderful flowering of Attic art in the second half of the sixth century B.C.; they attracted to Athens Simonides of Ceos and also Anacreon after the fall of Polycrates and they caused to be prepared the first careful edition of the Homeric poems. During the first half of the fifth century, at a time when the tyrannies of Greece proper had disappeared, the colonial tyrants Gelon and Hieron at Syracuse brought to their court the poets Simonides and Bacchylides of Ceos, as well as Pindar himself, who afterwards betook himself to Arcesilas IV at Cyrene.

The policy of the tyrants towards foreign states, whether Greek or Barbarian, can scarcely be defined without much consideration. Some of them yielded to the temptation to indulge in forays or schemes of conquest: Cypselus sought to promote the establishment of Corinthian colonies in northwestern Greece, e.g.

Leucas and Ambracia; Periander brought Corcyra back into subjection to Corinth and founded the city of Potidaea in Pallene, which soon became the most important of the Greek colonies in Chalcidice. Polycrates waged war with Miletus and took action in the Cyclades, where he conquered the island of Rhenea and joined it to Delos. Arcesilas III reduced the other cities in Cyrenaica, Barca and Euesperides. But on the whole the tyrants did not seek foreign adventures. Anxious to establish their power and, if possible, to ensure the survival of their dynasties, they developed their military strength in order to protect themselves as much from internal as from external threats, rather than to plunge into an imperialistic policy. Battus IV of Cyrene, towards the end of the sixth century, avoided encouraging the Spartan Dorieus, who was seeking his collaboration in founding a colony in the Carthaginian zone of influence, on the site where Leptis Magna later stood, and the abstention of the tyrant of Cyrene caused the enterprise to fail. Pisistratus confined his foreign ambitions to occupation of Sigeum, on the coast of Asia Minor, near the Dardanelles; apart from this, he showed himself adroit and peace-loving with his neighbours and established friendly relations with other tyrants, such as Lydgamis of Naxos and Polycrates. Polycrates himself, although he yielded on several occasions to the temptation of warlike adventures, sought to come to terms with the great eastern monarchies; he concluded an alliance with the Pharaoh Amasis, and later provided Cambyses with ships when the Persian king attacked Egypt; that did not prevent him from being assassinated shortly afterwards in a trap laid by the Persians. In the Ionian cities, the tyrants came to terms with Persian domination and consented to play the role of satraps. This was also the policy of the Battiad monarchs in Cyrenaica. In Sicily, on the other hand, at the beginning of the fifth century, circumstances made Gelon, and later Hieron, champions of Hellenism against the Etruscans and the Carthaginians.

The logic of tyrannical rule, even when, as at Cyrene, it was disguised as a hereditary monarchy, implied that it must eventually succumb to the violence of its opponents, that is to say the supporters of the aristocracy which had been ousted from power, the moment when the vigour and lucidity of the tyrant began to fail. Thus, in spite of the desire that each of them had to found a dynasty, there were very few who succeeded in doing so and none of these dynasties survived beyond the third generation: at Corinth, Cypselus and Periander managed to maintain their power from 657 to 586 (according to the traditional chronology,

27. SMALL GEOMETRIC JUG
On this eighth-century vase the naturalistic element is more fully developed: there is a frieze of the birds known as 'waders' on the belly, running hounds on the shoulder, and a very curious and lively scene on the neck. A shipwrecked man is bestriding the keel of an overturned boat, while his dead companions are scattered around him. We are tempted to identify it as a mythical scene, for example the shipwreck of Ulysses. The Museum antiker Kleinkunst, Munich.

28. FRAGMENT OF A LARGE GEOMETRIC CRATER
The lively scene is that of a battle near a ship. The ship is represented with great precision (ram, ornament on the prow, upper deck, thole-pins for the oars along the side). When painting the corpses stretched out on the left (in isometric projection), the painter gave their simplified outlines remarkably realistic attitudes. We are reminded of some passages in the *Iliad*. Louvre.

29. MODELLED VASE IN THE FORM OF A GALLEY (EIGHTH CENTURY)
At the stern, a figure acting as steersman. At the prow, the ram with a 'prophylactic' eye. Geometric decoration. Boston Museum.

30. POLYPHEMUS BLINDED BY THE COMPANIONS OF ULYSSES
This fragment was part of a large crater produced in an Argive workshop in the seventh century. Amid Geometric designs (zigzags and criss-cross patterns), there is a scene with human figures inspired (but with some variations) by the legend related in *Odyssey* IX. Argos Museum.

31. WINE-JUG
Fine example of Rhodian pottery (second half of the seventh century). Frieze décor, in which animals, admirably drawn, stand out against a field of varied designs. A braidlike ornamentation on the neck. We can perceive the influence of eastern textiles. Boston Museum.

32. CORINTHIAN WINE-JUG
In Corinthian pottery, which flourished particularly at the time of the tyrants (second half of the seventh century and first half of the sixth), we find the method of frieze décor consisting of animals, but with a very individual technique (solid silhouettes divided by incisions). Louvre.

33. ATHENIAN COIN
The reverse side has Athena's owl, with two olive leaves and the first three words of the Athenian people's name. Bibliothèque Nationale, Cabinet des Médailles.

34. COIN OF AEGINA
On the obverse side, a tortoise. This minting of the Classical period did not spread so far afield as the Archaic Aeginetan coins stamped with a sea-turtle. Cabinet des Médailles.

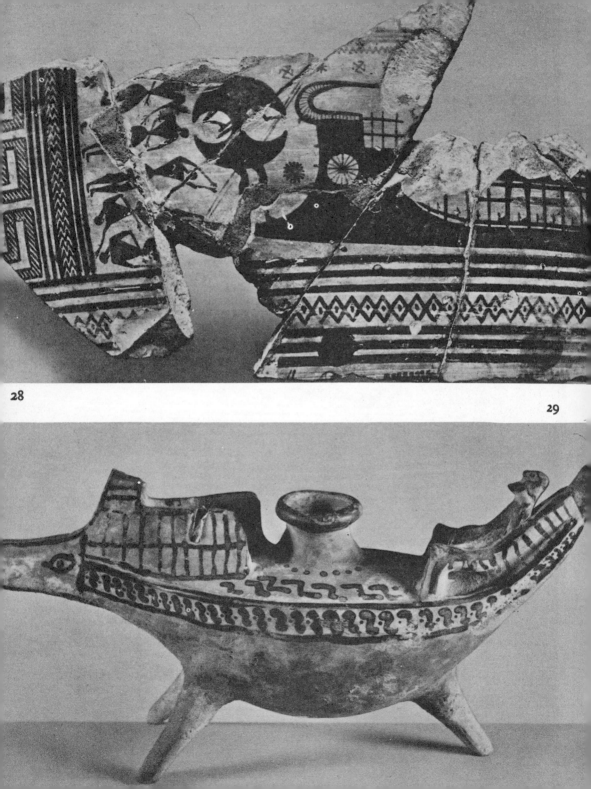

28

29

I

3

3

which some modern scholars put about thirty-five years later), but their successor was assassinated: at Athens, one of Pisistratus' sons, Hipparchus, was stabbed by the *tyrannoctoni* Harmodius and Aristogiton in 514, the other, Hippias, was expelled in 510; at Syracuse, Gelon, and then his brother Hieron, ruled from 485 to 466, but the tyranny was abolished in the same year in which Hieron died; at Cyrene, Arcesilas IV, the grandson of Arcesilas III, the third and last of the Battiad royal tyrants, was assassinated about 440 at Euesperides after having been driven out of his capital by a revolution. So, if tyranny was fairly widespread in the Greek world between the middle of the seventh century and the middle of the fifth, it did not last very long in each individual city. But if this short-lived form of government usually left a bitter memory because of the violent methods employed by the tyrants, nevertheless its effects were not wholly bad. In certain cases it represented a necessary stage on the road leading to democracy: this is particularly clear at Athens and also true at Corinth and Cyrene and in the Sicilian cities, such as Syracuse and Gela, where tyranny was succeeded by a moderate aristocratic régime. Often, to say the least, the tyrants gave the cities they governed a remarkably vigorous impulse on the economic and cultural plane, while playing their part in the abolition or relaxation of the old social limitations. Lastly, by virtue of their exceptional personality, the most illustrious of the early tyrants aroused the shocked or admiring curiosity which finds vigorous expression in Herodotus's *History*, where we find so many portraits of tyrants. While condemning their frantic ambition and inordinate aspirations, the subtle historian of Halicarnassus does not conceal the human interest that he finds in these paragons of the tyrannical form of government. The imagination of the Greeks dwelt upon the memory of men so clearly distinguished from the common run of mortals by their natural gifts, their energy, or their vices. It never forgot the proof they had given of the fact that it is men who make history, and that the masses, when one knows how to deal with them, are only too willing to submit to the prestige of the individual.

Sparta: formation of the Spartan state. Its conquests. Domestic wars in Greece. The Lelantine War. Development of commerce: prosperity of Corinth. Invention of money. Archaic Athens: Solon, the Pisistratids
It may well be that Sparta, the largest and most powerful of the Archaic Greek states, owed its freedom from tyranny (*atyranneutos* is Thucydides' expression)

to its distrust of the individual. The historian at least stresses the fact that Spartan policy was hostile to tyranny, and Sparta did in fact take action against Poly-crates and the Pisistratids. She overthrew Lygdamis of Naxos. She only drew Corinth and Sicyon into her alliance after the fall of their tyrants. The fact is that her political and social institutions, based upon a rigorous hierarchy, were in complete opposition to the demagogy which was a condition of success for the tyrants. It may even be true (as has recently been argued) that the Spartan régime was set up as an alternative 'to tyranny', to deal in a different way with an internal crisis experienced by Sparta as by all other Greek cities. These re-forms, whose economic aspect will be set forth later, were ascribed by ancient tradition to a famous lawgiver, Lycurgus, who is for us an entirely legendary figure, and who is supposed to have lived in the later part of the ninth century B.C. In fact Lacedaemon (another name for Sparta) seems to have ordered its institutions and customs progressively until about the middle of the sixth cen-tury, after which they remained unalterable to the end of the Classical period. A primary cause of this development lay in the policy of territorial expansion pur-sued by the Spartan state from the earliest stage of the Archaic period: it was to this that Sparta owed her greatness, her weaknesses, and her originality.

The Dorian invaders who had chosen the fertile valley of the Eurotas as their dwelling-place were not content to seize all Laconia between the parallel ridges of Taygetus and Parnon. They also wished to extend towards the east, over Parnon, as far as the Aegean Sea, and thus came into conflict with the interests of Argos, which had established its sway all over this coast down to the island of Cythera. The result was a long conflict in which Sparta eventually got the better of her rival, but which caused lasting hostility between the two neighbouring cities, though both of them were Dorian in language and institutions. In the north, the Lacedaemonians expanded at the expense of Arcadia and took from it several mountainous districts bordering on their own territory. But the decision most fraught with far-reaching consequences was that of invading Messenia, on the western side of the Taygetus barrier. It was during the second half of the eighth century that Sparta conquered this region, at the cost of a war that lasted twenty years (about 740–720) with the Messenians, who struggled desperately to defend their freedom. When at last their resistance was broken, the whole country was subjected to a rule of slavery and its inhabitants reduced to the con-dition of *helots*. The rich plain of Messenia, between Taygetus and Mount

Ithome, was henceforth cultivated by the helots for the benefit of the Spartans, providing them with their chief means of support. This conquest diverted Sparta from colonial enterprises, except for the colonization of Tarentum, which was a direct consequence of it, since the settlers led by Phalanthus were in fact bastards born at Sparta during the long absence of the Lacedaemonian hoplites.

Possession of Messenia made Sparta by far the most important state in the Peloponnesus. But the one ambition of the downtrodden Messenians was to shake off their chains. The rising of the helots, about the middle of the seventh century, brought Lacedaemon to the verge of ruin and compelled her to wage the Second Messenian War, from which she emerged victorious only after a struggle lasting thirty years (about 650–620); the warlike elegies of the poet Tyrtaeus helped to inspire the Lacedaemonian soldiers with the will to win. It was during this war that they perfected the tactics of the phalanx, and their discipline in battle enabled them to get the better of the insurgents and their Argive and Arcadian allies. But the need to maintain her hold on Messenia was to weigh heavily on the destiny of Lacedaemon. In order to be in a position to meet at any moment the danger which threatened them, the Spartans thenceforth submitted themselves to a rule of life entirely subject to military requirements: obedience, a communal life, constant military exercises, and concentration of command in the hands of a few persons. This rigorous system was destined, by a remorseless internal logic, to lead to ever-increasing austerity: after a brilliant period, following the Second Messenian War, Spartan civilization rapidly declined from the middle of the sixth century. The beautiful pottery which Sparta exported to Samos, Cyrene, Tarentum, and Etruria, and which rivalled that of Corinth, completely disappeared. The city ceased to welcome Ionian artists such as Bathycles of Magnesia, who had constructed the famous 'throne' of Apollo at Amyclae some time after the middle of the sixth century. Foreign poets no longer came to glorify her ceremonies, as Alcman of Sardis and Terpander of Lesbos had done in the seventh century. Lacedaemon was of course a formidable power, whose pre-eminence in Greece was undisputed The whole Peloponnesus, apart from Argos and Achaea, was included in a system of alliances in which Sparta played the leading role, as is well shown by the phrase 'the Lacedaemonians and their allies' generally employed from this time onwards. But this strength was not employed in the service of any great policy. Sparta was turned in upon herself, with no longer any ambition for new conquests, content to maintain those which she had already achieved and to enjoy in the eyes of the other Greek states a reputation for military valour and austere virtue.

Outside the Peloponnesus armed conflicts were no less frequent. The two cities of Euboea, Chalcis and Eretria, which had played the largest part in the earliest stages of colonization, engaged in a struggle with one another, towards the end of the eighth century, for possession of the Lelantine Plain, which lay between them in Euboea. Thucydides tells us that most of the Greek cities took part in this *Lelantine War*, in which Eretria was eventually defeated. That is almost all we know about it, but the remark shows how easily the smallest dispute could spread in the Hellenic microcosm. Early in the sixth century Megara and Athens were at war for possession of the island of Salamis: Solon, and then Pisistratus, secured the victory for Athens. A local quarrel between two little Phocian states, Delphi and Crisa, had considerable consequences, for Delphi was the seat both of an oracle of Apollo and of the Amphictyony, a league of twelve peoples of northeastern Greece. This league intervened and decreed the first *Sacred War* against Crisa (600–590): Crisa was defeated and destroyed and its land was dedicated to Apollo. Shortly afterwards, in 582, the *Pythian Games* were held for the first time. Delphian prestige greatly benefited thereby and the Thessalians, who had been put in charge of the operations against Crisa, for a long time held the leading position in the Amphictyony.

So war often broke out between the cities of Archaic Greece: they accepted it as an essential and constant activity. It did not, however, prevent economic development when circumstances were favourable to the latter. The case of Corinth is particularly significant: planted on its isthmus, with two ports, one to the west near the city, the other to the east on the Saronic Gulf, Corinth occupied a very favourable position, on the route taken by the goods trans-shipped between the Aegean and the Ionian Sea. She took full advantage of it, first under the rule of the noble family of the Bacchiadae, later under that of two successive tyrants, Cypselus and Periander. We have seen how she developed her colonial enterprises towards the seas and the markets of the west, and also in Chalcidice, where she founded Potidaea. In her own territory, she attempted unsuccessfully to cut a canal through the isthmus in order to join up the two seas; then she constructed a paved track, the *diolcos*, on which ships were hauled from one edge of the isthmus to the other. Corinth was not only a place of transit but also an important manufacturing centre. Its pottery, which begins with the Geometric

Period, was in extremely plentiful supply and widely distributed all over the
Greek world, especially in the west; the evolution of its style is very clearly
characterized (*Protocorinthian* until the last quarter of the seventh century:
Corinthian until the end of the sixth), and therefore provides archaeologists with
a valuable criterion for dating in the work of excavation. Of course some types of
vases, such as perfume bottles, did not travel empty, but were used in the exportation of Corinthian products. Another source of profit was metalworking:
weapons, mirrors and bronze vessels were turned out in great quantities in the
Corinthian workshops. To protect her commerce, she built up a powerful war-
fleet: it is to the Corinthians that Thucydides ascribes the invention of the
trireme, a vessel with three rows of oarsmen, which outclassed the pentekonter.
The craftsmen of Corinth, her fleets, and her commerce made her the most
thriving city in the Greek mainland during the first half of the sixth century.

The expansion of commerce was at this time facilitated by a still recent invention, the coining of money. Tradition ascribes to the Lydians, whose soil
contained deposits of electrum, a native alloy of gold and silver, the first step in
using it as currency. On the Greek mainland, the only metal that could be used in
this way was silver: it was King Phidon of Argos who minted the first silver
coins, about the middle of the seventh century, and at the same time he introduced a complete system of weights and measures. From then onwards, the
Greeks had at their disposal a much more convenient instrument of exchange
than the iron spits (*oboloi*) which in early times had performed this function.

The main cities soon had their individual currencies, distinguished and guaranteed in each case by a particular emblem: the 'turtles' of Aegina, the 'foals' of
Corinth, and the 'owls' of Athens. Phidon's system of weights and measures, also
known as *Aeginetan*, met with competition from other systems, particularly the
Euboean system, which was adopted by Corinth and later by Athens. This gave
rise to complications, which the Greeks never succeeded in clearing up entirely.
In spite of this, the circulation of coined money gave a remarkable impetus to
commerce.

Athens scarcely took an active part in the economic movement until she began
to mint money early in the sixth century. It is a strange thing that Attica, which
we have seen developing a brilliant civilization in the Mycenaean and Geometric
Ages, underwent a sort of eclipse in the seventh century. There was no question
of the creative abilities of the inhabitants having declined, since we still justly

appreciate the Protoattic pottery of this age: but its appreciation in foreign eyes was limited to the immediate neighbourhood of Attica, an infallible sign of internal weakness that is fairly clearly supported by our admittedly obscure historical evidence. Athens was suffering from the same political and social crisis as the other Greek cities: excessive concentration of power in the hands of the noble families or *gene*, intolerable load of debt on the shoulders of the country folk, faulty administration of justice by the aristocracy in whose hands it entirely lay, multiplication of private acts of vengeance. Some too hesitant attempts at reform came to nothing, and an ambitious young man called Cylon tried to set up a tyranny. He was prevented by the reaction of the nobles, led by the family of the Alcmaeonidae and Megacles, head of the family: the repression was carried out so rigorously that some of Cylon's followers, who had taken refuge in a sanctuary, were put to death in violation of the right of asylum. This sacrilege weighed for a long time upon the *genos* of the Alcmaeonidae, who were exiled with their leader: two centuries later Pericles, who belonged to this family on his mother's side, was blamed because of the hereditary pollution incurred through the massacre of the Cylonians. The Cretan Epimenides came and purified the city (632 B.C.).

After this setback, the Athenian lawgiver Draco was entrusted with the task of reforming the dispensation of justice: he drew up the very severe code that bears his name. While determining Attic law for the first time in written enactments, he established legal procedure before public tribunals in place of private vengeance. In addition, drawing a distinction between wilful murder and unintentional homicide, he clarified the concept of personal responsibility. Despotic action and overruling power as practised by the noble clans were henceforth radically cut back.

But this was not enough to settle the social crisis. That was the achievement of the wise Solon, a poet, statesman, and merchant, who was raised in 594–593 to the high office of archon, with plenary powers of legislation. He began by cancelling all debts and abolishing their effects upon persons and property. Slavery for debt was prohibited. Various legal measures weakened the tyrannical force of family ties within the *genos*. Sumptuary laws forbade displays of luxury at funerals, which had given the clans an opportunity to assert their wealth and power. A series of detailed economic measures was passed with the object of promoting agriculture and commerce. Solon reformed the system of weights and measures and introduced the Euboean system for currency; this reform freed

Athens from the threatened economic ascendancy of Aegina, which used the 'Phidonian' system. The silver from the publicly owned mines at Laurium, in the extreme south of Attica, soon bestowed upon the Solonian currency a value recognized in the international market.

Other measures were of a political nature. On the one hand the citizens were divided into the four traditional Ionian tribes, on the basis of their birth, and on the other into four classes based on a property assessment, determined by their annual income from land. Solon made no alterations in this twofold division, but he based participation in public responsibilities on classification according to income, thus making political advancement possible to anyone who acquired wealth. He set up an annually elected Council of four hundred members, one hundred per tribe, to prepare the business for the Assembly. Lastly he established a popular court, the *Heliaea*, whose members were chosen from the whole citizen body, and which was later to play a vital part in Athenian democracy, for, as Aristotle says in this connection, 'as a result of the vote which the people can cast in the court, it automatically has control over the government of the city'.

Solon's reforms at many points laid the foundations of what was later to be the democratic system of Athens. Yet they did not restore civic peace, since the two parties, both the nobles and the people, had hoped for more from this clear-sighted and moderate lawgiver. Thirty years later, in 561–560 B.C., Pisistratus, a noble from Brauron, seized the Acropolis by a bold *coup d'état* and set up a tyranny. Twice deposed from power, he managed each time to recover the tyranny, which he bequeathed on his death, in 528–527, to his sons Hipparchus and Hippias, who held it peacefully until 514, the year in which the *tyrannoctonoi* Harmodius and Aristogeiton assassinated Hipparchus for entirely personal grievances which had nothing to do with politics. Hippias held on to power until the Spartans, on the invitation of the Alcmaeonidae, who were opposed to the tyrant, and on the advice of the Delphic oracle, intervened and expelled him in 510.

Tyranny, which the Athenians afterwards remembered with such loathing, had nevertheless brought considerable advantages to Athens. An enemy of the great families whose wealth consisted of large estates, Pisistratus was, however, sympathetic towards the small rural landowners: he sought by various measures to promote the formation of a stable and independent yeoman class, firmly attached to the soil which it tilled with its own hands. Thus the agrarian problem which Solon had been unable to solve was settled from now on. Moreover, Pisistratus developed the minting of coins with the silver from Laurium and, in place of the various emblems of noble families, stamped the coins with the new types of Athena and the owl, symbols of the Athenian state. This currency spread abroad: it is found from Egypt to Chalcidice, from Chios and Cos to Tarentum. From about 550 B.C. onwards, the 'black-figured' Attic pottery replaces that of Corinth in all the foreign markets, in Etruria no less than in Egypt, at Cyrene and also in the Black Sea area. Buildings erected with an eye to prestige in Athens itself and the encouragement given to art are indications of the prosperity which the city largely owed to the prudent government of its tyrants.

After the fall of Hippias, two parties were formed, one in favour of the aristocracy and the alliance with Sparta, the other, led by the Alcmaeonid Clisthenes, in support of the people. After an attempted intervention by Sparta, which failed, Clisthenes got the better of his opponents and won the adoption of important new political reforms: this was the birth of Athenian democracy. A motley coalition consisting of Sparta, Corinth, Chalcis, and the Boeotians broke up without having achieved any success: the Boeotians and Chalcidians, who had continued the conflict alone, were soundly beaten in 506, and this victory put Athens in possession of some land in Euboea on which she settled for the first time colonists who were at one and the same time farmers and soldiers, known as *cleruchs*. The city of Pallas, endowed henceforth with a new political organization and an army that had brilliantly proved its valour, could now play a decisive part in the events which were about to bring the Greek world and the Asiatic empire of the Achaemenids into conflict with one another.

Ionia. Relations with Lydia under the Mermnadae. Orientalizing civilization in the Greek Archaic period. The threat from Asia
From the moment when they settled on the western shore of Asia Minor, the Greeks had never ceased to be in contact with the native states of the interior. The excavations still proceeding at Gordium, the capital of Phrygia, are making us gradually more and more acquainted with the civilization of the kingdom of Midas, to whom legend attributed fabulous wealth. When it was destroyed early in the seventh century by a Cimmerian incursion, it was Lydia, with Sardis as its capital, that became the main power in Anatolia. In the first half of the seventh century Gyges founded the dynasty of the Mermnadae, whose most distinguished

rulers were Alyattes early in the sixth century B.C. and Croesus (560–546). Under the impetus of these enterprising monarchs, Lydia developed its relations with the cities of Ionia to the extent of exercising a real protectorate over them. After a long period of hostility, Alyattes had succeeded in making peace with Miletus, signing a treaty of friendship with her, and opening up his states to Greek commerce. The result was a profitable trade between the Ionian ports, which imported merchandise from Egypt and the Black Sea, as well as from the Greek mainland and the far west, and the market of Sardis, which was famed as a city of luxury and pleasure. The Greeks put up fairly well with a subjection which was not very severe and was imposed by cultured rulers who showed every consideration for Greek civilization: Alyattes married a Greek wife and Croesus welcomed Solon at his court; both of them showered gifts on the Delphic sanctuary, and the Delphians in return granted citizen rights to Croesus. Thanks to these cordial relations with Lydia, the Greek cities of Ionia experienced a period of great prosperity during the first half of the sixth century B.C. The widespread diffusion of common Ionian earthenware, in which products for exportation were normally stored, provides ample evidence of this: it is found everywhere, in Etruria, Provence, and Spain, as well as at Naucratis and the Black Sea colonies. Concurrently with its economic development, Ionia at this time experienced a brilliant cultural development: while the great temple of Artemis was being erected at Ephesus, with which only the Heraeum at Samos could compete in size, Milesians such as Thales, who predicted an eclipse of the sun in 585, or Anaximander, who, about 546, composed the first Greek work in prose known to us, were giving science and philosophy their first rational form.

But the influence of Eastern thought and above all of Eastern art had already for a long time been exercising a constant influence on Greek civilization as a whole. The seventh century and the first half of the sixth are known in archaeological classification as the *Orientalizing period*. Trade with the eastern markets, first through the agency of the Phoenicians, and later directly, by the sea route and also by the Anatolian land route, had distributed the products of Asian craftsmanship throughout the Greek world: objects of the goldsmith's art, textiles, carved ivory, and bronze utensils. A phenomenon that we noted in connection with the Mycenaean Age now reappears: Asian influences reveal themselves to an extreme degree in manners, thought, and art. Eastern fashions— long and richly embroidered garments, magnificent jewels, perfumes, costly appurtenances, ease and luxury in everyday life—made their way into the Greek cities of Ionia and also into the rich colonies in the west, which traded with the east and also with the Etruscans, who themselves showed strong traces of their Anatolian traditions. Religious beliefs and myths took shape in imitation of Oriental traditions: the Ephesian Artemis, the Aphrodite of Paphos, the Apollo of Didyma, near Miletus, had several characteristics borrowed from Asian deities. The Heracles of Thasos was believed to be of Phoenician origin. The monsters readily adopted by mythology, such as the Sphinx, Griffin, Gorgon, Chimaera, Siren, and Pegasus, came from Asian folklore or were inspired by its creations. Decorative art, in the work of goldsmiths and silversmiths no less than in pottery, reproduced the familiar motifs of Eastern art in the forms in which they had already become familiar throughout Greece, chiefly from decorated textiles: indefinitely repeated animal friezes, as if printed with one of the cylindrical seals engraved by the artists of the Near East, were a prominent feature of the decoration on the fine Orientalizing Rhodian vases, as also in Corinthian pottery. Even in music, the Anatolian contribution was of notable importance: the Greeks owed to it two of the primary *modes*, the Phrygian and the Lydian.

But the peculiar originality of Hellenic civilization was in no more danger of letting itself be swamped by eastern influences than it had been in the Mycenaean Age, face to face with the impressive achievements of Crete. Even in Ionia architecture remained essentially Greek, and in the pottery of Chios as on the sarcophagi of Clazomenae or the Ionian hydriae from Caere we still find the imprint of the Greek's lucid instinct for order, his realistic observation, and the constant intervention of the artist who puts something individual into the work the moment it ceases to be an object of commonplace production for use alone. Archaic Greek civilization found means of self-enrichment in its contacts with the east and took the fullest advantage of them; but it refused to sacrifice its own purity. This is nowhere more clearly to be seen than in Attica in the second half of the sixth century, where the gracious company of the *korai* from the Acropolis have often a completely Ionian kind of elegance and adornment, and yet preserve in their carriage and expression a reserve and modesty in keeping with the ideal of Greek womanhood. The faint smile that plays upon their marble features is certainly not mere convention: it is the expression of an inner life that makes the statue an individual, and thus very different from the impersonal images of the east.

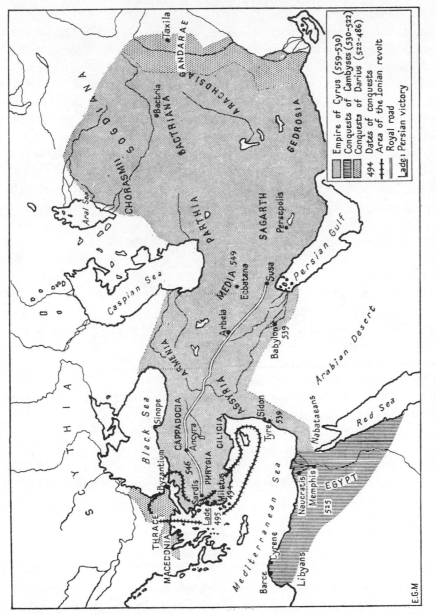

7. THE PERSIAN EMPIRE BEFORE THE PERSIAN WARS

Empire of Cyrus (559–530)
Conquests of Cambyses (530–522)
Conquests of Darius (522–486)
494 Dates of conquests
⌒ Area of the Ionian revolt
+++ Royal road
Lade: Persian victory

E.G.M

Now at the very moment when this art and civilization were benefiting by the contribution made by Asia without letting themselves be dominated by it, a formidable threat was taking shape; it came from that very east which until then had been a source of enrichment and profit and was now suddenly laden with deadly peril for the Hellenic world. A new power had burst into view in the middle of the sixth century: the Persian Empire, founded in the heart of Iran by the Achaemenid Cyrus. Within a few years, this conqueror and statesman of genius, starting from the kingdom of Media of which he had made himself the master, overthrew the power of Croesus (546), gained possession of the whole of Anatolia, and put under his sway the Greek cities of the coast and several islands in the Aegean Sea. Then he conquered Babylon and all the region of Asia extending from the Mediterranean to Mesopotamia. His son Cambyses conquered Egypt (525). From 522 a great king, Darius, ruled over the Achaemenid empire and was planning to extend its frontiers still further. On several occasions he had found the Greeks of the mainland in his path: Sparta had supported Croesus against Cyrus and maintained a hostile attitude towards the Persian Empire. Athens had refused to permit the return of Hippias, which was favoured by the Persians. In 499, a Persian expedition unsuccessfully attempted to reduce the island of Naxos in the Cyclades. This setback encouraged the Ionian cities to revolt: they obtained from Athens a reinforcement of twenty ships and five from Eretria; then they sent an expeditionary force into the valley of the Hermus, where they took and burnt Sardis, without sparing the sanctuary of Cybele, which was an object of veneration to the Lydians. Then all Asian Greece joined the insurrection, while the Athenians returned home. But Darius reacted vigorously and effectively: the revolt ended in 494 with the capture of Miletus, following upon the naval victory of Lade, in which the Ionian fleet had been defeated. The Milesians were deported in a body, the shrine of Apollo at Didyma was pillaged and its sacred offerings carried off as booty to Susa, where one of them has been found in our own time. Shortly afterwards, in 492, a Persian army commanded by Mardonius crossed the Straits and re-established Darius's authority in Thrace and Macedonia, which, along with the Greek cities of the region, had already been reduced on a former occasion, before the Ionian revolt. Two years later, in 490, an expedition led by Datis and Artaphernes set out from Cilicia: its immediate objective was to punish Athens and Eretria for the support which the two cities had given to the Ionian rising. But a more ambitious political aim was certainly being pursued: it was also a question of placing the whole of Greece under the domination of the Great King. In the ordeal of the Persian Wars, it was the future of an independent Greek civilization that was at stake. The glory of Athens is to have understood this from the very beginning and to have met the danger without faltering.

CHAPTER IV

THE CLASSICAL AGE

(From the Persian Wars to the accession of Alexander
the Great, 490-336)

The first Persian War: Marathon. Historical importance of the Athenian victory
THE expedition commanded by Datis and Artaphernes consisted of a considerable force of infantry and cavalry (perhaps 25,000 men), transported
by sea under the protection of a fleet of warships. Hippias, the son of
Pisistratus, formerly tyrant of Athens, accompanied the expedition, with the
purpose of re-establishing his rule in Attica with the help of the Persians. He
was counting on some collusion within the city, from those who remembered the
reign of Pisistratus as a 'golden age'. On its way the fleet set fire to Naxos, reduced the Cyclades, ravaged the lands of Carystus in Euboea, and then reached
Eretria, which fell by betrayal after a siege that lasted six days. Next it sailed to
Attica, where the invasion forces were disembarked at the Bay of Marathon,
facing Euboea. Hippias was advising the Persians in their operations.

Face to face with this urgent danger, Athens sent a runner to Sparta to ask for
aid. But the Spartans, prevented by religious scruples, did not march until full
moon, six days later: when they arrived, all was over. The Athenian assembly
had decided to fight in the open rather than await the attack within their city
walls. One of the ten selected generals, Miltiades, who had previously encountered the Persians during a colonial enterprise in the Thracian Chersonesus, had
won acceptance for this proposal. He also played a decisive part on the battlefield
by inducing the polemarch Callimachus, who was commander-in-chief, to take
the risk of battle without temporizing. The clash took place at dawn on a day in

September 490. Reinforced by 1,000 soldiers from Plataea, a faithful ally of Athens, the hoplites charged at the double and, after a hard hand-to-hand struggle, routed the Persian infantry, which was at least twice their number. The enemy fleet took the defeated survivors on board and weighed anchor. Callimachus and fewer than 200 Athenians had fallen in the battle, and they were buried in a common mound which still dominates the plain by the shore of Marathon, among the olive-trees. The Persians had lost nearly 6,500 men. Miltiades and the generals led the army back to Athens on the same day and arrived in time to forestall an attempt to land at Phalerum. Seeing that the shore was defended, Datis and Artaphernes made no further attempt but returned to Asia, carrying with them the booty and the prisoners taken in Euboea and the Cyclades.

From Darius's point of view the operation could be regarded as a partial success. Athens had indeed escaped from the Great King's vengeance, but Eretria, the other city guilty of aiding the Ionian rebels, had been heavily chastised. The captive Eretrians were deported to Ardericca, north of Susa in Luristan, a region in which an oil-well was already being worked; when Herodotus visited them fifty years later, they were still using their native language and customs. The plundering of the cities of Euboea and of Naxos and the large number of prisoners taken were positive results which the failure of the landing in Attica could not cause to be forgotten. Athens could wait: the Persians now realized that a landing force supported by a fleet was not enough to achieve the conquest of Greece. Darius resumed his plans for invasion on a large scale, but the revolt of Egypt delayed their fulfilment. In the meanwhile the king died (486) and his successor, Xerxes, had to restore order in Egypt before thinking of a new expedition to Europe.

What for the Persians was merely a minor reverse appeared on the contrary to the Greeks and rightly remains in the memory of mankind a victory whose results were of capital importance. For the first time the dreaded Persian army, which until then had seemed invincible, had been put to rout by the hoplites in open country. Athens had achieved this exploit by her own strength alone: the city of Cecrops, proud of her ancient traditions and her recent prosperity, was henceforth crowned with a halo of military glory such as even her success against Chalcis in 506 had not been able to confer upon her. Side by side with Sparta, which until now had been unrivalled in the military sphere, Athens was acquiring

35. CORINTHIAN COIN
On the obverse, Pegasus as the emblem of Corinth, because of which the Corinthian coins were sometimes called 'colts'. Beneath the horse there is an archaic letter (koppa), the initial letter of the name of the Corinthians. Cabinet des Médailles.

36. A DEER WITH ITS FAWN
A little Geometric bronze of the eighth century. The base of these figurines was sometimes used as a seal. A bird is perched on the deer's hindquarters. Boston Museum.

37. EARTHENWARE CHARIOT WITH TEAM OF FOUR
Found in Boeotia (seventh century). The simplification inherited from the Geometric style does not exclude a lifelike quality in the bearing of the horses and of the two warriors. The charioteer has his shield slung over his back, while his master keeps his on his arm. Only the latter is wearing a helmet. This work brings to mind the rich horse-rearing aristocracy in Greek society in the Archaic Age. National Museum, Athens.

38. A CATTLE-RAID. METOPE OF A SICYONIAN MONUMENT AT DELPHI
The sculptor (about 580–570) has portrayed the theft of a herd of cattle by the Dioscuri Castor and Pollux and two other heroes. Both men and cattle are walking at a measured pace, in triumphal procession. The warriors have their javelins in their hands. They are wearing the chlamys and have their hair long. Note the considerable number of planes in depth. Delphi Museum.

39. 'RAMPIN' HEAD
This masterpiece of Attic sculpture dating from 570–560 was bought in Greece by the French diplomat after whom it is named. The torso of the knight whose head this was, discovered later, is in the Acropolis Museum. The treatment of the beard and of the hair (adorned with a garland) is extremely delicate. There are traces of painting in several colours. Louvre.

40. BAY OF MARATHON (AIR PHOTOGRAPH)
In the middle, Mount Kotroni divides the modern town of Marathon (on the left) from the village of Vrana (on the right, against the wooded slopes of Mount Agriliki). The battle took place in the coastal plain, today covered with olive-trees, between the lowest slopes of Kotroni and the sea. A little to the left can be seen the long, narrow promontory of Cynosura, which encloses the bay. In the background, Euboea.

41. PAUSANIAS
Roman copy of a fifth-century portrait bust which has been identified with probability as that of the victor of Plataea. Oslo Museum.

35

36

37

38

42

43

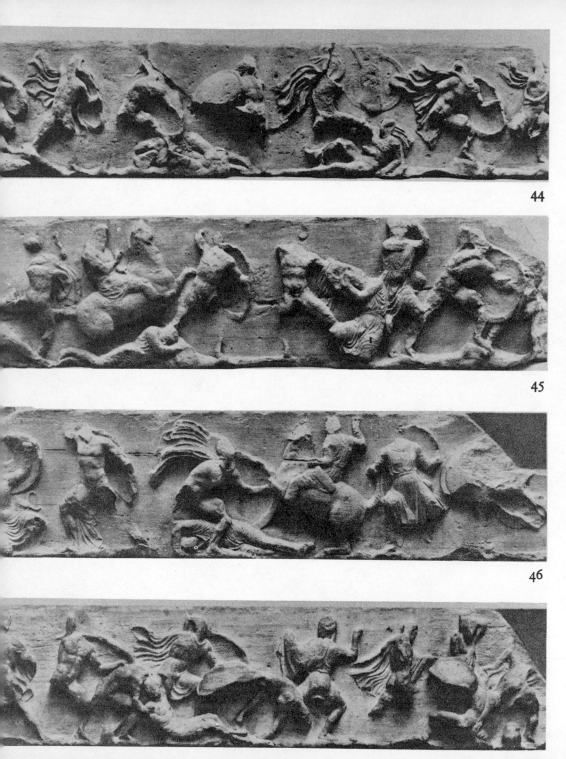

44

45

46

47

42. MILTIADES
On the shaft of the herm of the roman period bearing the copy of this portrait, there is a Greek epigram which reads: 'All the Persians, Miltiades, know your glorious deeds. Marathon is the sanctuary which preserves the memory of your valour.' The original was a complete statue erected in the fifth century, after Miltiades' death. Ravenna Museum.

43. THEMISTOCLES
A herm of the Roman period which faithfully reproduces a portrait of Themistocles done during his lifetime (about 470–460). The identification is made certain by an inscription. A face with vigorous features, worthy of this exceptionally gifted man. Ostia Museum.

44–47. BATTLE OF PLATAEA
The north, south, and west friezes of the temple of Athena Nike on the Athenian Acropolis, carved about 420, are no doubt rightly referred to the episodes of this battle. Greek warriors, represented in 'heroic' nudity, are shown in conflict with Orientals: long tunics, crescent-shaped shields (ills. 45 and 46), or with other Greeks (ills. 44 and 47), who could be Thebans, allies of Xerxes. British Museum.

H

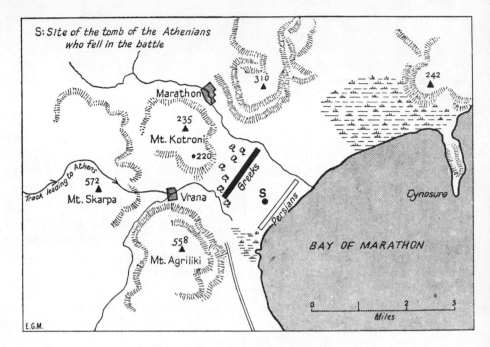

S: *Site of the tomb of the Athenians who fell in the battle*

Marathon

310 ▲

242 ▲

235 ▲
Mt. Kotroni

•220

Greeks

S

Track leading to Athens

572 ▲
Mt. Skarpa

Vrana

Persians

Cynosure

558 ▲
Mt. Agriliki

BAY OF MARATHON

0   1   2   3
Miles

E.G.M.

8. THE BATTLE OF MARATHON

(*After N. G. L. Hammond.*) The Persian army, with its back to the sea, was pro-
visioned by its fleet anchored in the bay. The Athenians and Plataeans came
down from the foothills of Pentelicus (Mounts Agriliki and Kotroni). The
polemarch Callimachus (who fell in the battle) was in command of the right
wing, and the Plataeans formed the left wing. Miltiades deployed his forces at an
arrow's flight from the Persians and then charged. In the centre, the Persians
had the advantage at first, but on the two wings the Greeks quickly got the better
of their opponents, then turned in on the victorious Persians in the centre and
overwhelmed them. Most of the Persian troops re-embarked in spite of the
efforts made to prevent them. It was at this stage that Aeschylus' brother,
Cynaegirus, had his hand cut off by a blow with an axe when trying to hold back
an enemy ship by grasping its stern.

a prestige that would serve her growing ambition. But above all, Darius's attempt upon Athens had given the Greeks a greater awareness than they had ever had before of what Hellenism stood for when confronted with the powerful Asian empire. It was not only the life and independence of a people that were at stake, but the future of a civilization. Whatever benefits Attica might formerly have enjoyed from the rule of the Pisistratids, the presence of Hippias in the wagon-train of the Persian army took on a symbolic meaning. The young Athenian democracy, which had chosen manfully to face foreign invasion, represented the whole Greek people declaring its resolution to reject slavery. Beyond a doubt many Greeks had experienced, and many would experience again, enslavement at the hands of other Greeks. But this time it was not a question of an ordinary struggle, in which 'war, the mother of all things', as Heraclitus said, brought human beings and their various forms of covetousness into conflict: the modest colonial expedition of Datis and Artaphernes was seen as an attempt to impose upon Greece not merely foreign domination, but also a political philosophy, that of the huge Oriental states ruled by sovereigns endowed with divine right, where the inhabitants were not citizens but subjects, a nameless, servile multitude in which the individual was submerged. Such was the destiny that the men who fought at Marathon, the *Marathonomachai*, refused to accept for themselves, their brothers, and their descendants. Confronted with an Asia whose nature they knew to perfection, its power, wealth, and splendour, based on the subjection of masses of humanity to the whims of an absolute monarch, they defended in battle the constitutional ideal of a city composed of free men. When in the fresh light of a summer morning Miltiades' soldiers, with the round shield on their arm and brandishing their long spears, charged at the double against the Persians, whose dark mass was silhouetted in the rising sun against the sparkling waves of the sea, they were fighting not only for themselves, but also for a conception of life which was afterwards to become a common possession of the Western world.

The Second Persian War. Xerxes' army. Battles of Thermopylae and Artemisium. Salamis. Plataea. Liberation of Ionia.

The Second Persian War had an entirely different character. Xerxes' preparations, beginning in 483, were obvious to everyone: he not only assembled large land and sea forces, but also had impressive works taken in hand, such as the

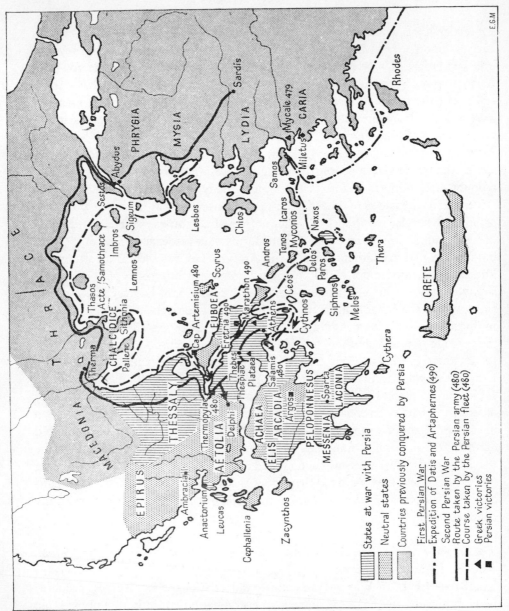

9. THE PERSIAN WARS

Sardis

Rhodes

PHRYGIA

MYSIA

LYDIA

CARIA

Mycale 479

Miletus

Abydus

Sestos

Samos

THRACE

Acte

Samothrace

Imbros

Thasos

Sigeum

Lesbos

Chios

Icaros

Sithonia

Lemnos

Pallene

CHALCIDICE

Scyrus

Andros

Tenos

Myconos

Delos

Naxos

Therma

Cap Artemisium 480

EUBOEA

Eretria 490

Marathon 490

Ceos

Paros

Thera

Athens

Cythnos

Siphnos

MACEDONIA

Thermopylae 480

Thebes

Salamis

Melos

Thespiae

Plataea

480

EPIRUS

THESSALY

Delphi

ACHAEA

ELIS

ARCADIA

Argos

Sparta

Cythera

Ambracia

AETOLIA

Anactorium

MESSENIA

LACONIA

Leucas

PELOPONNESUS

Cephallenia

Zacynthos

CRETE

E.G.M

States at war with Persia

Neutral states

Countries previously conquered by Persia

First Persian War

Expedition of Datis and Artaphernes (490)

Second Persian War

Route taken by the Persian army (480)

Course taken by the Persian fleet (480)

Greek victories

Persian victories

cutting of a canal through the isthmus of Acte (the peninsula of Mount Athos) in Chalcidice, in order to save his fleet from having to round this dangerous cape, where Darius's vessels had suffered heavy losses ten years earlier, during the operations on the northern shores of the Aegean in 492. It was clear that invasion was imminent and that this time Greece as a whole was the Great King's objective.

At Athens, Miltiades had died in disgrace after an ill-fated expedition to Paros. The most influential political leader, Themistocles, had foreseen the danger and taken measures to provide against it; on his recommendation the people had decided to spend the unusually high revenues derived from the silver mines at Laurium on the construction of a fleet of two hundred triremes. Sparta, strong in her ancient glory and the support of her allies, became the leader of the Greek states determined to fight side by side for their liberty. All wars between the cities were stopped. Meeting at the Isthmus of Corinth, the delegates of the various states discussed the strategy to be adopted and entrusted supreme command to the Lacedaemonian leaders. Argos, Achaea, Aetolia, and Crete remained neutral. Gelon, the tyrant of Syracuse, when asked to join, refused to do so because they would not make him the leader of the coalition. But it is also true that an understanding which had been reached between the Persian king and Carthage played a certain part in discouraging the Sicilian tyrant from involving himself in an adventure far from home at a time when the Carthaginian threat might be renewed at any moment.

Xerxes' forces, having assembled in the northwest of Asia Minor, began to cross the Hellespont at the beginning of June 480, using the pontoon bridges which the Persian engineering corps had thrown over the straits between Abydus and Sestus under the direction of the Greek engineer Harpalus. A fleet of 1,200 vessels covered the land operations and helped to supply the troops, numbering several hundred thousand men. All the provinces of the immense empire had provided contingents, whose picturesque and motley appearance Herodotus describes with complacency. The naval force included Phoenician, Egyptian, Cilician, and Cypriot squadrons and also 300 Greek vessels manned by Ionians or islanders who were subjects of the king. Crossing Thrace and the Greek colonies there, which had already been reduced to the status of a satrapy, and then Macedonia, which was an ally of the Achaemenid monarchy, Xerxes reached the region of Mount Olympus and entered Thessaly: the Greeks had withdrawn their line of resistance farther to the south. The Thessalians and the Boeotians (except Plataea and Thespiae) threw in their lot with Xerxes.

The first engagement on land took place at the Pass of Thermopylae, the only possible route between the sea and the mountain barrier of Callidromus, which was considered impassable by an army. During the first few days of August 480, the Persians forced the defensive position, which an enemy column had turned by way of a mountain path. Warned in time, the Greek forces had fallen back upon the Isthmus of Corinth, leaving at Thermopylae only King Leonidas and his three hundred Spartans who, with some Boeotians from Thespiae, fought and died to the last man. Their self-sacrifice inflamed the Greek determination to do or die, and was celebrated by the poet Simonides in the inscription later carved on the tomb where these heroes lay buried together:

> Go tell the Spartans, thou that passest by,
> That here, obedient to their laws, we lie.

Simultaneously the Greek fleet, which had assembled near Cape Artemisium, at the northern point of Euboea, had clashed for the first time with the squadrons of the Great King which were sailing down from Therma, a town on the site of the future Thessalonica. Although severely tried by a hurricane which had shattered 400 vessels on the rocky peninsula of Magnesia, the Egyptian and Asian ships had given a good account of themselves during two days of indecisive fighting. When news was received of the relinquishment of Thermopylae, the Greek fleet withdrew southwards and anchored near Salamis, from which position it could guard the flank of the fortifications on the Isthmus.

By way of Phocis, which they plundered, and Boeotia, which welcomed them as allies, the Persians reached Attica. In obedience to an oracle, the Athenians had abandoned their city and taken refuge in the fleet, which had evacuated them to Salamis and Troezen. The small garrison left on the Acropolis put up a courageous defence before being butchered. Athens was plundered and set on fire. Thus did Xerxes avenge the burning by the Ionians of the sanctuaries at Sardis, as Darius had wished.

Before attacking the defences of the Isthmus, the king had to destroy the Greek fleet, which was still mustered at Salamis. Messengers described to him the dissensions and uncertainties of the generals commanding the confederate Greek contingents under the supreme authority of the Spartan Eurybiades. The

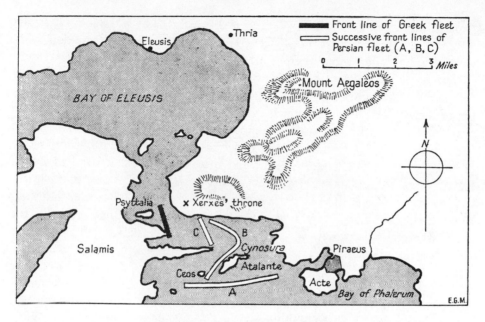

10. THE BATTLE OF SALAMIS

(*After N. G. L. Hammond.*) The experts still discuss the identification of the islet of Psyttalia, which some would place where the islet of Atalante appears on the map. The position of the two fleets and that of Xerxes' throne are also not fixed with certainty. According to Hammond, the Greek fleet occupied the northern part of the Strait of Salamis and its outlet into the Bay of Eleusis. During the day preceding the battle, the Persian fleet (A) came and closed the southern outlet of the strait, near Atalante. Then it entered the strait during the night (B) and in the morning found itself face to face (C) with the Greek fleet, which was itself advancing into the strait. The clash took place in the middle of the strait, which in some places is no more than 1 kilometre wide. Persian forces landed on Psyttalia were decimated by arrow-shot and later massacred by the hoplites, while the Greek ships, more capable of manoeuvring in this narrow space, rammed the Great King's vessels, which got in each other's way.

Athenian Themistocles held the view that they must fight without delay in the waters of Salamis, where lack of space would prevent the enemy from deploying all his ships and thus profiting from his superiority in numbers. He manoeuvred cleverly to obstruct a plan to withdraw towards the Isthmus: the Persians, whom he had taken care to warn, blocked with one of their squadrons the western channel of the Bay of Eleusis, by which the Greek ships could have withdrawn. So they were obliged to join battle. One morning, towards the end of September 480, the Great King's fleet, led by the Phoenician ships, entered the strait, barely one kilometre wide, between Salamis and the Attic shore. Xerxes had had a throne set up for him on the slopes of Mount Aegaleos, so that he might witness the victory of his squadrons. The Greek ships were ready for battle: following the tactics recommended by Themistocles, they employed their capacity for manoeuvre to ram the enemy ships, which hindered one another because of their too close formation. The hoplites in the Greek ships, who were better armed than their Asian or Egyptian opponents, had the advantage in combat when a ship had been boarded. The Athenians and the Aeginetans, the two most numerous contingents in the Greek fleet, rivalled one another in valour and skill. After a fierce and confused battle, the Great King's fleet went about and made off towards Phalerum, while the Greeks indulged until nightfall in a great massacre of shipwrecked enemies, whom they destroyed, as Aeschylus says, 'like tunnyfish'. Fewer than four hundred Greek ships had inflicted a ruinous defeat on a fleet three times as strong.

Though weakened by its heavy losses, this fleet was nevertheless still formidable. But Xerxes had had enough and the season was too far advanced for further action. He gave the order to retreat, sending the fleet back directly towards the Hellespont while he himself returned by land with the army: it cost him forty-five days of painful marching to get back to Asia. But he left in Thessaly one of his generals, Mardonius, with a large force which was to winter on the spot and renew operations in the spring.

In 479, just after the harvest, at the beginning of July, Mardonius invaded Attica, whose inhabitants had once more been evacuated to Salamis. Learning that the Greek confederate army was advancing from the Peloponnesus, he fell back into Boeotia, leaving the city in ruins and the countryside ravaged. He awaited the Greeks at the opening of the passes over Mount Cithaeron, near the river Asopus. His troops were numerous and of excellent quality: along with the infantry of Persia and other Asian nations were contingents of Boeotian and Phocian hoplites: his cavalry was specially formidable, reinforced as it was by squadrons from Thessaly, Boeotia, and Macedonia. The Greek army led by the Spartan Pausanias, a nephew of Leonidas, contained nearly 40,000 hoplites, of whom 10,000 were Lacedaemonians and 8,000 Athenians; there were light-armed troops in addition to these. It crossed Cithaeron and took up a position at the foot of the mountain, facing the Persian lines, near the town of Plataea. The opposing forces watched each other for three weeks, during which the Greeks suffered severely from harassing by the enemy cavalry. An attempted retreat ordered by Pausanias, but badly carried out by his subordinates, encouraged Mardonius to cross the Asopus with his infantry and attack the now disorganized Greeks. But the Greeks withstood the attack steadfastly: the Lacedaemonians above all gave proof of their traditional valour, shattered the Persian assault and, themselves charging in their turn, put the enemy to rout. Mardonius fell on the battlefield. The Athenians, on the left wing, had compelled the Boeotians to retreat. The Barbarians' camp fell into the hands of the Greeks, who massacred its occupants. What was left of the invading army retreated northwards, protected by its cavalry. Thebes, after a siege lasting twenty days, handed over the Persian supporters. The victors had every right to glorify their victory by setting up votive offerings in the great sanctuaries, such as the famous serpentine column at Delphi: this time Greece was definitely saved.

The Battle of Plataea, one year after Salamis, put an end to the threat which had been hanging over the Greek world for fifteen years, but it did not actually end the Persian Wars. On the same day when Pausanias was destroying Mardonius in the fields of Boeotia, the Greek fleet, commanded by a Spartan admiral, was winning another resounding victory. It had taken the offensive in answer to an appeal from the Ionians who wished to free themselves from the Achaemenid yoke. The Persian fleet, declining battle, had been hauled up on land near Cape Mycale on the coast of Asia Minor, opposite Samos, and the crews had joined the troops quartered in the district to form an entrenched camp. The Greeks landed and stormed the camp, while the Ionian units enlisted by the Persians were deserting. The victory of Mycale gave the Greeks naval supremacy in the Aegean Sea. Almost everywhere the Ionians drove out the Persian garrisons and the Great King's representatives. The Greek fleet proceeded to the Hellespont to destroy the pontoon bridges thrown by Xerxes over the waters of the strait, but storms had already done the job. The fleet then returned to Greece, but the Athenian contingent remained in the Straits and laid siege to Sestus, which fell during the winter. In the spring of 478, the Athenian general Xanthippus, the father of Pericles, brought back to Athens, along with substantial booty, the cables which had been used to fasten together the boats that carried Xerxes' pontoon bridges. These trophies, which were dedicated to the gods in the major sanctuaries, added to the glory of Athens, which from now on held the military and political initiative in operations against Asia.

Pentecontaetia. First Delian Confederacy. Cimon. The policy of Pericles. The Athenian Empire. Origins of the conflict with Sparta
'From the time of the Persian Wars until that of the Peloponnesian War,' Thucydides tells us, 'the Lacedaemonians and the Athenians, now making war against one another, now struggling with allies of their own who were trying to escape from their control, now forming a truce, never ceased improving their military resources and increasing their experience in warfare through the opportunities provided by these undertakings.' This period of fifty years, or *Pentecontaetia*, thus appears retrospectively to the historian as a preparation for the conflict in which the rivalry of the two great Greek states was inevitably bound to end. Sparta, whose authority had until then been unquestioned, saw with misgivings the extension of Athenian power to the point of counterbalancing her own influence even in the affairs of the Peloponnesus. This growth is a fact of primary importance not only for the history of Greece, but also for our whole civilization; for it was by attaining the leading role in the political and military arena that Athens was able to develop all her genius in the domain of thought, literature, and art. The half-century from 480 to 430 B.C. is justly known in the memory of mankind as the *Periclean Age*: it gave Greek civilization a decisive upward surge, a brilliance that has never ceased to dazzle.

From the winter of 478–477 onwards, Athens in concert with the Ionian cities of Asia Minor was organizing a league whose purpose was to continue the war with the Persians. The latter were still formidable and a new invasion might still well be feared. The cities of Asia Minor, the Straits, and the Aegean Sea, which were directly threatened, needed permanent protection based on a powerful navy. Athens alone could provide it; no doubt the common tradition shared by Attica and Ionia facilitated this union, but the primary cause was of course

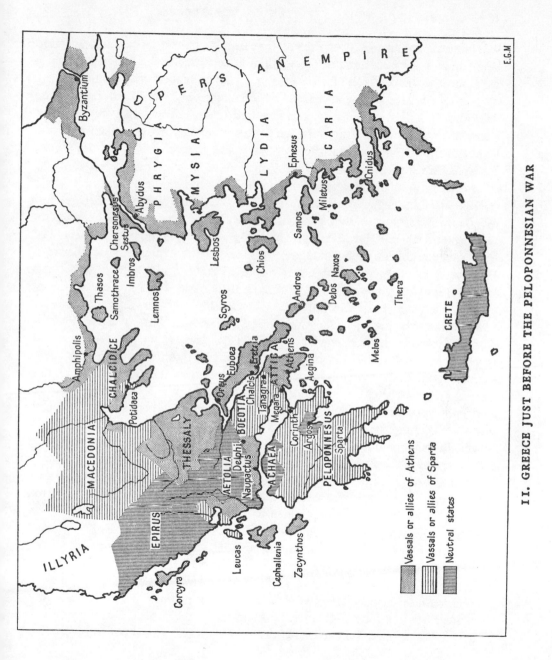

II. GREECE JUST BEFORE THE PELOPONNESIAN WAR

Map labels:

PERSIAN EMPIRE

PHRYGIA · MYSIA · LYDIA · CARIA

Byzantium · Chersonesus · Sestus · Abydus · Amphipolis · Thasos · Samothrace · Imbros · Lemnos · Scyros · Lesbos · Chios · Samos · Ephesus · Miletus · Cnidus · Andros · Delos · Naxos · Thera · Melos

CHALCIDICE · Potidaea · MACEDONIA · THESSALY · EPIRUS · ILLYRIA · Corcyra · Leucas · Cephallenia · Zacynthos

AETOLIA · Naupactus · Delphi · ACHAEA · BOEOTIA · Tanagra · Oreus · Euboea · Chalcis · Eretria · ATTICA · Athens · Megara · Aegina · Corinth · Argos · PELOPONNESUS · Sparta

CRETE

Vassals or allies of Athens
Vassals or allies of Sparta
Neutral states

E.G.M

self-interest. Athens put her fleet at the disposal of the league and assumed command of the confederate forces. The cities which could not contribute a naval force to the common effort agreed to pay an annual contribution in money, or tribute, whose total was calculated and assessed with great fairness by Aristides. The federal treasury, administered by Athenian treasurers, was put under the protection of Apollo in the sanctuary of Delos, in the centre of the Cyclades, which had for centuries past been an object of veneration for all the Ionians. Under the leadership of the Athenian generals, a series of campaigns ensured control of the Straits, drove the Persian garrisons out of Thrace, made possible the establishment of Athenian military colonies (*cleruchies*) at the mouth of the Strymon and in the island of Scyros, and repressed an inclination to secede on the part of Naxos. Lastly, about 467, Cimon the son of Militiades led a large squadron against the Persian fleet on the southern coast of Asia Minor; in Pamphylia, at the mouth of the river Eurymedon, he won a twofold victory on land and sea which was a repetition of the Battle of Mycale. The Greek cities in the Aegean Sea were henceforth safe.

Meanwhile the leading figures in the Second Persian War were disappearing from the scene in an atmosphere of scandal. Pausanias, the victor of Plataea, had revealed personal ambitions incompatible with the traditions of the Lacedae-monian state. Removed from his command, he had established secret contacts with the Great King: his intrigues were discovered and he was left to die of hunger in a sanctuary where he had sought asylum. Themistocles, the real victor of Salamis, also suffered disgrace. He had rendered his native city a new service by persuading it to rebuild its walls, which had been destroyed by the Persians, and to fortify the Piraeus, in spite of Spartan opposition. But the accidents of political life brought him into disfavour with the Athenian people and caused him to be ostracized. He had been implicated in Pausanias's dealings with Persia and was for this reason pursued by the agents of Sparta and Athens. His only way of escaping from them was to go and place himself under the protection of Artaxerxes the son of Xerxes, who received him with favour and gave him lands in Anatolia, where he died soon afterwards, about 460.

While Athens, though deprived of Themistocles, had found in Cimon a leader capable of inspiring her to follow an enterprising policy, Sparta was having to contend with serious difficulties. She had once again had to face the hostility of her neighbour and old enemy, Argos. Then a revolt of the helots broke out, involving a Third Messenian War that lasted nearly ten years (469–460). In 464 a violent earthquake almost entirely destroyed the city of Sparta: it needed all the energy of King Archidamus and the traditional Spartan discipline to save the state from utter disaster. Thus Sparta was not able to take advantage of the difficulties Athens was encountering in the earlier stages of her aspiration to hegemony: when, in 465–464, the island of Thasos, near the Thracian coast, wished to leave the Athenian alliance, she appealed in vain to Sparta for aid and Cimon was able to reduce the rebel city after a siege lasting two years. What is more, Sparta had to beg for Athenian assistance in order to bring the resistance of the Messenians to an end. Cimon was sent with an expeditionary force, but failed in his attempt to carry the fortress on Mount Ithome, where the insurgents had taken refuge. The Spartans dismissed him with blunt discourtesy. This led to an open rupture between the two states; armed conflict was about to replace the veiled rivalry that had kept them in opposition to one another for twenty years.

The internal political development of Athens was tending to promote hostility towards Sparta. Cimon had always been sympathetic towards the conservative traditions of Lacedaemon. But in spite of his victories he was ostracized in 461; he had not been able to prevent the democratic party, led by Ephialtes and Xanthippus's young son Pericles, from securing the adoption of reforms which took all political influence away from the Council of the Areopagus, consisting of ex-archons, leaving it only legal functions confined to cases of homicide and sacrilege. The Council of the Five Hundred and the court of the Heliaea, whose members were chosen on more democratic principles, inherited the other powers previously exercised by the Areopagus. Although Ephialtes was almost immediately murdered, these measures were kept in force, hence Aeschylus's warning in his *Oresteia* (458): 'Reject both anarchy and despotism' (*Eumenides*, ll. 526–527). At the same time, Athens was beginning offensive operations against the Lacedaemonians and their allies as well as the Persians. While increasing her means of defence by building the continuous fortification of the Long Walls from the city to Piraeus, she sent a fleet to aid a Libyan chief who was attempting, in the neighbourhood of Memphis, to raise Egypt against the Great King. After some initial successes, this expedition ended in disaster, in 454: almost all the force perished. In Greece itself, Athens obtained the support of Megara, hitherto an ally of Sparta, contended with Corinth and destroyed the power of Aegina (457), thus securing complete freedom of manoeuvre in the Saronic Gulf. In 457 she suffered defeat at Tanagra in Boeotia by a Lacedaemonian army which returned to the Peloponnesus after its victory. The Athenians took advantage of this to assert their authority in central Greece. Next the Peloponnesian coasts were harried in naval operations, partly conducted by Pericles. At Naupactus, in western Locris, the Athenians had established a strong base manned by the Messenians who had been exiled by the Spartans; they could thus control the Gulf of Corinth as they already controlled the Saronic Gulf.

The ten years between 460 and 450 were of vital significance for Athens: it was at this time that Pericles, born about 495 in a noble family connected by marriage with the *genos* of the Alcmaeonidae, became the leading influence in Athenian politics. Handsome, attractive, cultured, an excellent orator and a competent leader in war, he enjoyed the complete confidence of the democrats, who, aware of his high qualities, regarded him as politically and financially upright and remained faithful to him to the end, in spite of the attacks made on him by comic poets favourable to his opponents. He conceived vast ambitions for his native city and, as a sagacious statesman, was not troubled by excessive scruples about the means of realizing them. Being very properly convinced that the Athenian people possessed exceptional abilities, he held the view that these abilities entitled it to hegemony, which it was its duty to exercise: he was thus driven to the doctrine of imperialism, to which his compatriots felt no objection. The people benefited by it, since it thus became the ruling element, not merely in a confederacy, but in an empire, and the resources of the league would supply it with subsidies: the introduction of a daily wage for the jury of the Heliaea, the great increase in the number of officials in Athens and abroad, military pay and allowances, all this, according to Aristotle, provided a livelihood for more than twenty thousand citizens. Add to this the building for prestige which was being undertaken under Pericles' direction on the Acropolis and which kept hundreds of workmen busy for more than twenty years and we can see how greatly Pericles' policy promoted the material interests of the people, to say nothing of the satisfaction it brought to their national self-esteem. In 454–453, the federal treasury was transferred from Delos to Athens, thus passing from the protection of Apollo into that of Athena; although this step was justified by the dangers with which the Persian fleet threatened the Cyclades after the Athenian disaster in

Egypt, at bottom it was a political operation which indicated complete seizure by Athens of everything appertaining to the league. The allied states were in actual fact passing into the ranks of subjects and the league was changing into an empire.

Pericles, with the assistance of Cimon, who had been recalled from exile, acted with decision and vigour. The Egyptian disaster and the imperialistic tendencies of Athens had caused several allied cities to revolt, in which they were aided and abetted by Persia. In order to have their hands free, the Athenians concluded a truce with Sparta. They then devoted their efforts to restoring their disaffected allies to their allegiance. As soon as their authority was re-established, they renewed the war against the Persians: Cimon was in command of the naval force that went to seek action in the waters around Cyprus. He died of illness during the operations, after having won new successes. In 449–448 negotiations were undertaken and ended in a treaty known as the Peace of Callias, from the name of the chief Athenian negotiator. The autonomy of the Greek cities in Asia was guaranteed. The Great King's warships were no longer to let themselves be seen between Pamphylia and the Bosporus. Athens, on her side, undertook to respect the Great King's territories. The restoration of peace ensured the safety of the Ionians, which was the avowed object of the Delian League, and sea trade once more became free from hindrance.

Athens took advantage of the situation to assert her domination over her 'allies' still more: she increased the number of military colonies, or *cleruchies*, established in their lands; she frequently exercised control over the internal policy of the states in favour of the local democrats; she imposed the use of Attic currency and the Attic system of weights and measures. Economic and political imperialism went hand in hand. Sparta, however, was not inactive on the mainland. She launched the Second Sacred War against the Phocians, allies of Athens, to protect the autonomy of Delphi against their threats. Athens took action in reply, but she encountered serious difficulties in central Greece, where she was opposed by several Boeotian cities. An Athenian corps was heavily defeated at Coronea in 446; the inescapable result was a complete withdrawal from Boeotia. Megara revolted and all Euboea did the same. Finally a Lacedaemonian army advanced as far as Eleusis. Happily for Athens, the commander of this army did not press his attack, but beat a retreat. Pericles took advantage of this to chastise the rebel Euboeans with much severity. He then concluded a thirty years' peace with Sparta, in 446–445; it established a certain balance of

48. GREEK AGAINST PERSIAN

This Attic red-figure cup, unfortunately badly damaged and restored (the whole upper half of the warrior has been repainted), is a work of the vase-painter Duris. It represents the struggles between the Greek cities and the Achaemenid empire about the time of Marathon (490). The fallen Persian, with his close-fitting garments of gaudy design, was a standard-bearer. Louvre.

49. HEADING OF AN ATTIC DECREE

This decree, passed in autumn 405, confers Athenian citizenship on the Samians who remained faithful to their alliance with Athens after Aegospotami (on the same stele there are also two other decrees on behalf of the Samians, dated 403–402). The bas-relief shows Hera and Athena, the patron goddesses of Samos and Athens respectively, sealing their alliance with a handshake. The words are: 'Cephisophon of the deme of Paeania, was Secretary [of the Council]. For the Samians who remained faithful to the Athenian people.' Then follows the text of the decree. Cephisophon's name is mentioned in the heading because it was he who had to have the three decrees engraved in 403–402. Acropolis Museum, Athens.

50. PERICLES

A herm of the Roman period, identified by an inscription. The original statue, by Cresilas, was made shortly before or shortly after the great man's death, about 430–420. The helmet worn by Pericles is the mark of his office as strategus. There is classic nobility and dignity in the face, whose features approximate to an ideal type, but without losing all individual character. British Museum.

51. COIN OF PHILIP II OF MACEDON

In 356, the year of Alexander's birth, Philip, in order to celebrate the victory of his horse in the Olympic Games, had a series of tetradrachms minted, showing on the obverse a head of Zeus and on the reverse a horse with a nude rider on its back. The rider has a head-band round his hair and holds a palm-branch in his hand: these are the emblems of his victory. Beneath the horse there is a cantharus. Cabinet des Médailles.

ΚΗΦΙΣΟΦΩΝΠΑΙΑΝΙΕΥΣ
ΕΓΡΑΜΜΑΤΕΥΕ
ΣΑΜΙΟΙΣΟΣΟΙΜΕΤΑΤΟΔΗΜΟΤΟΑΘΗΝΑΙ
ΩΝΕΓΕΝΟΝΤΟΜ

49

power between the Athenian Empire, shorn of most of its mainland allies (save Plataea and Naupactus), but still lord of the Aegean, and the Peloponnesian coalition led by Sparta, which was now strengthened by the adherence of Megara and Boeotia. Each state was to refrain from any action against the allies of the other, but could act as it wished towards states not included in the treaty. Freedom of maritime trade was guaranteed both in the east and in the west.

In spite of her retreat in the Greek mainland, Athens was at the height of her economic and military power. On the instigation of Pericles, she devoted a part of the funds raised by tribute to the cost of monuments and statues being erected on the Acropolis: the Parthenon was being built from 447 to 438, and the sacred plateau was a huge building-site in endless activity until 432. The statue of Athena Parthenos, by Phidias, alone cost 700 talents, nearly twice the total amount of the yearly tribute of the allies. At the same time Athens maintained a navy of 60 triremes in a state of permanent alert during eight months of the year. These forces enabled her to intervene abroad in every region. It was the Athenians who in 443 established a colony, whose members were drawn from several Greek cities, at Thurii, near the site of the old town of Sybaris, in southern Italy; the historian Herodotus of Halicarnassus was one of its first citizens. In 440–439 Pericles suppressed with considerable difficulty a revolt at Samos and another at Byzantium. The harshness that accompanied the suppression of the Samians made clear to all eyes the transformation of the league into a tyrannically oppressive empire. With her authority thus reasserted, Athens was then able to send an expedition into the Black Sea to Sinope and Amisus, where colonists were settled side by side with the former inhabitants. In 436 Athens founded the important colony of Amphipolis near the mouth of the Strymon, with the purpose of strengthening her influence in Thrace and Chalcidice. In the west she formed an alliance with Acarnania.

In this region, as in Chalcidice, the interests of Athens clashed with those of Corinth, a member of the Peloponnesian League. Hostilities having developed between Corinth and her colony at Corcyra (Corfu), the latter requested and obtained an alliance with Athens; in a naval battle which took place in 433 in Corcyraean waters, the Corcyraeans owed the repulse of the Corinthian squadron to the arrival of Athenian reinforcements. The danger of a general conflict was becoming clearer, and Pericles, who was well aware of it, regarded it as something inevitable. So he increased his acts of provocation against Sparta's allies. In

I

432 a decree proposed by him excluded the traders of Megara from the ports and markets of Attica and the Athenian Empire: this was tantamount to economic strangulation of Megara, whose offence was to have harboured runaway slaves from Athens. Simultaneously an Athenian expedition was sent against Potidaea, the largest city in Chalcidice, which was a Corinthian colony and had maintained close relations with its mother-city. The Athenian intervention at Corfu, the siege of Potidaea, and the 'Megarian' decree were more than Sparta could endure. Supported by her allies and pressed especially by Corinth, she sent an ultimatum to Athens demanding at least revocation of the Megarian decree. On Pericles' advice the Athenians rejected this demand; this meant a rupture and a decisive trial of strength between the two rival cities. The war which began in 431 was to last twenty-seven years until it ended with the defeat of Athens in 404.

Peloponnesian War. The Archidamian War. Sphacteria. Victories and death of Brasidas. Peace of Nicias. Its instability. The Sicilian Expedition. The War of Decelea. Political and military difficulty of Athens. Aegospotami. Capture of Athens by Lysander

From the very beginning of the conflict, Pericles made his fellow-countrymen adopt a costly strategy, but the only one likely to offer Athens a real chance of success. He estimated to perfection how inferior the Athenian troops would be if they met the forces of Sparta and her allies in open warfare: not only were the Peloponnesians numerically stronger in this field but the acknowledged valour of the Spartan hoplites might well make their opponents disinclined to welcome an encounter. Obviously the Lacedaemonians would wish to seek action in order to have the issue decided by a single battle. Pericles' advice was to decline a pitched battle: the populace of Attica was to take shelter behind the fortifications of the city, the Piraeus, and the Long Walls, abandoning the countryside to the forays of the enemy. In compensation, Athens would make full use of her maritime superiority, not only to maintain the freedom of her seagoing trade from the Piraeus, but also to harry the coasts of the Peloponnesus with frequent landings and surprise attacks. Her 300 triremes, reinforced by those of Chios, Lesbos, and Corcyra, the quality of their crews, the bases in the west at Naupactus and in Acarnania, her domination of the Aegean Sea, and her ample financial reserves regularly supplied by the tribute, all these were factors favourable to Athens in her conflict with an enemy less well equipped at sea and less rich. It might be hoped that the Peloponnesian League, exhausted in the end by ruthless naval warfare, would finally disintegrate and that Sparta, deserted by her allies, would acknowledge defeat. So it was a matter of a war of attrition, in which the Athenians would have to show perseverance and moral strength, bringing themselves to let their lands be ravaged by the invader, but remaining confident about the final issue of the struggle. It needed all Pericles' prestige to have his policy adopted: half the population of Attica—all the country folk and the townsmen who owed country estates—was going to sacrifice its possessions and its way of life for the success of a strategy whose results would have to be long awaited.

The first part of the war, which lasted for ten years (431–421), is often called the Archidamian War, from the name of the Spartan king who conducted the first operations, but who, in fact, died in 427. After an unsuccessful surprise attempt by the Thebans on Plataea, an ally of Athens, the Lacedaemonian army invaded Attica and plundered the low-lying parts of the country, while the Athenian fleet was carrying out raids on the Peloponnesian coast. The following year (430), the Lacedaemonians invaded Attica again. Athens was then smitten by an unforeseen blow, the plague: the concentration of the whole population within the urban zone, where the country people camped on waste ground under very defective conditions of hygiene, was favourable to the epidemic, which lasted for more than a year and broke out again in 427. A third of the population was carried off. In the midst of this terrible trial, of which Thucydides has left us an impressive picture, the Athenians for a brief period turned against Pericles, but in the spring of 429 they put their trust in him once more and re-elected him as strategus. The great man died, worn out, in the autumn. His death deprived Athens of the only statesman who could have brought the war to a successful conclusion. After him, there was no leader who enjoyed comparable credit or possessed so clear an intellect.

The military operations continued with varying fortunes. In Chalcidice, the Athenians eventually took Potidaea (429) after two years of costly effort. In the waters of Naupactus, the strategus Phormion won a series of brilliant successes in the same year against a Peloponnesian squadron much superior in numbers; in commemoration of his victory the Athenians erected a portico in the sanctuary at Delphi. But they were faced with a revolt by Mitylene, the most important city on the island of Lesbos, which they had to reduce and punish. On the proposal of a democratic leader named Cleon, the instigators of the revolt were executed in great numbers. In the same year (427), Plataea, which had been besieged for two years, had to yield and the little garrison of Plataeans and Athenians was massacred. The war was taking on a cruel and pitiless character.

In 425, by a stroke of fortune, Athens had victory within her grasp. She had sent some troops into action in Sicily against Syracuse and the other cities allied to Sparta. A squadron carrying reinforcements to the west put in because of stormy weather in the roadstead of Pylus, on the western coast of Messenia. An Athenian general, Demosthenes, who had already distinguished himself in Acarnania, decided to remain at Pylus and to entrench himself there with a few soldiers in order to threaten, from this base of operations, the whole of Messenia, which was a vulnerable part of Lacedaemonian territory. In order to avert this threat, the Spartans sought to carry the Athenian position, which resisted their attacks: they occupied the little island of Sphacteria, just off the coast, enclosing the roadstead of Pylus. While this was taking place, an Athenian squadron appeared on the scene and blockaded the island with the 400 Spartans occupying it. The number of Spartan citizens properly so called (*Spartiatai*) in the city of Lacedaemon was so limited that this blockade of 400 of them was enough to make Sparta decide to ask for peace, offering the Athenians very advantageous terms. But the Assembly of the Athenian people, spurred on by Cleon, a demagogue inclined to extreme measures, showed itself uncompromising and, after animated debates, entrusted Cleon with the task of reducing those besieged on Sphacteria. Skilfully led by Demosthenes, the Athenian forces, which were greatly superior in numbers, broke the resistance of the Lacedaemonian hoplites: twenty days after setting out, Cleon was bringing back to Athens some 300 prisoners, including 120 Spartiates (425 B.C.). This brilliant operation strengthened the determination of the greater part of the Athenian people not to negotiate until total victory was won, though Aristophanes was ardently pleading for peace.

But luck turned. In 424, the Athenian army attempted an invasion of Boeotia. At Delium, near Tanagra, it met the Boeotians and was defeated in a pitched battle: Athens had been unwise to depart from the policy formerly recommended by Pericles. The Lacedaemonian general Brasidas, being sent to northern Greece, seized Amphipolis in spite of the efforts of the Athenian Thucydides, who was in command of the squadron stationed at Thasos; held responsible for the loss of Amphipolis, Thucydides was sentenced to exile, in which he devoted his enforced leisure to writing the history of this war. Meanwhile Brasidas was winning success after success in Chalcidice, where he detached a considerable number of cities from their alliance with Athens. Cleon obtained command of an expedition to recover Amphipolis; in the summer of 422 he was beaten by Brasidas under the walls of the city; both Cleon and Brasidas lost their lives in this action. The simultaneous removal of the best Spartan general and of the Athenian leader who stood for war to the bitter end enabled the two states to open negotiations, which ended in the Peace of Nicias, called after the Athenian statesman who negotiated it. This peace, which was due to exhaustion and concluded at the price of reciprocal concessions, did not settle the dispute for pre-eminence between Sparta and Athens. It could not last for long.

It was clear from the beginning that the clauses of this treaty would remain a dead letter: Athens did not succeed in regaining control of Amphipolis and Chalcidice, so she kept Pylus and Cythera, from which she continued to threaten Sparta. A complicated diplomatic game developed between Sparta and Thebes, Athens and Argos, in which Elis and the Arcadian states also took part. Athenian policy was pulled this way and that between Nicias, an advocate of peace by agreement with Lacedaemon, Cleon's successor Hyperbolus, who led the democratic party, and the young Alcibiades, a fascinating and unscrupulous schemer, an aristocrat by birth and a democrat from calculating ambition, a disciple of Socrates and a nephew of Pericles. The procedure of ostracism, which was employed in 417 for the last time, resulted in the exile of Hyperbolus, but left face to face Alcibiades and Nicias, who were at one and the same time partners and rivals. In the year before this, Sparta had restored her military prestige by winning a pitched battle near Mantinea against an Argive army reinforced by Arcadians and a small Athenian contingent. Athens, for her part, was seeking to make her control of the Aegean Sea complete. When the island of Melos refused to join the league, the Athenians took it by force and slaughtered all the adult males (416–415). This massacre aroused universal indignation, but the Athenian people cared nothing and decided to send an expedition to Sicily.

Syracuse had long held the leading place in Sicily. Early in the century, the enterprising policy of her successive tyrants, Gelon and his brother Hieron, had remarkably increased her territory and power. Their glory had eclipsed that of the other western tyrants, such as Theron of Acragas and Anaxilas of Rhegium. They had brilliantly defended Hellenism against the Carthaginians, by Gelon's

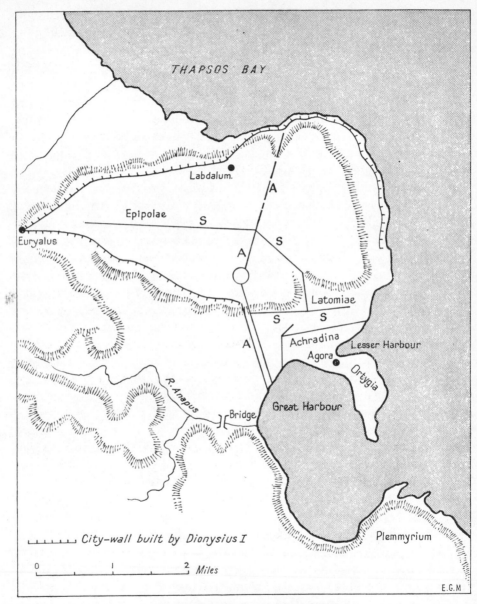

THAPSOS BAY

Labdalum.

Epipolae   S

Euryalus

A   S

A

Latomiae

S   S

A

Achradina

Agora   Lesser Harbour

Ortygia

R. Anapus

Bridge   Great Harbour

Plemmyrium

⊢⊢⊢⊢⊢ *City-wall built by Dionysius I*

0   1   2 *Miles*

E.G.M

12. THE SIEGE OF SYRACUSE

victory in the Battle of Himera in 480, and against the Etruscans, by Hieron's victory in the sea-fight off Cumae in 474. Several Etruscan helmets dedicated by Hieron in memory of his victory have been found at Olympia. Even after the fall of the tyranny in 466, a year after Hieron's death, Syracuse remained the most powerful of the Greek states in Sicily. Remaining faithful to the memory of its origins, it was on good terms with its mother-city Corinth, and, from the earliest stages of the Peloponnesian War, it had rallied most of the Greek cities in the island to the cause of Corinth and Sparta. From 427 to 424 Athens had tried hard to help Leontini and Camarina which, aided by Rhegium, were in conflict with Syracuse and her allies, but her intervention had produced no results. It was now a question of utilizing the respite which Athens enjoyed in Greece proper to resume an adventurous policy in the west. The opportunity was provided by appeals for aid from Segesta, an ally of Athens then involved in war with Selinus, an ally of Syracuse. Nicias, prudent as always, advised against this enterprise. Alcibiades was its warmest advocate. He prevailed in the debates before the people, who reckoned upon the material advantages of such an expedition in the form of pay and booty. The joint command was conferred upon Alcibiades and Nicias, and the expedition, fitted out in the most lavish way, set forth at the end of spring in the year 415 B.C.

A few days earlier, the Athenians had been stirred to indignation by an act of sacrilege: the pillars bearing a bust of Hermes, which popular piety had erected in large numbers in the streets and in the Agora since the time of the Pisistratids, had been mutilated by unknown hands during the night. An inquiry was initiated and an attempt was made to implicate Alcibiades, who was already suspected of having taken part in a burlesque of the Eleusinian Mysteries. A ship was sent to Sicily to fetch him, but he escaped and reached Sparta. There he painted in the most alarming colours his native city's ambitions in the west. The Lacedaemonians followed his advice, sent the Spartiate Gylippus to Syracuse to lead the resistance to the Athenian invasion, and decided to reopen hostilities in Greece proper. These measures were crowned with success: after two years of fruitless operations and in spite of the reinforcements sent under the leadership of Demosthenes, the best Athenian general, the expeditionary force failed in its attempts to take Syracuse by storm, and then suffered in its turn from the attacks of the Syracusans, skilfully led by Gylippus, to which attacks it finally succumbed in the summer of 413. Nicias and Demosthenes were put to death by the victors.

52. HOPLITE
This little bronze, found at Dodona, dates from about the end of the sixth century. The warrior, protected by his shield, advances brandishing his lance (lost). He wears a 'Corinthian' helmet with a large plume, a metal 'bell-shaped' cuirass, and greaves. He has long hair. Berlin Museum.

53. FUNERAL STELE OF THE ATHENIAN ARISTION
At the bottom we may read the artist's signature in archaic letters: 'The work of Aristocles' (about 520–510). The hoplite is wearing a turned-up 'Corinthian' helmet (of which part is lost) on his curly hair. On top of a thin tunic he is wearing a cuirass with lambrequins. He has greaves and he holds his spear in his left hand. Many details were shown merely by painting, some traces of which remain. National Museum, Athens.

54. FUNERAL STELE OF THE ATHENIAN DEXILEOS
This cavalryman, who died in action in 394 in the Corinthian War, is represented in the act of striking with his spear (lost) an enemy who has fallen on the ground. While the latter is shown in the state of 'heroic' nudity, Dexileos, with his tunic and chlamys, is wearing the military costume of the period. Ceramicus Museum, Athens.

55 & 56. TWO BRONZE 'CORINTHIAN' HELMETS
This type of helmet, with a round shell sometimes accentuated with a flange, nose-piece, cheek-pieces, and rear-peak, had no detachable part (except the plume, which is in all cases lost). Except during a battle (see ill. 58), it was worn turned back (see ills. 49, 53, 82). It might be decorated with incisions (ill. 56) or even bas-reliefs on the cheek pieces. It was provided with a leather lining. Olympia Museum.

57. GEOMETRIC ARMOUR
This helmet and cuirass, found in a tomb in Argos, date from the second half of the eighth century. The cuirass consists of a breast-plate and a back-piece joined by inter-locking and lacing. The helmet, provided with cheek-pieces, is surmounted by a high crest which held a horse-hair plume. Argos Museum.

58. 'CORINTHIAN' HELMET
This detail of the north frieze of the Treasury of Siphnos at Delphi, carved about 530, shows how the 'Corinthian' helmet was worn in battle. The giant who is taking to flight, in the middle ground, with his face turned backwards, has a helmet furnished with a crest in the form of a cantharus, with two plumes attached each to one handle of this cantharus. On the left, the face of Artemis. Delphi Museum.

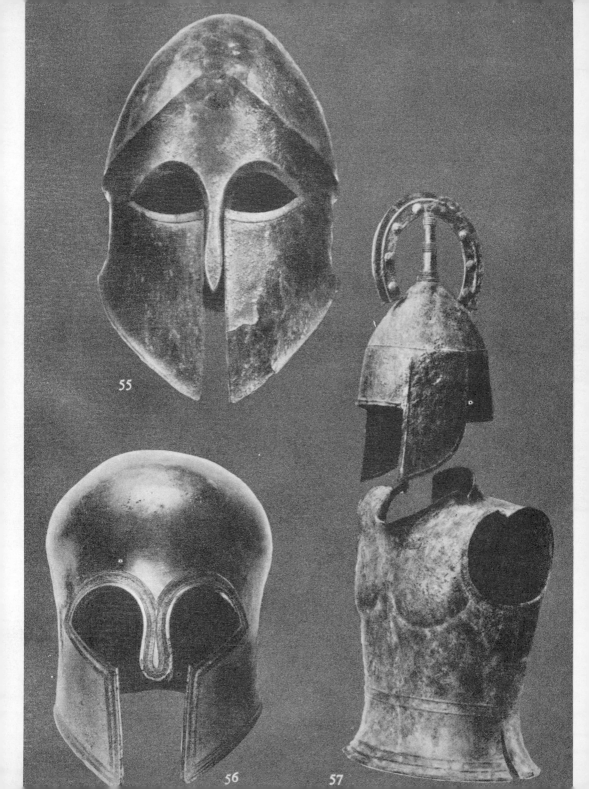

55

56 57

58

59

59. BRONZE SHIELD

The shield, circular in shape, photographed at the moment of its discovery, is crushed by the weight of the soil. Traces of a dedicatory inscription can be made out on the rim. Olympia.

60–62. ATTACK ON A FORTIFIED TOWN

These friezes are from the monumental tomb of a native prince at Trysa (Gjölbaschi), in Lycia (fifth century). A Greek sculptor carved them in the local limestone. Soldiers armed in Greek style are attacking a battlemented wall defended by other soldiers. The prince and his wife are seated in the midst of these, apparently little interested in the battle. It is a remarkable attempt to bring to life large groups of fighters in spite of the technical difficulties of bas-reliefs: the influence of large-scale painting is probable. This scene has been interpreted, no doubt wrongly, as the capture of Troy. Kunsthistorisches Museum, Vienna.

63. AMAZON ON HORSEBACK

This modelled Attic vase, signed by the potter Sotades (middle of the fifth century), was found in a pyramid at Meroë, in Nubia. The horsewoman wears a high-plumed 'Attic' helmet, with the cheek-pieces raised. Boston Museum.

The captured survivors suffered harsh imprisonment in the quarries, or *latomiai*, of Syracuse before being sold as slaves.

Meanwhile war was beginning again in Greece proper. In the same year 413, the Lacedaemonians, on the advice of Alcibiades, invaded Attica and fortified the small town of Decelea, at the foot of Mount Parnes, from which they now dominated the region of Athens. This post, being held throughout the year, henceforth enabled them to exercise a permanent blockade on the city by land, preventing it from utilizing the resources of the Attic countryside and in particular the silver mines of Laurium, whose slave miners took to flight. The extremely complicated history of the years 412 to 404 shows both the desperate efforts made by Athens to escape from the pressure of her foreign enemies and her repeated attempts to reform a political régime which was held to be responsible for the disaster in Sicily. The ambitions of individuals played their part in these activities amid the military operations whose success or failure often depended largely on them. It was a pathetic and merciless struggle, in which each contestant staked his own life as well as the fortunes of the Republic. Military exploits, diplomatic negotiations, shady schemes concocted by adventurers, popular movements stirred up by demagogues, intrigues of secret societies (*hetairiai*), political assassinations, death sentences, massacres of prisoners—these are the things met at every instant by the historian of this agitated period. Political figures bearing the stamp of originality, who are at the same time war leaders, tread their way through these vicissitudes: first Alcibiades, then, among the Athenians, Theramenes, a representative of the moderate party, the democrat Thrasybulus and the strategus Conon; among the Lacedaemonians, Lysander, an energetic and skilful general, a crafty and unscrupulous negotiator; among the Persians, the satraps Pharnabazus and Tissaphernes and the Great King's younger son, Cyrus, who afterwards organized the expedition of the Ten Thousand. For henceforth the Persians played a decisive rôle in the development of the conflict. The time was long past when the Greeks united against the threat from Asia. Instead they now competed for alliance with the Achaemenid monarch and his representatives in Asia Minor: they did not so much seek military support, of which there is little sign on the battlefields, as the king's gold; this they needed to meet the cost of war and to entice the mercenaries in the opposing camp by a higher bid at the right moment. This factor was to prove decisive in bringing final victory to Sparta.

The rest of the war was mainly fought at sea, where both the expense and the loss of life were heavier than on land. Athens was making desperate efforts to preserve her empire, which was revolting on all sides, and the lines of communication that were indispensable for her food supplies. The defection of Rhodes had cut her trade route with Egypt, one of her two chief suppliers of cereals, so now she would have to struggle to the end to keep the Straits open in order to receive the convoys of wheat grown in southern Russia. In Ionia, revolt after revolt took place: only the island of Samos, where the Athenians had established a democratic form of government, offered their fleet a reliable base of operations. But the sailors and soldiers stationed at Samos viewed with indignation the oligarchic revolution which, in their absence, had broken out at Athens under the combined influence of the aristocratic clubs (*hetairiai*), which drew their inspiration from the orator Antiphon, and the moderate party, led by Theramenes. For several months of the year 411, democracy was abolished and replaced by an oligarchic régime known as the rule of the *Four Hundred*. But the latter were unable to retain the support of Theramenes, who restored the previous form of government for the time being, after reaching agreement with the fleet at Samos commanded by Thrasybulus. Alcibiades, who had quarrelled with Sparta, now returned into his fellow-countrymen's good graces, and it was under his command that the united forces of Thrasybulus and Theramenes won a great naval victory at Cyzicus in 410. Sparta offered peace, which the Athenian Assembly was unwise enough to refuse. Until 408, the Athenian fleet won a good number of new successes in Thrace and in the Straits, but the arrival of Lysander as admiral commanding the Peloponnesian fleet and the financial aid which he received from Cyrus the Younger reversed the situation. Lysander enticed away the oarsmen of the Athenian triremes by offering them higher rates of pay, and gained the advantage in the first battle he fought. Alcibiades, who was held responsible, had to yield his command to Conon and fled to the Chersonese. In 406, Athens made a new effort: her fleet, considerably strengthened, defeated the Peloponnesian squadron at the Arginusae islands close to the coast of Asia Minor, facing Lesbos. This was fortune's last smile. The Athenian people could not take advantage of it; what is more, in a fit of unreasoning anger, they punished the victorious generals with death, blaming them for having neglected to save the men on board the vessels sunk in the battle. Among the generals who were the victims of these illegal proceedings was a son of Pericles. In the following year Lysander, by a clever strategem, surprised the Athenian fleet at anchor on the coast of the Chersonese, near the mouth of the Aegospotamus, and utterly destroyed it, capturing the ships and their crews, with the exception of a small detachment led by Conon, which escaped. This defeat was decisive. From November 405 the Piraeus was under blockade, and the people besieged in the city were beginning to suffer famine. They held out for four months and surrendered in April 404, accepting the victor's terms: destruction of the Long Walls, surrender of the remaining warships, obedience to Sparta in matters of foreign policy. Yet the Lacedaemonians had shown themselves generous by refusing to agree to the proposals of their allies Thebes and Corinth, whose desire was to inflict on Athens the murderous treatment that she had herself inflicted on Melos, Mitylene, and other cities. The Long Walls were at once demolished, to the music of flutes: it seemed that Greece was now entering upon an era of liberty.

Sparta and Athens after 404. The Thirty. Restoration of democracy at Athens. The expedition of the Ten Thousand. The Corinthian War. The Greek world of the west. Dionysius I

Though the collapse of the Athenian Empire may have given birth to such hopes as these, they did not last for long. Sparta, undisputed head of the victorious league, soon showed herself incapable of playing the role of leadership now incumbent on her in the reorganization of the Greek world: wedded to its traditional policy of mainland hegemony, embarrassed by its alliance with Persia, whose subsidies were necessary to it for its fleet, and weakened by an internal development, resulting from its political and social system, which progressively reduced the number of Spartiates properly so called in proportion to the lower classes and the helots, the Lacedaemonian state had not enough men, not a broad enough political vision, to impose upon the Greek cities, jealous of their autonomy, an authority capable of co-ordinating their efforts and settling their quarrels. The personal prestige of Lysander, on whom the Greeks conferred exceptional honours after his victory, certainly enabled him for a period to lord it over Athens' former allies by putting the oligarchical parties everywhere in power, supported by Lacedaemonian garrisons under the order of a Spartan governor called a *harmost*. But by the end of 403 Sparta, distrustful as ever of outstanding individuals, was withdrawing power completely from this 'uncrowned king' and returning to her old absorption in hegemony within the

Peloponnese by repressing the Eleans, who were showing some inclination to assert their independence.

After the defeat of Athens, the city underwent a violent antidemocratic re-action that lasted several months. The government was in the hands of a com-mission of thirty citizens, including Theramenes and Critias, an intelligent and cynically ambitious aristocrat, a disciple of Socrates and an uncle of Plato. Strengthened by the presence of a Lacedaemonian garrison installed by Lysander, the Thirty set up a reign of terror in the city, handing over to the executioner more than fifteen hundred citizens and numerous resident aliens (*metoikoi*), and confiscating for their own benefit the property of the condemned and of those who had sought safety in exile. Theramenes, still a moderate, tried in vain to oppose these acts of violence: Critias had him executed by his henchmen, while the Council of the Five Hundred, terrorized, did not dare to interfere. But the exiles, united under the leadership of Thrasybulus, who had found refuge in Boeotia, returned to Attica, seized the fortress of Phyle, and then took possession of the Piraeus. After a fratricidal struggle between the people in the city and people in Piraeus, during which Critias fell in battle, the Thirty were driven off, and then, under the threat of a new Lacedaemonian army sent to Attica, a reconciliation between the two parties took place. In 403–402, under the archon-ship of Euclides, a general amnesty was arranged, from which only the Thirty and some magistrates were excluded, and the traditional democracy was fully re-established.

The people scrupulously observed the amnesty agreement and even under-took the repayment of the debts which the people in the city had incurred to-wards the Lacedaemonians in fighting against the people in the Piraeus. Nevertheless, the memory of the excesses committed by the oligarchs was slow in fading away, and the hatreds which they had aroused played a part in the trial of Socrates: by imputing to him the crime of impiety and that of corrupting the young, his accuser Meletus, supported by the democrat Anytus, was arousing in the jury a vague feeling that the philosopher was partly responsible, not only for the daring speculations and destructive criticisms which undermined the moral foundations of the city, but also for the scandalous behaviour of his disciples, insolent and sceptical aristocrats like Alcibiades, Charmides, and, worst of all, Critias. The surprising thing is not that Socrates was condemned, but that he was found guilty by such a small majority of votes. His heroic resignation in the face of death and the respect which he showed for the city's laws by refusing to take to flight in order to avoid condemnation made a powerful impression on his friends, which Plato and Xenophon transmitted to their contemporaries. The dramatic circumstances of his death helped to spread his teaching.

Thus occupied with her internal restoration, Athens quietly left it to Sparta to take the lead in relations with Persia. The latter had recently undergone a serious crisis, in which Greeks had become involved. On the death of King Darius II, his younger son Cyrus, who had played an important rôle during the closing years of the Peloponnesian War, rose against his elder brother, who had become king as Artaxerxes II. He recruited a corps of Greek mercenaries to strengthen his existing army in Anatolia and marched on Babylon. In the autumn of 401 B.C., he met the king's army at Cunaxa, in Mesopotamia, and was killed in the battle. The Greek mercenaries, numbering about 13,000, left to themselves, retreated northwards along the Tigris, then crossed Armenia and in the following spring arrived at Trebizond, on the Black Sea, whence they found their way back to Europe. The epic of the Ten Thousand, which was so called from the approximate number of the survivors, struck the imagination of the age: it revealed the basic weakness of the Achaemenid empire, which had not been able to stop this little force in the course of its long retreat, and it vastly increased the confidence of the Greeks in their military superiority over the Orientals. Brilliantly related by Xenophon in his *Anabasis*, which he composed as an eyewitness and leader in this adventure, it was later to provide inspiration for Alexander's plans.

During this same year 400 B.C., Sparta broke off her relations with the Great King, whose satrap Tissaphernes wished to re-establish Persian domination over the Greek cities in Ionia. The war was a series of disconnected operations in Asia Minor by Lacedaemonian armies prevented from pursuing an effective strategy by the need to carry off booty to replenish their treasury. The Spartan king Agesilaus distinguished himself by his activity and energy. At Cyprus the Athenian Conon, who had taken refuge with King Evagoras after his defeat at Aegospotami, organized a squadron for the Persians. The emissaries of the Great King were also travelling through mainland Greece, openhandedly distributing gold in order to rouse against Lacedaemon all the cities that were jealous of her authority.

In 395 their efforts culminated in the formation of a coalition comprising

Thebes (at this time directly threatened by Sparta as the result of an incident in Phocis), Athens, Argos, and Corinth. Lysander was killed in an unsuccessful battle in Boeotia. Agesilaus, recalled from Asia as the Great King had wished, won a victory at Coronea (394) over the confederate forces. But Athens was re-building the Long Walls and Conon's fleet defeated a Peloponnesian squadron off Cnidus. Soon the Laconian coast was again experiencing sea raids. Other operations were taking place in the neighbourhood of the Isthmus of Corinth—hence the name *Corinthian War* given to this war as a whole. Now for the first time was seen in action the light infantry (*peltasts*) of the Athenian Iphicrates, who was introducing a new element into the military art. The reconstructed Athenian fleet won successes in the Aegean Sea under the command of Thrasybulus. Sparta retaliated by intercepting in the Straits the supply convoys sailing to Athens and by carrying out surprise attacks on the Piraeus from Aegina. Then exhaustion on the part of Sparta's enemies brought the war to an end. The Spartan Antalcidas negotiated with the Persians, and Artaxerxes made known the conditions which he proposed to the Greek states. After long hesitation, the latter eventually accepted the *King's Peace* (386). They recognized the Achaemenid sovereign as master of the Greek cities in Asia and in Cyprus. The other Greek cities, both small and large, were to remain autonomous. Athens kept Lemnos, Imbros, and Scyros, where she had re-established cleruchs. The King was the guarantor of these agreements: he was also the one who benefited by them, since he recovered control of the Greeks in Asia Minor, while European Greece, because of the principle of the autonomy of individual cities, remained a medley of states, powerless to attempt any great enterprise. This was a revenge for the Persian Wars.

In the west, the Greek world had had to face a formidable offensive from the Carthaginians, who took advantage of the dissension between the Greek cities to resume their expansion in Sicily, which had been held in check since Gelon's victory at Himera in 480. The Carthaginian troops took Selinus and Himera by storm in 408, captured and razed Agrigentum, occupied Gela, and threatened Syracuse. The last-named city had, during military operations, put itself under the authority of an energetic young officer, Dionysius, who, elected as strategus, had established a tyranny by massacring his opponents. A plague which had broken out in the camp of the Carthaginians obliged them to seek terms: Dionysius agreed to acknowledge the suzerainty of Carthage over the greater part of Sicily (404). Then he concentrated his efforts on building up his strength: he extended the fortifications of Syracuse until he made it the largest city in the Greek world; he collected large forces of mercenaries both Greek and Barbarian; he set up a park of war-engines and built a fleet of 300 ships, not only triremes but also vessels with four and five banks of oars. With these powerful armaments he attacked the Carthaginians in 397 and, after a long war in which he won brilliant successes, but also suffered reverses, he concluded in 392 a new treaty, which substantially reduced the Punic zone of influence. Dionysius then devoted himself to other enterprises in southern Italy, where, relying on the support of the native populations of Lucania, he conquered all Bruttium with the Greek cities of Locri, Croton, and lastly Rhegium, possession of which gave him control of the Italian shore of the straits (387). At the same time, his fleet dominated the Ionian Sea and enabled the Syracusan traders to penetrate to the upper end of the Adriatic: they established trading posts at Lissus in Illyria, at Hadria in the delta of the Po, and also at Ancona, an excellent port on the Italian coast. A sea raid on the territory of the Etruscan town Agylla (Caere) established the threat of the Syracusan fleet in the Tyrrhenian Sea. Yet, in spite of two further wars with the Carthaginians, Dionysius did not succeed in expelling them from Sicily: in the end the opponents agreed to observe as the respective boundaries of their territories the stream Himera in the north and the river Halycus in the south. The Carthaginians thus kept the western third of the island, with Selinus and Segesta. The rest remained in the possession of the Greeks, under Syracusan control.

These achievements won great prestige for Dionysius the Elder (so called to distinguish him from his son and successor Dionysius the Younger): when he died in 367, he was beyond dispute the most illustrious Greek of his age. His power rested upon force, that is to say basically upon his well-paid and well-armed mercenaries, and upon a complete freedom from scruples. His originality lay in the fact that he was the first to organize a great state in which Greeks of the most diverse origins, Sicilian and Italian Barbarians, soldiers of fortune and traders from every country, lived side by side under his personal authority, more in the condition of subjects than of citizens. Of course he did not succeed in welding these disparate elements into a genuine political unit, but he basically altered the old framework of social relations. On the other hand, he gave a strong impetus to economic life and made Syracuse the great market of the west. The

Empire of Dionysius

Territories held by Carthage in 387

* Italian cities allied to Dionysius I after 379

• Trading stations set up by Dionysius

IAPYGES allied to Dionysius

13. SYRACUSE IN THE TIME OF DIONYSIUS I

K

brilliance of his court, his interest in literature (he prided himself on being a writer of tragedies), and the attraction of his unique personality drew to him the interested curiosity of philosophers. He was visited by Plato and Aristippus, but neither of them had reason to be pleased with the experience. Isocrates, whose dream was to see the Greeks united against the danger from Persia, thought for one brief moment that Dionysius might undertake the realization of this great plan. The Athenians, shortly before the death of the Syracusan tyrant, conferred upon him the freedom of their city and gave him the first prize in the dramatic competition of the Dionysia in 367. This honour paid to his tragedies must have flattered his vanity more than any of his military victories. But the example of autocratic government which he had given in Sicily could never be forgotten: he was destined to have several imitators.

Conflicts in Greece proper. Second Delian Confederacy. Epaminondas and the hegemony of Thebes. Battle of Mantinea
During this period, Greece proper was floundering in the anarchy created by the King's Peace with the connivance of Sparta. Sparta's main object was to repress any attempts of her allies to assert their independence: so she intervened, first at Mantinea in Arcadia, then at Phlius, near Corinth, to establish governments favourable to her policy in these places. In response to an appeal from two cities in Chalcidice, which refused to join a confederacy arranged by Olynthus, the largest city in this district, a Lacedaemonian army intervened to break up this league and thus secure observance of the 'autonomy' laid down in the King's Peace. During this expedition to northern Greece, a Spartan corps passing through Thebes was solicited by one of the two factions competing for power and, at its request, occupied the citadel of Thebes, the Cadmea. This occupation lasted for several years, but one night in winter, in 379, some Theban patriots, led by Pelopidas, massacred the pro-Spartan magistrates and liberated the city, compelling the Lacedaemonian garrison to withdraw. The armies which Sparta subsequently sent to Boeotia proved unable to compel Thebes to come to terms.

Athens, in spite of her old distrust for her northern neighbour, had quite quickly sided with her against Sparta: the new men who were controlling the destiny of the city, the orator Callistratus, the generals Chabrias, Iphicrates, and Timotheus, the son of Conon, were determined to take advantage of circumstances to restore the prestige of their native city. In 377 their efforts culminated in the foundation of the second maritime Confederacy which, exactly a century after the first, associated with Athens most of the island states of the Aegean Sea and the Greek states of the Thracian coast. A series of bilateral treaties, concluded in 384–383, had prepared the way for this new organization, which joined Athens and the totality of her allies on a plane of equality. The allies met in a Council (*Synedrion*) of which Athens was not a member. The decisions of this Council were decided by a majority of votes, each city having one vote. The Athenian state made its own decisions. If these coincided with those of the Synedrion of the allies, then, and then only, the Confederacy acted as such, Athens being entitled to lead their common operations. To meet the federal expenses, the allies paid contributions fixed by the Synedrion, not a tribute. Athens, on her side, assumed responsibility for the maintenance of her own military forces. She thus furnished a considerable effort which enabled her to win several successes at sea against the Peloponnesian ships, not only in the Cyclades but also in the Ionian Sea, where Timotheus led a squadron to Corcyra and Acarnania. In 374, anxious to reduce her expenses and worried about the advance made by Thebes, Athens made peace with Sparta on the basis of the *status quo*: she had regained maritime superiority.

During this time Thebes had reconstituted the league of the Boeotian cities to her own advantage, while in Thessaly an energetic leader, Jason the tyrant of Pherae, was unifying the country under his authority. This pupil of the sophist Gorgias had collected a powerful army of mercenaries, supported by the excellent Thessalian cavalry; his presence introduced a new element in central Greece. This gave Athens some grounds for anxiety which prompted her to draw closer to Sparta, in spite of new difficulties which had caused hostility between them in connection with the affairs of Corcyra. In 371, a peace conference met at Sparta, with representatives of the principal Greek powers, including Dionysius of Syracuse, and a representative of the Great King. It was agreed to reaffirm the principles of the King's Peace. But a dispute broke out about the position of Boeotia: Epaminondas, the Theban plenipotentiary, wished to sign the treaty on behalf of all the Boeotians and not of Thebes alone. The Spartan King Agesilaus peremptorily opposed this request and Epaminondas left Sparta without signing the treaty.

Sparta at once ordered the Lacedaemonian army stationed in Phocis to march against the Thebans, who were refusing to acknowledge the autonomy of the other Boeotian cities. About ten miles southwest of Thebes, near the small town of Leuctra, the clash took place (371). Epaminondas, who was in command of the Theban forces, employed a tactical innovation of the greatest importance: contrary to the traditional practice, he concentrated his best troops on the left wing, drew them up in depth and crushed the Lacedaemonian right wing with a massive attack: King Cleombrotus and 400 Spartiates perished in the battle. This victory put an end to Sparta's military superiority in open warfare and established Thebes as a new claimant to hegemony on the Greek mainland. The Theban success was closely linked with the personal activity of Epaminondas. His integrity and patriotism, and, above all, his military genius were about to raise his country to the first rank.

The assassination of Jason of Pherae in 370 removed a formidable neighbour: Thebes seized the opportunity to extend her influence in Thessaly. At the same time Epaminondas was leading his army into the Peloponnese, where the Arcadians who had risen against Sparta were appealing to him for aid. In 370–369 he invaded the hitherto inviolate Laconia, where old Agesilaus could only defend the city of Sparta, leaving the Thebans to lay waste the country. Messenia, which had risen in revolt once more, was finally delivered from the Spartan yoke: it had as its capital the newly-founded city of Messene, on the slopes of Mount Ithome, where its strong walls still stand. The Spartan state thus lost its main source of livelihood; its decline was henceforth inevitable. In Arcadia, the states united in a confederacy and provided themselves with a capital by founding a new and unusually large city, Megalopolis; standing as it did not far from the frontier of Laconia, it was to bar the way to any new venture on the part of Lacedaemon. Sparta's hegemony in the Peloponnese was at an end.

These brilliant Theban successes led to an alliance between Sparta and Athens, which tried to secure support from the Persians, but Pelopidas, the Theban delegate at Susa, succeeded in winning the favour of the Great King, who recognized the independence of Messenia and demanded that the Athenian fleet should be put out of commission (367). War was resumed on all fronts. While Thebes was installing a garrison at Oropus, on the very frontier of Attica, the Athenians, thanks to the efforts of Timotheus, were occupying Samos, from which they expelled the Persians, and settling cleruchs in the island. They did likewise at Potidaea in Chalcidice and reduced several other cities in this region. But Thebes was not idle: she was building a fleet based on a seaport in Locris

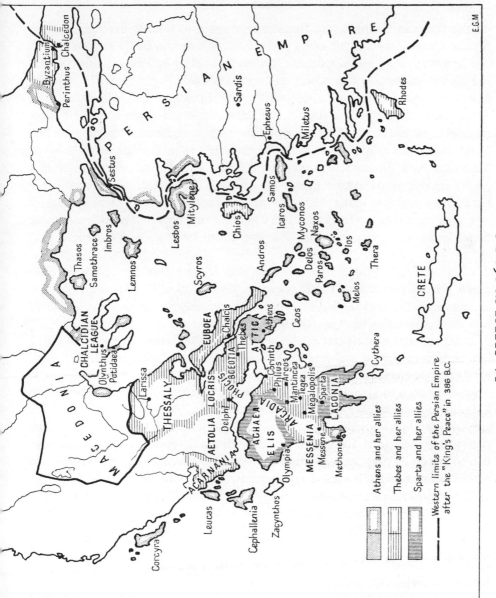

Athens and her allies

Thebes and her allies

Sparta and her allies

Western limits of the Persian Empire
after the "King's Peace" in 386 B.C.

14. GREECE IN 362 B.C.

PERSIAN EMPIRE

Byzantium
Perinthus
Chalcedon
Sestus
Sandis
Ephesus
Miletus
Rhodes
Samos
Icaros
Mitylene
Lesbos
Chios
Thasos
Samothrace
Imbros
Lemnos
Scyros
Andros
Myconos
Delos
Naxos
Paros
Ios
Thera
Melos
Ceos
CRETE

MACEDONIA
CHALCIDIAN
LEAGUE
Olynthus
Potidaea
Larissa
THESSALY
AETOLIA
LOCRIS
PHOCIS
Delphi
BOEOTIA
Thebes
Chalcis
EUBOEA
ATTICA
Athens
Corinth
Phlius
Argos
Mantinea
Tegea
Sparta
LACONIA
ARCADIA
ACHAEA
ELIS
Olympia
Megalopolis
MESSENIA
Messene
Methone
ACARNANIA
Leucas
Cephallenia
Zacynthos
Corcyra
Cythera

E.G.M

on the Euboean Channel, and Epaminondas went to raise Byzantium and the Straits against Athens. The naval prestige of Athens was badly shaken.

The situation in the Peloponnesus, where hostilities had broken out between the Eleans and the Arcadians, was still very confused. Then dissension between Mantinea and Tegea developed within the Arcadian confederacy. Sparta, Athens, and Elis supported Mantinea. Thebes supported Tegea and sent Epaminondas to her aid in 362. A Lacedaemonian army, strengthened by Athenian and Mantinean contingents, awaited the Theban attack in the neighbourhood of Mantinea. As at Leuctra, Epaminondas formed his left wing 'in the shape of a prow' and shattered the resistance of the Spartans. But he fell in the battle at the head of his hoplites; along with this man of genius Thebes lost her hopes of assuming control of Greek affairs. The Theban army, deprived of its leader, took no advantage of its victory. More than ever, disorder reigned in Greece.

The difficulties of the western Greeks: Dionysius II, Timoleon. Growth of the kingdom of Macedonia. Philip II. His conquests. Third Sacred War. Fall of Olynthus and Peace of Philocrates. New enterprises of Philip. Fourth Sacred War. Battle of Chaeronea. Corinthian League. Death of Philip

The outlook was no brighter in the west, where the death of Dionysius I had left the government of Syracuse in the hands of his son Dionysius II (367–357), who had not his father's qualities. To provide the young sovereign with wise counsel, Dion, a brother-in-law of his father, invited Plato to Syracuse again, but the philosopher's second visit to Sicily was no happier than the first. Dionysius very soon fell out with Dion, who was exiled and retired to Corinth. Some years later he returned victoriously to Syracuse with Carthaginian support. Dionysius fled to Locri, leaving Dion to wield the tyranny, which he did by resorting to acts of violence which led to his assassination in 354. This was the beginning of a period of grave disorder during which the Syracusan Empire, passing from one hand to another, broke up. Dionysius himself, having returned to power in 347, was quite unable to restore it: in every Sicilian city, at Catana as at Tauromenium, at Messana as at Leontini, local tyrants had sprung up. The Syracusans turned to their mother-city, Corinth, which sent them a mediator, Timoleon, in 344. Being favourably received by the tyrant of Tauromenium, Timoleon managed to arrange that Dionysius should renounce the tyranny. Since his opponents had appealed to the Carthaginians, he had to get rid of this threat first of all. He won a victory at the river Crimisus in 341 and concluded a peace treaty two years later, after having reconquered the Greek territories in Sicily up to the frontier formerly agreed on by Dionysius I, namely the stream of Himera and the river Halycus. Then he re-established internal order, abolishing all the tyrannies except that of Andromachus at Tauromenium, who had aided him from the beginning: the Greek cities were formed into a confederacy led by Syracuse. In Syracuse itself he set up a mixed form of government; side by side with the assembly of the people, there was a council with 600 members in control of administration. Having thus finished his task and brought back peace to Sicily when it was worn out by twenty years of anarchy, Timoleon resigned in 337 from the supreme magistracy that had been conferred on him with the title of Strategus invested with full powers and he ended his days peaceably in Syracuse as a private citizen, giving a rare example of moderation and good citizenship in such a troubled period.

In Greece proper, the creation of a new order, which the Greek cities had been powerless to establish themselves, was brought about by foreign intervention, that of the kingdom of Macedonia. The question whether the Macedonians were ethnically Greeks is still under discussion. It is at least certain that this nation of rough peasants and mountaineers, dwelling around the Thermaic Gulf and in the neighbouring mountains, between the Pindus range and the lower valley of the Strymon, remained for a long time on the fringe of the Hellenic world. But from the early part of the fifth century B.C., its hereditary sovereigns, the dynasty of the Argeadae, took an active part in Greek life. Towards the end of the fifth century, King Archelaus, who was interested in literature, welcomed to his court at Pella the poets Euripides and Agathon, the musician Timotheus of Miletus, and the painter Zeuxis. Macedonia played a part in international affairs and on several occasions joined an alliance with Greek states. She had much appreciated resources at her disposal, in particular timber, indispensable for shipbuilding. The king, supported by a noble caste bearing the proud title of the king's 'companions' (*hetairoi*), could also count on the loyal support of a peasantry which provided excellent infantry, the *pezetairoi*. This military monarchy, based on strong feelings of personal allegiance to the sovereign, could become a potent political instrument in the hands of an energetic and ambitious king. It was Philip the son of Amyntas who brought this to pass.

After the death of Amyntas III in 370 B.C., the Macedonian kingdom had

64. A CORNER OF THE FORTRESS AT ELEUTHERAE
Inner side of the rampart near a tower in the north wall. Only the lower part of the wall
is preserved. Fine regular stonework. The gate in the middle led into the tower. On the
right there is a postern-gate (see ill. 67).

65. THE SURROUNDING WALL OF GELA
The upper part of the wall, of unbaked brick, is partly preserved above the footing of
stonework. To protect these fragile remains, a framework and a roof of plastic have
been installed. Note the pointed postern-gate, like those of the besieged city in the
Trysa frieze (ills. 61–62).

66. FORTIFICATIONS OF AEGOSTHENA (AIR PHOTOGRAPH)
The little city stood on a hill near the sea at the foot of Cithaeron, in an isolated district
of Megaris. The fairly well preserved surrounding walls are still dominated by several
high towers (note particularly the corner tower on the right).

67. THE FORTRESS OF ELEUTHERAE (AIR PHOTOGRAPH)
Built in the second half of the fourth century, it stands on a rocky height dominating
the main pass of Cithaeron, on the road from Athens to Thebes. All the northern part
of the surrounding walls is still clearly visible, with the square towers projecting outwards. The tower shown in ill. 64 is the last on the left (where the gradient changes).
The opening for the postern-gate can be seen just to the right of it.

68. ACHILLES
Attic red-figure amphora, dating from the third quarter of the fifth century (contemporary with the Parthenon). Achilles is represented as a hoplite of the period, who has
laid down his helmet and shield. He is wearing a cuirass with lambrequins and shoulder-
pieces. On the breast-plate, a Gorgon's head. His garments are a short tunic and a
cloak rolled over his left arm. He has no greaves. He holds in his left hand a long spear
strengthened in the middle, with a metallic tip fastened to its heel for sticking it in the
ground. A short baldric holds the sword, whose hilt can just be seen under the left
armpit. Vatican Museum.

69. THREE-BODIED GERYON
Attic black-figure amphora (third quarter of the sixth century). Heracles' adversary is
shown as a three-bodied hoplite. His monstrous hound has two heads. The design
gives a good view of the front and back of the round shield used in Greek armies. On
the front there is an emblem with magical powers, painted or in relief: it is supposed to
frighten the enemy and keep off deadly blows (here it is the head of Silenus). On the
back, the shield has a padding (sometimes painted or embroidered) on which are fixed,
by metal clips or straps, a band crossing the middle for the forearm to be passed under
and a handle at the side for the hand to grasp. Cabinet des Médailles.

70

71

73

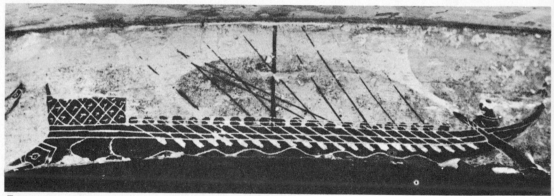

74

75

70. SINGLE COMBAT

Corinthian crater (second quarter of the sixth century). Two heroes armed as hoplites face one another over the body of a man called Hippolytus (name written in the Corinthian alphabet). Behind each fighter there is a mounted squire. Louvre.

71. SPARTAN WARRIORS RETURNING FROM BATTLE

Laconian cup (middle of the sixth century). The painter has, so to speak, cut out a small section from a frieze to decorate the bottom of his cup. The nude warriors are bringing back the bodies of their dead comrades. The poignant ruggedness of this funeral procession gives a good illustration of the military ideal of Sparta. In the space below, there are two fighting cocks, quite unconnected with the principal scene. Berlin Museum.

72. ACHILLES AND PENTHESILEA

Attic red-figure cup (about 470–460). Achilles falls in love with the Amazon at the moment when he is giving her the death blow. He is represented in a state of 'heroic' nudity and Penthesilea is dressed like a Greek girl (short tunic, and a headband holding up her hair). But the warrior on the left has the equipment of a hoplite of the fifth century (see ill. 69), wearing an 'Attic' helmet with the cheek-pieces lowered, while the dead Amazon on the right is wearing the close-fitting costume of the Orientals (see ill. 48). Munich Museum.

73. WARSHIPS UNDER SAIL

Attic black-figure cup by the potter Nicosthenes (about 530–520). The two ships, with oars shipped, are racing along together before the wind. We can see only the steersman at the rudder and a look-out man at the bow. The ram is shaped like an animal's snout. Behind, under the ornament of the stern (aplustre), is fixed the ladder used to climb down to the ground when the ship has touched land. Louvre.

74. ATHENIAN PENTECONTER

Attic cup by the potter Exekias (third quarter of the sixth century). The ship, similar in type to the preceding one, is propelled by oars with some help from a wind astern. The painter has only shown twenty-two rowers (instead of twenty-five). Rome, Villa Giulia.

75. ATHENIAN TRIREME

This bas-relief, unfortunately mutilated, gives very precise indications for the seating of the oarsmen in a trireme. We see the thranites (topmost row), whose oars are supported upon the gallery projecting outwards. As for the zeugites and thalamites, we can only see their oars passing through portholes, between the wales. Above the thranites, there is an upper deck supported on an openwork timber frame. Acropolis Museum, Athens.

suffered from a series of dynastic quarrels. Philip, a younger son of the late king, was still quite young and spent several years in Thebes as a hostage; there he knew Epaminondas and Pelopidas and became familiar with Greek politics. He was twenty-two years of age in 359, when he was appointed regent of the kingdom on the death of his brother Perdiccas III, whose son was still a child. Before long, the young regent restored a situation which seemed fraught with much danger: he got rid of the other pretenders to the royal title and reached an understanding with Athens by promising to assist her to recover Amphipolis, from which he withdrew the Macedonian garrison placed there by Perdiccas; then he defeated the Illyrians to the west and subdued the Paeonians to the north of Macedonia. With his phalanx of *pezetairoi* and his heavy cavalry led by the *hetairoi*, he had organized a powerful army which, in recognition of his triumphs, declared him king.

His first aim was to provide Macedonia with a free outlet to the sea. The best seaports on his shores, Pydna and Methone, were Greek colonies allied to Athens. But for years past Athens had been struggling with diplomatic and financial difficulties in her effort to maintain control of the Straits and keep her maritime Confederacy together. The latter was seriously weakened when in 357 Chios, Rhodes, and Byzantium, supported by the Carian dynast Mausolus, who governed Halicarnassus on behalf of the Great King, formed a separate alliance, independent of the Confederacy. There followed a war in the course of which Athens failed in her efforts to bring the rebels back to their allegiance. The peace concluded in 355 explicitly acknowledged the weakening of the Confederacy: at Athens the moderate party, led by Eubulus, an able statesman and financier, had won acceptance for its views and the people no longer wished either to pay or to serve. Philip took advantage of the situation: first he seized Amphipolis, which Athens had for years been vainly attempting to recover, then Pydna, and finally Methone, during the siege of which he lost an eye (354). Macedonia's outlets to the sea were henceforth secured. Meanwhile he had taken Potidaea in Pallene, but had ceded it to the Chalcidian Confederacy after expelling the Athenian cleruchs. Eastwards, he had crossed the Strymon beyond Amphipolis and conquered Crenides, a colony of Thasos in the plain at the foot of Mount Pangaeum. Here he introduced an innovation of great significance by creating a new city named Philippi from his own name, the first instance of a practice that was to become general in the Hellenistic Age. The gold mines of Pangaeum provided him with the means of paying his mercenaries and conquering the scruples of his opponents. Philip's coins were henceforth to play the part which Persian gold had played for a century in the Greek world.

In 356 a grave international crisis had broken out in central Greece, providing a convenient pretext for interference by the Macedonian. The sanctuary of Delphi was once more the cause of a Sacred War, the third. It was the Phocians, as it had been a century earlier, who were accused of sacrilege: among the members of the Amphictyony, it was Thebes who showed herself the most rabid enemy of these neighbours to whom an old rivalry had already made her hostile. But the Phocians, supported by Athens and Sparta, put at their head an energetic man named Philomelus, and took possession of the sanctuary: the sacred treasury provided them with the means of recruiting an army of mercenaries, with which Philomelus and, after his death, his successor Onomarchus gained successes. Onomarchus even made his way into Thessaly, where the tyrants of Pherae and Crannon were on his side. Other cities of Thessaly then appealed to Philip. After a serious repulse in 353, the Macedonian returned to Thessaly in the following year and crushed the forces of Onomarchus, who perished in the battle. This did not put an end to the Sacred War, since Philip could not pass Thermopylae, which was held by the Phocians' allies, to enter central Greece, but at least he had become the ally and protector of Thessaly. He then turned towards Thrace, where he forced his alliance upon the native kings and led his army as far as the Propontis. Athens, which had just re-established a footing in Sestus, became alarmed once more. She soon had other reasons for alarm when Philip decided to subdue the cities of Chalcidice and captured them one by one. The most important, Olynthus, fell in 348. In spite of the fiery appeals of the orator Demosthenes, who saw the danger growing, Athens had proved unable to help Olynthus in time. The city was razed and all Chalcidice was incorporated into the Macedonian kingdom. At the same time Philip's intrigues had severed Euboea from Athens' maritime Confederacy.

The Athenians then decided to negotiate: an embassy sent to Pella, the capital of the Macedonian kingdom, in 346, drew up the Peace of Philocrates, thus called from the name of the chief Athenian plenipotentiary, who was accompanied by Demosthenes and the orator Aeschines. The latter allowed himself to be suborned by Philip and became a convinced supporter of his policies. According to the terms of the treaty, each was to keep the possessions he held at the moment, but

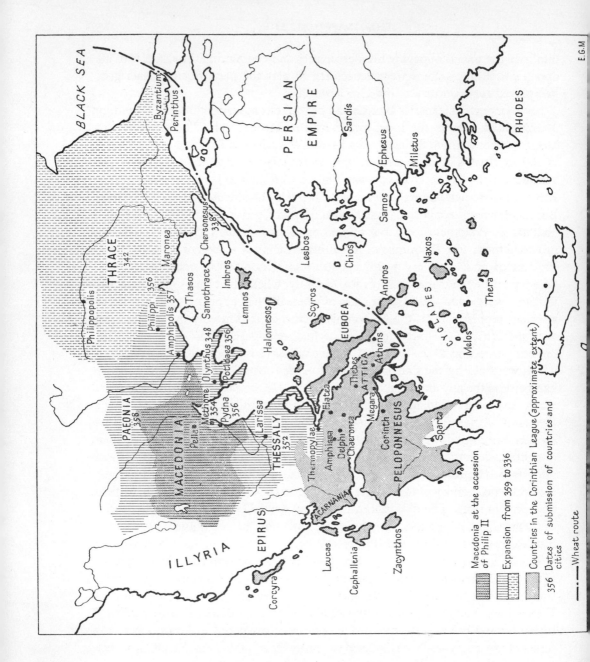

BLACK SEA

PERSIAN EMPIRE

RHODES

Sardis

Ephesus

Miletus

Samos

THRACE

Byzantium
Perinthus

Maronea 342

Philippopolis

Philippi 356

Thasos

Amphipolis 357

Samothrace

Chersonesus 338

Imbros

Lemnos

Lesbos

Chios

Scyros

Andros

Naxos

Thera

C Y C L A D E S

Melos

EUBOEA

Halonnesos

PAEONIA 358

MACEDONIA

Methone 354
Olynthus 348
Potidaea 356
Pella
Pydna 356

Larissa

THESSALY 352

Thermopylae

Amphissa
Delphi
Chaeronea

Plataea

Thebes

Athens

ATTICA

Megara

Corinth

Sparta

PELOPONNESUS

ILLYRIA

EPIRUS

ACARNANIA

Leucas

Cephallenia

Zacynthos

Corcyra

E.G.M

Macedonia at the accession
of Philip II

Expansion from 359 to 336

Countries in the Corinthian League (approximate extent)

356 Dates of submission of countries and
cities

Wheat route

Philip had refused to include the Phocians among the allies of Athens who benefited by the agreements concluded: he quickly settled their fate, in the same year
346, by occupying their country. The Amphictyony condemned the Phocians to
a heavy fine, payable annually, in reparation for the pillage they had committed in
the Delphian sanctuary. Their two votes in the Amphictyonic Council, and also
the presidency at the Pythian Games for the current year, were transferred to
Philip. The king of Macedonia was from that moment officially admitted to the
company of the Greek states.

Many were glad of this, particularly those who, like the old rhetor Isocrates,
already saw in the Macedonian monarch the leader needed by Greece to settle
its quarrels and unite its strength in a common enterprise against Achaemenid
Persia. But others, among whom Demosthenes was very prominent, looked on
the Peace of Philocrates as a temporary armistice, merely providing time to prepare for the decisive struggle, which they considered inevitable. This became
clear enough when, in 343, Demosthenes accused Aeschines of having betrayed
his country on the occasion of the embassy in 346: Aeschines was acquitted, but
the policy of Philip and his supporters had been attacked with great violence
during the trial and popular passions on the subject were again mounting high.

Philip, for his part, made the best use of the respite at his command. A new
campaign against the Illyrians, followed by intervention in Epirus, removed any
threats in the rearward areas. In Thessaly he reorganized the administration of
the country, thenceforth divided into four provinces, whose governors, called
tetrarchs, were his devoted adherents. Then he turned his attention to Thrace,
which he subdued eastward of the Nestus as far as the Propontis and the Black
Sea: all the country became a royal possession governed by a strategus appointed
by Philip. The Greek cities on the coastline, such as Byzantium and Perinthus,
and the Athenian positions in the Chersonese were directly threatened. Fearing
for the wheat route, vital for her provisioning, Athens again prepared for war, as
Demosthenes was urging her to do. So when in 340 the Macedonian forces
besieged Perinthus, and then Byzantium, the Athenian fleet intervened in force.
Philip, who had failed in his attempt on Perinthus, was also obliged to raise the
siege of Byzantium, which was succoured by the Athenian general Phocion.
This setback convinced the king that success against Athens must be sought by
intervention in Greece proper.

Affairs connected with Delphi were soon to provide him with his opportunity.

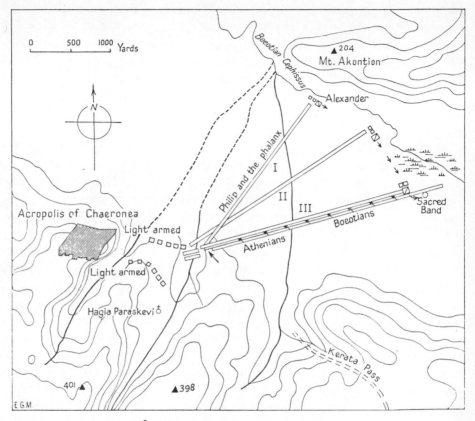

16. THE BATTLE OF CHAERONEA

(*After N. G. L. Hammond*). The Greek forces, with the Athenians on the left wing and the Boeotians on the right, were flanked by the marshes of the Cephissus on the right and by the foothills close to Chaeronea on the left. Philip joined battle with his right wing which he was commanding himself (position I), then fell back of his own accord (position II) before his left wing made contact. The Athenians, thinking that victory was within their grasp, advanced incautiously in pursuit of Philip, thus throwing the Greek lines into disorder. A gap opened between the centre and the Sacred Band. Into this gap Alexander charged with the Macedonian cavalry, while the whole phalanx moved forward again against the now disordered enemy. The Sacred Band was annihilated, the Greeks broke

In order to divert attention from a complaint against Athens submitted to the Amphictyonic Council, the Athenian representative, Aeschines, accused the Locrians of having improperly put under cultivation land consecrated to Apollo. To expiate this sacrilege, it was decided to declare a Sacred War on the Locrians, and the conduct of it was entrusted to Philip (339). Acting with great speed, he moved his forces into Phocis, with the consent of the Phocians, to whom he promised remission of the fine that had been imposed on them. By means of this stratagem he succeeded in turning the key position of Thermopylae, occupied by the Boeotians, on the westward side and thus debouching at Elatea in central Greece. This news threw Athens into commotion: it was the 'Elatean surprise' and Demosthenes had to exert himself to raise the courage of his compatriots. Fully realizing the danger, Athens made an alliance with Thebes to organize the common defence. An army consisting of the forces of the two states assembled in Boeotia while Philip was busying himself with the chastisement of Amphissa, in accordance with the mission entrusted to him by the Amphictyons. During the summer of 338, Philip returned with his troops from western Locris to the upper valley of the Boeotian Cephisus, where the enemy army was waiting for him near Chaeronea. The Macedonian left wing, commanded by Philip's young son Alexander, broke the resistance of the Boeotian hoplites opposing it; the 'sacred band' of the Thebans fought and died to the last man. The Athenian contingent suffered heavy losses, and then dispersed in rout (2 August 338).

The victory at Chaeronea was decisive. All resistance to Philip's will came to an end. Thebes was harshly treated, got a Macedonian garrison in the Cadmea and lost its leading position in Boeotia. Athens got out of it as lightly as possible: she only surrendered her positions in the Thracian Chersonesus and consented to dissolve the maritime Confederacy; she kept her foreign possessions, Lemnos, Imbros, Scyros, and Samos, and even recovered Oropus, on the Bocotian frontier, which she had formerly lost; she at last joined Philip's alliance.

---

into rout, and the survivors fled towards Lebadea through the Kerata Pass. The commemorative lion said to have been erected after the battle to mark the common grave of the dead of the Sacred Band has been replaced on its original site, at the foot of the rising ground, nearly in the middle of the site occupied on the plan by the reference to light-armed troops. Contour intervals 50 m. Heights in metres.

76. THE APOLLO OF MANTICLUS

A bronze statuette of the early part of the seventh century, representing a nude male figure standing (Apollo?). The left hand, stretched forward, no doubt held a bow. A dedication to Phoebus Apollo, in two epic verses recalling a passage of Homer, is carved on the thighs. A good example of 'Daedalic' art. Boston Museum.

77. ZEUS AMMON

On the coins of Cyrene, in the Classical Age, Zeus appears furnished with ram's horns, by assimilation of the Greek god with the ram-headed Egyptian god Ammon, who had an oracle at Siwah, in the desert of Libya. But this animal attribute remains unobtrusive and does not prevent the face of Zeus from recalling the nobility of the bearded gods created by Phidias and his emulators. Cabinet des Médailles.

78. HERA (COIN OF ARGOS, FOURTH CENTURY)

On the obverse, the profile of the goddess Hera, wearing a crown decorated with palmettes connected by volutes and ear-pendants shaped like truncated cones. This face with regular features may be a reflection of the chryselephantine statue which Polycletus had executed for the Heraeum at Argos about 420, but, according to Pausanias's description, the crown of that statue was of a different type. Cabinet des Médailles.

79. DIONYSUS (COIN OF NAXUS)

The Sicilian city of Naxus (which should not be confused with its namesake, the island in the Cyclades) minted admirable tetradrachms in the fifth century with a profile of Dionysus on the obverse and on the reverse an astonishing front view of a seated Silenus (see ill. 207). This Dionysus, with long hair wreathed with ivy and collected into a knot on the nape of the neck, is a masterpiece of the severe style. Cabinet des Médailles.

80. POSEIDON

The statue fished up from the sea off Cape Artemisium, near Histiaea in Euboea, is (with the Charioteer of Delphi) the best representative of great sculpture in bronze in the severe style (about 460). It is a nude Poseidon, drawing back his long-shafted trident in readiness to strike an objective which he is pointing to with his left hand stretched forward. The divine countenance, on which coloured eyes (now lost) must have conferred a very lifelike quality, is impressive in its strength and majesty. National Museum, Athens.

77

78

Nevertheless, even in its defeat the Athenian people preserved enough dignity to entrust to Demosthenes the traditional task of delivering the funeral oration in praise of the soldiers who had died at Chaeronea.

Philip's victory was a turning-point in Greek history. A monarchical and centralized state had brilliantly demonstrated its superiority to the ephemeral leagues formed by independent cities. The future belonged to the great kingdoms, not to the little republics limited to the land belonging to a single city. The classical conception of the *polis* was from now on left behind. This was clearly seen when, in 337, Philip summoned a general assembly of the Greeks at Corinth. All the cities except Sparta sent representatives. They jointly organized the Corinthian League, which for the first time gave a federal form to a sort of panhellenic state. Universal peace was established between the cities and it was forbidden to disturb this peace on pain of military sanctions. Respect for the domestic constitution of each state and for its autonomy was laid down by proclamation. Piracy and brigandage were forbidden. A federal Council (*Synedrion*), to which the states were to send delegates in a number proportional to their importance, would meet each year in one of the great sanctuaries. Its decisions, reached by majority voting, would be binding on all the members of the League.

Macedonia was not a member of the Corinthian League, but formed an offensive and defensive alliance with it, and Philip was appointed as commander of the federal army. In 337 he proposed that the league should undertake warfare against the king of Persia. At this time the Achaemenid monarchy was passing through a serious crisis of succession which made the moment propitious for an attack. But Philip was not himself to set the enterprise afoot: in the summer of 336, during a festival in celebration of his daughter's marriage to the king of Epirus, he was assassinated by a certain Pausanias for reasons of personal hostility. With his son Alexander, whom the people immediately proclaimed king of Macedonia, begins a new era, the one which we call the Hellenistic Age.

CHAPTER V

POLEMOS

Importance of war in the Greek world

'POLEMOS', says Heraclitus, 'is the parent and ruler of the universe.' By this the Ephesian philosopher, who was writing early in the fifth century, means that the cosmos is the scene of an endless struggle between opposing elements, resulting in perpetual change: Polemos, war, therefore appears to him as the very law of the universe. This disillusioned reflection could well have been suggested to Heraclitus by the spectacle of what was happening all around him, since for the Greeks of the Archaic Age war was a matter of perpetual concern. It is not without good reason that the preceding historical account contains so many descriptions of military operations: it has been calculated that, during the century and a half between the Persian Wars and the Battle of Chaeronea, Athens was on the average at war more than two years out of three, without ever having enjoyed peace for as long as ten years on end. Of course it is true that other cities, with more modest responsibilities and pretensions, had a less warlike history. But none of them could stand entirely apart from armed conflicts if it wished to survive: war was truly the 'brazen law' of the Greek world.

There were, indeed, economic reasons for this. Since fertile areas are not plentiful in Greece, they could arouse the covetousness of greedy or overcrowded neighbours. Athens used armed force to establish settlements of a military character (*cleruchies*) outside Attica. Sparta was impelled to conquer Messenia by the internal logic of her political and social system. Later, the need to keep an essential trade route open could lead to war: throughout a century Athens engaged in repeated military ventures to control the region of the Straits, through which passed the convoys of wheat from southern Russia. Again, we have seen the part played in the outbreak of the Peloponnesian War by the famous 'Megarian Decree' by which Pericles established the economic blockade of Megara. Lastly, the covetous desires aroused by the Thracian mines led to a series of conflicts in the regions of Thasos and Mount Pangaeum.

But economic rivalries were not the main cause. If the Greeks devoted so much time and effort to war, it was primarily for psychological reasons connected with the Hellenic conception of the city. The city represented supreme authority in the eyes of its members. Absolute independence was its rule: if it joined an alliance, it did so, in principle, on a footing of equality, without surrendering the autonomy on which it prided itself. In default of a recognized arbiter to settle disputes, every clash of interests could easily degenerate into armed conflict. The passion for liberty, which inspired orators and poets to so many fiery appeals, implies that war will be accepted and even that it will be waged with enthusiasm: only the city that could fight for its freedom had the right to remain free. So the first object of civic organization was to prepare the citizens for the inevitable contingency of battle. This was perfectly understood by Plato, who makes the Cretan Clinias say, in *Laws* 625 e, 'the whole citizen body spends its life in maintaining endless warfare against all other cities'. In a Greek city of the Archaic and Classical Ages, the citizen was first of all a soldier, just as the statesman had often to change into a military leader. Everything depended upon the fortune of arms: each man's personal future, that of the state, and ultimately that of Hellenism as a whole. The decline of Athens revealed itself as irretrievable when she no longer wished for other guides than financiers and lawyers, and when the Athenians, deaf to Demosthenes' solemn entreaties, refused to serve in person, abandoning the protection of their country to mercenaries.

The land army: hoplites. Equipment of the heavy-armed infantry
As we have seen, the main element in the Greek army was a corps of heavy infantry, the *hoplites*. The hoplite had a complete equipment of weapons of offence and defence, which we can see in detail in sculptured representations and vase paintings. But we must distinguish between such representations of warriors as faithfully reproducing contemporary reality and those, by far the more

numerous, which remove it into the world of myth: the completely naked fighters on the frieze of the Mausoleum of Halicarnassus never encountered any other foe than the Amazons. In compensation, the famous little Dodona bronze at Berlin, the stele of Aristion carved by Aristocles, and the Achilles vase in the Vatican are trustworthy pieces of evidence. Here the hoplite appears clad in a short tunic leaving the legs entirely free. He may also wear a cloak. The feet are bare or shod with ankle-boots or sandals. We have some evidence suggesting that Greek soldiers sometimes felt more at ease bare-foot on difficult ground.

The chest was protected either by a metal cuirass or by a leather or linen one strengthened with metal plates. The cuirass worn in the Archaic Age was the stiff 'bell-shaped' one, consisting of two bronze plates, one for the chest and one for the back, joined by clasps on the shoulders and under the arms. A splendid specimen has recently been found at Argos. Later, flexible models were more in favour: unlike the bell-shaped cuirass, which only came down to the waist, they were usually lengthened beneath the belt by rows of hanging strips of leather, or *lambrequins*, which protected the abdomen. On his head the hoplite wore a metal helmet with a leather or felt lining, often furnished with one or several crests bristling with tall plumes. The officers were distinguished by the great size and richness of their plumes, of which Aristophanes on occasion makes fun. The shape of the helmet fell into various, generally well-defined, types, to which tradition gives somewhat arbitrary names. The *Corinthian* helmet, with a nose-piece and fixed cheek-pieces, was worn in a raised position when the wearer was not actually fighting. The *Attic* helmet, with no nose-piece, had movable cheek pieces which could be raised at will. The *Boeotian* helmet, in the shape of a conical cap, had neither cheek-pieces nor covering for the back of the neck. There were other types as well, but these were the types most commonly found on monuments decorated with figures. Excavations have brought to light many bronze helmets, especially at Olympia, where some very fine specimens have recently been found. Some bear dedications which enable them to be dated.

The same holds true of bronze shields, which were very often dedicated as offerings in sanctuaries. Their shape varied in the course of the centuries, from the 'figure-of-eight' shield of Creto-Mycenaean tradition to the round shield of the Classical Age, between which had come the 'Geometric' shield, with two broad lateral indentations, and the Boeotian shield, developed from the 'Geometric' but with indentations on a smaller scale. In the fifth and fourth centuries,

the round shield had a diameter of about one yard, or 90 centimetres. It had a
fairly strong outward curve. Its wooden framework was covered on the outer
side with leather or hides, or even a complete facing of bronze. There was sometimes an ornament in metal projecting in the middle: it was often a Gorgon's
head, whose gruesome appearance was expected, if not to terrify an opponent,
at least to ward off bad luck. Various devices, engraved on the metal or painted
on the leather, might adorn this outer surface of the shield, as can be seen on vase
paintings and in the descriptions, largely based on imagination, of the armour
worn by the Argive leaders attacking Thebes, given by the poet Aeschylus in
Seven against Thebes, and by Euripides in *Phoenissae.* As for the famous shield of
Achilles, described at length by Homer in *Iliad* XVIII, it belongs to the world of
myth. On the other hand there are ceremonial arms, such as the shields devised
by Phidias for his colossal Athenas on the Acropolis at Athens, whose convex
surfaces were embellished with reliefs portraying the conflict of the Greeks with
the Amazons and that of the Centaurs and the Lapithae. Even the inner concave
surface could receive a decoration, woven or painted on the linen covering the
padding of fabric or vegetable substance with which the inner side of the shield
was lined: on the shield of Athena Parthenos, Phidias had here painted the battle
of the gods and the giants. It was on this side too that the two handles which
enabled the hoplite to hold and manipulate the shield were attached. The one
which encircled the arm sometimes had a decoration of repoussé bronze reliefs:
the excavations at Olympia have yielded several specimens from the Archaic Age,
constituting an interesting series. The inner side of the shield was also furnished
with straps of rope or leather fastened near the upper rim: these were used for
carrying the shield when it was not being held in the fighting position and they
also enabled it to be hung on a prop. Because of its great weight, the shield was
entrusted during marches to a slave, the hoplite's indispensable attendant. The
military equipment carried by this camp-follower, over and above the shield,
which was enclosed in a canvas cover, included the blankets for bivouacking
and a stand on which the shield was hung in the open before battle.

During the Archaic Age, the heavy-armed warrior's defensive equipment also
included greaves (*cnemides*) to protect his shins; but this accessory fell into disuse
from the fifth century onwards.

The hoplite's weapons of offence were for all practical purposes the spear and
the sword. In the Classical Age the spear was both solid and long (about two and

a half yards, or 2·25 metres). In addition to the point, it was often furnished with a metal heel, to enable it to be planted in the ground. The wooden shaft was sometimes fitted with a leather band that made it thicker at the place where it was grasped, in order to give the hand a firmer grip. The spear was usually handled with the right hand alone, while the left hand held the shield. Like the shield, it was kept in a protective cover when not in use. The 'Dorian' spear was regarded by the poets as the characteristically Greek weapon. For Aeschylus it is the symbol of Greek valour as opposed to the Persian bow. Athena, the warrior goddess, preferred the spear to the sword.

The sword, which was the weapon for hand-to-hand fighting, served as a last resort for the fighter deprived of his spear. In the Classical period it had an iron blade of moderate length, rarely more than half a yard, or 45 centimetres. The blade was two-edged. The hilt was fitted with a narrow guard and a pommel. The sheath hung from a short shoulder-belt passing over the right shoulder. The position of the sheath was so high that the pommel of the sword almost reached the height of the left armpit: to draw the sword, it was necessary to tip it forward while wedging the sheath under the left arm. In this way the soldier could draw the sword without letting go his shield, which would not have been possible with a longer shoulder-belt. The sword was used both to cut and to thrust. While the handling of spear, bow, and javelins formed the subject of systematic training, the Greeks of the Classical period do not seem to have paid much attention to swordsmanship. Indeed one can easily imagine that the hoplite, burdened as he was with his shield and breast-plate, could scarcely have made good use of a subtly developed science of feinting and parrying.

Light troops. Their equipment. Role of peltasts in the fourth century
Side by side with the main fighting force consisting of the hoplites, the Greek armies had also light-armed troops and cavalry. We know much less about the light troops than about the cavalry, a fact which can easily be explained by their social origin. While the heavy infantry, who had to procure their costly armaments at their own expense, belonged to the well-to-do class, the archers, slingers and javelin-throwers were recruited from the ranks of the poorer citizens. They did not need weapons of defence, since their role was not to seek or withstand the shock of battle, but to harass the enemy from a distance. Their missiles cost little: they were the same as for hunting. The double-curved bow was the

most highly perfected of these weapons: although the poets on occasion regard
the bow as a characteristically 'Persian' weapon, yet it enjoyed a very ancient
tradition in the Greek world, illustrated by the legend of the bow of Ulysses in
the *Odyssey*, to say nothing of the myth of Heracles and Philoctetes. The Cretans
were regarded as the best archers. Archery was very effective when fire was concentrated on a body of troops in close order. Even in naval warfare, the threat of
arrows was formidable enough to cause warships to be provided with protective
sheets of canvas set up along the gunwales before each naval engagement.

Javelins, commonly used for hunting, also served a purpose in war. They had
normally been used by heavy infantry in Homeric times: in the *Iliad*, single
combat usually begins with a javelin cast, which rarely misses the mark. On the
Dipylon vases we see processions of warriors armed cap-à-pie, generally with
two javelins in their hands rather than a single spear. This heroic tradition provides the reason why all young men continued in classical times to be trained in
throwing the javelin, although this weapon had disappeared from the hoplites'
equipment. Moreover, the cavalry never ceased to use it. The javelin was considerably shorter than the spear, its length ranging from four and a half to six
feet (1·35 to 1·80 metres). Like the spear, it might have a point fitted to each
end. Its range was increased when it was thrown not simply by being grasped in
the hand but by means of a strap attached to the middle of it, which acted as a
propeller.

The sling was the simplest of the missile weapons: two straps or cords, about
two feet (roughly 60 centimetres) long, were attached to a sort of pouch made of
leather. The other end of the strings was held by the slinger, who placed the
missile in the leather pouch and twirled the weapon as fast as possible. When he
let go one of the strings, the missile, driven by centrifugal force, flew off at great
speed. A skilful slinger was capable of very exact aiming and, according to an
ancient author, could send the missile as far as a stade (600 feet, or about 180
metres). Stones were thrown with the sling, and also balls of clay or metal,
chiefly lead, specially manufactured for this purpose. These balls, ellipsoidal in
shape, could be sent farther and with more precision. A great many of them have
been found, particularly at Olynthus, where they remain from the siege of the
city by Philip in 348. Several of these balls bear inscriptions: these are names of
peoples, sometimes in an abridged form, or names of men. It is not surprising
to be able to recognize here the names 'Olynthian' and 'Chalcidian', that of

Philip himself, and perhaps those of his principal officers. Philip's name also appears on arrow-heads.

It must not be forgotten that side by side with these light weapons the ancient Greeks, at all periods of their long history, also fought with the most rudimentary natural weapons provided by their native soil, namely sticks and stones. In epic, we often see heroes brandishing a block of stone in order to crush an adversary with it. Even in the Classical Age it was with a shower of pebbles thrown by hand, as well as with arrows, that the Athenians overwhelmed the Persians who had been landed on the islet of Psyttalia, near Salamis, after the naval battle was over. The same tactics were used when Demosthenes got possession of the island of Sphacteria, defended by the Spartans, in 424. Towards the end of the century, we have an explicit statement from Xenophon that in the battle at Munychia, a district of Piraeus, between the supporters of the Thirty and those of the democracy (403 B.C.) the forces of the democrats included stone-throwers. Several texts refer to the use of cudgels as war weapons: the bodyguard of 300, armed with clubs, who, according to Herodotus (I, 59), enabled Pisistratus to seize power at Athens, were just as much soldiers as the 'spearmen' (*doryphoroi*) who normally formed the personal bodyguard of Greek tyrants.

Though light infantry played a minor part in the great conflicts of the Archaic Age and the fifth century, it was to acquire greater importance in the following century. Some episodes in the Peloponnesian War were already providing lessons for the future. For example, the Athenian general Demosthenes, before distinguishing himself in the Sphacteria affair, had suffered a severe defeat in 426, in the passes of Aetolia, from the mountaineers of the district: the latter, who had no heavy infantry, had caught the Athenian expeditionary force by surprise in difficult country, inflicted heavy losses on it with arrows and javelins, and driven it into headlong retreat. These lessons were not wasted. Early in the fourth century, the Athenian strategus Iphicrates organized a force of light-armed mercenaries, or *peltastai*, thus named because, instead of the heavy round shield, they carried a very light wicker-work shield, the *pelte*, which was crescent-shaped like the shields ascribed by legendary tradition to the Amazons. The peltast had no metal cuirass. His weapons of offence were a long javelin, which could also serve the purpose of a spear, and a short sword for hand-to-hand fighting. When fighting with hoplites, he relied on his agility to avoid being hit.

These troops performed wonders on many occasions, even when facing Lacedaemonian hoplites.

Cavalry. The Archaic chariots. The Greek cavalryman: his equipment. His tactical role. Aristocratic character of Greek cavalry

As we have already seen, the function of horses in the Greek art of war was at first confined to chariot fighting. The use of harnessed horses came before their use by mounted riders. The two-horse chariot was already in common use in the Mycenaean Age, as we can see on Cypriot vases. It was also the usual engine of war of the Homeric heroes: on this point, the evidence of Geometric pottery fully confirms that of epic. The noble rides in his chariot to the place of combat and then fights on foot as a hoplite. He has a charioteer to drive the team, and the charioteer remains in charge of the chariot while his master is engaged in battle. While the chariot is on the move, the warrior, who alone is provided with a shield, stands on the left of the charioteer. The Homeric chariot had two wheels; the light framework rested directly on the axle. The two horses were on each side of a single shaft, to which they were coupled by a yoke resting on their necks. Sometimes a trace-horse was added to the two yoked ones. No doubt it was this custom that led to the introduction of three-horse teams, which can be seen on a few monuments decorated with figures towards the end of the Geometric Age and in some Etruscan representations of the Archaic Age. Four-horse chariots were coming increasingly into fashion in the seventh century: but at this time the use of the chariot in warfare was gradually disappearing, as we have said above, because of the progress made by heavy infantry. From now on the four-horse chariot was a vehicle used for ceremonial purposes, as we see it on the Parthenon frieze, or for chariot-racing, which was an event of primary importance in the Panhellenic games. In Greek armies, war chariots were no longer employed except in outlying states such as Salamis in Cyprus, where the preservation of this tradition may be explained by Asiatic or Cyrenian influence; in Cyrene, squadrons of four-horse chariots were maintained until the Hellenistic Age to give swift pursuit to the bands of plunderers that came to raid the agricultural settlements on the Cyrenian plateau.

While the war chariot was passing out of use, its place was being taken by cavalry. The Homeric poems never mention cavalry as taking part in battle and contain only very rare allusions to equitation. But as early as the seventh century representations of armed horsemen appear on vases, on bas-reliefs such as the famous frieze of Prinias in Crete, and among terracotta statuettes and bronze figures. However, the part played in war by cavalry in the Archaic and Classical Ages was rarely of a decisive character. Greece proper was not a country suitable for the rearing of horses, owing to the lack of adequate pasture-land except in some favoured regions such as Thessaly or, to a lesser degree, Boeotia and Euboea. This is why the Thessalian cavalry possessed such a great reputation; Thessaly was the only part of Greece where the proportion of cavalry to infantry in the forces was even as high as one in three. In the Boeotian army, where the cavalry likewise had the advantage of a firm tradition, it never played an important part in battle until Epaminondas' tactical innovations were introduced. On the other hand, in certain colonial states whose land lent itself to horse-breeding, in Cyrene, for example, and Tarentum and Syracuse, the cavalry always retained considerable importance and reputation.

Over a long period the horsemen rode bareback, later upon a piece of cloth or hide. The use of saddle and stirrups was unknown. The horse was driven by means of a metal bit and reins, but the tongue-bit was not known. In order to make the action of the snaffle more effective, a very savage kind of bit was used, with sharp edges or a surface bristling with points. The horse's mouth was cruelly punished in consequence; hence the bloody foam mentioned by writers and represented in equestrian paintings. The head harness consisted of the same principal elements as are used today, nose-band, head-band, head-stall and cheek-straps, adorned, from the close of the fifth century onwards, with *phalara*, small metal discs embellished with reliefs or inlaid work, which were fixed to the straps by means of rings attached to their inner surface.

Though they possessed great skill in driving their steeds, as we know from Xenophon's treatise *On Horsemanship*, the Greek cavalry could not achieve the same effectiveness in impact as medieval knights who, firmly settled on their saddle and stirrups, drove home their lance with all the force amassed by a horse at full gallop. The Greeks could only strike with the force of their arms; otherwise they would easily have been thrown from the saddle. So, instead of a long lance, they preferred two shorter and lighter javelins, which could either be thrown or used for thrusting. They rarely used the bow, leaving this weapon to Barbarian horsemen such as Scythians and Persians. Their other weapon of offence was a sword. Often they had no weapon of defence, relying entirely on their speed and agility to avoid the enemy's blows. Sometimes, however, they carried a round shield, smaller than that of the hoplites. Their customary outer garment was the *chlamys*, a short cloak held by a clasp on the right shoulder. Under this the horseman wore a tunic. On his head he had either a wide-brimmed hat (*petasos*), a fur cap, or a helmet. On his feet were sandals or top-boots of limp leather. Such is the picture we see in the Parthenon frieze of the young knights of Athens mustered in a brilliant cavalcade.

Thus equipped, the Greek cavalry was not a force of shock-troops: it reconnoitred for the main body of the forces, protected the flanks of the army during a battle, and pursued the disordered enemy after a victory. The Thessalians alone seem to have made systematic use of their mounted squadrons, which wore breast-plates, to decide the issue of an encounter. It was only after having secured their co-operation that Philip created a force of heavy cavalry, commanded by his son Alexander, whose mass attack made a brilliant contribution to the victory at Chaeronea.

The knight, like the hoplite, did not have his equipment provided by the state; in addition, he had to procure his own horse. This accounts for the aristocratic character of the Greek cavalry, like that of the chariot-riding warriors of earlier days. Horse-breeding (*hippotrophia*) was a privilege of noble, and at the same time rich, families: an interest in horses was evidence of aristocracy, or at least a form of snobbery, as in young Phidippides, the son of the countryman Strepsiades, in the *Clouds* of Aristophanes. At Athens the cavalry was recruited from the two propertied classes with the highest incomes; the second of these classes was in fact called the *Knights*. It is they who appear in Aristophanes' comedy thus named (*Hippeis*) produced in 424 B.C.: he represents them as devoted to ancestral traditions and eager to destroy the credit of the demagogue Cleon. Xenophon, himself a horse-lover, gives perfect expression to the interests and the prejudices of Greek 'cavaliers' during the first third of the fourth century.

Tactical organization. Athens as an example. The ephebic system at Athens
The organization of these armed forces varied in different states and at different periods. In the Classical Age, we have an approximate knowledge of it in the cases of Athens and Sparta. But the names given to the various units do not always refer to similarities of fact: thus the word *lochos* at Sparta meant a numerous

infantry corps, corresponding to a big battalion, whereas the same word was used at Athens for a smaller unit, something like a company. The responsibilities of a *lochagos*, the officer commanding a *lochos*, were therefore different in the two armies. Nevertheless the principles of organization were everywhere the same: the soldiers were organized in units of increasing size, analogous to our platoons, companies, and battalions, whose effective force was in each case a multiple of 10. The titles of the officers commanding them were normally derived from the term used to describe the unit: thus an *enomotarchas* at Sparta commanded a platoon (*enomotia*); a *lochagos* led a *lochos*; at Cyrene, a *triakatiarchas* was the commander of a company of 300 men; a *taxiarchos* at Athens was the leader of a battalion (*taxis*).

Large units, capable of conducting a campaign and composed of elements from the various branches, were under the command of generals, whose title varied: at Athens, they were the *strategoi*, assisted by two *hipparchoi* in command of the cavalry; at Sparta, one of the two kings was in control of operations, aided by commanding officers (*polemarchoi*). The term *strategos* was the one most widely used to designate a general officer.

Recruitment was closely bound up with the social and political organization of the city. Social classification was carried on into the army: at Athens, about which we are better informed than about any other city, this correspondence was rigorously ensured, since each of the ten tribes constituting the whole body of citizens supplied the army with a *taxis*, or battalion, of hoplites, commanded by an elected taxiarch belonging to the same tribe. It was the taxiarch who chose the *lochagoi*, who commanded the companies. It was also he who drafted members of his tribe to serve in a given campaign—a very heavy responsibility, which might give rise to disputes and abuses. The cavalry was provided for in the same way: each tribe contributed a *phyle*, or squadron, of 100 cavalrymen commanded by an elected *phylarchos*, whose prerogatives were analogous with those of the taxiarch. The recruitment of both cavalry and hoplites was, as we have seen, based on the principle of qualification by property: citizens who had not the required means served in the light-armed forces or in the fleet.

The citizen received a special training to prepare him to bear arms. This training was most highly developed at Sparta, where every effort was directed to making a warrior of the young Spartan. But even the Athenian democracy, whose ambitions by no means took the same direction as that imposed by the

Spartan constitution, devoted particular care to its future soldiers. With this in view it created the institution known as *ephebeia*, very characteristic of the military aspect assumed by the citizen's condition in an ancient city-state. We are familiar with the details of the system only for the period subsequent to the battle of Chaeronea, thanks to Aristotle's *Constitution of Athens*, a work written during the reign of Alexander the Great, at a time when the system of *ephebeia* had recently been reorganized. Yet it is probable that, at least as far as its principle is concerned, the institution was already an ancient one. As described by Aristotle, it took the form of compulsory military service for all young Athenians from eighteen to twenty years of age, at least for those of them who belonged to the classes qualified by property to serve as cavalrymen or hoplites. These young men, drafted to units based on the tribes under the command of leaders elected by the people, were subjected to physical training and preparation for military service under specialized instructors. They took their meals together at public expense. During their second year of service, they were sent out of Athens and stationed as garrisons in frontier fortresses such as Eleutherae, Phyle, and Rhamnus; they also carried out manoeuvres in open country. At the end of this second year, they were released from service and were now regarded as fully qualified citizens. After this they remained liable to mobilization between the ages of twenty and sixty: each annual contingent, designated by the name of the *archon eponymos* of the year in which it was entered in the ephebic roll, could be mobilized in its entirety or in part on the initiative of the strategi. However, the last ten classes, composed of citizens between fifty and sixty years of age, could only be called up for the defence of the territory and did not take part in expeditions outside Attica.

Thus the Athenian was subject to military duties for more than forty years of his life: two years as an ephebe, thirty years on the reserve list of the regular army, ten years in the territorial reserve. The great city's manpower enabled it, as Thucydides tells us, to muster 13,000 first-line hoplites, and 1,200 cavalry, not counting light troops, auxiliaries, and veterans entrusted with garrison duties. In 369, when Athens mobilized to aid Sparta, threatened by Epaminondas, the expeditionary force put under Iphicrates' command amounted to 12,000 hoplites. About the same time, the Boeotians could muster approximately 13,000 hoplites and 1,500 cavalry. Sparta could never put in the field such substantial forces as these: at Plataea, in 479, her heavy infantry did amount to 10,000 men, of whom one half were genuine Spartiates, but subsequently she could no longer muster such a large force as this and had to rely on the outstanding valour of her soldiers to make up for a lack of numbers that made itself increasingly felt as time went on. These figures refer to the more important operations; but the forces engaged were usually considerably less numerous, amounting to no more than a few thousand, sometimes a few hundred, men. It is understandable that, in comparison with such limited forces, the Greeks credited the great armies of Darius and Xerxes, in which were mustered the contingents furnished by an immense empire, with strength of numbers probably far in excess of reality.

Tactics and strategy. Rôle of soothsayers. The Spartan doctrine of massed frontal attack. Tactical innovations of Epaminondas. Ineffectiveness of the traditional methods. Defence of fortified positions: defence walls. Forts and watch-towers. Usual development of a military operation in the Classical period

The tactics employed by Greek armies were usually extremely simple. The object was to bring about a frontal clash between the opposing armies in open country. The hostile forces were drawn up in a well-defined traditional order: the main fighting force was in the centre, the light troops and the cavalry, when there was any, on the flanks. In the main force, which would play the decisive part in the encounter, the hoplites were drawn up in close formation to a depth of eight to twelve ranks. According to a well-established tradition, the best troops were posted on the right wing. This custom is no doubt to be explained by the fact that, the shield being carried on the left arm, the right was the most vulnerable side, whether of a soldier standing by himself or of an organized unit; therefore the most exposed position had to be entrusted to picked fighters. The officers were in the front rank and the general himself often took part in the battle: many were the famous leaders who died in battle.

It was customary to perform certain religious rites before joining battle. In war, as in all other things, the Greeks knew that the gods and destiny decided the result; this was Homer's belief and, on this point as on many others, both Archaic and Classical Greece remained faithful to the teaching of the *Iliad*. Every military leader was accompanied by soothsayers and exegetists who consulted the gods and interpreted the signs which they sent. Herodotus, mentioning a celebrated soothsayer Tisamenus, a native of Elis in the service of Lacedaemon, holds him directly responsible for five great victories won by the Spartans, from the battle of Plataea to that of Tanagra. At a later date, when the Lacedaemonian Lysander, the victor of Aegospotami, had a likeness of himself, accompanied by his chief officers, set up in the sanctuary of Delphi in commemoration of his victory, he had a statue of the soothsayer Agias, who had followed him on this campaign, placed beside his own. Thus, whether by virtue of sincere belief or merely to gratify public credulity, whether the general was actuated by profound piety, like the Athenian Nicias, or was frivolous and sceptical, like Alcibiades, he took great care to perform libations and a sacrifice and to investigate the omens. If these were not favourable, he shrank from giving battle. Herodotus, in his account of the battle of Plataea, tells us that the Lacedaemonians, though they were the target of showers of arrows from the Persian bowmen, stood motionless at their post without attempting to hit back until their general Pausanias had succeeded, by repeated prayers and sacrifices, in obtaining a favourable signal from the gods. Mardonius, the leader of the Persian army, had also secured (by payment in gold) the services of a famous Greek soothsayer, who hated the Lacedaemonians and performed sacrifices on behalf of the invader.

As soon as favourable omens had been obtained, the action began. After the light forces, bowmen or slingers, had softened up the enemy line by bombarding it with their projectiles, the hoplites would strike up the *paean*, an ancient war-song in honour of Apollo, and then move forward for the final assault. The main clash would develop into a series of hand-to-hand fights with spear and sword, until one of the two opponents gave ground and broke into flight. In the melée, morale no less than tactics would help the better side to win: in order to keep the line of attack or defence in a state of cohesion, to close the ranks and take the place of those who fell, not only the sure reflexes which a well-trained unit acquires by practice in manoeuvring together were needed, but also dauntless courage based on a spirit of self-sacrifice. These supreme virtues of the warrior were for a long time the glory of the Lacedaemonian soldiers, who since the second half of the seventh century had been reciting the martial elegies of the poet Tyrtaeus: 'Come now, young men, do battle, each keeping his place in the line! Do not yield to fear or the shameful urge to flee! Make the hearts in your breasts stout and valiant! Forget love of life when you confront the foe! . . . Let each withstand the onset, with his legs wide apart, his two feet firmly planted on the ground, biting his lip with his teeth!'

A tactical revolution was needed to put an end to the recognized superiority of

81. THE VICTORY OF PAEONIUS AT OLYMPIA

One of the very few surviving originals whose attribution to a great classical sculptor is certain. Mentioned by Pausanias, whose statement is confirmed by the discovery of the inscription with the artist's signature, this Victory, set on a triangular pillar, was dedicated in front of the temple of Zeus soon after 455. The head is lost, but the body whose outlines are clearly perceptible beneath the garments pressed against her body by the wind in her flight, is of extreme sculptural beauty. Beneath her feet flies the eagle of Zeus. It is possible that this same Paeonius carved the pediments of the neighbouring temple ten years earlier. Olympia Museum.

82. 'MELANCHOLY' ATHENA

A small votive relief (middle of the fifth century) showing the goddess in pensive mood in front of one of the quadrangular pillars which marked the starting-line on the running-track in the stadium. Athena thus appears as the patroness of the Panathenaïc Games, held in her honour. Acropolis Museum, Athens.

83 & 84. THE LENORMANT ATHENA

A marble statuette, made in the Roman period, in imitation of the Athena Parthenos. Although unfinished and incomplete (the chief elements lacking are the Victory that stood on the right hand, which was supported by a column, the spear in the left hand, and the rich decoration of the helmet), it enables us to imagine quite well the total effect produced by Phidias's colossus, with the decoration in relief on the front side of the base (creation of Pandora, the first woman, amid the watching gods) and on the shield (Amazonomachy). National Museum, Athens.

85. VOTIVE RELIEF FROM BRAURON

One of the fourth-century reliefs discovered in the excavations at the sanctuary of Artemis (see ills. 97, 98, and 117), near the eastern coast of Attica. Artemis is on the right, bringing back from the chase a hind alive and rearing up (nothing but its front legs is visible). Beside her we should in all probability identify, from right to left, her brother Apollo, their mother Leto, and their father Zeus, seated. National Museum, Athens.

86. POSEIDON, APOLLO, ARTEMIS

A fragment of the Ionic frieze which extended beneath the external portico of the Parthenon, above the walls of the temple. This slab was part of the east frieze, above the entrance porch, where one could see the gods seated to welcome the procession bringing Athena's peplos. Acropolis Museum, Athens.

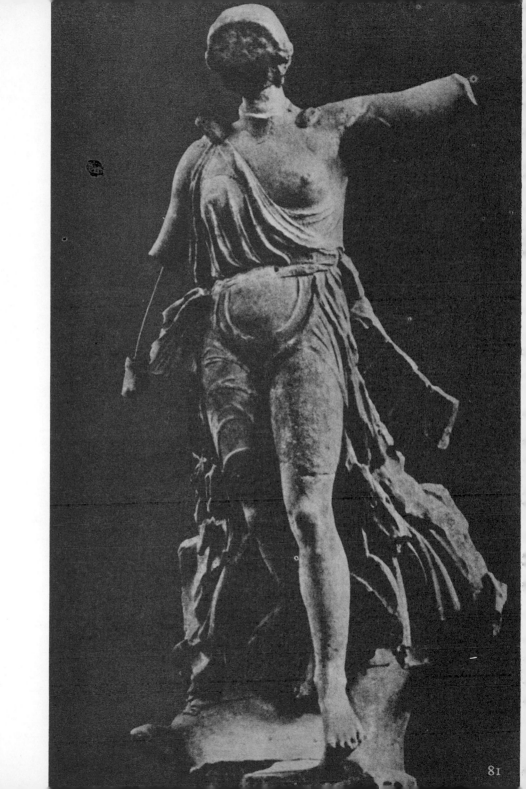

85

86

the Lacedaemonian hoplites, a revolution effected by the military genius of
Epaminondas. At Leuctra, in 371, and at Mantinea, in 362, the Theban made
use of a decisive innovation: instead of placing his own phalanx on the right
wing, according to the traditional tactics, he replaced the line formation with a
wedge formation, withdrawing his right wing and advancing his left. The 'wedge'
was composed of his hoplites drawn up to a depth of fifty ranks. This compact
mass 'like the prow of a trireme' crushed the Lacedaemonian phalanx opposed to
it, which was drawn up, according to custom, to a depth of twelve ranks. Having
thus first broken the main strength of the enemy by a well-planned blow in the
right place (the fundamental Clausewitz principle already in operation!), he
found it easy to deal with the rest of the opposing army, even although it had
enjoyed a clear numerical superiority. The invention of the 'oblique phalanx',
with which, at Mantinea, Epaminondas combined the use of his cavalry as
shock-troops, put an end to tactical methods that had been established since the
seventh century and showed what a shrewd leader might achieve by manoeuvre.
The Athenians had long been aware of this in naval warfare, but on land the
conservative spirit of the Lacedaemonians and the respect felt for their warlike
valour had hitherto prevented the art of war from seeking improvement: Philip
of Macedon, learning the lesson taught by Epaminondas, was soon to make it
progress in its turn.

When one of the opposing sides had taken to flight, the victor's cavalry pursued the fugitives, but the pursuit was rarely pressed to the bitter end. The victorious army, satisfied with the enemy's acknowledgment of its superiority, set
up a *trophy*, a kind of framework covered with weapons, which was the visible
symbol of its triumph, and sang the paean of victory. The dead were buried and
the enemy's dead handed over to him; by requesting a truce for this purpose, he
acknowledged his defeat. All that remained to be done was to take advantage of
success by imposing advantageous conditions of peace on the vanquished and to
thank the gods by consecrating to them a tithe of the booty in the form of offerings in the national sanctuaries, or even, on occasion, in the Panhellenic sanctuaries.

Described in these terms, war might seem nothing but a sort of bloody game
with well-defined laws, enabling rival cities to settle their differences in a manner
admitting of no dispute. Nevertheless, armed conflicts by no means always took
on this character. In fact, decisive encounters were the exception in Greek history,

M

and wars often dragged on for a long time, bringing their train of countless miseries year after year. The chief cause of this was the strange inability of Greek armies to take fortified cities by storm. Hardly any progress was made in this respect between the Trojan War and the Classical Age: just as Agamemnon's forces lingered for ten years outside the walls of Ilium and only captured it in the end by a stratagem, so the Lacedaemonian hoplites, in spite of all their confidence in their superiority in open warfare, never succeeded in forcing the fortifications of Athens and the Piraeus throughout the Peloponnesian War, and only over-came Athenian resistance by blockade and famine. The fact is that a wall stoutly defended was practically impregnable against assault, for lack of suitable siege engines.

It was Dionysius I of Syracuse who, early in the fourth century, first con-structed a kind of artillery and made progress with siege engines, perhaps following the example of the Carthaginians. Practically all that can be cited earlier than this is Pericles' use of machines during the siege of Samos in 440, the use of battering-rams in certain circumstances during the Peloponnesian War, and such a stratagem as the flame-thrower with which the Boeotians set fire to the wooden fortifications of Delium in 424. The art of siege (*poliorketike*) was not destined to develop in Greece, following the example given by Dionysius in Sicily, before the military revolution of the fourth century and the achievements of Philip of Macedon.

Up to this time, the art of defence had outstripped that of attack, as we learn from the *Treatise on the Defence of fortified Positions*, composed about 360 B.C. by an Arcadian officer, Aeneas Tacticus. The precepts, counsels, and stratagems that form the subject-matter of this work enable us to understand why Greek armies so often failed in the siege of fortified cities up to the middle of the fourth century. Such fortified cities had become very numerous in the Greek mainland from the time of the Persian Wars. The Mycenaean tradition of powerful rings of fortifications had long been forgotten, and the cities of the Archaic Age were satisfied with the refuge afforded to their population by their acropolis, which alone was defended by walls. But in the sixth century the Ionians, alarmed by the threats hanging over them as a result of Cyrus's conquests, had surrounded their cities with defensive walls. Those of Phocaea, raised by means of the re-sources acquired by trade with the west, were built with freestone, to the astonish-ment of contemporaries, who were accustomed to the brick-built walls of eastern cities: but Cyrus's forces, which had besieged many a city, captured Phocaea by raising banks that enabled them to scale and counter-batter the walls. At Athens only the Acropolis was fortified up to the end of the sixth century, at which period, according to the latest researches, the city itself would appear to have been provided for the first time with a ring of fortifications. This wall having been destroyed by the Persians in 480, Themistocles hastily had it rebuilt, adopting a technique which was often employed for the walls of Greek cities: a rampart of unfired brick was erected upon a strong base of stone. At first, for the sake of speed, stones from older buildings and even funerary stelae were used, according to Thucydides (I, 93), to build the stone base. More care was taken later with the fortifications of the Piraeus, the blocks even being bound to one another with metal clamps, a practice normally reserved for the walls of buildings designed for ostentation, but unusual in those merely designed for use. In walls of this type, the courses of unfired brick have usually disappeared, while the stone base alone remains, more or less destroyed. In the Sicilian city of Gela, however, recent excavations have revealed a thick wall of brick, preserved to a considerable height. According to Greek writers on tactics, these ramparts of brick stood up very well to battering rams.

When financial resources or the presence of quarries within easy reach of the workers made it possible, the fortifications were constructed entirely of stone. At Thasos the walls were built of marble and gneiss, materials which were plentiful in the island, towards the end of the Archaic Age, and later restored after the Persian Wars and again after 411. In Greece proper, the best-preserved fortifications are those of Aegosthena in the Megarid, at the foot of Cithaeron: they show fine examples of classical fortifications, with rectilinear curtains, from which project square towers twice as high as the walls. The construction of the walls is magnificent, with fine regular courses of stone blocks with bossages. The curtains were topped with merlons and crenelles or with a continuous breastwork containing loop-holes. The towers often had a roof. They were about 20 or 30 metres apart, so that the wall could be effectively protected from each flank by the fire of arrows and javelins. Later, when the use of the catapult, invented by the engineers of Dionysius I, became common, the considerable range of this missile weapon made it possible to lengthen the curtains and even to replace the towers by mere redans in the wall, which henceforth had a jagged outline: these innovations spread from the time of Philip of Macedon.

Apart from the fortified cities, the Greeks built fortresses to guard passes and protect frontiers. Thus Attica was guarded against invasion by a number of strongpoints: Eleutherae, Phyle, Rhamnus, whose remains are still standing. Eleutherae in particular, dominating the pass of Cithaeron which leads towards Plataea and Thebes, still raises its towers and walls on the summit of a rocky peak; they are quite well preserved, with fine isodomic construction of the fourth century. Certain of these forts, such as Phyle and Decelea, played an important part in the political and military history of Athens. In the fifth century, most of the fortifications of this kind were less fully developed: the entrenchment erected by the Athenians at Delium in 424 was mainly of wood, which made it easy for the Boeotians to set it on fire. In every region of Greece there are isolated fortlets, generally nothing more than square towers, solidly built of freestone, rising in the middle of an agricultural or pastoral area, no attempt having been made to place them in a specially strong position. The date of these buildings, found in mountainous regions and in islands as well, is often difficult to determine, but some of them, as far as we can judge from the masonry of their walls, go back at least to the fourth century. They were in all probability places of refuge or watch-towers erected in frontier districts or isolated spots exposed to the forays of plunderers coming by land or by sea: the peasants and shepherds of the district could use them to hold up an enemy who appeared unexpectedly.

All these defensive arrangements made the invaders' task difficult, as long as the art of siege had undergone no new developments. A normal land campaign pursued the following course during the fifth century and the first half of the fourth: after the declaration of war, made through the agency of a herald, the attacking side marshalled its forces, joined by the allied contingents, and invaded the enemy territory. They had naturally consulted the gods before entering upon hostilities, either by sending a delegation to one of the famous oracles or by relying on the local oracles and the customary rites. The favourable seasons were spring and summer. Winter campaigns, which exposed the army to bad weather, were avoided: in Aristophanes' *Acharnians* we find the taxiarch Lamachus, who had been ordered to go in the depth of winter to repel a Boeotian invasion on the Attic frontier, raving about the snow and the wintry weather in general. As soon as they were in enemy territory, the army proceeded to systematic plunder and ravaging: it set fire to the farmhouses, seized the livestock, destroyed the standing crops, cut down the fruit-trees and the vines, and even went so far as to dig up

the cloves of garlic with sticks to make sure of having ruined everything. Faced
with such an invasion, the country folk sought safety in flight: there were fortified
towns to shelter them, and the development of city fortifications, often enclosing
large unbuilt areas along with the genuinely urban districts, was intended precisely to enable cities to serve in this way as places of refuge. Thus the country
people of Attica crowded together promiscuously during the Peloponnesian War
in the waste ground and in the sanctuaries of Athens and Piraeus, and also between the Long Walls: this sudden influx of inhabitants driven from their villages
and camping in deplorable hygienic conditions caused the terrible plague during
the early years of the war. If the invading army was not opposed by the enemy
forces in a decisive battle, it would advance as far as the city walls. The gates
might sometimes be opened to it through surprise, treachery, or fear, as at
Plataea in March 431, when an accomplice enabled 300 Theban hoplites to enter
by night, or at Amphipolis, which surrendered at Brasidas's first summons in
424. If this did not happen, the only hope of reducing the city was by blockade,
which it was difficult to maintain effectively for a long period: it took Athens
more than two years (431–429) to reduce Potidaea, in Chalcidice. Usually, after a
demonstration beneath the walls of the city, the attacker, little inclined to expose
himself to the rigours of a winter siege in a district already plundered and deprived of all its resources, returned home and released his troops until the following spring. Such was the pattern of operations year after year during the Peloponnesian War, at least until the Peloponnesians, by seizing Decelea, occupied a base
of operations which enabled them to establish themselves permanently, even
throughout the winter, in Attic territory.

States which had not adequate forces for a pitched battle or which did not
wish to run the risk of one countered the conventional tactics described above by
guerrilla warfare, which might take the form of ambushes like the one laid by the
Aetolians for the Athenian Demosthenes in 426 or the one in which the Athenian
Iphicrates, leading his peltasts, destroyed a force of Spartan infantry during the
Corinthian War. Maritime retaliation was even more effective. Naval superiority
enabled its possessor to strike unexpected blows at the enemy. During the
Peloponnesian War, Athens was not slow to plunder the Peloponnesian coast
during the summer months, even penetrating deep into the Laconian Gulf; for
several years she maintained a base of operations at Pylus in Messenia, doing the
utmost harm she could to the sea trade of Sparta and her allies. This great conflict

was, as was perfectly realized at the time, largely a struggle between a naval power and a military one, and Sparta did not gain the final victory until, thanks to Lysander and Persian gold, she had succeeded in smashing the Athenian fleet. The vital part played by naval warfare was one of the most characteristic features of Greek history.

Naval war. Homeric ships. The penteconter. The trireme: its size and complement of rowers. Trierarchy at Athens. Boat-houses. The Skeuotheke at the Piraeus. Athenian trieremes. Naval tactics: diekplous and periplous. Combined operations As early as the Mycenaean Age, the Greeks used ships for warfare and for piracy, two allied activities which were to remain associated in their eyes right down to the Hellenistic period. A famous Pylus tablet refers to a naval expedition. The Trojan War was but the most renowned of a series of similar operations in which a fleet and a land army co-operated. We know little of the Mycenaean ships: some engraved stones, a few drawings or graffiti, are too slight and imperfect records to provide us with adequate information about Greek navigation in the second millennium B.C. But there is no reason to doubt that the vessels used at this period were already capable of quite long voyages: this is sufficiently indicated, as early as the later part of the thirteenth century, by the invasion of Egypt by the Peoples of the Sea, among whom there were Achaeans.

We are much better informed about ships in Homeric times, thanks to the Homeric poems and the representations that appear on Geometric vases. The latter, as we have seen, quite often show naval battle-scenes or conflicts close to ships, which offer striking similarities to Homeric descriptions. By combining the information drawn from these two sources, we can draw a fairly exact picture of these large open galleys, provided with a ram, having a forecastle and a quarter-deck, both raised and surrounded with hand-rails. The oarsmen were arranged in two rows on the same level, pulling their oars in rowlocks in the form of hooks fixed vertically on the gunwale. Between the two files of oarsmen there was a raised passage (or gangway) from one end of the ship to the other. This was the place occupied by the soldiers on board. The ship was steered by means of two long oars acting as a rudder, placed on each side of the stern. The steersman could pass from one to the other by a 'foot bench' reserved for his use, crossing the whole width of the ship, which at this point close to the stern was about two metres. It was on to this bench that Ajax, in *Iliad* XI, leapt brandishing a great handspike to repel the assault of the Trojan battalions as he fought from the decks of the Greek ships beached upon the shore.

Such was the 'long-ship'—the *galère subtile*, as V. Bérard calls it, reviving the expression used in the seventeenth century—commonly employed in the Greek navies of early Archaic times. It was propelled both by oars and by a sail. The single mast, which was removable, rose in the centre of the ship through a hole in the central gangway, the heel of the mast being fixed in a wooden block or *step* attached to the keel. A horizontal yard, hoisted with leather halyards, carried the square sail, a single sail supported and trimmed by means of sheets and braces. This rigging, which shows no advance on that of Egyptian ships, did not make it possible to sail close to the wind: the only modes of sailing that it allowed were with wind astern or wind on the quarter. When it was a question of hauling the wind, the only possible course was to take in the sail and use the oars. The oarsmen might be as many as fifty, twenty-five on each side of the ship: so we have already practically the fifty-oared type of ship, the *pentekontoros*, common in the seventh and sixth centuries.

The long ships of the Homeric age, being provided with a beak, were capable of destroying an enemy ship by ramming it: although we have no direct evidence of an authentic sea-fight at this period, it is clear that naval tactics had already come into existence. They were brought to perfection by the great maritime powers, mainly by Corinth. This important city, standing on the Isthmus and looking out on both the seas, developed its navy in order to protect its trade and its communications with its colonies; with this end in view, it built a fleet of warships of a new type, open vessels lower in the water, swifter and easier to handle, propelled by fifty rowers whose oars were no longer fastened in rowlocks but passed through openings made in the gunwales. These *pentekontoroi*, about 100 feet long, were fully comparable in Mediterranean waters to the Norman *drakkars* of later days in the Atlantic; they were superior to the Homeric ships in manoeuvring to make use of the ram. Along with the thirty-oared boats called *triakontoroi*, similar in type but smaller, they formed the main strength of Greek fleets in the Archaic period and made colonial expansion in distant seas a possibility. For example, it was on two penteconters that Battus and his followers sailed from Thera to Libya to found Cyrene.

The dimensions of the penteconter (100 to 115 feet in length) are about the maximum possible for an ordinary wooden ship: as soon as this length is

87. RELIEF FROM CHRYSAPHA

Small funeral stele (third quarter of the sixth century) from the little Laconian town of Chrysapha. A 'heroized' dead couple, seated on a throne and accompanied by or furnished with chthonian or funerary symbols (serpent, cantharus, pomegranate in the woman's right hand), are receiving offerings from a living couple. The latter are represented on a smaller scale, to stress the superior dignity of the deceased pair. Their offerings are a cock, an egg, and a pomegranate. Berlin Museum.

88. GIUSTINIANI STELE

A funeral stele, probably sculptured in the Cyclades about the middle of the fifth century. The girl, wearing a peplos, is throwing incense, taken from a box, on a tiny round altar (another view is that she is drawing an invisible trinket from a box whose lid has been placed on the ground). The serene gravity of her attitude and expression is typical of the funeral monuments of the Classical Age. Note the splendid palmette crowning the stele. Berlin Museum.

89 & 90. THE PREPARATIONS FOR THE SACRIFICE TO ATHENA (PARTHENON FRIEZE)

In the procession at the Panathenaea appear the beasts intended for the hecatomb and men carrying hydrias, bronze vessels containing the water for purification. At the extreme right of ill. 89 can be seen the hands and the instrument of a flute-player whose tunes accompanied the march of the procession and kept it in time. These two slabs (Nos. VI and II of the frieze on the north side) are of exceptional quality as sculpture. Acropolis Museum, Athens.

91–93.

Crater with volutes attributed to the 'Painter of Cleophon' (third quarter of the fifth century). This Attic red-figure vase, discovered in the Etruscan cemetery at Spina (in the Po delta), is contemporary with the Parthenon frieze. It shows the procession of the bulls for sacrifice (91: cf. ill. 90). The participants are garlanded with laurel. Two of them are standing on each side of a thymiaterion, a bronze censer, ovoid in shape, mounted on a stand. Next comes a woman carrying offerings, richly attired, holding on her head an offerings-basket with three triangular handles. She is welcomed by the priest of Apollo, a bearded man with a long staff in his hand. At his feet there is the omphalos, with a tripod standing behind it. Finally, between two columns symbolizing the temple, Apollo is seated on his throne, holding a laurel branch in his hand. Hanging on the wall are his bow and his quiver, which have partly vanished in a crack. A second tripod stands on a base in the form of a column with a capital of pendent leaves (ill. 93). Lifelike representation of the ceremonies at Delphi. Ferrara Museum.

89

90

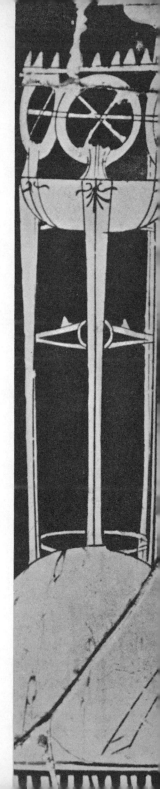

I

94. RITE AT THE SKIRA

This Attic red-figure lecythus of the late fifth century portrays a strange ceremony in the cult of Demeter and Kore in Attica. During the festival of the Skira (late May-early June), women threw live animals (generally young pigs, here a small dog) into deep hollows in the ground (in the country), where they were left to starve to death. Their remains were collected in the autumn and mixed with the seeds for sowing in order to ensure their fruitfulness. The woman is leaning forward to throw the animal into the fissure in the ground, from which emerge two torches, Kore's symbol. In the basket for offerings (see ill. 92) there were ritual cakes which were also thrown into the hole. National Museum, Athens.

95. SACRIFICIAL SCENE

Attic red-figure vase of the third quarter of the fifth century. While the priest is placing the entrails of the victim on the altar, where they will be entirely burned up, a young participant is pouring a libation from a wine-jug. Another is roasting in the fire on the altar, on the end of long spits, the meat which is to be eaten at the ritual feast to follow. A young man, garlanded with laurel like the other figures, is holding a long branch in his hand. A laurel tree behind the altar suggests that the sacrifice is being performed in honour of Apollo. Louvre.

96. DIONYSUS AND TWO MAENADS

Attic black-figure vase by the potter Amasis (third quarter of the sixth century). We can read above the figures the words: 'Dionysus. Work of Amasis.' The god is holding a large cantharus. He welcomes two dancing Maenads wearing gaily-coloured dresses (one also a panther skin), each with one arm round the other's shoulder. They have necklaces and ear-pendants. Each of them is holding a spring of ivy, the Dionysiac plant, and an animal (one a hare, the other a deer represented in miniature). They are going to tear these animals asunder and eat them raw, according to the rite of omophagy. Cabinet des Médailles.

97 & 98. TWO 'SHE-BEARS'

These fourth-century statues, recently discovered in the sanctuary of Artemis Brauronia (see ills. 85 and 117), are charmingly natural representations of the little Athenian girls who took part in the cult of Artemis Brauronia with the cult title of Shebears. National Museum, Athens.

exceeded, there is danger of the keel breaking as a result of the strain that may be imposed on the boat when sailing in the open sea. In order to increase the speed, the number of rowers had to be increased. How could this be done without increasing the length of the ship? The solution of the problem was to place the oarsmen above one another: hence the types of vessel with two or three banks of oars, *biremes* and *triremes*, which, but particularly the latter, were to be especially favoured during the Classical Age. In fact, the trireme represents the culminating point of Greek naval construction: this delicately manoeuvrable ship was the main element in the Athenian fleet at the period of its greatest power and so deserves special attention.

The hull, about 115 to 125 feet long, was narrow: 13 to 16 feet in width at the midship frame, on the water-line. The ship drew less than 3 feet of water, and the displacement was about 80 tons in terms of international tonnage. The hull, strengthened with wales, was fitted with a ram. The arrangement of the rowers, which has long been a subject of debate, can be inferred pretty clearly from extant representations on bas-reliefs, etc. From literary texts we learn that the three banks of rowers, beginning at the top, were known as *thranitai*, *zeugitai*, and *thalamitai*. Those corresponding to the traditional oarsmen of the pente-conter and earlier vessels were the rowers of the midmost bank, who were seated, as formerly, directly on the beams of the ship: a beam was called *zeugos* ('yoke' or 'traverse beam'), hence the name *zeugitai*. As in the penteconter, their oars passed through openings in the gunwales. The *thranitai* sat two feet higher than the *zeugitai* and their seat or bench (*thranos*) was set right against the upper part of the gunwale, each one half-way between the benches of the *zeugitai*. The *thranitai* were therefore 'staggered', in relation to the *zeugitai*, both vertically and longitudinally, and also latitudinally, since they were about a shoulder's breadth farther from the axis of the ship than the *zeugitai*. To make up for this outside position, the device was invented of fitting the trireme with a gallery, about two feet wide, jutting out at the level of the gunwale and supported by props joining the wales at an acute angle. On the edge of this gallery, above which there was an openwork guard-rail, were the rowlocks for the oars of the *thranitai*.

Thus the latter, though seated right against the gunwales of the ship, had enough leverage at their command to handle their long oars without excessive fatigue. As for the *thalamitai*, they were seated in the hold (*thalamos*), exactly level longitudinally with the *thranitai*, but a shoulder's breadth nearer to the axis of the ship than the *zeugitai* and about three feet lower down in the ship. Their oars, like those of the *zeugitai*, passed through ports in the side of the vessel, situated exactly beneath the rowlocks of the corresponding *thranitai*. This seemingly complicated arrangement was in reality extremely simple: it consisted of making the best use of the available space by 'staggering' the three ranks of oarsmen both vertically and latitudinally and by arranging them longitudinally in quincunx formation. In this way each had enough room to handle his oar without being impeded by a too near neighbour, an advantage of particular value with regard to an operation, essential for the safety of the ship, which consisted of drawing in the oars quickly on command, when an enemy ship was approaching with the intention of breaking them, and of putting them out again with all speed as soon as the danger had passed. The ports used by the *thalamitai* were scarcely more than 19 inches, and those of the *zeugitai* about 3 feet above the surface of the water: so, in order to avoid shipping water in a heavy sea, the ports had to be blocked with leather covers, attached to the hull and at the same time tightly gripping the oar, yet leaving it freedom of movement. The *thranitai* were in the open, $4\frac{1}{2}$ or $4\frac{3}{4}$ feet above the water. In the fifth century, an upper deck was usually built above them, to protect them from enemy missiles and to accommodate the soldiers on board. In addition, canvas shields were put up on the sides of the ship before a battle, as a protection against arrows.

An Athenian trireme would have a crew of 170 oarsmen: 62 *thranitai*, 54 *zeugitai* and 54 *thalamitai*. Since the *thranitai*, occupying the highest position, had also the longest oars, they were regarded as having the hardest task: hence the expression 'the thranite people' used by Aristophanes of humble folk at Athens, who provided the rowers. There would also be some sailors on board, no more than ten or so, to handle the sails, the anchors, and the cables. With regard to rigging, the trireme showed no advance upon earlier warships: like them, it had only one main-mast with a single square sail, and sometimes a small foresail, also square. The staff consisted of the captain or *trierarch*, a 'pilot officer', a second officer called the 'commander of the bow' who was in charge of the forward part of the ship, the 'boatswain' in control of the oarsmen, who set the stroke with the help of a flute-player giving the time, and probably several leading seamen. The ship's company would also include some hoplites or archers (*epibatai*) who would normally number some 200 men.

With a well-trained crew, a trireme could make five or six knots. The training of the rowers was a serious undertaking: the physical effort required was great and might last for hours on end. Perfect cohesion of the crew in delicate man-oeuvres could only be brought about by constant practice. As Pericles said in his address to the Athenians just before the outbreak of the Peloponnesian War, 'if there is any occupation that requires technical training, it is that of a seaman. Practice in it cannot be left to odd times, as though it were a hobby; on the contrary, it precludes the pursuit of any hobby.' Yet the Athenian crews were re-cruited from the ordinary people: it was the class of the *thetes*, the citizens with-out means, that provided the oarsmen. On occasion, metics too were enlisted or even slaves. These seamen received daily pay varying in amount, according to circumstances and the resources of the Treasury, from two obols to one drachma (six obols). During the later stages of the Peloponnesian War, the Lacedaemonian admirals, with Persian subsidies at their disposal, resorted to outbidding in the matter of pay, thus causing many oarsmen in the service of Athens to desert.

The commanding officer of the trireme (*trierarch*) was not a professional sea-man. He was a rich citizen appointed by the strategi to hold this office, which was at the same time a heavy financial responsibility. The *trierarchy* lasted for a year: it entailed taking over command of the ship, putting it into a seaworthy condition, and maintaining it. The hull, mast, and sail, and the main tackle were provided by the state, but the trierarch had to complete the equipment, have repairs carried out, and keep the zeal of the crew alive by gifts or bounties in addition to the pay provided by the Treasury. The expense was so heavy that, from 411 B.C. onwards, it was found necessary to allow two citizens to meet it jointly and later, in 357–356, to organize the more complicated system of *symmories*, which shared the burden between a considerable number of joint contributors. This meant abandoning the basic principle of physical and individual involvement in the service of the city: the citizen no longer risked his person, but only his money, and his mental attitude to war was in consequence profoundly altered. It need scarcely be said that, at the time when trierarchs themselves went to sea in their ships, they did not always possess the qualities and experience of a naval officer: hence the importance of the 'pilot officer', who was a professional seaman and whose function was to give effective advice to the trierarch. The latter, however, remained fully responsible for his ship. This was clearly seen in the Arginusae incident, when some trierarchs keenly opposed the strategi at the meeting of the

Assembly, because they felt personally responsible for the execution of the orders they had received.

At the time of her greatness, the power of Athens depended mainly on her naval squadrons. During the Second Persian War, she could put in line almost 300 triremes. In 431, she had at least as many, not counting those of her allies who had kept an independent fleet, such as Lesbos, Chios, and Corcyra. On many occasions she was able to build dozens of new ones and fit them out. Aristophanes gives us, in the *Acharnians*, a lively picture of one of these naval mobilizations: 'The whole city is full of the hubbub of war: there are calls for the captain, pay is handed out, the statues of Pallas are being gilded. The colonnades re-echo as the rations are measured out. Everywhere you can see leather bottles, thongs, people buying jars, string bags full of garlic, olives, and onions, garlands, anchovies, flute-girls and black eyes. There is also turmoil at the dockyard: spars are being planed into oars, there is the noise of pegs being driven home, the covers are being fixed on the port-holes. Nothing can be heard but tunes on flutes, the shouts of boatswains, the sound of pipes and blasts on the whistle.'

In the intervals between periods of action, the hull of the trireme was put under cover in sheds specially constructed for this purpose: these were roofed slip-docks on an inclined plane, opening directly upon the harbour basin. The trireme was hauled up on rollers, stern first, having been first cleared of its rigging. Here it remained high and dry, so that seaweed and shells could be removed and the hull caulked. Remains of these boat-sheds have been identified at many ancient sites. Their length, about 130 feet, confirms the calculations fixing the average length of a trireme at 115–125 feet. As a rule, these sheds were made to accommodate a single ship: but Dionysius I had some constructed at Syracuse to take two vessels at the same time. Already in Homer we find mention of the boat-sheds in which the Phaeacians, who were experienced seamen, kept their ships under cover. Hesiod, less well acquainted with maritime affairs, only speaks of berths in the open air. At Corinth, and at Samos in Polycrates' time, roofed dry-docks had already been in existence since the Archaic Age. Strabo informs us that the harbour of Cyzicus had 200. But of course Athens was the city best provided with berthing of this kind, with its three harbours at Piraeus, viz. the commercial harbour of Cantharus, on the western side, and the two roadsteads of Zea and Munychia, reserved for the war-fleets: in the middle of the fourth century, there were as many as 300 such sheds for vessels.

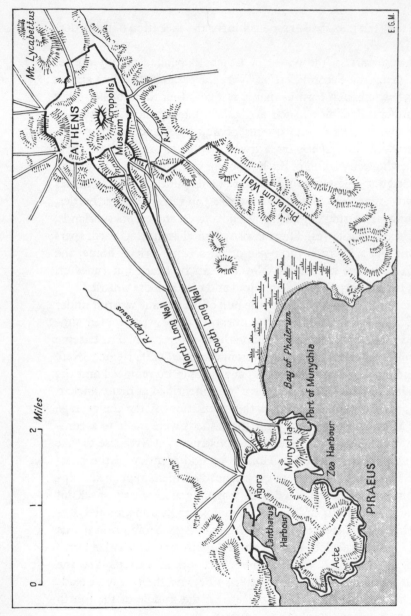

17. ATHENS AND PIRAEUS

(*After R. E. Wycherley.*) Placed at the foot of Acropolis and protected by its walls, the city of Athens was also connected with Piraeus and the open roadstead of Phalerum by the Long Walls, built on the instigation of Themistocles and, later, Pericles. The huge fortified area thus created defied all enemy attacks as long as the Athenian navy maintained supremacy at sea. The three harbours of the Piraeus, viz. the naval harbours of Zea and Munychia and the commercial harbour of Cantharus, were also protected by walls. The hill of Munychia was the key to the defence of Piraeus, just as the Acropolis and the hill of Museum were the keys to Athens.

E.G.M.

The mast, the oars, and the rudder (consisting of two long stern oars) of the laid-up trireme were put under cover in the same shed in which the hull was placed. As for the rigging, sails and ropes (a category described in official documents as 'hanging gear'), they were collected in a special building, the arsenal or *skeuotheke*. In 347–346, the Athenians undertook the construction of a new *skeuotheke* near the harbour of Zea on plans prepared by the architect Philon of Eleusis: we possess the specification for building, which has been preserved in an inscription and is a document of primary importance for Greek architecture. It was a very carefully designed building, 425 feet long and 60 feet wide. Inside, 134 large cupboards, in which the sails were to be stored, were set in the aisles on each side of a central gallery lined with high columns. The ropes were placed on rows of shelves above the cupboards. Precautionary measures had been taken to avoid outbreaks of fire: for example, the window-frames were of metal instead of wood.

The building of triremes was in the hands of specialists, the engineers of the naval construction department, who were also regarded as naval architects. In official documents, the ship's name was followed by that of the builder, who was thus committed to responsibility for the quality of the craft. The methods of working made it possible to get on quickly when necessary: cases are mentioned of an entire fleet being completed in a few months. The great problem was to obtain the wood necessary for such naval construction. Attica was poor in timber: it had to be imported from Chalcidice or Macedonia. The kings of Macedonia knew how to profit by this important resource of their kingdoms and to make Athens pay a high price for a friendship which it was greatly in her interest to cultivate.

As in modern navies, each trireme had a name, always a feminine one. Names of goddesses or heroines: *Amphitrite, Thetis, Hebe, Galatea, Pandora*; names of virtues or abstract ideas: *Justice, Strength, Virtue, Freedom, Peace*; laudatory epithets: *Beloved, Swift, Golden, Lucky*; geographical adjectives: *Nemean, Delian, Delphian, Salaminian*. The *Salaminian*, along with another trireme named *Paralos*, was specially commissioned to carry official dispatches. The Athenians were naturally greatly attached to a navy on which their fortunes depended. Aristophanes humorously conveys this sentiment when, in the *Knights*, he imagines the triremes meeting in council to put a stop to a projected expedition with which they are not greatly pleased. The eldest of them addresses the meeting: 'Are you unaware, ladies, of what is taking place in the city? It is said that a certain orator, a bad citizen, is demanding a hundred of our company for an attack on Carthage. . . .' The triremes protest that they will take no part in this fatal project, even if it means seeking asylum, like runaways, in some inviolable sanctuary! The hearts of the Athenians must also have been filled with pride when they went down to Piraeus to witness the departure of the fleet for an enterprise in distant waters or to welcome it back after some resounding success. Thucydides paints an unforgettable picture of the departure of the Sicilian expedition in the middle of the year 415: 'When all the ships had been manned and everything necessary for the voyage had been put on board, the trumpet sounded and silence fell on the throng. Then the prayers that are customary before putting out to sea were offered, not on each individual ship, but by them all together, led by the voice of a herald. Throughout the fleet wine was drawn from mixing bowls and the officers and marines made libations with gold and silver cups. The rest of the multitude, standing on the shore, both citizens and others who wished success to the expedition, joined in these prayers. When they had sung the paean and finished the libations, they put out to sea, sailing at first in single column, and then raced one another as far as Aegina.'

The historians give us numerous accounts of battles that enable us to estimate the progress made in naval tactics. Operations only took place in the summer months: winter storms would have been fatal to these narrow, long, open ships. The fleets spent the winter in some naval base and only put out to sea in spring. They rarely went very far from the shore, in fact only in cases of absolute necessity (for the long crossings to Africa or southern Italy, for example), since lack of space made life on board very uncomfortable for a long journey. Night sailing was avoided and it was usual to land even for meals. This accounts for the fact that the history of Greek warfare records hardly any battles on the high seas, but battles close to the coast, often in a strait, in which the vessels tend to attempt to reach the shore and in which land forces often play a part. Nevertheless, developments in the conduct of operations can be observed. In the Archaic period, although warships had a ram on their prow, sea-fights tended to resemble fights on land. Each vessel sought to close alongside an enemy ship and the hoplites on board would then attack those of the enemy: so the only tactics were those of boarding and the battle was little more than a series of single combats between one ship and another, without anything that could be called general manoeuvring.

This kind of fighting is represented on a number of Archaic vases, for example on the famous crater of Aristonothus, dating from the seventh century.

Later, and particularly in the fifth century, naval tactics underwent a transformation, largely under the influence of Athenian admirals, who showed great ability to make good use of well-trained crews. Already at Salamis the Greek ships had made considerable use of their manoeuvrability to ram the enemy vessels, which got in one another's way in a too confined space. Later on, complicated manoeuvres were brought to a high pitch of perfection, enabling a squadron that was ably led to get the better of much larger forces in the open sea. The manoeuvre known as *diekplous* consisted of sailing in single column through the lines of enemy vessels drawn up in front: attempts were made, while sailing through, to break the oars of some of the opposing ships, but the main object was to oblige the enemy squadron to avoid the danger of being taken in the rear by resorting to a change of direction that was likely to produce confusion and gave opportunities for ramming. The still more delicate manoeuvre known as *periplous* consisted in sailing at top speed, always in single column, round and round the enemy fleet: the risk of an attack on the flank was a real one, but each vessel could be protected against it if the vessel following was always ready to ram any ship attacking the one in front. Provided that formation was kept and speed was uniform, the manoeuvre would finally oblige the enemy to close up his lines until the ships got in one another's way, or else to break his battle order, thus presenting the attacker with a favourable opportunity. A brilliant example of the use of *periplous* was provided by the Athenian Phormion in the naval battle in the Gulf of Patras in 429: with his twenty triremes, he encircled the forty-seven triremes of a Peloponnesian squadron, compelled them to draw in close to one another, and when, as he had foreseen, the fresh morning breeze stirred the waters in the gulf, increasing the disorder in the enemy fleet, Phormion attacked, put the Peloponnesians to rout and captured twelve triremes without losing one.

Other battles took the form of a combined operation, with disembarkment and participation in the action by infantry landed on the shore. This is what happened, for example, in the Battle of Aegospotami in 405, in which Lysander destroyed the Athenian fleet: by declining battle for several days in succession, the Spartan admiral had led his opponents into a false sense of security. Learning through one of his look-out ships that the Athenians, after their daily demonstration in the middle of the strait, had returned to the shore of the Chersonesus for their evening meal, Lysander at once put out to sea, surprised the enemy tri-remes while they were riding at anchor, with their crews on land, and captured or destroyed nearly all of them, thus giving Sparta her final victory in the long struggle that had begun twenty-six years before.

The law of war. Its merciless character. Development of moral scruples that mitigated its harshness. The idea of a just war. Military duty and longings for peace
With these naval and military forces, the cities waged war upon one another with-out respite and often without pity. For the Greeks always held that the rights of the victor over the person and the property of the vanquished were in principle subject to no restrictions. The victor could, without breaking the laws of war, massacre or enslave the population, take possession of the land or destroy the crops, appropriate chattels and furniture, burn the villages and towns, subject to one condition only, that he should respect sacred lands so as not to provoke the gods. This was the intention of the Achaeans when attacking Troy. In the fourth book of the *Iliad* we can hear Agamemnon describing to his men the fate awaiting their enemies: 'Let us make no doubt of it: the vultures will feed on their defenceless flesh, and we shall carry off their wives and little children in our ships, when we have conquered the city.' Later Ulysses, while on his way home, feels no scruples about plundering the country of the Cicones, on the coast of Thrace: he spares nobody except the priest of Apollo, out of respect for the god, but at the same time accepts splendid presents from him by way of ransom. The epic shows that every man lived under the shadow of an anxious desire to avert from his children and his city the fatal day, the 'pitiless day' of defeat and servi-tude. One of the seven Argive heroes who led the assault on Thebes had inscribed on his shield a device consisting of the words: 'I shall set the city on fire.'

This indefeasible right of the stronger was never called in question by the Classical Age, even if in practice it could apply some restraint to it. Socrates himself, in the *Memorabilia* (IV, 2, 15), bases one of his lines of reasoning on this evidence: 'If a general, having taken by storm an enemy city which has been guilty of some misdeed, reduces its population to slavery, shall we say that he is guilty of wrongdoing?—Certainly not!—Shall we not say that he is acting in conformity with justice?—Of course!' So the victor was entitled to dispose of the vanquished according to his whim, and any restriction that he imposed on him-self was regarded as a measure of clemency. The Athenians, in spite of the moderation and 'gentleness' on which they were prone to pride themselves, sometimes showed extreme severity: they expelled some inhabitants of Euboea from their country in 446, the Aeginetans and the inhabitants of Potidaea in 430, and the Delians in 422. They pronounced sentence of death in 427 against all the inhabitants of Mytilene, which had revolted, but on the following day went back on this cruel judgment so that the trireme *Paralos*, rowing at full speed, succeeded in bringing the counter-order in time to the strategus Paches, who had been instructed to carry out the execution. Later, in 422, Cleon, who had proposed the massacre of the Mytilenaeans, had the inhabitants of Torone in Chalcidice sold as slaves. In the following year Scione, another city in Chalcidice, suffered a still more cruel fate: the Athenians killed all the able-bodied men and reduced the women and children to slavery. Lastly in 416–415 they treated in the same merciless way the island of Melos in the Cyclades, which had refused to submit to them. Thracian mercenaries in the pay of Athens utterly destroyed the Boeotian city of Mycalessus in 415, massacring the whole population, including women and children, so that the very site was finally abandoned, as Plutarch remarks in the second century A.D. The Spartans behaved no less cruelly: they executed the men captured at Plataea in 427, and treated in the same way those of Hysiae, a small town in Argolis, in 417–416. We can easily understand that Athens, having capitulated to Lysander in 404, feared that she would suffer the same fate. That was in fact what certain allies of Sparta, Thebes and Corinth for example, demanded for their old enemy, now at last struck down. Xenophon tells us in the *Hellenica* how greatly his fellow-Athenians, remembering the cruelties they had themselves inflicted on their opponents, feared that they would find the law of retaliation applied to themselves. 'But,' he adds, 'the Lacedaemonians refused to reduce to slavery a Greek city which had rendered such services to Greece in the greatest dangers that she had incurred.'

It is therefore clear that moral considerations could on occasion intervene to mitigate the violent customs sanctioned by tradition. It is one of the glories of Hellenism that it could express, by the mouths of some of its thinkers, writers or statesmen, humanitarian scruples that gradually tended to make the laws of war less merciless. In the first place there were religious influences, especially that of Delphi: the text of an Amphictyonic oath quoted by the orator Aeschines in his speech *On the Embassy* contains an undertaking not to 'depopulate' by war any of the cities belonging to the Delphic Amphictyony. This oath seems, in fact, to have been respected all through the sixth century, the period in which the Delphic oracle enjoyed the highest moral prestige. The text of the 'oath of Plataea' is no doubt apocryphal in the form in which it had been handed down to us in a fourth-century inscription, but it mirrors the objects that preoccupied men's minds at the date when it was carved: it repeats the same undertaking, now applied, not to the Amphictyonic states, but to Athens, Sparta, and Plataea, and also to the cities that were members of the defensive alliance against Xerxes. In this case, the scruples of conscience that led to the formulation of the restriction in question were not so much religious as moral: they arose from a feeling of Hellenic brotherhood and community of race and language, to which writers and orators were ever ready to give expression and which, though they never succeeded in bringing an end to the oversensitive spirit of independence cherished by every city, did nevertheless sometimes impose a little restraint on its more violent manifestations. Plato re-echoes this concern when, in the *Menexenus* (242 d), he attributes the Athenian decision to spare the Spartiate hoplites captured at Sphacteria to respect for the bond of brotherhood between Greeks: 'They judged that in war against a sister nation it is enough to fight until victory is won and that the principle of Greek unity must not be endangered in order to gratify the individual resentment of one city.'

Violence in itself finally aroused disapproval and shame in some minds less inclined than others to conform to traditional forms of behaviour. This was true in the case of Euripides, who did not hesitate in his *Trojan Women*, produced in 415, to condemn the principle of a war of conquest, because of the undeserved miseries and suffering that it involves. He puts this condemnation in the mouth of a god, Poseidon, at the beginning of the play, whose whole theme is the unhappy lot of the captive women, Hecuba, Andromache, and Cassandra, immediately after the fall of Troy: 'Mad is the mortal who lays cities waste! He has made desolate the temples of the gods and tombs, the sacred domain of the dead: and soon he will perish in his turn!' Later the poet makes Cassandra say: 'All wise men should avoid war. Yet, if this calamity is suffered, it is a glorious honour to die bravely for one's native land.' Thus we find a new conception gradually developing of a just war, in which glory is not associated only with the exercise of military virtues, but also with the justice of the cause which they have to defend. Even if the possibility of the supreme sacrifice is envisaged, it must be made for the sake of a noble ideal. Hence the insistence, in epitaphs and funeral orations in honour of fallen warriors, not only on obedience to the laws of the fatherland (the Spartiates needed no other motive), but also on the fact that they died in defence of liberty. It was to ensure the freedom of their city that they were ready to die. This obsession is already apparent in certain funerary epigrams composed after the Persian Wars, such as the following one, attributed to Simonides, which expresses in very general terms an extremely widespread sentiment:

> The highest prowess is to die as a brave man:
> Fate gave this lot to us more than to any other.
> It was because we offered freedom to Greece
> That we sleep, clothed in undying glory.

This idealistic conception of military duty was very generally accepted in the Classical Age, at least in theory, whatever may have been the reality underlying it. In any case, little attempt was made to set up any other in opposition to it. The 'pacifism' of Aristophanes, as it is sometimes called by a too modern and certainly anachronistic term, by no means disputes the obligation to serve the interests of one's native city in arms: what the author of the *Acharnians*, the *Peace*, and *Lysistrata* advocates is simply a peaceful foreign policy, contrary to that of the demagogues Cleon, Hyperbolus, and Cleophon, who saw in the pursuit of war a means of gratifying the aspirations of their following by military pay and allowances, the funds derived from tribute paid by the allies, and the establishment of cleruchies outside Attica. While these advantages were appreciated by the urban lower class, the farmers in the country bore the brunt of hostilities: driven from their homes in the country, they watched from the walls of the city the plundering of their property, the destruction of their olive-trees and vines, and they fretted and fumed at being unable to raise a finger in their defence. That was why they longed for peace, being persuaded, on somewhat illusory grounds, that the enemy would agree to conclude peace on reasonable terms. Aristophanes made himself their spokesman because he loved and respected them and loathed the demagogues and their shameless manoeuvres to gain support. But if he shows us the honest countryman Dicaeopolis concluding a private truce with the Lacedaemonians and holds up to mockery the taxiarch Lamachus, his braggadocio, the gigantic plume on his helmet and the horrific Gorgon on his shield, he does not mean to advocate a policy of surrender or to ridicule genuine bravery. On the contrary, his perhaps short-sighted patriotism inspires him to write several eloquent hymns in praise of Attica, and no one sang better than he the glories (idealized, if the truth be told) of the *Marathonomachai*, the heroes of the Persian Wars, models of civic and military virtues. As a *laudator temporis acti*, Aristophanes had no originality in the matter of political principles, and his propaganda in favour of peace is fully understood when we envisage it as an argument directed to domestic policy. Did he perceive that war, by impoverishing the rural population in a lasting way, was undermining the very foundations of society and was fated to result in its utter transformation? It would be rash to say so: at least, even if the process of this deterioration escaped him, he clearly recognized its symptoms and did all he could to combat them.

Social consequences of war. Mercenary troops. Their historical importance
Now it was in fact this social crisis, of whose imminence Aristophanes felt a fore-boding and of which war was indeed the immediate cause, that was to bring in its train a consequence of great importance to Greek military traditions: the re-appearance of mercenaries, which began to take place in the final stages of the Peloponnesian War and was already perceptibly changing the methods and con-ditions of warfare in the fourth century, before entirely overturning them in the Hellenistic Age. The use of mercenaries, as has been recently pointed out, reveals a deep-seated lack of balance in society: in order that large numbers of men should consent to live a life of discomfort and risk their lives, no longer under the stress of civic duty, but merely to serve any master who pays them, it must be the case that the society to which they belong leaves them no other choice. The phenomenon is all the more remarkable because the mercenaries' rate of pay, far from being high, seems to have been normally lower in the fourth century than that of a skilled workman. Nevertheless the number of soldiers of fortune serving in the Greek armies of this period was considerable: in the early part of the cen-tury there were, according to recent calculations, at least 40,000, about half of whom were in Sicily, in the service of Dionysius I; in 366, at the time when Thebes was at the height of her power, when Athens was resuming an imperial-istic policy under the leadership of Timotheus and when Dionysius II, who had just succeeded his father, was sending forces to Greece to support Sparta, there were about 20,000 mercenaries serving in the various theatres of war; at the middle of the century, there were at least as many, a great number of whom were in the service of the Phocians, who, engaged in the Third Sacred War, made use

of the treasures of Delphi to enlist mercenaries and thus succeeded in holding their enemies at bay for ten years. So we have here a new phenomenon which made its presence felt fairly frequently in the organization of Greek armies during the fourth century.

Mercenaries had certainly been employed as early as the Archaic Age. A. Aymard has brought to light, in a penetrating analysis, the links between mercenary service, colonization, and tyranny: they were three different, but approximately concurrent, symptoms of the social crisis that was rife in the Greek world in the seventh and sixth centuries. At this period we already find Greek mercenaries in the armies of the Saitic Pharaohs, from Psammetichus I to Amasis and the latter's son, Psammetichus III, whom the devotion of his foreign soldiers could not save from defeat at the hands of Cambyses. Apart from the references to these mercenaries that occur in Herodotus, their presence is attested by the graffiti that some of them, in 591, carved on the legs of the gigantic stone statues at the entrance to the great temple at Abu Simbel in Nubia. Among the foreigners or *alloglossoi* who thus left a record of their presence, there were Semites, Carians, and Greeks from Ionia and Rhodes. Asian monarchs such as Nebuchadnezzar, the king of Babylon, and the dynasty of the Mermnadae, in Lydia, appealed on occasion to Greek warriors. Finally, the Greek tyrants themselves readily recruited their henchmen from among soldiers of fortune from other parts of the Greek world. The dynasty of the Battiadae, in Cyrene, the last three kings of which behaved like tyrants, provides good examples of this line of action: Arcesilas III, driven from Cyrene by a revolution in about 530, took refuge with Polycrates at Samos and there recruited a band of mercenaries with whose aid he reconquered his kingdom. His grandson, Arcesilas IV, entrusted his own brother-in-law Carrhotus, in 462, with the task of recruiting mercenaries on the occasion of his journey to Greece to take part in the chariot race at the Pythian Games as Arcesilas' representative.

Nevertheless, as far as we can judge by the records at our disposal, mercenary service does not seem to have developed in the Archaic Age to a point approaching that which it reached in the fourth century. No doubt colonization provided a sufficient outlet for the homeless and destitute. In the fifth century at least, apart from the case of Arcesilas IV, mentioned above, recruitment of mercenaries seems to have ceased. It was during the Peloponnesian War that it began again: thus Athens called in Thracian auxiliaries for the Sicilian expedition, and it

99. TEMPLE OF HERA AT OLYMPIA

This temple, among the pines that shade the Altis, is the oldest in the sanctuary (about 600 B.C.). Photograph taken from in front of the main façade. The two columns still standing, near the southeast corner, have archaic capitals with a low, spreading echinus. On the shaft of one of them there is a recess to house a small votive panel of painted wood. We can see the footing of the side walls of the building, with the front wall, containing a large doorway, which separated the entrance porch from the main body of the temple. At the rear, there is a wall without a door between the main part of the temple and the opisthodomus. In the distance are the columns of the Hellenistic palaestra.

100. RUINS OF THE TEMPLE OF ZEUS AT OLYMPIA

The temple, built between 468 and 456, of local limestone, is in a very ruined state. Here we see a part of the outer colonnade on the south side. On the right is the foundation of the wall; on the left, drums of columns in position on the stylobate.

101. TEMPLE OF APOLLO AT DELPHI

Except at the front, where some columns have been reassembled, practically all that remains is part of the sub-foundation of the building, i.e. of the temple as rebuilt in the fourth century, after the catastrophe of 375. The main part of the structure was in limestone from Parnassus. It is no longer possible to reconstruct in detail the lay-out of the interior, where consultation of the oracle took place. In the background is the rocky cliff of one of the Phaedriades, at the foot of which passes the road to Lebadea.

102. THE THOLOS AT DELPHI

This rotunda, built in marble in the first half of the fourth century, stood in the sanctuary of Athena Pronaia, some distance from the sanctuary of Apollo, on the road to Lebadea. It was a masterpiece of the architect Theodorus. It had an exterior Doric colonnade (partly set up again) of twenty columns, surrounding a circular hall. Inside, against the wall, there was a colonnade with Corinthian capitals standing on a continuous plinth which formed a bench (visible to the right in the photograph). The religious purpose of the building is not known.

103. THE TREASURY OF THE ATHENIANS AT DELPHI

Built in marble about 500 B.C., it is typical of the little Doric treasuries, with a porch of two columns between the antae, leading to a small windowless chamber. There is sculptured decoration on the metopes (Amazonomachy and exploits of Heracles and Theseus). The building has been entirely reconstructed with the ancient components replaced in their original positions.

102

103

104

105

108

109

110

111

104. THE SERPENTINE COLUMN FROM PLATAEA

After the victory in 479, the allied cities dedicated a joint offering at Delphi: a gold tripod on a bronze column formed with three interlaced serpents. This column was later removed to Constantinople, where it stands on the site of the ancient Byzantine hippodrome. The upper part is lost, but we can still read on the eleven lower coils the list of the thirty-one peoples who fought side by side against Mardonius's forces. Istanbul, Atmeidan.

105. THE OMPHALOS OF DELPHI

There was in the sanctuary (most probably beside the statue of Apollo; see ill. 93) a cone-shaped sacred stone, covered with a network whose meshes were made of woollen yarn. It was called the omphalos ('navel'), because it was supposed to mark the centre of the world. Several replicas of it were in existence, such as the present one, found to the east of the temple. Delphi Museum.

106. ELEUSIS: ENTRANCE TO THE SANCTUARY

The esplanade paved with stone flags in the foreground and the Great Propylaea, whose ruins can be seen on their supporting platform with six steps, date from the Roman Age. To the left of the Propylaea was the well of Callichoros, beside which Demeter rested, as the story told, when she was wandering all over the world in search of her daughter Kore, carried off by Hades. The ascending path in the background, to the left, leads to the Telesterion, situated behind the rocky spur on which a chapel of the Blessed Virgin now stands.

107. ATHENS: CEMETERY OF THE CERAMICUS

In this district just outside the city walls, near the Dipylon Gate, excavations have revealed many graves, some marked by high funeral stelae, sometimes sheltered in a little edifice like a lean-to (right background), others by a simple cylindrical cippus. The cypresses, planted in recent times, hide the modern houses of this popular district of Athens.

108 & 109. CHARON AND HERMES PSYCHOPOMPOS

On an Attic white ground funerary lecythus of the fifth century, the painter has portrayed Hermes the Guide of Souls. He has a broad-brimmed hat (petasus) and a chlamys (worn by travellers), and he is holding the caduceus in his right hand. Close to him Charon, the ferryman of the Underworld, handles the pole by means of which he is driving his boat to the bank. He is wearing a workman's tunic, leaving one shoulder bare, and a fur cap. The artist has put an element of caricature into his profile, which is very different from the classical beauty of the god. National Museum, Athens.

110. THE FUNERAL OFFERING

Attic white-ground lecythus of the fifth century. These vases are very commonly decorated with funerary scenes, since they were intended to be laid on tombs. The young woman represented here is in fact holding one of these lecythi, which she is about to place on a tomb, seen on the right, surmounted by a stele with a high palmette. In her left hand she has a large basket containing offerings. National Museum, Athens.

111. LAMENTATION FOR THE DEAD

Attic red-figure vase of the fourth century. Around the bed on which the dead man is lying in state, his head encircled with a garland, two women are lamenting, with their hands raised in token of mourning. Von Schoen Collection, Lugano.

112. FUNERAL STELE OF THEANO

A good specimen of Attic funerary relief (end of the fifth century). The dead young woman, whose name is given in the inscription at the top, is seated on a backless chair, with her feet resting on a footstool. Her husband Ctesileos, leaning on a long staff placed under his left armpit, gazes with an intense expression at the wife whom he has lost. The scene proclaims without any grandiloquence that the bonds of affection which united the living are not broken by death. Note the architectural décor which, with its pediment furnished with acroteria and its two pillars serving as antae, makes the stele resemble the front of a little temple. National Museum, Athens.

was a contingent of these mercenaries, which arrived too late, after the fleet had already left for Syracuse, that Diitrephes was instructed to lead back to Thrace and that ravaged the Boeotian town of Mycalessus on its way home. As hostilities dragged out, an ever-increasing number of professional soldiers hired themselves out for service in the various Greek countries: this is why such a large number of them were unemployed after the end of the war and could thus put themselves at the disposal of Cyrus the Younger when he attempted to overthrow his brother Artaxerxes. The Retreat of the Ten Thousand in 401–399, after the Battle of Cunaxa, illustrates both the great number and the military valour of these mercenaries.

From this time onwards, whatever the causes may have been, the part played by professional soldiers in Greek armies continued to increase at the expense of citizen soldiers. Their technical abilities increased as a result of the training imposed on them by gifted generals such as the Athenians Conon, Iphicrates, and Timotheus, the Spartan Agesilaus, and even less important officers, mere leaders of mercenary companies, of whom Menelaus the Pelagonian was a characteristic specimen: he was a Macedonian who entered the service of Athens in 363 and received various honours, including the freedom of the city. The modifications of military tactics, as described above, are largely due to the employment of mercenaries: this applies to Iphicrates' peltasts, and we shall not be surprised to observe that the Macedonian Menelaus served as a hipparch in command of his cavalry squadrons, thus exemplifying the increasing importance of cavalry in the armies of the fourth century.

Did these professional soldiers show themselves more merciless to the civil population than the traditional forces of earlier days? To tell the truth, both these classes of soldiers practised plundering, which was regarded as the victor's privilege. But it is a fact that contemporaries viewed with great alarm the increase of these bands of mercenaries, composed of 'stateless persons, deserters, and individuals guilty of every kind of crime'; they were held guilty of 'exactions, acts of violence and contempt of law'; in the end they were regarded as 'the common enemies of all humankind'. Such at least are the terms employed by Isocrates in 356 in his speech *On the Peace* (44–46). All allowance being made for rhetorical exaggeration, the tone of the speech reveals a sentiment that was becoming widespread. In the same speech, the Athenian orator rebukes his fellow-citizens for depending on these foreigners to defend the interests of the city in warfare. The same reproach is several times expressed by Demosthenes. These texts give us a good idea of the direction in which the military habits of the Greek world were developing. War had until then been the public concern of each city, and at the same time, at least in principle, the concern of each citizen as an individual. But from now on a certain degree of specialization became established in this field, as in all others: even if such institutions as ephebia were designed to make military service more effective and better organized, it was no longer in fact regarded as the first duty of a citizen, a duty carried out with conviction, even if without enthusiasm. The citizen was quite ready to shift his responsibility to a class of specialists enlisted abroad for pay. The development of individualism, the relaxation of the ties binding the individual to the city, the desire to avoid the risks and obligations imposed by membership in the citizen body, all this is in keeping with the creation of an international market of mercenaries following upon a social and economic crisis. Supply and demand increased simultaneously. There was also the factor of increasing complications in military techniques—in armament, tactics, and the use of engines—which emphasized the superiority of a professional force over a citizen army. The Age of Alexander might for a time conceal the reality of this development because of the outstanding part played in this period by the national army of Macedonia. But when this leader of genius was no longer on the scene, it soon became evident to what degree the development of mercenary forces favoured the designs of ambitious generals: henceforth, in the Hellenic world, war was no longer the business of cities but of princes.

CHAPTER VI

RITES AND GODS

The sources for our knowledge of Greek religion: literary texts and mythological tradition. Pausanias. Archaeological objects and inscriptions

FOR most of our contemporaries, Greek religion is mainly a collection of legends which our poets and artists have often drawn upon, since the Renaissance, in imitation of their Greek and Latin predecessors. These mythological memories are associated with the visible image of some impressive sites: Delphi, the Acropolis at Athens, or Cape Sunium, where beautiful or pathetic ruins still stand in the midst of an abandoned sanctuary. Since Leconte de Lisle and the 'Parnassians', the genuine names of the Greek gods, more or less correctly transcribed, have been substituted for those of the corresponding Latin gods, with whom they had long been confused. But even if we now speak of Zeus, not Jupiter, of Aphrodite in place of Venus, and of Hermes in place of Mercury, we generally continue to regard them as a reader of Ovid's *Metamorphoses* would do, rather than with the eyes of an Athenian of the fifth century. This way of thinking is due to a long tradition in our schools whose influence it is not easy to shake off. But it scarcely corresponds at all to the realities of Greek religious sentiment in the Classical Age: that is of course the truth that we desire to reach. Is it still accessible to us, and what is the way to reach it?

Literary texts are still our richest source of information, and also the one least likely to mislead us. In fact the imagination of the Greeks always liked to play upon the legends of the gods, entirely free from scrupulous regard for tradition.

The Greeks knew no such thing as immutable dogma in the sphere of mythology: the great number of cult sites, the wide dispersion of the population, and the particularism of Greek cities easily led to the multiplying of legends and to extreme diversity in their forms. Aware of these variations, which in no way shocked their feelings about divinity, the poets were by no means disinclined to add to them as occasion offered. Such a deeply religious mind as Pindar's did not hesitate to depart from a well-established tradition: in his first *Olympian Ode* he criticizes sharply the tale according to which Tantalus killed his son Pelops and had his flesh served up to the gods at a banquet: 'It is man's duty to ascribe only honourable actions to the gods. . . . For me it is impossible to call one of the Blessed a cannibal: I refuse to do it!' Thus, on several occasions, he changes a legend to make it more in keeping with his moral requirements. The tragic dramatists acted similarly: they had little compunction in adjusting tradition as their fancy inclined them, and so the subject-matter of the old myths, as treated by them, showed astonishing variability. Later, in the Hellenistic Age, scholars, mythographers, scholiasts, and compilers in their turn devoted themselves with extreme liberty to elaboration of a mythology that was already overabundant and full of accepted incoherencies. These alterations and these attempts to enrich the hoard of Greek legend in the Hellenistic Age were inspired by different motives: the aim was to introduce some degree of coherence between contradictory traditions, in order to satisfy the rationalistic demands aroused in men's minds by the philosophers, or else, by means of picturesque inventions, to give some spice to accounts that had been too long served up in identical form to gratify the public's now jaded appetite. It was from these late authors rather than from Homer or the tragic dramatists that Latin writers drew the information which they have handed down to us. From this we can see what difficulties the information they give us creates for the historian of religion. What they have handed down is not so much the common sentiment of the Classical Greeks as the product of a learned elaboration, in the midst of which it is a very delicate, and often impossible, task, to sift out genuine evidence drawn from a good source from what is pure fancy.

There is, beyond a doubt, in the very richness and malleability of the mythological tradition an original quality that reveals the underlying nature of Greek religion. But it must be used with infinite caution. The only texts which can be employed without great critical reservations are those which with obvious honesty and objectivity inform us of traditions associated with rites. For it is the realities of worship, rather than legends, that make us really familiar with the Greeks of former days and give us an immediate understanding of their religious behaviour. Their actual practice is the only valid field of reference in this domain, whether it is revealed to us by an author, an inscription, or an archaeological object. For here we are in contact with social realities, with beliefs revealed by actions, not mere intellectual speculations. So the study of Greek religion is a matter of listing, describing, and, if possible, interpreting the practices of religious worship, which are always local, rather than of uniting in a dubious synthesis pieces of mythological evidence that are often artificial and rarely consistent. Legend is never a useful document unless it is linked with some cult reality which it illustrates or explains. Where such positive confirmation does not exist, legend is really little more than a literary exercise which informs us more about its author than about anything else.

Our knowledge of the details of religious practice is derived from varied sources of information, whose interpretation calls for very different methods. First of all there is the evidence of literary texts, which sometimes make passing mention of rites and at other times describe them with a wealth of detail which is of the greatest value to us. Thus the Homeric poems contain several scenes of prayer and sacrifice, the Attic tragedies describe certain funeral rites, Aristophanes gives a lively and precise representation of the celebration of the rustic Dionysia. Next we have the indications given by historians and writers on general subjects: Herodotus in the fifth century B.C. and Plutarch early in the second century A.D. are full of information about the religious life of the Greeks, in which they were both very keenly interested. Finally there are the compilers of later periods, whose work has been handed down in a fragmentary form through the Byzantine lexicographers of the Middle Ages, such as the anonymous author of the compilation entitled *The Souda*, who in consequence of an old error is often called *Suidas*. These citations and brief notes, though often altered in the course of manuscript transcription, nevertheless enrich our knowledge of ancient Greek religion to a considerable degree.

But our irreplaceable treasure is Pausanias. This rhetor of the second century A.D., who composed a description or *Periegesis* of Greece (Attica, Peloponnesus, Boeotia, and Phocis), had the most lively curiosity about facts and traditions of religion. As his journey through each region brought him to the smallest villages, he made a point of noting down in an admirably conscientious way the legends he was told and the cult practices he observed in each place. But for his evidence, varied and abundant as it is, and also reliable, we should on many points have only a sketchy and partial knowledge of Greek religion. He had great respect for the prohibitions applied to certain aspects of the cults, knowledge of which was confined to initiates, so he takes care not to reveal these secret practices, but informs us that they existed, which normally we might not have suspected. As for the public rites, these he is glad to describe, sometimes with great wealth of detail, especially if strange or surprising customs are involved; in connection with them he reports the explanation that he has been given on the spot or that he has picked up in the course of reading. Let us add that the great topographical precision of his itineraries has made it possible to identify on the site a number of sacred monuments of which traces still survive: but for him we should have great difficulty in putting a name upon most of the buildings or offerings in the great sanctuaries at Delphi and Olympia. But for his descriptions, which are certainly quite devoid of picturesqueness and any sense of atmosphere, but generally exact and sometimes detailed, we should have no idea of what the interior of the great temples looked like. It can be seen how immense a debt historians of Greek religion owe to Pausanias.

Side by side with literary texts, archaeological and epigraphical records also constitute a very rich and varied source of information. Inscriptions concerning religious institutions are extremely numerous: sacred laws, dedications, inventories of offerings and sacred treasures, accounts of miraculous cures, oracles, decrees concerning religious festivals, sacred calendars, funerary epigrams—all such texts carved on stone or metal, which have been collected either in excavations or by the chance of accidental discovery, disclose aspects of Greek religion about which writers, apart from Pausanias, are usually silent or at least far from informative. Their interest for us is increased by the fact that they are 'uncooked' records, composed in order to satisfy immediate practical considerations and as a rule never subjected to any interpretative elaboration or to the alterations inseparable from manuscript tradition. That is what makes their evidence so outstandingly valuable.

As for the specifically archaeological evidence for the history of religion, it falls into two categories: architectural monuments and those decorated with figures. Ruins, more or less intelligible according to their present state of preservation or destruction, increase our knowledge of the lay-out of sanctuaries and the arrangement of sacred buildings: temples, treasures, altars, special buildings designed for the ceremonies of the mysteries, porticos and miraculous springs. In some more fortunate instances, it is possible (more or less hypothetically) to reconstruct the elevation. Partial reconstructions, which are today sometimes referred to by the slightly pedantic newfangled term *anastyloses*, give the scale of the sites and help us to reconstruct in our imagination the religious scenes that they once witnessed. Monuments decorated with figures contribute further precision to such a picture: statues which have been discovered, whether genuine offerings or late copies of famous works, restore for us the divine image; votive or funerary reliefs show us the faithful in the presence of the god, or else around the departed one whom death has ushered into the world of everlasting peace, the forms of those he has left behind; the sculptured decorations of religious buildings, pediments, metopes, continuous Ionic friezes, cymas and architraves decorated with scenes containing human figures, unfold before our gaze representations that were not chosen at random but always included at least a partial element of instruction for the spectator; paintings on vases, in their infinite variety, offer some ritual scenes of lively interest, but also countless mythological representations which enormously enrich the indications we receive from texts. A good number of these records still present specialists with enigmas not yet resolved. Nevertheless the study of them is making gradual progress and the representations thus receive the necessary commentary, while the information derived from texts is endowed with new life by collation with evidence drawn from archaeological sources. The method which consists of thus comparing the two kinds of evidence, so that each may shed light upon the other, this synthetical method which demands of the scholar multifarious skills and very extensive knowledge, certainly proves fertile in results in every field of the study of antiquity, but nowhere is it more indispensable than in the history of religion: the admirable *Handbook* by the Swedish scholar M. P. Nilsson is a brilliant illustration of this. Any general exposition of Greek religion must take these various elements into consideration and use the information derived from them in combination.

Religion and the social group. Elementary religious sentiment. Familiarity with the sacred. Anthropomorphism. Rôle of the poets and artists
In the light of these forms of evidence, we see Classical Greek religion as some-

o

thing closely bound up with the social group. This is obviously to some degree due to the character of the records from which our information is derived, texts giving regulations for corporate ceremonies, public buildings erected in honour of the city's gods, works of art illustrating beliefs held in common. But it is also a fundamental characteristic of the Classical Greek man. He did not regard himself as an individual in isolation, whose personal welfare could be ensured independently of the social groups to which he belonged: he was an outstandingly social being, or, in Aristotle's phrase, a 'political animal', who set great value on his relations with others and felt that he could really achieve his own destiny only through this communication with others. We have already noted this when analysing the phenomenon of war. We shall see it again when we study the organization of the city. Now religion is the essential psychological element that ensures the cohesion of groups and their continued existence. That is why its manifestations, even when individual, usually assume a more or less strongly marked social character: even if they are directed towards divine beings, they also take for granted a public that witnesses them and to which the thoughts of the celebrant turn while he is performing his act of piety.

This does not mean that elementary religious sentiment, in its individual and spontaneous form, was unknown to the Greeks. On the contrary, they had a word, perhaps borrowed from the vocabulary of a pre-Hellenic language, to express the mixture of respect and awe that man feels in the presence of whatever seems to him in some way dependent upon a mysterious and supernatural force, animated by a will of which man has a kind of presentiment though he cannot always fathom its purposes. This feeling was called *thambos*: the Greeks seem to have experienced it with extreme force and frequency, especially in the face of nature and the inspiring spectacles she reveals to man in a country so favoured by nature as Greece. It was a kind of immediate sense of a divine presence suddenly inspired by an imposing landscape or some secret spot, a light or a shadow, a sound or a silence, the flight of a bird, the sight of a passing beast, the majesty of a beautiful tree, the shape of a rock, the coolness of a spring, the strong flow of a river, the rustling of reeds, the caress of the wind, a clap of thunder, a moonbeam, the noonday heat, the ceaseless murmur of waves. The attentive and responsive spirit of the Greeks eagerly welcomed these impressions of nature, which filled them with a kind of uneasy delight mingled with ecstasy, which seemed to them obviously the work of a god. This omnipresence of divinity, felt with singular intensity, provided the principal and permanent element in Greek religion. The fact that the gods are everywhere to be found is the reason why they are so numerous: the origin of polytheism lay in the very lively sentiment that all nature is permeated by the divine. This deeply religious people was at the same time extremely devoted to logical reasoning (these things are by no means mutually exclusive); their taste for social life and for discussion fostered this inclination. So they were naturally impelled to divide a divine presence so frequent and so polymorphous into manifold individualities, conceived in human terms. Hence the great number of cult sites, rustic altars, heaps of stones, sacred trees, caves of Pan, offerings to the nymphs, nameless heroes, and also the vast number of sanctuaries in which the major divinities were honoured in a specifically local form, indicated by a particular epithet.

If and when he felt *thambos*, the Greek drew the conclusion that he was in contact with some divine personality. He would at once make the community of which he was a member acquainted with the divinity thus revealed, or, which more often happened, he would identify the deity whose power he had just experienced with one of those already held in reverence by the community. Thus the traditional cults maintained their vigour and influence; sometimes some new cult would be added to them. The intervention of the social group, transforming an individual's reaction into a rite, gave a concrete and lasting value to what in its beginning had been only a transitory sentiment. Inversely, participation in an identical belief and the conviction of being subjected to the authority of an identical god endowed the group with permanence and homogeneousness. So Greek religion, like most others, had both a subjective and a social aspect. One would have been nothing without the other. If the social element was the dominant one, this was due to the Greek's instinctive tendency to live his life in the communal setting. The personal value of his faith was not weakened thereby, but rather strengthened.

This somewhat abstract analysis has seemed necessary to make it understood that Greek religion, even if its essential manifestations were ritual acts, that is to say the rites of a cult that was normally collective, was no more confined to these ceremonies than to the brilliant display of mythological legends. It would not have aroused the fervour of crowds and individuals for centuries if it had not spoken abundantly to the soul. Over and above the city's homage to its gods and the mere exchange of services between the faithful and the deity, in which the offering was made to win divine favour, there was daily familiarity between the Hellene and the sacred powers. As far as we can define this familiarity by means of the documents that reveal it, it had little of the nature of a mystical outpouring of the soul: it was, rather, a realization that the gods exist, that they are close to us in their feelings as well as in their forms, and that, for all their power, they are interested in the fate of mortals. Thus the relations between the Greeks and their divinities readily assumed a personal tone. The god, like his worshipper, was an individual: his protection was prayed for with trust and love, not only with respect and awe. The bonds established between the god and his devotee sometimes contain an element of complicity. Such indeed is the attitude of Athena to Diomedes in the *Iliad* and to Ulysses in the *Odyssey*. The help she gives them is given with a touch of affection and her counsels are humanized with a smile. Whatever may have been said in the past, divine grandeur lost nothing by such direct dealings with mankind: the mortal who felt himself the object of such favour could not commit sin without exposing himself to the direst penalties. He knew that the gods were of another race and were more powerful than mankind. But he was not surprised to meet them close at hand.

This should be seen as the proper background to the legends recording the amours between gods and mortals, which so shocked the Christian Fathers. In the Classical Age the rites of 'hierogamy', or sacred marriage, were still performed with fervent zeal, and popular belief credited them with real validity: the famous athlete Theogenes of Thasos, early in the fifth century, was supposed to have been conceived during a ceremony of this kind, in which his father, the priest of Thasian Heracles, performed the god's function with his own wife, and the very name of the offspring (*Theogenes* means 'born from a god') recalled his sacred origin. At Athens a similar rite took place each year, in which the 'queen', who was the wife of the king archon, a magistrate who enjoyed universal respect, was united to Dionysus, who was probably represented on this occasion by her husband. Similarly the legends that represent humans as admitted to the table of the gods were ritually kept up in the sacred banquets (*theoxenia*), known to have formed part of religious cults, particularly that of the Dioscuri. So the sincerely religious Virgil was not false to the Greek tradition when he wrote at the end of the fourth *Eclogue*: *Qui non risere parenti, nec deus hunc mensua, dea nec dignata cubili est.* 'Those who have not in infancy smiled at their mother, no god receives them at his table, no goddess welcomes them to her bed.'

It was in this way that anthropomorphism, a basic feature of Greek religion, took shape. It sprang from the combination of three characteristics that distinguished the soul of this people: a sense of the divine, practical rationalism, and creative imagination. In order to represent to themselves in a concrete manner the divinity of whose existence they had a direct perception, the Greeks conceived it in terms that could be easily assimilated by the community in which they lived, that is to say in human form, while attributing to it a higher level in the social hierarchy. Their capacity to translate ideas into material or verbal images and their natural gift for art and poetry aided them powerfully to fix this conception in such a way that it would last and could be handed on to others, and also to systematize and enrich it. They were themselves aware of this fruitful effort. Herodotus has strongly, indeed excessively, emphasized the importance of Homer and Hesiod in the field of religion: 'It is to them that we owe the poetical account of the theogony [genealogy of the gods]; they gave the gods their ritual names; they defined the details of their various cults and their respective functions; they made known their forms.' Being better informed today, especially by means of the Myccnacan records, we know that Hellenic polytheism was already fully alive some centuries before Homer. But it is true that the Homeric poems and those of Hesiod served as a 'catechism' for a whole people, which, accustomed to read them from childhood, drew from them its basic ideas about religion. In these works men found, not only a lively portrayal of the immortals, but also moral principles, sanctioned by the authority of Zeus, the supreme god, and the ritual precepts whose detailed enumeration has so large a place in *The Works and Days*.

Important as the elaboration contributed by these two poets was for Greek religion, the part played by artists, especially sculptors, was no less decisive. From their labours religion derived the advantage of becoming even more humanized than in works of literature. Poetic creation indeed preserves relative mobility and leaves some scope for the reader's imagination. Plastic creation, on the contrary, being solid and immutable, is filled with concrete presence in three dimensions. The idea of divinity very soon became closely associated with the cult statue. Here it found the solid support which it needed. No religion has depended more strictly on the image, to which the Greeks, in their normal if not unvarying linguistic usage, gave a special name, *agalma*. By this word they meant a sacred image, in opposition to one representing a mortal, which was an *eikon*.

It was only as the result of a very late change of meaning that the word 'icon' came to mean, in Byzantine Greek, a sacred image in contrast to the meaning usually given to the word in Classical Greek. The agalma was at one and the same time a representation of the god and a token of his presence: the statue *was* the god, though he was not entirely identified with it. No doubt the divine nature was not wholly confined to the image: the worshipper would have no difficulty in acknowledging that there were many images of one god. But he believed that all of them contained their part of the divine essence, which thus manifested itself fully in each of them.

However, these images had to be easily identifiable. We have seen from the Cypriot bronze of Apollo *Alasiotas* (if the suggested identification is correct) that the Mycenaean artists were well able to express effectively the idea of an anthropomorphic god. Their successors in the early Archaic Age were at first less skilful: the stiff sacred effigies from Drerus in Crete, made of wood coated with bronze plaques hammered and fixed with nails, and the lean-flanked Apollo, cast solid, which was dedicated by the Boeotian Manticlus furnish good examples of their degree of accomplishment. The subsequent development which led Greek art along the path of naturalism until the zenith of Classical culture was reached only strengthened the anthropomorphic tendency in religion. It soon helped it to get rid of the vestiges of primitive *aniconism*, which saw gods in objects lacking human shape, such as uncut stones, pieces of wood, or even trees, and also of the after-effects of *theriomorphism*, which worshipped beast-gods or monsters. Certainly some traces of these ancestral aberrations, which the Greek people, like all others, experienced, were always to remain: piety is naturally conservative, and in the second century of the Christian era Pausanias can still report many instances of the worship of sacred stones, while he draws our attention to a horse-headed Demeter in Arcadia. Along with the statues of gods by the great masters of Classical art, rudimentary images of wood or stone, a legacy from the Archaic Age, were piously preserved in the sanctuaries; they were known as *xoana* and they continued to be objects of very lively devotion: for example, on the Acropolis at Athens, the most greatly venerated image of Athena was not Phidias's colossal gold and ivory statue in the Parthenon, but the old olive-wood *xoanon* preserved in the Erechtheum, which was believed to have fallen from heaven and to which the citizens came every four years with the solemn offering of the *peplos* on the occasion of the great Panathenaïc Festival. We should not then ignore these survivals, which were tenacious of life, yet we must note that they are of small importance compared with the pantheon of humanized gods whom the exacting intelligence of the Hellenes, served by the brilliant accomplishments of the artists, could arrange in a hierarchical community, active, accessible, and sympathetic to moral and civic anxieties and to a certain form of spirituality.

Ritual purity. Prayer. Offerings

These gods, who for the most part already had in the Mycenaean Age the names they were thereafter to bear, received from the Greeks a form of worship in conformity with traditional customs that we find already well established in the Homeric poems. The regulations are extremely complicated in detail: they vary according to the places and the deities in question. We can at least distinguish between the principal acts of worship which, amid all the diversity imposed on them by circumstances, share certain well-defined features: these are prayer, offering, sacrifice, public festivals and games. We shall study them successively.

We should however begin by defining the idea of ritual purity, which appears in all these operations as an indispensable preliminary condition. This idea is linked with that of the sacred and the profane. If certain places or certain acts are held to be sacred, it is understandable that, to approach the former or to perform the latter, one must submit to certain demands which evince the respect one feels for them: such demands as cleanliness and decency in dress and behaviour. Anyone who neglects these rules is impure: he has failed to remove the pollution that makes him unfit to approach the gods. In principle it is a question of physical pollution: the idea of moral impurity, in so far as it plays a part, can only have appeared subsequently. So, before every act of piety, precautions must be taken for cleanliness. When Achilles, in Book XVI of the *Iliad*, addresses a prayer to Zeus, he chooses a cup of great price, purifies it with sulphur, washes it in water from the river, then washes his own hands before making a libation and uttering his prayer. It is the same when Telemachus, in Book II of the *Odyssey*, utters a prayer to Athena: as he was then on the sea-shore, he washed his hands in sea-water before praying. When, in Book III of the *Iliad*, the Achaean leaders are about to swear oaths accompanied with prayer and sacrifice, the heralds who attend them first pour water on their hands. What Homer shows us in practice, Hesiod states as a precept in *The Works and Days*: 'You must never offer libations of dark wine at dawn to Zeus and the other gods without

113. THE TEMPLE OF HEPHAESTUS AND THE WESTERN EDGE OF THE AGORA
    AT ATHENS

This model offers a restoration of this district as seen by Pausanias in the second
century A.D. Beginning at the south end, we see in the foreground, behind a wall interrupted by a propylaeum, the rotunda or tholos of the prytanes. Further on is the temple
of the Mother of the Gods and its annexes, and in front of it a long portico. More to the
left there is a taller building, with an entrance porch facing southwards, viz., the
Bouleuterion, used for the meetings of the Council (*Boule*). Further north, standing
slightly back, is the façade of the little temple of Apollo Patroos. At the north end is the
Royal Portico, or Portico of Zeus, with its two wings projecting forwards. The purpose
of the large Hellenistic building raised on the slope to the left of the Royal Portico is
not known. Higher up, the temple of Hephaestus occupies the top of the hill of Colonos
Agoraios and dominates the whole Agora: this is the temple still standing, traditionally
known as the Theseum. Agora Museum, Athens.

114. THE ATHENIAN ACROPOLIS

A model constructed by the American archaeologist G. P. Stevens. It shows the monuments on the sacred plateau in the first century A.D. To the right of the ascent leading
to the Propylaea is the bastion and the little temple of Athena Nike. The central
structure of the Propylaea is flanked on the left by the Pinakotheke and on the right
by the portico leading to the bastion. Further behind is the enclosure of Artemis
Brauronia and its portico with projecting wings, then the Chalkotheke with a portico
along its front, in an enclosure furnished with a small propylaeum. More to the left, in
front of a wall, is Phidias's colossal bronze Athena Promachos. Still more to the left,
behind a building for the maintenance service, is the Erechtheum with its tall north
porch, its east front facing the enclosure of Pandrosos, and, behind the sacred laurel,
the gallery of the Caryatids. Beyond this we can see the enclosure of Zeus Polieus,
which contained nothing but an altar. Between this enclosure and the Parthenon there
is the little rotunda of Rome and Augustus. The harmonious mass of the Parthenon
dominates everything else. Agora Museum, Athens.

115. ATHENS AND THE ACROPOLIS, SEEN FROM THE MUSEUM (HILL OF THE
    MUSES)

Beginning at the left, we can make out the buildings of the Propylaea (with the entrance
porch of the Pinakotheke) enframing the temple of Athena Nike on its bastion, the
Erechtheum (we see the western side of the north porch and the gallery of the Caryatids)
and the Parthenon (western front and south side). The wall built by Cimon to support
the embankment on the south side of the plateau is now largely concealed by mediaeval
and modern alterations. Below the Propylaea stands the tall Roman façade of the Odeum
of Herodes Atticus (second century A.D.) extended towards the right by the long
Portico of Eumenes II (second century B.C.). On the horizon, the outline of Mount

117

118

Pentelicus, in the form of a flattened triangle, stands up against the sky like a pediment, behind the Parthenon. Nearer, to the right, is the high, sharp-pointed hill of Lycabettus.

116. THE THEATRE AT EPIDAURUS (AIR PHOTOGRAPH)
The huge shell-shaped structure rests on the hillside. Behind the temporary stage set up for a modern production, we can see a part of the orchestra. Even the large crowds of modern spectators only occupy a small part of the theatre, which could accommodate about 14,000 people on its fifty-six superimposed rows of seats.

117. PORTICO IN THE SANCTUARY OF BRAURON
A view from within of the northwest corner of the Doric colonnade (restored) in the portico with projecting wings (fifth century) which marked the limits of a rectangular courtyard open on the south side. On two sides, the back of the portico consisted of rooms opening on the colonnade. In the foreground we can see the doorway and threshold of one of these rooms. The building was of local limestone, except for the capitals, which were of marble.

118. THE DIOLCOS ON THE ISTHMUS OF CORINTH
Recent excavations have uncovered for several hundreds of metres the track (*diolcos*) by means of which ships were carried across the isthmus from one sea to the other. There was a causeway, paved with flags of limestone, about four metres wide, in which were cut two parallel grooves 1·5 metres (about 5 feet) apart. In these 'rails' rolled or glided the waggons or frames on which the vessels were pulled across. The work appears to date from the sixth century.

119. THE AGORA OF CORINTH (AIR PHOTOGRAPH)
The photograph has been taken facing south. On the left is the road leading to the harbour of Lechaeum (to the north, on the Gulf of Corinth). To the right of this road, there is rising ground, overlooking the Agora, on which stands the temple of Apollo, built about 540 B.C.; several columns are still standing (west front and southwest corner). The Agora is a large rectangle, fringed with porticos and buildings of the Roman period: it was here that St Paul preached. To the left of the spot where the road from Lechaeum is about to enter the Agora is the spring called Pirene, with artificial channels, caverns, etc., hollowed out in the rock. On the right of the photograph, in front of the modern buildings of the museum, we see the remains of another fountain, called Glauke.

120. THE STONE-QUARRIES (LATOMIAE) OF SYRACUSE
The workman in the picture gives the scale of these imposing works. It was in these man-made caverns that the Athenian prisoners were penned in 413.

having washed your hands: for then they do not listen, but reject your prayers with disgust.' The custom of these ritual ablutions was maintained throughout the Classical Age: that is why a basin of lustral water was always placed at the gate of a sanctuary for the use of visitors. Pausanias mentions, as standing near the entrance to the Acropolis at Athens, a bronze statue by Lycius, a son of Myron, representing a boy carrying a 'holy-water basin' for this purpose (*perirrhanterion*): it dated from the second half of the fifth century.

One of the most serious pollutions was that due to the shedding of blood: Hector, who had momentarily withdrawn from the battle, replied to his mother Hecuba, who summoned him to make a libation to Zeus, that he could neither make a libation nor utter a prayer because he was bespattered with blood (*Iliad* VI, 264–268). Similarly Ulysses, after the slaying of the suitors, hastens to purify his palace by having sulphur burned in it (*Odyssey* XXII, 493–494). Closely connected with this ancient prejudice are the instructions concerning purification of a murderer as known to us from various texts. It was not a question of cleansing him of a sin, since the perpetrator of unintentional homicide was subject to the same ritual requirements as a murderer: it was the fact of having shed blood that caused the pollution, even if the action was justified or excusable. This pollution had to be washed away to prevent it from spreading through contact with the one affected by it. So the killer was banished from his city until he had been purified. Vase paintings show the purification of Orestes, the murderer of his mother, by sprinkling with the blood of a young pig. This widespread rite shocked the philosopher Heraclitus, who remarked: 'It is vain to purify men polluted by murder with blood: does a man who has trod in mud wash himself with mud?' The sacred laws of Cyrene, the text of which is preserved in a fourth-century inscription, give a detailed account of the proper treatment of a suppliant who, guilty of murder, seeks to be admitted to the city: they contain the strictest precautions to avoid any contact between the citizens and the stranger as long as he remains unpurified.

Death was, like blood, a cause of impurity. Pausanias tells us that at Messene, in the Peloponnese, it was an established rule that a priest or priestess, one of whose children happened to die, had to resign his or her priestly duties: such a close family bereavement involved a contamination which rendered the bereaved unfit for the service of the gods. It was normally forbidden to bury the dead within sacred precincts (except, of course, in the case of 'heroes'). In 426–425

the Athenians, who were in control of Apollo's sanctuary at Delos, received instructions from an oracle to purify the whole island: a century earlier Pisistratus
had already had the whole area visible from the sanctuary purified. In order to
conform to the god's command, they destroyed all the tombs that still existed at
Delos and removed to the neighbouring island of Rhenea the funerary material
(mainly earthenware vases) which had been gathered from these tombs. It has
been discovered by modern excavators in a common grave-pit. From then onwards, no one was allowed to die in the holy island: those at death's door were
carried across to Rhenea to breathe their last.

The same rule was applied to women in travail: they had to go to Rhenea to be
confined. For confinement, no doubt because of the blood, also involved impurity.
The laws of Cyrene state that the presence of a woman in childbed made the
whole household impure, including any person under the same roof. Another
paragraph deals with cases of miscarriage: if the foetus has a human shape, the
impurity is like that occasioned by death; if not, the miscarriage is on the same
footing as a normal delivery. Even sexual relations could in certain cases lead to
ritual impurity: the fact is worthy of note, because Hellenic morality never
applied, as Christian morality later did, the idea of sin to physical love as such.
But it was a cause of physical impurity, as is clearly indicated by a passage of
Hesiod, in *Works and Days* 733–736, whose crude terms are very revealing.
Sexual intercourse was forbidden in sanctuaries. Herodotus, who ascribes the
invention of this rule to the Egyptians, informs us that the Egyptians and the
Greeks were the only peoples who observed it and who also bathed after coition
before entering a sacred site. The historian's remark is confirmed by the laws of
Cyrene, which state with regard to this matter that copulation by night involves
no impurity; if, on the contrary, it takes place by day, it must by followed by
ritual ablution. The legend of Atalanta and her husband Hippomenes illustrates
this ritual prohibition with regard to sanctuaries: because they yielded to their
mutual passion within the enclosure of a sacred place, the bride and bridegroom
were punished by the divine wrath, which changed them into a couple of lions.
Ovid tells the tale in Book X of his *Metamorphoses*.

Thus, in order to have the right of entry to religious ceremonies, a man had to
conform to clearly stated conditions: he had to be clean of all contact with the
disturbing mysteries of birth and death. Euripides gives very clear expression to
this through the mouth of Iphigenia, the priestess of Taurian Artemis: 'The

man who has taken part in a murder, one who has laid his hands upon a woman in childbed or upon a corpse, him the goddess will not allow to approach her altars because in her eyes he is stained with pollution.' The rites of purification, as precise as they are various, which were observed in the Greek states, made it possible to cope with these temporary prohibitions by restoring the requisite purity. At the same time, by a kind of inevitable impulse, they led enlightened spirits, naturally preoccupied with the problem of good and evil, to question themselves about the value of this ritual purity, which they felt impelled to extend to the moral plane. Hence there existed in the religion of the Greeks, at least as envisaged by the best of them, an ambiguity, which never completely vanished, as between the ethical and the sacred. That is why Apollo and Zeus, the great purifying gods, were at the same time those to whom—though still on a very moderate plane—was attributed the role of protectors of justice and morality. Hesiod's appeals to the justice of Zeus and Apollo's rôle in the *Eumenides* of Aeschylus enable us to perceive this shift of opinion which corresponded to a deep spiritual need. But Hellenic polytheism was not yet in a position completely to satisfy it.

Prayer was the elemental religious act by which the worshipper entered into explicit communication with a god, whether he thus responded to an inner call which had touched his soul or himself spontaneously opened the dialogue. In either case there was indeed a dialogue. The god either answered or did not, according to his will, but at least he had heard what the man had openly put into words. So prayer was essentially verbal and uttered audibly. The ancient Greek world scarcely knew silent or even muttered prayer, which is a revealing indication of the social character of its religious behaviour. No doubt we should also see in this the after-memory of a very primitive sentiment, which ascribed a kind of magic virtue to the word: yet magic, though never absent from Hellenic thought, played only a minor and restricted part in it. To the mind of the Classical Greek, the object of prayer was not to constrain the divine will by some mysterious power attributed to the word, but to make the suppliant understood by the god, as one makes oneself understood by a fellow-mortal. So it ought to have a meaning: meaningless cries, onomatopoeic exclamations—the *io Paian* or *ie Paion* of Apollo's worship, the Dionysiac *euoi*, the war-cry *alale* or *alala*, the women's cry of lamentation *ololuge* (comparable to the *you-you* of Arab women) —are not prayers. On the other hand, the mere invocation, in which the deity is called upon by his name, is in itself already a prayer, since it has the force of a greeting and is an expression of reverence for the god: in this sense, the single word *god* or *gods*, in the nominative (the case employed for exclamation and interpellation), which often appears on stelae above decrees, by itself stands for a prayer.

Apart from invocation, prayer usually included the expression of a request addressed to the god whose protection was sought; the better to win his favour, he is sometimes reminded either of the favours he has already granted before, which bind him, or of the pious acts which the petitioner has performed in his honour; to these appeals may be added a promise of future offerings. Here, for example, is the prayer which Penelope utters to Athena in Book IV of the *Odyssey*: 'Hear me, daughter of aegis-bearing Zeus, Atrytone [an appellation of Athena]! If formerly wise Ulysses had thighs of fat victims, heifers or ewes, burnt in your honour in this palace, remember it today in my favour and save my son. Frustrate the shameless intentions of the suitors.' The prayer was uttered while standing, in front of the statue or the shrine, with the right hand or both hands raised and the palm turned towards the god. The supplicant prostrated himself only in some funerary cults or in those of earth-deities: in this case he beat the earth with his hands while praying. Kneeling was hardly practised except in magic rites: Theophrastus, in his *Characters*, represents it as one of the distinctive traits of a superstitious man.

The prayer was often accompanied with an offering. Was it not natural to try to win the favour of a powerful being by bringing him some gift? This gesture should not, however, always be interpreted as a piece of bargaining, corresponding to the purely juridical notion expressed in the Latin phrase *do ut des*, 'my gift invites yours in return'. This sentiment certainly lay behind many offerings, and is well illustrated by the dedication of a statue by an Athenian in the sixth century who says to the goddess in his artless way: 'May you grant me reason to offer you another!' But ordinarily it is merely a question of expressing in a tangible way the donor's respect or gratitude towards the deity. The offering may be an occasional one, like the modest gifts deposited by the faithful in rustic sanctuaries: a fruit, a handful of ears of grain, some flowers, cakes, or a wild beast's hide. These tokens of popular piety later inspired the Hellenistic poets, who vied with one another in composing epigrams to accompany such offerings, as a kind of literary exercise: 'Receive as a token of gratitude, Laphria [an appellation of

Artemis], from Leonidas the vagabond, the down-and-out, the starveling, these bits of pancake done with oil, this olive (a treasure!), this green fig freshly gathered: take also these five grapes picked from a fine cluster, mistress, and as a libation the heeltaps from my tankard! You have delivered me from illness: rescue me likewise from the poverty that plagues me, and I will sacrifice a kid to you!' What for Leonidas of Tarentum, in the third century B.C., was merely an Alexandrian poet's literary game, had throughout centuries been for the Greek peasant a gesture of ingenuous and sincere devotion.

Apart from these occasional offerings, there were those prescribed by regular custom: such, for example, were libations which, according to Hesiod's instructions, should be made each morning and evening, by sprinkling a few drops of wine on the ground. The same act was performed at meals before drinking: the god was thus honoured with a share of the beverage which was about to gladden the heart of man. Other offerings corresponded to local traditions to which the people long remained faithful: Pausanias informs us that in his time the people of Lilaea (a town in Phocis) on certain appointed days still threw cakes characteristic of the country and other traditional offerings into the source of the Cephisus (a river of Phocis and Boeotia). He tells us that after a mysterious underground journey these cakes were said to reappear in the fountain of Castalia at Delphi.

In other cases, it was precious objects rather than food that were offered to the deity. Gifts of clothes were frequent: is it not fitting that statues should be provided with garments? This is why Hecuba, praying to Athena at Troy, is about to place on the knees of the goddess the most beautiful veil in her wardrobe. There was no more venerable festival in the Athenian calendar than that of the Great Panathenaea, at which, every four years, the goddess received the *peplos* woven for her by the Ergastinae, girls of the most noble Attic families, who reproduced on their loom a pattern designed by the best artists, representing the struggle of the gods with the giants. As can be seen on the Ionian frieze of the Parthenon, it was the whole city which on this occasion participated in the offering. It was thus that the sacred treasures were built up, by public gifts and no less by those of individuals: garments, weapons, vessels of previous metals, jewels, reserves of gold or silver in ingots or in specie, objects of every kind dedicated to the deity by the piety of his worshippers. They were preserved in the temples or in special buildings, generally of small dimensions, very comparable to chapels, except for the fact that they contained no cult statue, and were called treasure-houses.

Priests and magistrates were in charge of these riches, for which they were responsible, not only to the god, but also to their fellow-citizens, to whom they presented detailed accounts after retiring from office. Hence the curious epigraphical documents consisting of sacred inventories, enumerating offerings with a statement of their main characteristics and their weight: in specially favourable instances, as, for example, at Delos, these texts have been preserved in sufficient numbers for a study of them to reveal a whole aspect of the life of the sanctuary, which can be reconstructed through the survival and renewal of these collections.

Some of these offerings were in effect votive offerings: they were dedicated in testimony of the worshippers' gratitude to their god for some service rendered. These are not inspired by the motive of *do ut des*, but by the desire to express feelings of gratitude, whose reasons are often revealed in the inscription accompanying the votive offering. Private individuals, if rich, dedicate a statue, or, if they are people of modest means, a humble terracotta statuette. Often an unskilful hand has engraved the name of the deity in the glaze of a very simple earthenware vase. In the sanctuary of the divine healer Asclepios, an image of the limb or organ cured by the god was dedicated in relief. Sometimes it is the life-saving action of Asclepios himself that is represented in a picture or on stone: these offerings become more numerous from the fourth century onwards, as the Epidaurian cult developed and extended. Other votive offerings recall athletic or military exploits. The great sanctuaries of Olympia and Delphi were filled with statues of victorious athletes, which Pausanias enumerates with evident satisfaction: the inscriptions on their pedestals copied by him have sometimes come to light in the course of excavations, thus confirming the conscientiousness and truthfulness of the author of the *Periegesis*.

It was customary to offer to the deity a tithe of any exceptional profit gained in hunting, fishing, trade, or the capture of booty. Herodotus records a number of such dedications, such as that offered by the Samian Colaeus, a seventh-century merchant who went and made a fortune in Spain, the land of tin, and who, on his return, dedicated in the Heraeum of his native city a colossal bronze mixing-bowl adorned with projecting griffins' heads, a type of vase well known today as a result of archaeological discoveries. Later, towards the end of the sixth century, the engineer Mandrocles, also a Samian, received magnificent presents from Darius as a reward for the skill with which he had constructed a pontoon bridge over the Bosporus for the passage of the Great King's army during the Scythian

121. JUMPER

Exterior of an Attic red-figure cup (end of the sixth century). In the presence of their trainer, who is holding in his hand a rod as the emblem of his profession, two athletes are practising the jump. They are holding halteres (weights) to give them more impetus. Boston Museum.

122. DISCUS-THROWER

Bottom of an Attic red-figure cup (end of the sixth century). The nude ephebe (note his long hair drawn back into a sort of knot on the nape of the neck) is preparing to hurl the discus. The movement, which it has been found possible to reconstruct in detail, was noticeably different from the modern method of throwing. Behind the young athlete there is a mattock with which to level or loosen up the ground. In the field, two halteres for the jump. Boston Museum.

123 & 124. THE PALAESTRA BASE

These bas-reliefs adorned the sides of the base of a statue (late sixth century), later (after 480) used as building material in the wall built by Themistocles. They show scenes in the palaestra: ball-players (ill. 123) in a great variety of attitudes, and ephebes amusing themselves by egging on a dog and a cat, both on the leash, to fight (ill. 124). Note the relationship with contemporary vase-paintings. These sharply sketched bas-reliefs were enriched with painting, of which some traces remain. National Museum, Athens.

125. EPHEBES AND YOUNG BOYS

This Attic red-figure amphora (late sixth century) illustrates the relations of exclusive friendship which in the circles of Athenian aristocracy, devoted to Dorian customs, grew up between young boys and grown men. The promiscuous contacts of the palaestra lent themselves to intimate relations. Louvre.

126. WOMEN PLAYING THE LYRE

On an earthenware pyxis (box with a lid), decorated with the same polychromatic technique as the white-ground lecythi, the Attic vase-painter has represented two female musicians (middle of the fifth century). One, seated on a folding stool, is holding a seven-stringed lyre, with a sound-box of tortoise-shell (see ill. 128). In her right hand she has the plectrum, a little stick with which to strike the strings. The woman on the left, standing, is playing a cithara, a seven-stringed instrument like the lyre, but fashioned in a more complicated way, with a wooden sound-box, which amplified the sounds more. Boston Museum.

127. BEFORE THE CONCERT

An Attic red-figure crater, signed by Euphronius (late sixth century). In the middle of a circle of seated youths, a player of the double flute steps up on to a platform to give a recital. In his hand he holds his instrument, the aulos, whose two pipes are pressed against one another. They are bound together only at the mouthpiece and the musician draws them apart when he plays (see ill. 129). Louvre.

123

124

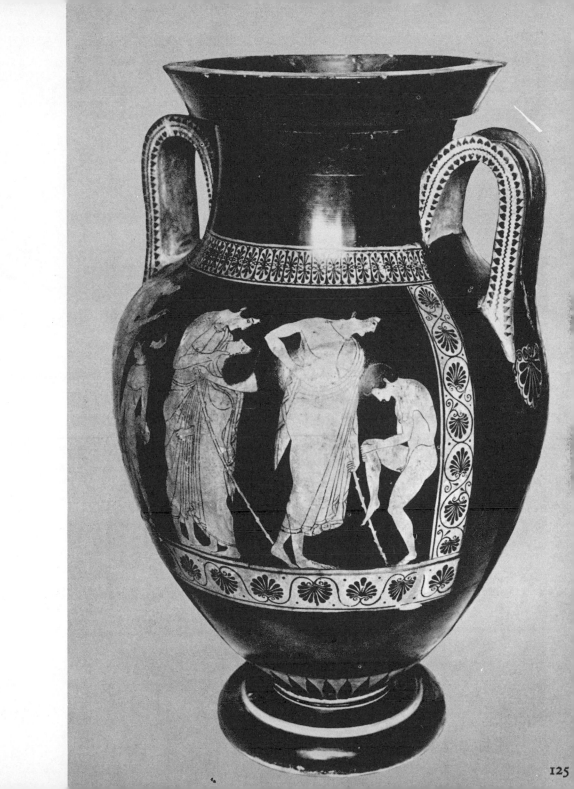

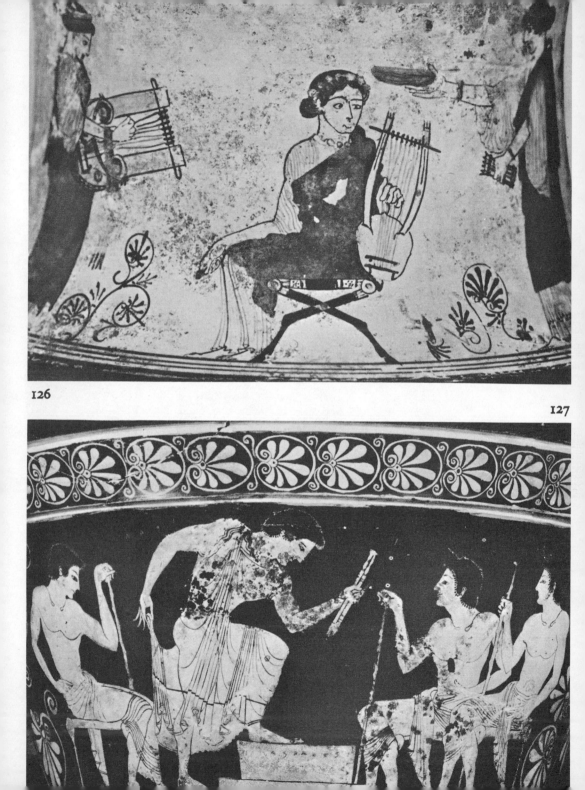

126

127

expedition: Mandrocles had a picture painted, which showed Darius looking on as his army crossed the bridge, and he dedicated it in the Heraeum at Samos, with an inscription in verse preserved in Herodotus's *History*. We can see that such offerings were not merely a display of piety: they also gratified the pride of the donor, who was handing down his achievements to the memory of posterity.

Communities were no less keenly inspired with such sentiments than private individuals. Pausanias mentions an offering by the Corcyraeans at Delphi, dating from the first half of the fifth century, which is very characteristic of the religious behaviour of a Greek city at this period: 'At the entrance of the sanctuary there is a bronze bull, the work of Theopropus of Aegina, dedicated by the Corcyraeans. The story concerning it is that at Corcyra a bull used to leave the herd, come down from the pastures, and bellow on the shore. As this happened every day, the herdsman came down to the sea, where he saw a countless shoal of tunny-fish. He informed the Corcyraeans in the city, who tried in vain to catch the tunnies. So they consulted the oracle at Delphi, sacrificed the bull to Poseidon and immediately after the sacrifice caught the fish. With a tithe of their catch they dedicated offerings at Olympia and Delphi.'

Since we are aware of the importance of war in the Greek world, we shall not be surprised to note that the majority of the votive offerings made by cities refer to military exploits. Not only did each Greek state celebrate its victories by dedications in their national sanctuaries; they also made a point of immortalizing them by offerings in the Panhellenic holy places, where all Greece could see them. This is where human pride played the greatest part in what was nevertheless, in principle, a gesture of gratitude towards the deity. Innumerable dedications followed upon the Persian Wars. Athens offered to Delphian Apollo the spoils of the Persians defeated at Marathon, laid out upon a pedestal leaning against the southern wall of her treasury: the insufficiently explicit dedication of this votive offering is referred by Pausanias to the treasury itself, which was probably constructed some years earlier. In memory of the Persian defeats there also stood at Delphi a second Athenian votive offering (at the very entrance to the sanctuary), dedications by Carystus in Euboea and Plataea, a mast adorned with golden stars offered by the Aeginetans, and two offerings dedicated in common by the allied states: an Apollo holding a prow in memory of the victory at Salamis, and a tripod resting on a bronze column to commemorate the Battle of Plataea. This bronze column, formed by three intertwining serpents, has been partly preserved at Constantinople, to which Constantine had it removed. We can still read on it the names of the thirty-one cities which joined in the dedication.

While we can easily understand the sentiment that impelled the Greeks to erect monuments as an expression of their gratitude to the gods who had ensured the salvation of Greece, we can less readily accept the frequency of dedications in memory of victories won by Greeks over other Greeks. Yet the Greek cities, which met each other incessantly on the battlefield, proudly celebrated their fratricidal triumphs by offerings in the great sanctuaries. In front of the façade of the temple of Zeus at Olympia, the Messenians who had been settled at Naupactus by Athens raised a triangular pillar, nine metres high, topped by a statue of Nike, Victory, shown in full flight, with her wings outspread and her drapery swollen by the wind or pressed against her beautiful young body. The marble statue has been discovered, with its dedicatory inscription, in the place mentioned by Pausanias: the Messenians' purpose was to thank Zeus for victories won over their Acarnanian neighbours. The work, signed by the Ionian sculptor Paeonius of Mende, probably also the artist of the temple sculptures, dates from the years 455–450 B.C. In the sanctuary of Apollo at Delphi, all the first section of the Sacred Way was like a tilting-yard in which the rival cities challenged each other: facing the Athenian offering for Marathon, the Lacedaemonian Lysander had set up the group commemorating the defeat of Athens at Aegospotami. But thirty years later, in 369, the Arcadians of Tegea, who had ravaged Laconia with the help of Epaminondas, set up in front of Lysander's offering a pedestal supporting statues of Apollo, Victory, and several Arcadian heroes, in memory of the reverses that they had inflicted on Sparta. Close to these, several Argive offerings recalled successes won by Argos over Lacedaemon. A little further on was the treasury built by Thebes after the Battle of Leuctra (in 371) and the one which the Syracusans had dedicated after the Athenian disaster in Sicily: it was not by chance that they had chosen for the erection of this treasury a site quite close to the Athenian treasury, which was more than a century older! All these manifestations of piety towards Apollo were so many opportunities to exalt the glory of victorious cities and to humble those defeated.

Sacrifice. 'Uranian' and 'chthonian' ritual. The great religious ceremonies as an expression of civic sentiment. Processions. Sacred drama in the cult of Dionysus
In his dialogue *Euthyphro*, Plato introduces a soothsayer thus named, who was

well known for his learning in religious matters in late fifth-century Athens. Euthyphro, expressing current opinion, gives the following definition of piety: 'Piety consists of knowing how to pray and sacrifice, saying and doing what is acceptable to the gods: it ensures the safety of families and of states' (14b). Prayer and sacrifice, such were the two essential acts of religious behaviour in the eyes of the Greeks. We have studied the former, with the offering which often accompanied it. Sacrifice can in truth be regarded as a particular form of offering: Socrates declares in reply to Euthyphro (14c): 'To sacrifice is to make an offering to the gods.' But in fact sacrifice, and especially public sacrifice, occupied so large a place in the religious life of the Greeks that it deserves special study and now demands our attention.

What distinguishes sacrifice from ordinary offerings is the importance of the part played in sacrifice by ritual regulations. Each sacrifice, whether public or private, was a complicated operation that followed rules settled by long tradition. It consisted of a solemn offering to the deity, in conformity with the rites, of consumable property, seeds, vegetables, beverages, or animal victims. In this sense, even libations of milk or wine or offerings of cakes are sacrifices, provided that they are carried out in accordance with the rites determining the nature, the time, and the procedure of these offerings. But even if sacrifices without shedding of blood existed in a number of cults, blood sacrifices, with cutting of the throat (and sometimes even quartering) of an animal victim, were much more frequent and more important: in the usual meaning of the word, only the last were envisaged, and a sacrifice without a victim was scarcely thought of. Ancient scholars of a later age thought they could establish a chronological succession between bloodless forms of sacrifice, which they regarded as primitive, and blood sacrifice, introduced later; such, for example, is the theory expounded at length by Ovid in Book I of his *Fasti* (ll. 335–456). But this is merely a rationalistic speculation, to which only the Pythagorean tradition, which disapproved of blood sacrifices, gave some appearance of truth. In reality, our earliest records, the Homeric poems, already provide descriptions of blood sacrifices: for example, in Book I of the *Iliad*, when Ulysses, sent by the Greeks, restores Chryseis to her father, he at the same time puts ashore the victims whose immediate sacrifice is to appease Apollo's wrath.

Even in this early reference, the principal phases of the ceremony are already clearly distinguished. The animals for sacrifice are arranged in order around an altar: they form a *hecatomb*, etymologically consisting of one hundred oxen; but at a very early date, and even in Homer, the word had taken on a less exact sense, and meant merely numerous victims, whether cattle or smaller livestock. The celebrants wash their hands to purify themselves and take handfuls of barley-grains. The priest of Apollo utters a prayer, the barley-grains are sprinkled as a first offering, then the victims' throats are cut, their muzzles being pressed backwards, so that the blood spurts into the air towards the altar. Then the dead beasts are dismembered. The thighs are set apart, wrapped in fat and burnt in the fire kindled on the altar, while the priest pours libations of wine upon them. When these pieces have been consumed in the fire, the rest of the meat is cut up, put on the spit, and forthwith roasted; then all those taking part join in a banquet and eat the flesh together. In most blood sacrifices these essential characteristics are found: a solemn formation around the altar, purificatory gestures, a prayer, cutting of the victims' throats at the altar, cremation of part of the animal, libations, and immediate consumption of the remainder of the flesh by the participants.

This procedure, though very frequent, was not always rigorously observed: the variety of rites was extreme. In certain cults, for example, eating of the victim's flesh was forbidden and the whole animal was burnt (this is what was called a 'complete burnt offering' or *holocaust*); this was the usual practice in sacrifices accompanying an oath, in certain expiatory rites, in the cults of earth-deities and gods of the underworld, and in most funerary cults and those of hero-worship. We have already encountered comparable variations in connection with prayer. Certain modern scholars have interpreted these differences as evidence that the deities of Hellenic polytheism belonged to two great main categories, that of the divinities of the sky ('uranian') and that of the gods below ('chthonian'). The assumption is that the former are helpful to man, the latter dangerous. The ritual employed for the former is in that case a ritual of trustful homage and participation: that is the ritual described above. The chthonian ritual is then, in contrast, an 'averting' ritual, designed to dispel the threat of a maleficent or hostile power. Hence the importance of the sacrificial feast in the former, in which the worshippers share the flesh of the victim with the god, while in the latter the whole victim is handed over to the divinity.

There is no doubt that this duality existed. But it by no means always applied as rigorously as has been asserted. Certain deities sometimes showed uranian and sometimes chthonian characteristics, according to the place of worship. Zeus, pre-eminently the sky-god, appears as an earth-god when invoked by the title of Zeus *Meilichios*, who had the form of a serpent: we know from Xenophon, who mentions him in *Anabasis* (VII, 8, 1), that holocausts were offered to him. Heracles was worshipped at Thasos in two forms of cult, one in conformity with divine (that is to say, in this case, uranian) ritual, the other according to a chthonian ritual characteristic of hero-worship. Pausanias, ever interested in curiosities pertaining to cults, points out that, in a small town in Phocis called Tronis, when sacrifice was offered to the local hero, the victim's blood was allowed to flow through an opening into the hero's tomb, a feature proper to funerary and chthonian ritual, but that the flesh of the victim was eaten, which was a characteristic of uranian ritual. It would, then, be wrong to base a too systematic interpretation of Greek religion on a distinction that was not always observed in practice. Even if, as is possible, the two main categories of deities were originally very clearly distinguished, we cannot discover the reasons for this division and we must be content to take note of their subsequent effects in the details of ritual, without really understanding them.

Here again, the essentially local character of the cults should be emphasized. Within the framework of the general picture of the most usual type of blood sacrifices outlined above, the regulations varied perceptibly from one sanctuary to another, and even according to the diverse aspects of a single god. The nature of the victims could be specified either negatively or positively. At Thasos, several cult regulations of the fifth century forbade the sacrifice of pigs or goats in the case of certain deities. The same prohibition is found at Delos; at Cyrene, however, the instruction was to sacrifice a russet-coloured kid to Apollo *Apotropaios*. At Lampsacus, on the Hellespont, asses were sacrificed to the local god Priapus, while at Sparta Enyalius, the god of war, had dogs sacrificed to him. The pig was habitually chosen for purificatory or expiatory sacrifices. Socrates' final injunction before his death, as recorded by Plato in the *Phaedo*, shows that a cock was sacrificed to Asclepios. These few examples show the extreme variety of the rites: to transgress them, to offer a victim not in accordance with custom, meant committing sacrilege, against which pecuniary and religious sanctions were provided. The same variety can be seen in the matter of libations: wine, so often used for this purpose, was prohibited in certain cults. A Thasian regulation forbade the singing of the paean, which elsewhere accompanied the ceremony. Pausanias, describing an annual festival held by the inhabitants of Sicyon in the rustic sanctuary of the Eumenides, tells us that they sacrificed ewes with lamb, that they made libations of honey and water, and that, instead of garlanding themselves for the festival (which was a very general custom), they merely brought flowers: such are the details of ritual practice recorded by the author of the *Periegesis* (II, 11, 4).

The very complexity of these practices gives the operation of sacrifice a very definitely technical character. It is understandable that, in order to avoid errors which would be regarded as sacrilegious, specialists were called in to assist. It is no accident that in Greek the word meaning 'to sacrifice', *hiereuein,* is closely connected with the word for priest, *hiereus.* The priest or priestess, usually a single individual, was attached to a sanctuary to supervise the performance of ritual. Chosen by election or by the casting of lots from among the best families in the city, the priest exercised functions comparable to those of a magistrate. He enjoyed a prestige indicated by a place of honour in public ceremonies and benefited by certain material advantages, such as a larger share of the meat from victims, the right to claim sacrificial fees, and exemption from taxes. For the rest, the priests were citizens like everyone else and by no means constituted a priestly caste. Their priesthood was an office usually conferred for a period, rarely for life. It certainly imposed upon them rules of propriety and dignity which might sometimes, for example, involve an obligation to wear white clothes or the observance of chastity (quite usual in the case of priestesses). But, on the whole, the office of priest should be identified with that of a magistrate endowed with technical functions. Hellenic society never had any rigorous separation between the priesthood and the laity.

These facts once more reveal the fundamentally social character of Greek religion: the supreme importance attached to ritual, inherited from an ancestral tradition, and the part played by the priest in the preservation of this tradition show that this religion, in terms of what we know best of it, that is to say the practice of worship, was essentially the business of a group. The family group had its own cults: the cult of the hearth in front of which Alcestis in Euripides' play addresses her last prayer to Hestia before she dies; the cult of Apollo Patroos and that of Zeus Herkeios, in which future archons at Athens had, according to Aristotle, to prove that their families had a share; the cult of *Agathos Daimon,* the 'good spirit of the home', represented in the form of a serpent, to whom a libation of unmixed wine was offered at the end of the daily repast; the cult of Hermes and that of Hecate *Prothyraia*, at the house door. The largest civic association, the *phratry*, was organized around common cults, with its peculiar festivals, such as that of the Apaturia in the Ionian cities: membership of this subdivision of the citizen body and, consequently, participation in its religious life, were, in many Greek states (to a lesser degree, it is true, in Athens), a formal condition of the right to enjoy the privileges of citizenship. In Athens the tribes, a main division of the civic body, drew their names from a local hero, who was accordingly called the 'eponymous' hero, and they rendered religious honours to this 'patron'. Even the Attic demes, which were merely administrative units on a territorial basis, founded at a comparatively late period, had their sanctuaries and their cults, just like the villages in the other Greek states, faithful to their ancient traditions.

As for the city itself, it was, as has been said, pre-eminently the setting for religious life. Its sanctuaries and its cults claimed the interest of the citizen, who felt himself a member of the civic body only in so far as he shared in its common beliefs. The fatherland was for him in the first place the religion handed down by his ancestors. This is clearly shown by the oath of the Athenian ephebes as preserved in an inscription of the fourth century B.C.: 'I will fight to protect the shrines and the city . . . I will honour the ancestral cults.' Women too were bound from childhood by these religious obligations in the service of the state. The chorus of Athenian women which Aristophanes introduces in his *Lysistrata* (ll. 638–647) recalls the stages of an Athenian girl's ideal *curriculum vitae*: 'I had barely reached the age of seven when I was chosen as an *arrephoros*. At ten I prepared the sacred cakes for the goddess Archegetis. Then I put on the saffron-coloured robe as a *bear* at the Brauronia. Finally, as a young woman, I carried the baskets of offerings, wearing a necklace of figs.' Of course these duties did not fall to the lot of every girl in Athens, being confined to the small company of the elect. But the poet's detailed account of them has nevertheless a symbolic value: every woman, like every man, felt herself a member of a single social body, kept in a state of cohesion by religion.

This is why the Greeks attached such importance to the great sacred ceremonies, of which public sacrifice was the main feature. It was only on these occasions that they had a feeling of sharing actively and completely in the life of the city in its most important and most valued aspect. Such communal celebrations were of course attended by material advantages that were by no means negligible: because of the scarcity of cattle in Greece, many people never ate butcher's meat except at public sacrifices, and the sacred feast, as well as being lavish, had the additional attraction of being free. But there was something more than this. The solemnity and splendour of the festivals delighted a public whose amusements were few and far between and whose daily life was austere: on such occasions the people admired the dignity of the magistrates, the splendid bearing of the knights as they performed caracoles on their horses, the beauty of the girls (*canephoroi*) who carried the offerings, and the fine appearance of the victims offered for sacrifice.

Every festival began with a procession, which might have a propitiatory quality, but which above all offered the spectators a brilliant and well-ordered tableau. Far from being passive spectators of the parade, the bystanders were not slow to make remarks about its details in their lively Mediterranean way, sometimes even exchanging buffoonery with the members of the procession. In certain cases, this kind of jesting was even a regular custom, as during the procession to Eleusis, when the spectators, clustering round a bridge, bombarded the pilgrims with traditional obscenities, known as *gephyrismoi*, 'banter from the bridge'. The 'gibes from the waggons', hurled down from the crowded vehicles during the Anthesteria and the Lenaea, festivals of Dionysus in Attica, played a part in the origins of comedy. The movements of these processions were regulated by officially appointed organizers, whom we can see in the Parthenon frieze turning in an opposite direction to the march of the procession. The processions passed through the streets and squares, ending at the sanctuary, on the esplanade surrounding the altar. The genius of Phidias, inspiring a homogeneous team of sculptors, has wonderfully succeeded in expressing the animated scene of such a procession, in all its rich complexity, on the occasion of the Attic festival of the Great Panathenaea. Men and beasts, horsemen and chariots, girls and bearers of offerings—nothing is missing in the long frieze, containing 360 figures, which stretches above the walls and the inner porches of the Parthenon: and, no doubt in harmony with the fervour which the reality inspired in the people of Athens, the religious spirit that breathes through the work is so lively and sincere that it seems quite natural that human beings should emerge, above the entrance to the temple, in the presence of the assembled gods.

After the procession came the sacrifice, which took place close to an altar. The altar was intended for the fire in which all or part of the victim was to be consumed. It might be merely a site reserved for this purpose or a hole dug in the ground, or a small dome-shaped heap of soil, without any architectural addition. In such cases it was usually known by the same name as the hearth, *eschara*; this was the usual form of altar for chthonian deities, heroes and the dead. But this very primitive type of altar is also found in other cults: at Olympia, for example, the great altar of Zeus, no trace of which remains on the site, was a hillock entirely formed by accumulation of the ashes from sacrifices. Pausanias describes it with great precision as a truncated cone (frustum of a cone) whose circumference measured 37 metres (125 feet) at the base and 9·5 metres (32 feet) at the summit. Its height was 6·5 metres (22 feet). A stairway cut in the solid mass of ashes gave access to the upper surface; up this stairway fuel could be carried, and also the flesh of the victims, which was burnt on top of the altar. In this Panhellenic sanctuary, which was at the same time the national sanctuary of the Eleans, there were daily sacrifices even when no *panegyris* was taking place. Once a year, on an appointed day, the soothsayers (for there was an oracle attached to the altar) added to the altar all the ash collected during the year, after having mixed it with water from the Alpheus, the river of Olympia. Thus the hillock was ever increasing little by little as a result of the piety of the faithful. In Apollo's sanctuary at Didyma, near Miletus, there was another altar of ashes, which was reputed to have been built by Heracles. Apollo's altar at Delos was stranger still: it was known as the altar of horns, *Keraton*, because it was entirely composed of goats' horns. The legend related by Callimachus in his *Hymn to Apollo* asserted that the god had built it himself with the horns of the wild goats which his sister Artemis shot down with her arrows while hunting throughout the island.

But the majority of the altars were made of stone, being either monolithic or constructed by the hand of the mason. Their shape was that of a cylindrical or rectangular table, on whose upper surface the sacrificial fire was lit. Side by side with modest altars, mere stone cubes sometimes bearing the deity's name carved on a lateral surface, monumental altars were to be found in the important sanctuaries. They were structures of large dimensions, composed of a solid oblong rectangular mass serving as a table, sometimes raised upon a plinth with several steps. The lateral edges of the table could be developed into high solid barriers to cut off the wind and prevent the ashes from falling from the altar. This architectural construction was sometimes embellished with a marble facing, mouldings, and bas-reliefs. The famous Ludovisi Throne, the pride of the Museum of the Terme in Rome, is no doubt nothing other than a decoration for the lateral surface of an altar, carved by an Ionian sculptor in the second quarter of the fifth century B.C. The dimensions of these altars could be very considerable. As early as the Archaic period, they reached horizontal dimensions of 66 to 98 feet by 19 to 43 feet; it is so in the case of the altars of the 'Basilica' (temple of Hera) at Posidonia–Paestum, of temple 'D' at Selinus, of the temple of Apollo at Cyrene, and of the temple of Aphaea in Aegina. In Classical times, we find dimensions of the same order in the temple of Hera at Agrigentum and in the temple of Alea Athena at Tegea. At the Olympeum of Agrigentum, the altar, as colossal as the temple, measured 183 by 39 feet. The Hellenistic Age increased these dimensions still further, since Hieron II, king of Syracuse, had an altar one Olympic stade (607 feet) long constructed in his capital in the middle of the third century B.C. But, without reaching colossal dimensions, the altar erected by the city of Chios in front of Apollo's temple at Delphi, in the first quarter of the fifth century, was an impressive edifice (28 by 7 feet). It has been partially reconstructed, with its main part built in dark limestone, its base and its white marble table. Dominating as it does the final bend in the Sacred Way, it helps the modern visitor to imagine the ceremonies of other days.

   The altar was practically always in the open air. For this there were two reasons: firstly the smoke from the sacrifices would soon have made the air impossible to breathe in a closed building, and secondly there had to be enough room round the altar for the crowd of people taking part. Indoor altars (except for small domestic altars) were therefore rare and were associated with unusual forms of worship. On the other hand, no close link existed between the altar and the temple: the more important of the two, contrary to what is often thought, was the former, not the latter. A temple without an altar was inconceivable, but the Greeks had sanctuaries without a temple, in which they were content to sacrifice upon an altar in the open air. This was the case in the sanctuary of Zeus at Olympia right through the Archaic Age until the temple was built by the Elean architect Libon in the second quarter of the fifth century. It was the same at Dodona. Though the altar usually stood in front of the temple, if there was one, this was not a strict necessity, merely an architectural convenience: on the Acropolis at Athens, Athena's altar was not situated in front of the Parthenon, nor in front of the eastern *cella* of the Erechtheum, but in front of the site formerly occupied by the Archaic temple of Athena, and sacrifices always continued to be performed here until the end of paganism.

Around the altar there was generally a clear space consisting of an esplanade, large enough to accommodate those performing and those watching the sacrifice. In front of the altar-table, an iron ring was fastened, either in the soil or in the actual flagstone (known as the *prothysis*) on which the sacrificing priest stood; to it the victims were haltered to keep them still at the moment of the fatal blow. Archaeologists sometimes find this ring *in situ*, a trivial detail that speaks to the imagination with singular force. It helps to bring before the mind's eye the animals of the hecatomb, the group consisting of priest, magistrates, and temple-servants by the altar, and the crowd of citizens forming a circle around. A highly-coloured spectacle it must have been, at once lively and solemn: flames and smoke rose into the clear sky and the smell of incense mingled with that of sizzling flesh, while music on flutes and the hymns of a choir sounded as the ceremony proceeded. Sometimes the murmurs of the people would grow still for a brief moment of silence, disturbed only by the lowing of a victim. At other times, all those present would repeat with one voice some ritual acclamation. The façade of a temple with gaily coloured pediment, the colonnades of a portico, the offerings and the bronze statues sparkling in the sunshine, the foliage of a sacred wood, the slopes of a near mountain or the vast horizon of the sea, provided the setting for these open-air festivals, at which an atmosphere of gaiety was maintained by the trust that the people put in their gods and the prospect of the feasting that was soon to follow.

The respect for traditional regulations sometimes made certain episodes in the ceremony seem like a kind of sacred play, in which the players followed a scenario going back to ancient beliefs now forgotten. So it was, for example, at the *Dipoleia* in Athens, a festival in honour of Zeus Polieus, the guardian of the city, whose cult was celebrated on the Acropolis in an open-air enclosure in which no temple stood. Aristophanes, in the *Clouds* (423 B.C.), regards this festival as typically Archaic (ll. 984–985). It was celebrated in the middle of the month of *Scirophorion* (corresponding to May–June) and included a sacrifice which was called the *Buphonia*, or 'slaying of the ox'. This is how it is described by Pausanias: 'As for Zeus Polieus, I shall describe the customary mode of sacrificing to him, but I shall not add the traditional explanation which is given. Upon the altar they place barley mixed with wheat and leave them unguarded. The ox which has been made ready for the sacrifice approaches the altar and partakes of the consecrated grains. Then one of the priests, who is called the "ox-slayer", kills the beast with an axe and immediately, throwing down the axe on the spot, as the ritual prescribes, takes to his heels and disappears. The others, pretending not to know who has killed the ox, bring the axe to trial before the court.' It is a pity that, on this occasion as on others, the scrupulous Pausanias has respected the rule of silence concerning the secret interpretation of this peculiar rite set forth by the priests; modern scholars have offered lengthy speculations on the reasons for such a sacred comedy. They are inclined to see in it the survival of an old rustic belief, according to which the sacrifice of a plough-ox, man's companion in husbandry, even for a religious purpose, is still a scandalous act, a downright murder, which necessitates judicial redress. Whatever the truth may be, we can see from this that cult ceremonies easily allowed of a certain rudimentary form of dramatic fiction. We find it more fully developed in the ritual of Delphi: here, every eight years, there was enacted on the *halos*, an open 'piazza' half-way up the Sacred Way, a veritable 'mystery', called the *Stepterion*, which commemorated an ancient Delphian legend, the slaying of the serpent Python by Apollo. The action, which included the burning of 'Python's hut', specially built for the occasion, was accompanied with the flute, whose imitative effects, suggesting the hissing of the serpent, are specially mentioned by Plutarch. At Sparta, too, during the festival of the Carnea, a kind of drama was played, on a warlike theme as was fitting in this city of soldiers: nine temporary hutments, similar to those in a camp, were set up, each occupied by nine men, under the orders of a leader who instructed them in the details of their rôle. Athenaeus, a compiler of the third century A.D., regards this episode at the Carnea as 'a representation of a military expedition'. In other cases, it was dances, more or less rich in symbolic import, that accompanied the sacrifice.

No cult gave a more prominent place to these ritual performances than that of Dionysus. This god of vegetation, and more particularly of the vine and of wine, was long considered to have been a foreign god belatedly brought into Greece from Thrace or the east. Great was the surprise when his name appeared on a Mycenaean tablet. Henceforth he must be regarded as one of the ancient members of the Hellenic pantheon. Yet it was only at the very end of the Archaic period that actual dramatic performances appeared in his cult. The Dionysiac ritual, like many others, included singing and dancing choruses as well as processions.

The choruses in honour of the god sang a special kind of hymn, known as the *dithyramb*. The processions, which were particularly mirthful and boisterous, carried an image of the male organ, the *phallos*, a symbol of fertility and of universal rebirth in spring. Dionysus aroused his worshippers more than did the other gods to mystical ecstasy, violent contortions, and unbridled rapture: wine no doubt played a part in this, but so also did a rustic tradition, fully in keeping with this agrarian cult, the tradition of the merry festivals that followed the heavy toil of summer and autumn. The members of the Dionysiac procession (*thiasos*) readily identified themselves with the god's legendary companions, the goat-footed *satyrs*, and adopted their costume, a bearded and snub-nosed mask and a goat-skin around the loins, furnished with a tail and an imitation *phallos*. According to Aristotle (*Poetics*, IV, 1449 a), the dithyramb was the origin of tragedy, whose name (*goat-song*) recalls the he-goat, *tragos*, the animal sacred to Dionysus. The Attic poet Thespis, a native of the deme of Icaria, on the slopes of Mount Pentelicus, was credited with having been the first to make an actor engage in dialogue with the chorus and its leader, thus introducing into the lyric hymn of the dithyramb a dramatic element which developed rapidly. The *Parian Marble* gives 534 B.C. as the date of the first dramatic performance at Athens: it is not the least claim to glory of Pisistratus' government. The literary genre of drama, as we understand the word, had now come into existence.

Henceforth the main Dionysiac festivals in Athens, the *Great Dionysia* or city Dionysia at the end of March and the *Lenaea* at the end of December, like the *Rustic Dionysia* at the end of November in the Attic villages, included theatrical performances, organized by the magistrates responsible for these festivals, and providing occasions for competitions. The religious nature of these ceremonies remained clearly defined down to the end of the Hellenistic period: the stage provided for the spectacle, at first made of wood and later of stone, was always set up in a sanctuary of Dionysus: the circular space set apart for the movements of the chorus had an altar of the god at the centre of it; the priest of Dionysus had a seat of honour reserved for him. The performances only took place during religious festivals and were preceded by other rites, processions, sacrifices, and purifications. From Demosthenes' speech against Midias, one of his enemies, who had struck the orator when he was exercising his functions as a *choregus*, we can see to what degree, in the middle of the fourth century, the dramatic competitions still had a sacred character in the eyes of the people.

As for Attic comedy, which gained its place a little later side by side with tragedy and the ancient dithyramb, it originated, as Aristotle tells us, in the phallic processions and the songs and *lazzi* which accompanied them. The choruses of satyrs which, from the beginning of the sixth century, formed the retinue of Dionysus on Attic vases, were just as favourable to the birth of comedy, which suited their shameless and lascivious character, as to that of tragedy. It was between the two Persian Wars, probably in 486 B.C., if we accept the statement of 'Suidas', that the first competition in comedy took place at the Great Dionysia, about half a century after the first competition in tragedy. Comedy, like tragedy, was always an important element in the Dionysiac festivals in Attica. Making very free use of the licence granted to them by tradition to raise a laugh by any means, however audacious, the poets did not, on occasion, even refrain from mocking the god who was the patron of their art. Aristophanes in the *Frogs* (405 B.C.) presents Dionysus as a ridiculous character: disguised as Heracles, the god wishes to descend into the underworld, but, unlike the hero whose dress he has assumed, he shows himself cowardly and pusillanimous, which involves him in comical misadventures and even a cudgelling! Heracles himself, in spite of being a son of Zeus, is often depicted as a toper and a guzzler: he appears in this light in Euripides' *Alcestis*, which is not strictly speaking a tragedy, but somewhat like a satyric drama, that is to say a play containing an element of burlesque.

We have some difficulty in recognizing that this way of representing the gods on the stage can go hand in hand with sincere piety, and yet there can be no doubt of it. There is here a kind of popular familiarity with the anthropo-morphic deity, which did not shock the ancients, apart from some particularly fastidious or delicate spirits. The masses had no difficulty in accepting the idea that the divine nature, having the same form as man, should also assume some of his weaknesses. But this did not lessen their respect for the formidable power of the Immortals: it was because men felt that they knew and could trust the gods that they were quite ready to poke fun at them in their own festivals when tradi-tion permitted. On the other hand, when an opportunity arose, the comic dramatist could invoke the gods of the city in noble strains: 'Pallas, Mistress of our city, protectress of this sacred land which surpasses all others in its warlike valour, its poets and its power, come into our midst and bring with you Victory, who was our comrade in military expeditions and in battles.' So speak the

Knights in Aristophanes' play (ll. 581–589). Elsewhere the same poet shows us the honest countryman Dicaeopolis celebrating the festival of the Rustic Dionysia (*Acharnians*, ll. 241–279): this scene is of great interest, since it gives us a life-like picture of the way in which popular piety found expression in these rustic rites out of which Attic comedy arose. Dicaeopolis, as head of the family, directs the ceremony in which the whole household takes part: he leads a little procession followed by his daughter, who, carrying the basket of offerings, plays the role of *canephoros*, and by his two slaves, whose task is to flourish aloft a great *phallos*, the Dionysiac emblem. He offers a modest bloodless sacrifice to the God: a cake with thick vegetable soup poured over it. Then he utters a prayer: 'Lord Dionysus, may you take pleasure in this procession which I lead and in this sacrifice which I offer you with all my household! Grant that I may celebrate your country festival with good luck to us all.' Then the procession begins to move, while Dicaeopolis intones the phallic hymn and his wife watches him from the flat roof of their house.

The Games. Their rôle in Greek religion. The Olympian Games: their programme; their outstanding importance. The Pythian Games. The Isthmian and Nemean Games. The glory showered upon the victors: Theogenes of Thasos as an example

Dramatic contests, which made such an important contribution to the development of European literature, were merely one particular aspect of Greek contests; these were a very common feature of religious festivals and they played a vital rôle in the social and moral life of the Hellenes. These contests were originally, and during the earlier period, athletic: musical competitions, for example, did not appear until later. The first games known to us are those arranged by Achilles, in *Iliad* XXIII, at the funeral of Patroclus. Other funeral games appear in the epic legends: for example, the games in honour of Pelias, the king of Iolcus, in Thessaly, in which a number of illustrious heroes took part, were represented on the famous Chest of Cypselus, which the tyrant of Corinth dedicated at Olympia in the second half of the seventh century. This is why certain modern authorities regard athletic competitions in Greece as having originated in funeral ceremonies. Nevertheless, it should be noted that in *Odyssey* VII we find Alcinous, the king of the Phaeacians, suggesting athletic contests to his subjects for the entertainment of his guest Ulysses; in this case the games had no funerary, or even

128 & 129. ATHENIAN EDUCATION

This famous cup by the painter Duris (early fifth century) is decorated on the exterior with scenes of lessons given by the music-master and the *grammatistes* (master teaching juniors). Ill. 128 shows lessons in lyre-playing and reading aloud (it will be observed that the text which can be read on the papyrus roll is, for the convenience of those looking at the picture, written down in a manner contrary to actual practice), while ill. 129 shows a lesson in playing the double flute and correction of a written exercise (the master, holding his stylet, is reading the exercise in order to point out the defects). In each there is, on the right, a bearded man watching the lessons, presumably the father of one of the boys. Hanging on the wall are musical instruments, a basket, drinking-cups, and writing-tablets. Berlin Museum.

130. PLOUGHING

In spite of the simplicity of the means employed, this terracotta group (Boeotia, seventh century) is full of life. A pair of oxen are drawing a wooden swing-plough of the most primitive type, like the one described by Hesiod (*Works and Days*, 427 ff.). The peasant is driving them and, bent by his effort, is leaning heavily on the single handle to drive in the wooden ploughshare. Louvre.

131. SILPHIUM

This wild plant, which modern botanists have not yet succeeded in identifying at all precisely, grew in the sub-desert steppes of Cyrenaica. It was gathered by the natives, who brought it as tribute to the Battiad kings (see the Arcesilas cup, coloured plate II), and it provided a juice employed for medicinal purposes and as a condiment. Throughout the Classical period the Cyrenaeans used it as the regular emblem of the city on their coins. Reading from left to right and from top to bottom, we have the name of the Cyrenaean people almost complete, in letters enframing the plant. Cabinet des Médailles.

132. EAR OF WHEAT

As the emblem of the city of Metapontum (whose name can be read in part on the left), in southern Italy, an ear of wheat appears on the reverse side of its coins. It symbolizes the fertility of the Italian soil, which greatly impressed Greek farmers. Cabinet des Médailles.

133. BOAR-HUNT

Attic red-figure cup (first half of the fifth century). The hunter, wearing a tunic and a chlamys, is defending himself with a sword against an attacking boar. He is holding a hunting spear-in his left hand. Louvre.

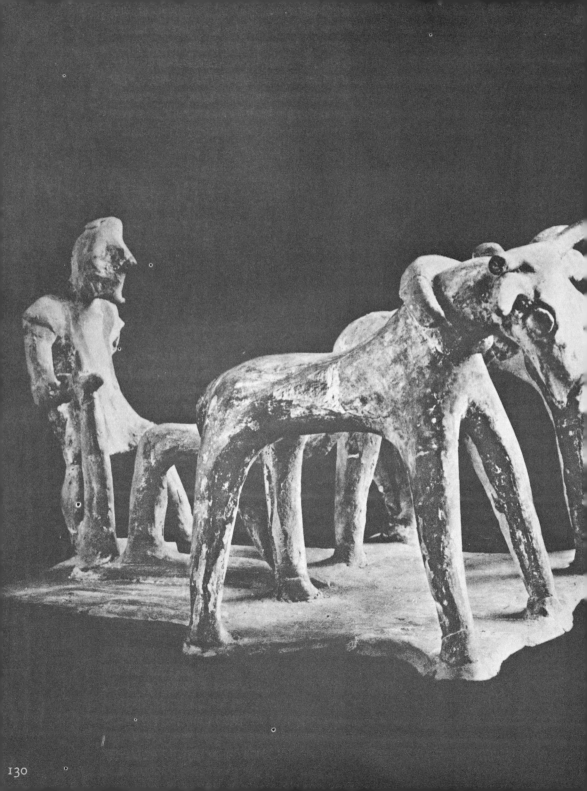

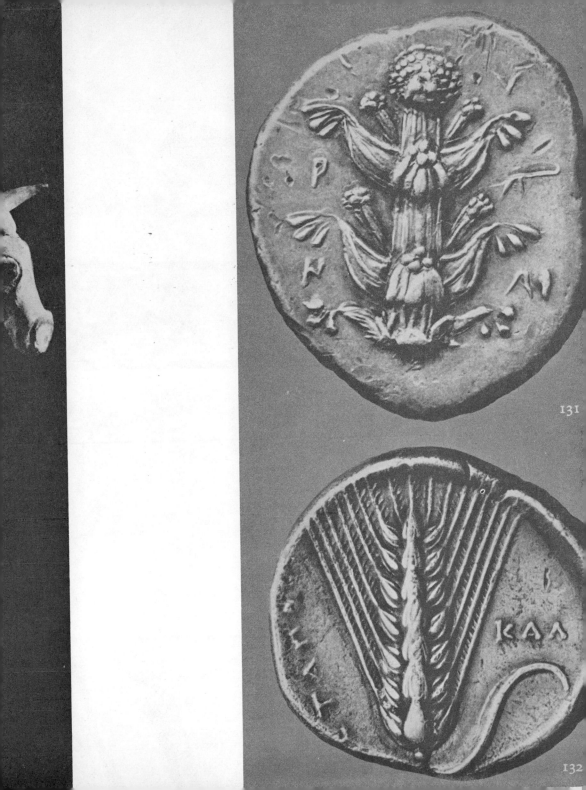

133

134

135

134. PLOUGHING AND SOWING
Attic black-figure cup (so-called 'little masters' series, third quarter of the sixth century). The nude ploughman, with a goad in his hand, is driving a team of two enormous bulls (see ill. 130). Behind him, another peasant is walking along the freshly ploughed furrow dropping seeds which he is drawing from a bag. A lifelike and evocative sketch, with a touch of caricature. British Museum.

135. KNOCKING DOWN OF OLIVES
Attic black-figure amphora (third quarter of the sixth century). Three countrymen, armed with long sticks, are striking the branches to make the olives fall: one of them has climbed the tree to reach the high branches. A fourth is picking up the olives and putting them in a basket. British Museum.

Q

religious character. But it is a fact that as a rule the Greek contests were organized as part of a sacred ceremony.

There were games everywhere in the Greek world, connected with the most varied cults. Thus Pindar, extolling the merits of a Cyrenaean foot-race champion in the ninth *Pythian Ode*, mentions among the games held at Cyrene contests in honour of Athena, others for Olympian Zeus, others for Mother Earth, and this list is not intended to be complete. These local games enabled the young men to face one another in various events, both for individuals and for teams. Sometimes the contest distinctly preserved the character of a religious rite: this is true, for example, of the torch-races (*lampadedromiai*), a familiar type of relay race at Athens, and of the race of the *staphylodromoi* ('grape-race'), which was an event in the great festival of the Carnea at Sparta, in honour of Apollo *Carneios*, a rustic deity. But it was most frequently a question of simple athletic competitions, in which young men exercised their qualities of strength and skill in honour of the god. As we can already see in Homer, in the eyes of the Greeks victory in the games, as in war, primarily depended on divine favour. Man does his best, but Destiny and the will of the gods decide the issue. At Olympia, as we learn from Pausanias, several altars in honour of various deities had been erected near the starting-point for the chariot-race, including altars of the *Moirai*, or Fates, and of *Moiragetes*. 'It is clear,' adds Pausanias, 'that this is a title of Zeus, who knows the destinies of men, what is granted to them by the *Moirai* and what is withheld' (V, 15, 5). This fact reveals an attitude of mind that was very common in Greece: man is conscious of his own deserts, but he knows that in every enterprise what may be a decisive part is played by chance. It is this element of contingency that brings down man's vainglory and reveals the overriding intervention of a supernatural power in human affairs. In athletic contests, at least in the earlier period, before they were debased by the appearance of professional athletes, there was an implicit recognition of divine will which gave them nobility and grandeur: it is fully understandable that Pindar found in them subject-matter to inspire the loftiest flights of lyric poetry.

So the victor in the games was regarded not only as an individual endowed with outstanding physical qualities, but also as the favourite of the gods: hence the custom of dedicating an offering after the victory in the sanctuary of the god who was the patron of the contest. Among all the games that aroused the ambition of athletes, there were some whose fame spread far beyond the frontiers of one state and extended all over the Greek world. Four of them especially attracted great multitudes: those of Olympia, Delphi, the Isthmus, and Nemea. Thanks to the brilliance of their festivals, the quality of the competitors who met in them, and the number and variety of the spectators, they genuinely deserved the title 'Panhellenic Games', by which they are generally known. It was for the victors in these glorious competitions that Pindar composed the triumphal odes (*epinicia*) which remain as the only complete specimens of his poetic genius and which were divided by ancient editors, in terms of the various contests, into *Olympian, Pythian, Isthmian,* and *Nemean Odes.* Leaving on one side the technical and sporting aspect of these games, we shall for the moment deal only with their religious importance.

The Olympian Games, in honour of Olympian Zeus, were the most famous. From 776 B.C. onwards, according to the traditional chronology adopted by the historian Timaeus of Tauromenium, who popularized the habit of computation by olympiads, these games were held every four years, in the height of summer (July–August). During the Classical Age, the festival lasted seven days. From 572 onwards, it took place under the patronage of the Eleans, who controlled the district and appointed from their own number the board of *Hellanodikai* ('judges of the Greeks') which was responsible for the organization of the games. Thus even a Panhellenic ceremony, open to all the Greeks, remained under the direction of a single people, in accordance with the political and religious principle which subordinated everything to the city-state. Some time before the beginning of the games, delegates called *spondophoroi* were sent round all the cities of Greece to announce the festival. A sacred truce was then observed in honour of Zeus, suspending all wars between Greek cities for the duration of the Olympic festival. Athletes and spectators set out for Elis, where accommodation was provided to receive them: a town of tents and huts stood for several weeks around the sanctuary.

The first day of the games was given over to sacrifices and the swearing of the Olympian oath by the competitors. They had to be Greeks, free-born, and un-sullied by any condemnation. This was a religious rather than a moral or political requirement: the games formed part of the worship of the god, in which a man could not fully participate unless he belonged to a civic community and was unstained by any pollution. That is why Barbarians, slaves, and convicts were excluded. The regulation which forbade women to enter the sanctuary and attend the contests was also a religious one: a single exception was made in favour of the priestess of Demeter *Chamyne*, which indicates the sacred character of the prohibition. The swearing of the oath was particularly solemn. It took place before the altar of Zeus *Horkios*, the guardian of oaths, whose statue stood in the *Bouleuterion* (the local senate-house) and held a thunderbolt in each hand with which to strike perjurers. On the quartered body of a boar sacrificed for the occasion, the athletes and their fathers and brothers, bound together by the ancient unity of the family clan, swore to respect the rules of the competition. Pausanias, to whom we are indebted for this information, adds a revealing remark: 'It did not occur to me to ask what is done with the boar after the athletes take the oath: it has been an established rule since the remotest times that a victim on which an oath has been sworn must not be eaten.' (V, 24, 10). At the foot of the statue of Zeus Horkios there was a bronze plaque with a poem in elegiac couplets reminding the reader of the punishment in store for perjurers. In cases of fraud, the Hellanodikai inflicted a heavy fine on the culprit and excluded him from the games for life. With the money derived from the fine they erected a bronze statue of Zeus; these statues of Zeus, which were called *Zanes* in the local Dorian dialect, stood in a row within the sanctuary, near the entrance to the stadium, at the foot of the Terrace of the Treasures. Some of the pedestals on which they stood can still be seen in their original position.

At the end of the contests, which lasted five days, the final day was spent in the distribution of the prizes. In the presence of an immense crowd, which greeted them with applause, the victors, who were styled *Olympionikai*, came forward when their names were called to receive their prize: a simple garland of wild olive woven with leaves from the sacred tree which Heracles, Pindar tells us, had brought back from the land of the Hyperboreans and planted at Olympia. These garlands were set out upon a magnificent table for offerings, inlaid with ivory and gold, the work of Colotes, a pupil and collaborator of Phidias. This table appears on the reverse side of one of the commemorative coins minted by the Eleans in A.D. 133, during the reign of the emperor Hadrian. There was no greater honour, in Greek eyes, than the Olympic garland, awarded in the presence of assembled Greece in the sanctuary of the king of the gods. This is the implication of the famous anecdote, told by Cicero in the *Tusculan Disputations* (I, 46, 111) about Diagoras and the Laconian. Diagoras of Rhodes, a celebrated boxer, had won at Olympia and had his success celebrated by Pindar in the seventh *Olympian Ode*.

In his old age he had the joy of seeing his two sons victorious in their turn, both on the same day. 'A Laconian approached the old man, congratulated him and said: *"Die now, Diagoras, for never again will you know such heavenly joy!"* . . . The man who spoke these words felt that it was a unique honour for one family to have produced three Olympic victors and that Diagoras would be exposing himself unnecessarily to the blows of fate if he lingered longer in this world.'

So desire for glory, thirst for praise, national pride, and sincere piety towards the god simultaneously aroused the ardour of the competitors. The spectators were also impelled by curiosity to see famous men at close quarters, for, in addition to the athletes, there came writers, philosophers, rhetors, and artists, all eager to take advantage of this great concourse to make their works known by public readings or to obtain commissions. While the athletic competitions and the sacred ceremonies pursued their course, there was also an animated scene, with much jostling and conduct of transactions. In the enclosure of the *Altis*, the plot of land dedicated to Zeus, all the Greek dialects could be heard. The by-standers would be pointing out to one another such famous visitors as Themistocles, Alcibiades, or Plato, whose visit to Olympia is definitely attested, and many others whose presence has not been recorded. Herodotus read his *History* at Olympia, to the applause of the crowd, which on this occasion, so Lucian tells us, gave the nine books of the work the names of the nine Muses. The sophist Gorgias of Leontini aroused admiration by his eloquence, in memory of which his brother-in-law had a statue of him erected, which Pausanias saw still standing. Through rubbing shoulders for several days, taking part in the same sacrifices, and feeling the same thrill of enthusiasm, men from every part of the Hellenic world learnt to know one another better. They felt a basic unity that transcended the divergent interests or conflicting vanities which kept their respective cities apart. They gave the very concept of Hellenism a more visible reality. So this concept was strengthened in these great recurring religious gatherings which the Greeks called *panegyreis*. This was expressed to perfection by Isocrates, the great Athenian rhetor of the fourth century, in the speech which he published, though it was never actually delivered, on the occasion of the hundredth Olympiad (380 B.C.), and which for this reason is called the *Panegyric*: 'We have good reason to praise those who established the *panegyreis* and have handed them down to us as a tradition. Thanks to them we gather in a single place after having declared the truce and put a stop to our enmities. Then we offer prayers and sacrifices together to the gods and revive the memory of our common origin. We derive better attitudes to one another for the future, we renew our ancient hospitable relations and form new ones. Neither for the masses in general nor for outstanding individuals are these meetings a waste of time: in the presence of the assembled Greeks, the latter display their natural gifts and the former find pleasure in gazing upon these contests. There is no danger that any of them will be bored. All have something to satisfy their personal pride, when the spectators see the athletes putting forth their best efforts to please them and the athletes realize that all these people have come to admire them.'

The other great Panhellenic games provided opportunities for *panegyreis* of the same kind. The Pythian Games at Delphi had been established in honour of Apollo after the first Sacred War, in 582. They gradually acquired the same pro-gramme of contests as those at Olympia. But their original feature was the im-portant place given to musical competitions, a very ancient tradition at Delphi: a story was told that Homer and Hesiod had both wished to take part in the com-petition and that both had been excluded, the former because he was blind and could not play the cithara, the latter because, good though he was as a poet, he was not a good enough citharist. This anecdote, related by Pausanias, is clearly apocryphal, but it shows that Apollo, the god of the arts, was as much interested in musical compositions as in athletic contests.

The festival took place every four years, in the third year of each Olympiad, and so two years after the Olympic Games, towards the end of summer (August–September). Some time before, the Delphians sent envoys, *theoroi* (or *thearoi*, as they were called at Delphi), into the various regions of the Greek world, to make official announcement of the forthcoming celebration of the *Pythia*. In the course of their religious embassy, these *theoroi* were welcomed and put up, in each sovereign state, by official representatives, known as *theorodokoi*, who had the responsibility of facilitating their mission. The list of these *theorodokoi* was from time to time carved on stone in the sanctuary; we have a fragment dating from the end of the fifth century, a very extensive text for the end of the third, and other fragments for the middle of the second. These records are very informative with regard to historical geography and the forms of proper names. As at Olympia, the prize for each contest was a simple garland of leaves. It was woven with laurel, Apollo's favourite tree, cut under special conditions in accordance with religious requirements: a boy whose father and mother were still living had to go and bring the branches from the valley of Tempe, in Thessaly. The glory of Apollo and the reputation of his oracle added to the attraction of the Games and brought to Delphi crowds comparable to those that thronged to Olympia.

The Isthmian and Nemean Games likewise took place every four years, alternating with those of Olympia and Delphi, that is to say in the second and fourth years respectively of each Olympiad. The Isthmian Games were held in honour of Poseidon in his sanctuary on the Isthmus of Corinth, the remains of which have recently been partly excavated. The Corinthians were the organizers, but the Athenians enjoyed a privileged place among all the visitors. The season for the games was spring (April–May). They were officially announced and on this occasion there was a sacred truce, which was observed even at the height of the Peloponnesian War: Thucydides explicitly mentions this with regard to the games in 413 B.C. The prize awarded to the victors was at first a pine wreath, soon replaced, before the time of Pindar, by one of wild celery. The garland at the Nemean Games was made of the same plant. The Nemean Games were held in the sanctuary of Zeus at Nemea, in Argolis. The organization was under the control of the people of Cleonae, a small town in the neighbourhood, until the age of Pindar, but the Argives, whose influence was spreading to this region of the Peloponnese, eventually supplanted them. Although the memory of the famous lion slain by Heracles always remained associated with the little plain of Nemea, it was Zeus who was worshipped there, in a close planted with cypress-trees. The competitions were like those at Olympia, and, as at Olympia, the judges of the contests bore the title of *Hellanodikai*. This festival, being recognized as a *panegyris* of all the Greeks, was also the occasion of a sacred truce.

The admiration aroused by victories in the great games was especially keen when a single athlete gained the crown in the series of four festivals in succession: he then bore the title of *periodonikes*, or 'victor in the cycle'. The renown of such champions lasted throughout the ages and could, in favourable circumstances, gain the athlete a place among the gods. This is well shown by the case of Theogenes of Thasos. This son of a priest of Heracles was credited with having the god himself as his real father, a legend no doubt to be explained, as we have seen, by a rite of 'hierogamy'. He was an unbeatable boxer for twenty-two years, winning numerous victories: nine times champion at Nemea, nine times at the Isthmus (plus a victory in the pancratium at the same festival), three times

136 & 137. TERRACOTTA ANIMALS

These statuettes from Tanagra (second half of the sixth century) reveal, in the same way as that in ill. 130, the liking of the Boeotian peasantry for rustic scenes. Two enormous Molossian hounds are holding a ram (of remarkably small dimensions) in their jaws. On the back of a dog, with his ears pricked up, there is a bird perched in a familiar manner. All these terracottas were painted. Louvre.

138-140. COOKS AND BAKERS

Boeotian terracottas of the late sixth century. A cook sitting on a stool is leaning over a large rectangular tray or basin; beside her, on the ground, are two bowls (ill. 138). Another is stirring with a long spoon the contents of a large cooking-pot; on the ground there is a round dish and a pet dog (ill. 139). Four bakers are kneading dough, keeping time, while the flute player is keeping them in rhythm (ill. 140). Louvre.

141. INDOOR SCENE

Moulded terracotta bas-relief (middle of the fifth century). A young woman wearing a peplos without a girdle is putting a carefully folded garment away in a large chest. The framework of the chest is decorated with a key pattern, the panels with mythological scenes (on the left, we can identify a scene from a gigantomachy: a goddess is throwing an armed giant to the ground). Behind the woman there is an armchair with cushions, on the wall a cantharus, a lecythus, a mirror, and a work-basket (upside down). It shows the calm atmosphere of the gynaeceum. Taranto Museum.

142 & 143. WOMEN'S WORK

Attic black-figure lecythus (third quarter of the sixth century). Two women are weaving a piece of material on a large vertical loom. One is passing the shuttle between the threads of the warp. the other is beating up the threads of the weft with a reed (ill. 142). Further to the left, a woman is filling a distaff with wool taken from a basket, while her neighbour is spinning. Two other women are folding and piling up the pieces of material. Metropolitan Museum, New York.

144 & 145. DOMESTIC SCENES

Boeotian terracottas (late sixth century). A man is having his hair cut with a razor by a barber, who is concentrating carefully on his task (ill. 144). A grandfather with a wrinkled forehead and white hair is handing a bunch of grapes to his grand-daughter (ill. 145). Some traces of painted decoration. Boston Museum.

146 & 147. KITCHEN SCENES

Boeotian terracottas (early fifth century). The modeller makes up for his lack of skill by an innate capacity for observation and a sense of life. There are traces of the white coating, or glaze, which took the painted decoration. Boston Museum.

138

139

140

144

145

146

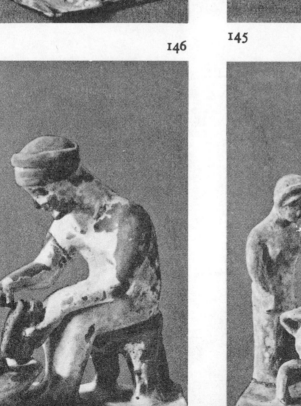

147

148

149

151

152

148. AT THE COBBLER'S

Attic black-figure amphora (late sixth century). An Athenian lady of fashion has stepped onto the cobbler's bench to have her measurements taken, while her husband is standing at the right, looking on. The master-cobbler, on the left, holding a shoemaker's knife, is taking the measurements, while his assistant, on the right, is busy with his work. On the wall are pieces of leather, a basket, and boots. The young woman has chosen her leather, which she is handing to the cobbler. On the ground there are a basin and a pair of sandals. Boston Museum.

149. IN THE SMITHY

Reverse side of the preceding amphora. Two blacksmiths are at work, watched by a pair of onlookers, who are exchanging remarks about the work. One of the workers is shaping with blows of a sledge-hammer on the anvil a piece of iron which his mate is holding with a pair of long tongs. On the wall there are a wine-jug, tools, and a cloak. Other tools are lying on the ground. Boston Museum.

150. WEIGHING

Attic black-figure amphora (third quarter of the sixth century). On a large pair of scales similar to the one on the Arcesilas cup (coloured plate II), a man is bringing up to weight a basket of goods, probably grain or dried vegetables, to allow for the weight of the receptacle placed on the other pan. Two assistants are aiding in the operation by keeping the pans of the balance in position. In the field we can read the complimentary inscription: 'Clitarchus is a beauty', and the potter's signature: 'Work of Talides'. Metropolitan Museum, New York.

151. IN THE SCULPTOR'S STUDIO

Red-figure crater from a workshop in southern Italy (first half of the fourth century). The artist, wearing a petticoat and the conical bonnet of felt worn by workers, has finished carving a marble statue of Heracles. He is putting the finishing touches to it by colouring it, as was usual, to produce a realistic effect. Heracles is watching the operation in person. The Victory hovering above symbolizes the artist's success. Metropolitan Museum, New York.

152. IN THE POTTER'S WORKSHOP

Attic red-figure crater (early fourth century). Three workmen are at work. One is painting a crater, another is shifting a vase of the same type, while the third is carrying away a large goblet. On the wall are cups, a goblet, and a long cylindrical bag containing a double flute. Oxford Museum.

crowned at the Pythian Games (on one of these occasions by a walk-over, no rival having dared to face him), he reached the summit of his career by winning the boxing tournament at Olympia in 480 and the pancratium at Olympia in 476. Statues of him were set up at Olympia, Delphi, and on the island of Thasos, his native place. The pedestals on which these statues stood have been discovered, more or less seriously mutilated: on the one at Delphi we can still read both a complete list of Theogenes' victories and a twelve-line epigram extolling the really outstanding merits of a champion who boasted of having won 1,300 matches! His achievements were remembered for centuries: in the third century B.C., a composer of epigrams, Posidippus of Pella, refers to the prodigious appetite of the boxer, who was capable, he claims, of devouring a whole bull all by himself. In the second century A.D., the rhetor Dio Chrysostomus, the philosopher Plutarch, and the traveller Pausanias refer at length to Theogenes, to his hot temper and his athletic exploits.

But the most remarkable thing is not so much his extraordinary series of victories in the ring as the religious honours conferred on him after his death, in circumstances recorded in detail by Pausanias: 'After the death of Theogenes, one of his enemies used to come every night and beat his bronze statue with rods, imagining that he was thus ill-treating Theogenes himself. The statue put an end to these outrages by falling on the man and thus killing him, and the victim's children prosecuted the statue for murder. The Thasians had it flung into the sea, applying the law of Draco, which, in the criminal code that he framed for Athens, punished even lifeless things with banishment if one of them chanced to fall on a man and kill him. After this the soil of Thasos was stricken with barrenness. The Thasians sent envoys to Delphi and the oracle instructed them to bring back any whom they had sent into exile. But the return of the exiles, which was decreed on receipt of this command, did not remedy the barrenness of the soil. So the Thasians consulted the Pythian priestess again, complaining that the wrath of the god continued to afflict them although they had obeyed the oracle. Then the Pythian priestess answered them thus: *"But you have forgotten your great Theogenes."* They were at a loss how to recover the statue of Theogenes, when, as the story tells, fishermen who had put out to sea to fish caught the statue in their net and brought it back to the shore. The Thasians set his statue up again in its original position, and have preserved the custom of sacrificing to him as to a god.' Various epigraphic records, interpreted in the light of the literary

texts, have confirmed this witness of Pausanias. It must have been towards the
end of the fifth century or early in the fourth that the worship of Theogenes
was established at Thasos, at the time when the statue was set up again. Later, as
we learn from an inscription of the first century B.C., the subsequent part of
Pausanias' account and a passage of Lucian, Theogenes was mainly regarded as a
hero who healed the sick, specially capable of protecting his worshippers from
malaria, and his worship spread outside the island of Thasos.

Here we can see in action, in connection with an illustrious athlete, the way in
which glory gained in the games, which was a striking proof of divine favour,
could, in specially favourable circumstances, raise a man to the ranks of the gods:
the hyperbole with which poets flattered their clients in their triumphal odes
thus became a reality. Yet this elevation could only take place after death, because the Greeks regarded the dead with special reverence. Side by side with the
worship of the Olympians, they attached extreme importance to the cult of the
dead. This is what we have now to study.

*The cult of the dead. Funerary ritual and beliefs in Homer and during the Geometric
Age. Funerary stelae and statues in the Archaic Age. 'Heroization' of the dead.
Eschatological myths: Orphism. The Eleusinian Mysteries*
In Mycenaean society, an aristocratic society, we know about the worship of the
dead only through tombs and the furniture they contained. The monumental
architecture of the domed tombs, the richness of the contents of the shaft-
graves, and certain indications that reveal the existence of a funerary cult show
well enough what attention the Mycenaeans paid to honouring their dead. But
we do not know how they envisaged their destiny in the after-life. In Homer,
funeral rites are described at length in connection with the funeral of Patroclus:
the cremation of the corpse upon a pyre, the sacrifice of Trojan prisoners and pet
animals, horses and dogs, offerings of honey and oil, the gift of hair offered by
the survivors as a token of mourning, a funeral banquet, athletic sports in
memory of the deceased, the erection of a tomb—Book XXIII of the *Iliad* relates
all this in detail. Such funeral honours could hardly be thought of without some
belief in an after-life. Homer does in fact believe in a form of survival: it is in his
works that the idea of a soul (*psyche*) appears for the first time clearly expressed
in European literature. Being distinct from the body, it parts from it at the
moment of death and flies away to Hades, the abode of the dead. It is an image

(*eidolon*) of what the man was in life, but an image without weight or solidity, yet still capable of suffering and regretting the loss of life. The poet makes it appear on several occasions in dreams, as Patroclus's soul appears to Achilles: but it evades the vain embrace of its friend. It is only a magical performance, carried out by Ulysses in *Odyssey* XI, that enables the dead to be summoned up—the *Nekyia*, later to be portrayed by the great Polygnotus in the hall (*lesche*) of the Cnidians at Delphi: on drinking the blood of the victims collected in a trench, the souls recover for a little while some semblance of human existence. But it is only a false appearance of life and, though Ulysses can thus exchange some words with his mother's soul, it is in vain that he stretches out his arms to embrace it: 'Three times I moved towards her: with all my heart I longed to embrace her. Three times, like a shadow or a dream, she slipped out of my grasp.' These shades wandered in a meadow of asphodel, somewhere beneath the earth, beyond the gates of Hades, the abode of the dead, ruled over by a god of the same name. Funeral honours, especially cremation, were a necessary condition for the soul to reach this abode and there enjoy its cheerless repose. Such a conception of life beyond the grave offered little comfort to mortals. Homer's heroes love life and are distressed at the thought of losing it: but a feeling of inevitability fills them with a sort of resigned pessimism. The shade of Achilles, who was the most handsome and valiant of men, utters these bitter words: 'How I would rather, as a mere farm labourer, serve a poor countryman, in whose house there is little to eat, than reign as king in the world of the dead.'

Was it merely to bring some comfort to these desolate souls? Was it rather a dim realization that the dead, in their strange after-life, possess some supernatural power that could bring suffering to the living? Whatever may be the reason, it is a fact that Geometric burying-places and those of the early Archaic period preserve traces of a funeral cult: in Attic cemeteries we find sacrificial ashes near the tombs and the great vases standing above them served for libations. Moreover, a large stone set up in the grave or near it served as a mark, *sema*. By a development peculiar to the Hellenic world, this stone was later to become the funerary stele. At first the name of the dead person was inscribed on the barely rough-hewn block of stone, as we see in the necropolises of Thera (Santorin). Then towards the end of the seventh century, in Attica, a more exacting taste developed: the carefully cut stele, high and narrow and slightly tapering, was from now on fixed in a wider base. Before this time, about the middle of the century, the idea had already occurred, in Crete, of adorning funerary stelae, as in the Mycenaean Age, with the portrayal of a human form, at first in incised carving: a woman with a spindle or an armed warrior. God or mortal? Most probably the dead, in an idealized form, to whom homage is being rendered by the living. Subsequently such portrayals become very numerous and their meaning is no longer a matter of doubt. In Attica in the sixth century the most luxurious tombs are decorated with bas-reliefs representing the dead person, as for example, at the end of the century, the stele of the hoplite Aristion or, better still, the statues carved in the round which form the beautiful series of funerary *kouroi* ('youths'). Here the idealization is evident, although the inscriptions clearly show that the figures are portraits. For the portrait in no way aims at physical resemblance, which the Greeks never thought of seeking at this period: it is an ideal portrayal of the deceased, in the fullness of strength and beauty, as if death has endowed him with everlasting youth. Some stelae in Laconia, like the Chrysapha relief, dating from the middle of the sixth century, enable us to grasp more clearly the meaning of these funerary portrayals: here a deceased couple sit enthroned upon a chair of state, behind which rises the serpent associated with the earth-gods. The man holds a drinking-cup, the woman a pomegranate. Two small figures are bringing offerings to this divine couple: a cock, a flower, a pomegranate, and an egg. Here we have a funerary cult scene, in which the living are honouring their departed parents, henceforth regarded as divine. The deceased has been transformed into a *hero*, in the religious sense of the term, which means a man ranked among the Immortals after his death.

This phenomenon of 'heroization' is fundamental in Greek thought. Based on the dread and reverence spontaneously inspired by death, it continually developed from the early Archaic period down to the Hellenistic Age. Certainly the idea that every deceased person becomes a 'hero' did not become general until quite late, but it corresponded to a deep-seated tendency and indeed explains many aspects of Archaic and Classical funerary decoration. A bas-relief delicately carved on the bulge of a large marble funerary vase shows the dead woman, with her name Myrrhine inscribed beside her, being led to the Underworld by Hermes *psychopompos*, the divine 'conductor of souls', in the presence of three men, her relatives. The Athenian artist who, about 430–420 B.C., carved this bas-relief has represented Myrrhine, like Hermes, as taller than the three living men, thus implying that she is already one of the Immortals. The Attic vases of painted earthenware known as funerary *lecythoi* (perfume-bottles), belonging to the fifth century, show us many scenes of offerings at a tomb: the living, young women or youths, approach the tombstone, decorate it with fillets, place offerings of fruit, cakes, and perfume, make libations or simply meditate, recalling the image of the departed one. The series of sculptured Attic stelae is interrupted between the latter part of the sixth century and about 440 B.C.: in all probability they were forbidden by a sumptuary law soon after the overthrow of the Pisistratids. But from 440 until the end of the fourth century (when the philosopher Demetrius of Phalerum had them forbidden again), they number hundreds, with the image of the deceased sitting or standing, often surrounded by his kin, whose hand he is sometimes clasping. With a touching discretion, they convey to perfection the complex feelings of the Athenians of the Classical period when face to face with death: sorrow at separation, resignation in presence of the inevitable, the desire to assert the permanence of the bonds of kinship or friendship (that is what the hand-clasp means), and also the idea that the deceased enjoys a new dignity in the new world to which he has passed. Aristotle has expressed this conviction in very clear terms in a passage of his *Eudemus*, preserved by Plutarch: 'Not only do we believe that the dead enjoy the felicity of the blessed, but we also judge it impious to say anything false or slanderous about them, because we regard this as an outrage on beings who have become better and more powerful.'

Was this title 'blessed' (*makarios*) really promised to all the dead? It was tempting to think so, but no less tempting to ensure by means of some guarantee, acquired during one's life on earth, that one would thus enjoy eternal blessedness. This very natural precaution explains the popularity of Orphism and the Mysteries. Orphism was a philosophical and eschatological doctrine which the ancients ascribed to the mythical poet Orpheus. Although Herodotus, Euripides, Aristophanes, and Plato explicitly mention this doctrine, it remains very obscure for us: it found expression in poems ascribed to the Thracian singer, whose touching life-story was often called to mind, his musical and poetical genius, the part he played with the Argonauts in the quest of the Golden Fleece, his inconsolable mourning for the death of Eurydice and his tragic death at the hands of the frenzied Maenads on Mount Pangaeum. He was supposed to have taught mankind an ascetic ideal for living, based on abstinence from every kind of meat, rejection of blood sacrifices, and a rule that the dead must not be buried in woollen cerements. Moreover, Orphism propounded an eschatology of its own, describing the lot that awaits men in the world to come, where sinners would be harshly punished, while the just would enjoy a life of delight in the *Isles of the Blest*. The second *Olympic Ode* and a fragment from the *Threnoi* of Pindar are clearly inspired by this conception of the after-life, which the poet expresses in majestic verses. Orphism may also have taught the doctrine of *metempsychosis*, or transmigration of souls. The philosopher Pythagoras of Samos, who lived at Croton in Magna Graecia in the sixth century, came under the influence of Orphism and helped to spread it through his own teaching.

That these speculations about the other world must have played an influential rôle as early as the Classical period is shown by a recent discovery: in a tomb at Pharsalus, in Thessaly, a bronze urn dating from the middle of the fourth century has been found. It contained, hidden among ashes and fragments of bones, a little sheet of gold, five centimetres by one-and-a-half, bearing an inscription in cursive writing. It is a short poem, already known with some variants from Hellenistic records. Its text is as follows: 'On the right-hand side of Hades' palace you will find a spring. Near this spring stands a white cypress. Beware of approaching this spring. Further on you will find the cool stream that flows out from the Lake of Memory: guardians stand above it. They will ask you why you have come. Reveal the entire truth to them. Say: I am a son of Earth and of the starry Sky. Stellar is my name. My throat is parched with thirst: so let me drink from the spring.' The Pharsalus text goes no further, but a similar tablet, found at Petelia in southern Italy, gives us what follows: 'They will let you drink from the holy spring and then you will reign among the other heroes.' The properly 'Orphic' character of this poem has been questioned, but its connection with the eschatology outlined above seems clear. The Pharsalus tablet is a 'viaticum' which the deceased carried on his journey beyond the grave: by obeying the instructions which it contained, the soul was sure to obtain everlasting happiness.

Such was also the object aimed at by initiation into the Mysteries of Eleusis, whose connection with Orphism is clearly indicated by ancient writers such as Plutarch and Pausanias. The latter writes, with regard to the ritual taboo concerning the bean (I, 37, 4): 'Anyone who has been initiated at Eleusis or has read the poems known as Orphic knows what I mean.' The Mysteries, linked with the worship of Demeter, were believed to have been established by the goddess herself. 'When, after Kore had been carried off,' says Isocrates in his *Panegyricus* (IV, 28), 'Demeter in the course of her wanderings arrived in our country, she

153. HOMER

In the course of antiquity there were several types of 'portraits' of Homer, all entirely imaginary. This one, known from several Roman copies, corresponds to the idea of the poet current in the Hellenistic and Roman periods: an old man blind and inspired. Naples Museum.

154. CITHARA-PLAYER

Attic red-figure amphora (about 480 B.C.). The musician is striking the strings with the plectrum, which is attached to the cithara by a long cord. With his left hand he stops the vibration of the strings at the desired moment. The cithara was probably suspended from the left shoulder by a shoulder-belt (for the difference between lyre and cithara, see ill. 126). The cithara-player is singing while he plays and he has his head thrown backwards under the effect of inspiration. Boston Museum.

155. MAN PLAYING A DOUBLE FLUTE

Attic red-figure amphora by the painter of Cleophrades (about 500 B.C.). The double flute or aulos was held against the lips by a thin strap fixed by two strings. Over his long tunic the musician wears a sleeveless jacket of a very unusual type. The movement of the folds of his tunic shows that he is swinging vigorously to and fro while playing. British Museum.

156. ALCAEUS AND SAPPHO

Attic red-figure vase (about 480–470 B.C.). On this very unusual type of vase (an opening at the base enables it to be emptied without being moved), a vase-painter of great talent has portrayed the two great lyric poets of Lesbos, who had died nearly a century earlier. These imaginary 'portraits' show how one imagined these poets whose songs were accompanied on the lyre. Munich Museum.

157. ANACREON

Roman copy of a fifth-century statue. The original, which was certainly of bronze, is considered with probability to have been the work of Phidias. It is an imaginary portrait, executed half a century after Anacreon's death. The tree-trunk is an addition by the copyist. The poet was represented as playing the lyre (the instrument has disappeared along with the hands which held it): he was staggering slightly under the intoxicating influence of inspiration. Ny Carlsberg Museum of Sculpture, Copenhagen.

158. SOPHOCLES

Roman copy of a fourth-century statue. Although it was a posthumous portrait, there is no doubt about its individual character: the sculptor of the original (about 340–330 B.C.). must have been inspired by genuine portraits of the poet. Lateran Museum, Rome.

159. AESCHYLUS

Bust of the Roman period after an original portrait executed during the last years of the poet's life, shortly before his death in 456. The identifications have recently been put forward with sound reasons. Several engraved gems of the Roman Age are derived from this portrait. Capitoline Museum, Rome.

153

felt well disposed towards our ancestors, who rendered her services which only the initiates have the right to hear spoken of. She then gave them two gifts, the most precious that exist: agriculture, which enables us to live differently from wild beasts, and the Mysteries, which cause the faithful to form comforting hopes of what awaits them at the end of their lives and throughout the aeons of eternity.' There are close links between these two blessings, for, however imperfect our knowledge of the secret ceremonies of initiation, it is quite certain that rural rites, and especially rites of fertility, played an essential role. The initiate, who was known as a *mystes*, was made to handle objects and recite formulas connected with a form of sexual symbolism, then an equally symbolical spectacle was put on, a kind of sacred drama recalling the sorrowful quest of Demeter wandering in search of her lost daughter, and also various other scenes, including perhaps a 'sacred marriage', a fertility rite well known in other cults. The ceremony was completed by the presentation to the congregation of an ear of wheat. The indignant allusions made by the Christian Fathers, some of whom, like Clement of Alexandria, had perhaps themselves been initiated into the Eleusinian Mysteries before being converted to Christianity, are our main source of information about these Mysteries, whose secrets were very well kept, throughout the centuries, until the close of Antiquity. The polemical character of the information derived from these sources renders it somewhat suspect. In fact we find it hard to see how such rites succeeded in comforting the participants about the lot that awaited them in the after-life. Perhaps the mere fact that Demeter's daughter Kore, who, as Persephone, was the wife of Hades, was the queen of Hell, gave anyone who shared in her worship a sure hope of finding a kindly welcome in the world below. In any case, this confidence is an attested fact: it is particularly evident in Aristophanes' play the *Frogs*, performed in 405 B.C., at the worst moment of the Peloponnesian War. The poet presents to his audience, in the Underworld where Dionysus is venturing, a chorus of initiates which dances gaily in the meadows of the world beyond the grave, 'where for them alone the sun joyously sheds its light, because they have received initiation and have behaved as pious men towards strangers no less than towards their fellow-citizens' (ll. 454–459).

By way of compensation, we have a better knowledge of the social and non-secret aspect of these ceremonies, which, in the Classical Age, formed part of the great festivals of Athens. They were organized by priests traditionally belonging

R

to two great Eleusinian families: the *hierophant* belonged to the family of the Eumolpidae, the *dadouchos* and the sacred herald to that of the Kerykes. The ceremonies consisted of several parts and were divided into the Little Mysteries, held at Agra, a suburb of Athens on the banks of the Ilissus, in February, and the Great Mysteries, held at Eleusis at the end of September. The latter lasted several days, with defiling, in which the ephebes played an official part, sea-bathing by the *mystae* at the Piraeus, purifications, public prayers, a procession in waggons from Athens to Eleusis along the Sacred Way (it was during this procession that the incident of the *gephyrismoi* or 'banter from the bridge' took place), a night vigil at Eleusis close to the sanctuary of the Two Goddesses, a solemn sacrifice, and finally the actual ceremony of initiation. This took place in a hall specially built for this purpose, namely the *Telesterion*. On the site of the primitive building, Pisistratus had had another constructed, which was destroyed by the Persians in 480. Pericles commissioned Ictinus, the architect of the Parthenon, to erect a new building better suited to its purpose. In collaboration with other architects, Ictinus made the plans for the *Telesterion* whose ruins can still be seen today: it was a large square hall measuring fifty metres on each side, furnished on all four sides in the interior with tiers of seats cut in the rock; the roof was supported by six rows of seven columns. A central lantern-light provided lighting and ventilation. In the centre of the hall, a small structure, called the *Anactoron*, sheltered the sacred objects, like a sort of 'Holy of Holies'.

Foreign Greeks (but not Barbarians) could participate in the Mysteries with the same rights as Athenians. Still, the national character of the cult was never lost sight of: a senior magistrate, the king–archon, had as his main duty to provide for the celebration of the Eleusinian Mysteries, as Aristotle states in his *Constitution of Athens* (57). The Athenian government made it its business to provide for the worship of the Two Goddesses: an inscription has preserved the text of a decree, made about the time of the Peace of Nicias (421 B.C.). By this decree the people decided to dedicate to Demeter and Kore the firstfruits of the cereal harvest, in the proportion of $\frac{1}{600}$ of barley and $\frac{1}{1200}$ of wheat. The allied cities were expected to imitate Athens and the other Greek states were invited to join in this pious gesture. The sums derived from these firstfruits were to meet the religious expenses of the sanctuary. This attempt to associate the Greek cities as a whole with a specifically Attic cult does not seem to have met with great success. But many individual Greeks from other states associated themselves with the cult in the course of the centuries, and, to judge by the loyalty with which the secrets of the ritual were kept, they did so with conviction and sincerity.

Oracles and divination. Fortuitous omens. Verbal predictions. Sibyls and prophets.
Sanctuaries with oracles. Dodona. Delphi: its history, method of consultation, the
sanctuary. Gods as healers: Asclepios

Apart from the Great Games, which we have already dealt with, the only cults in the Hellenic world that drew large audiences were those of deities possessed of oracular powers and, towards the end of the Classical period, that of the god of healing. The desire to foresee the future and the desire to recover health are so natural to the heart of man that, in some specially favourable cases, they led the Greeks to rise above the traditional exclusiveness of the city-states.

The great number of the oracles and the trust placed in their predictions is a cause of astonishment in our age, which is, or at least professes to be, rationalistic. Yet it is an indisputable fact that the Greeks, inclined as they were to reasoning and scepticism, habitually consulted the oracles, no less in public affairs than where private interests were concerned. The historians, even those most anxious, as Thucydides was, to reconstruct the logical sequence of events, do not fail to draw our attention to the oracles and to the influence they exercised on the actions of men. As for Herodotus, who was more in sympathy with traditional beliefs than Thucydides, he mentions no fewer than eighteen sanctuaries possessing an oracle and ninety-six consultations of oracles, fifty-three in the case of Delphi alone. So his work is incomparably full of materials for anyone who wishes to study this original aspect of Greek religious thought. Later historians— Xenophon, Diodorus Siculus, Plutarch, and, once again, our good friend Pausanias—also add much to our information. Finally, oracular responses have been preserved in inscriptions from the later part of the fifth century onwards. Here, for example, is one of the earliest, found at Troezen and connected with the cult of Asclepios: 'Euthymidas dedicated [this offering] wishing to learn under what conditions he ought to approach the god after performing the ritual ablutions.' [*Reply*]: 'After having sacrificed to Heracles and Helios, after having seen a bird of good omen.'

This oracle, as we see, alludes to divination by means of birds. Prophecy and divination were, in fact, closely linked, and the Greeks practised both. Divination, the science of portents, was in constant use. A sacred law of Ephesus, dating from the second half of the sixth century, gives us information, unfortunately of a fragmentary kind, about the rules which made it possible to interpret the flight of birds: not only the direction, but also the manner of flight (in a straight line or in zigzags, with or without beating of wings) affected the meaning of the omen. As early as Homer's time, the Greek and Trojan soothsayers Calchas and Helenus were regarded as very skilful in this art. This form of divination was so popular that the very word bird, *ornis*, came to mean 'omen': Aristophanes plays on this ambiguity in a passage of his comedy *The Birds* (ll. 719–721).

There were, indeed, other kinds of divination: by signs in heaven, claps of thunder, earthquakes, or even a mere drop of rain, like the one that served as a pretext for Dicaeopolis, in Aristophanes' *Acharnians* (ll. 170–171), to procure a suspension of the session of the popular assembly and veto a decision that was not to his liking; by dreams, a frequent medium of heavenly apparitions from the Homeric Age onwards and a normal means of receiving the counsels of the god in several sanctuaries, particularly those of Asclepios; by inspection of the entrails of victims, especially the liver, from which favourable or unfavourable indications were derived: in the *Electra* of Euripides (ll. 825 ff.), Aegisthus is warned of his impending death by his inspection of the liver of a bull which he has just sacrificed, and in fact Orestes, who is standing beside him incognito, takes advantage of his agitation to slay him. The very flame that burnt on the altar could also provide portents: the soothsayers at Olympia had the responsibility of watching for omens in the fire upon the great altar of Zeus. Sacrificial divination, as we have seen, played an important part in the conduct of war. In the opinion of the Greeks the will of the gods also revealed itself by other means whose naïvety or vulgarity is astonishing to us: a word heard by the merest chance, which, by some twist, even an unintentional play on words, fitted the situation of the moment, or even a mere sneeze. In *Odyssey* XVII, it was a sneeze from Telemachus that decided Penelope to send for the beggar in rags who was really Ulysses in disguise. In *Anabasis* III, 2, 9, when the Greek mercenaries, deprived of their leader whom the Persian Tissaphernes had treacherously killed, were about to give way to despair, Xenophon, whom they had just elected as their commander, was trying to encourage them with a speech. While he was speaking, a man sneezed, and, when the soldiers heard it, they all spontaneously hailed the god with a gesture of reverence and Xenophon resumed as follows: 'Since at the moment when we were discussing means of achieving our salvation,

Zeus the Saviour revealed himself to us by an omen, I propose that we should make a vow to offer sacrifices of thanksgiving to that god as soon as we reach friendly territory.'

Side by side with these physical and fortuitous omens, there were plenty of predictions in verbal forms of an elaborate kind. They were derived from men to whom the gods had given the gift of prophecy, 'those who,' says Plato, 'by virtue of inspired divination so often guide many of us on the path of the future by means of their predictions' (*Phaedrus*, 244 b). Female prophets were known as Sibyls: Pausanias devotes a whole chapter to them (X, 12), which may have partly inspired Michelangelo when he painted on the ceiling of the Sistine Chapel the Sibyls of Delphi, Erythrae in Asia Minor, and Cumae in southern Italy. Male prophets were called Bakides. Collections of their prophecies were hawked around, and interpreters, known as *exegetai*, undertook to apply them to particular occasions, as was done in France for the prophecies of Nostradamus. These collections included the famous Sibylline Books which Tarquin the Proud was said to have bought from the Sibyl of Cumae and which were lost in the conflagration that destroyed the Capitol in 83 B.C. Of course there were impostors among the soothsayers: during the reign of the Pisistratids, a certain Onomacritus was banished from Athens for having included oracles made up by himself among those ascribed to the Athenian Musaeus. The professional soothsayers were not always favourably regarded by the public as a whole: Aristophanes on several occasions makes mockery of oracle-mongers (*chresmologoi*). But several of them played an important rôle in the political life of Athens: for example, Lampon, a friend and collaborator of Pericles, who reappears as the author of an amendment to the decree concerning the Eleusinian firstfruits, Diopithes, who put the philosopher Anaxagoras on trial for impiety, and Euthypro, whom we find in Plato discussing with Socrates the proper definition of piety in the dialogue named after him.

Omens and collections of oracles could not answer every need. When in difficulties, both private individuals and cities applied to the sanctuaries containing an oracle and submitted to it the problem that was troubling them. Such oracles, which issued prophecies on request, were numerous in the Greek world and new ones continued to be established down to Roman times. But they did not all enjoy the same repute, far from it! Most of them only catered for a local public, for example, the oracle in Demeter's sanctuary at Patras, in Achaea:

'Here,' says Pausanias (VII, 21, 12), 'there is a reliable oracle. It is not consulted about all kinds of questions, but only about the sick. A mirror is hung at the end of a fine string and let down as far as the spring, care being taken not to let it sink into the water, but merely to touch the surface. Then, after having prayed to the goddess and burnt incense, the inquirer looks in the mirror, which now shows the patient as either alive or dead.' Other oracles had a more widespread renown, for example that of Amphiaraus, on the borders of Attica and Boeotia, that of Trophonius at Lebadea in Boeotia, and that of Apollo in the sanctuary of the Branchidae (the *Didymeion*), near Miletus, in Ionia. These three oracles were consulted, so Herodotus tells us, along with those of Delphi and Dodona, by Croesus, the famous king of Lydia, who wished to test their respective veracity: we are told that only the oracles of Amphiaraus and Delphi provided him with satisfactory replies.

At Dodona, in a remote valley in the mountains of Epirus, about twenty kilometres southwest of Lake Janina, Zeus delivered his oracles at the foot of Mount Tomarus, by the voice of his oak-trees rustling in the wind. Hardly any traces remain of the buildings of the Classical Age, which must have been quite rudimentary. The tall sacred oak referred to by Ulysses in *Odyssey* XIV, 327–328, has of course disappeared: only a large walnut-tree still stands not far from the Hellenistic and Roman ruins. But our texts tell us of the priests who ministered in the sanctuary, the *Selloi*, who slept on the bare ground and never washed their feet, and of the three priestesses who told Herodotus a legend about the Egyptian origin of the oracle, which the historian refuses to accept as true. Zeus *Naios* spoke by the rustling foliage of the oak-trees, which was interpreted by the priests. There was also another means of knowing the will of the god, described by Strabo. The Corcyreans had offered to the sanctuary a bronze cauldron resting on a column. Beside it, on another column, rose a statue of a child holding a whip formed of three bronze chains: these chains when shaken by the wind struck the cauldron, whose vibrations the soothsayers interpreted as oracles. This is the reason why Callimachus, in his *Hymn to Delos* (1. 286), calls the Selloi 'the servants of the cauldron which is never silent'. It is rather as if we regarded bells as speaking! We must assume that the replies given by Zeus satisfied the pilgrims, since, from the Homeric Age to Roman times, Dodona was always a well-known and respected oracle. Certainly its remote and inaccessible situation, in the midst of the wild mountains of Epirus, hardly encouraged the Greek cities to send delegations to consult it. But this ancient oracle was always regarded with particular reverence and the inhabitants of the district never ceased to submit ingenious questions to it about their humble personal destinies. Excavations have brought to light, not only very fine bronze statuettes, but also large numbers of lead plates engraved with formulas for consulting the oracle, extending from the fourth century B.C. to Roman times. We can, for example, read the following inscription: 'Heraclidas asks the god if he will have offspring from his wife.' The oracle's reply is not known.

But no oracle could rival the one at Delphi. Apollo's sanctuary, resting upon the southern flank of Parnassus, beneath the precipitous Phaedriades, still offers the traveller an imposing view of the 'rocky site shaped like a theatre' described by Strabo (X, 417): 'In front of the town, on the southern side, rises Mount Kirphis with its steep escarpments. Between them the Plistus flows in the depths of the gorge.' On all sides there are steep slopes or precipitous rocks: this is certainly the *rocky Pytho*, as it is called in the Homeric *Hymn to Apollo*. Some greenery can be found today only on the slopes stretching down from the sanctuary to the torrent, on which the toil of man throughout the ages has planted olive-woods and reclaimed a little land by hoeing. The landscape, with its marked differences of level, is vast and awe-inspiring: Delphi is at a height of nearly 600 metres, the summit of the Phaedriades rises above 1,200 metres, and Cirphis, opposite, reaches nearly 900 metres. But the effect is not at all oppressive: a broad extent of sky stretches above the ridge of Cirphis, up which winds the road to Anticyra on the Gulf of Corinth; eastwards, the high valley of the Plistus opens out broadly towards the modern Arachova, on the road to Lebadea, Thebes and Athens; finally, though the view westward from the sanctuary is obstructed by a projecting spur of the mountains, continued lower down by the enormous mass of rock on which stood Crisa (now Chrysso), one need only climb a little or go a few hundred metres towards the west to reach a viewpoint overlooking the mountains of Locris, the olive-clad plain of Amphissa, and the upper end of the Bay of Galaxidi, where, in ancient times as today, there was, close to Itea, the landing-place for the district of the sanctuary. Such was the site on which the most famous oracle in the ancient world stood and prospered.

Homer has only one reference to it, in *Odyssey* VIII, 79–81. But as early as the seventh century the influence of Delphi became considerable. This was the period of colonization, and, influenced by religious scruples, intending colonists did not embark on the adventure without appealing to a god for advice. Cicero was later to write in *De Divinatione* I, 3: 'Is there a single Greek colony that was founded without an appeal to the oracles of Delphi or Dodona or that of Ammon?' Delphi was by far the one most patronized, as the stories of Battus at Cyrene and Phalanthus at Tarentum have shown. For the Mycenaean and Geometric Ages, excavations have brought to light only very simple buildings, crude earthenware statuettes of a female deity with her arms outstretched (the 'crescent-shaped idols'), some small bronzes representing male human figures, and pottery for everyday use. However, as early as the seventh century, discoveries begin to be of greater consequence: bronze shields with reliefs or incised decorations, helmets, bronze utensils including *tripods*, bronze cauldrons mounted upon three-legged stands, which later became the normal offering to Delphian Apollo. The first Sacred War (600–590 B.C.), by delivering Delphi from Phocian ascendancy and giving the sanctuary the permanent protection of the Amphic-tyonic League, increased the splendour of the oracle still more. The second part of the Homeric *Hymn to Apollo* (the 'Pythian sequel') must have been composed just after these events. A stone temple had been built in the seventh century. It was burnt down in 548. But around it the sanctuary already contained some ten buildings, mostly treasuries built by Greek cities. In order to rebuild the temple, an appeal was made to public generosity, which responded magnificently. The subscriptions poured in from every side, and that of the courtesan Rhodopis, for whom Sappho's brother had beggared himself at Naucratis, was received as gladly as the gifts of the Philhellenic Pharaoh Amasis: the reputation of the oracle, to which splendid offerings had already been sent some time before by Croesus, spread far beyond the boundaries of the Greek world. A powerful Athenian family, the Alcmaeonids, then in exile, undertook the rebuilding of the temple, and completed it in about 510 B.C., more magnificently than had been estimated for.

During the Persian Wars, the oracle was said to have been miraculously pre-served from invasion and plundering and it was enriched by the dedicatory offerings of the victorious Greeks. We have noticed elsewhere how, in the course of the fratricidal struggles which followed, the pride of the various cities was displayed at Delphi by rival offerings. In the fourth century, a new catastrophe, most probably a landslide, destroyed the Alcmaeonid temple (373 B.C.): once more the solidarity of the Greeks was revealed by the voluntary contributions made by cities and private citizens. The restoration, which was interrupted or delayed by the third and fourth Sacred Wars, continued down to the time of Alexander: the new temple, little different from the one it replaced, was to survive until the close of Antiquity. This is the one that was seen by Pausanias, several columns of which have recently been set up again by French archaeologists. In the fourth century, in spite of the plundering of the god's treasures by the Phocians, the sanctuary still continued to be embellished with offerings: Thebes and Cyrene, among others, set up elegantly designed treasuries to take their place beside those which the other Greek cities had erected in the course of earlier centuries.

This brief outline of a history which literary texts, monuments, and inscriptions will provide the means of studying in detail, will at least enable the reader to understand how great the prestige of Delphi was in Archaic and Classical times. The god had to give guidance, not only in colonizing enterprises, but also in religious matters, which were often closely connected with political matters. When the reformer Clisthenes had to give names to the ten tribes which he had established in Attica to replace the four traditional tribes, he left it to the Delphian oracle to choose ten names from among those of the hundred heroes proposed as possible patrons (*eponymoi*) of these new tribes. Even in the relationships between cities the oracle often had a word to say: that is why those whom its predictions did not favour sometimes accused it of self-interested bias, whether to the advantage of the Persians at the time of the Persian Wars, or in favour of Sparta in the second half of the fifth century, or lastly for the benefit of Philip of Macedon. The insinuation on these occasions was that the Pythia 'medized', 'laconized', or 'philippized'. In any case, whether these accusations were well founded or not, they hardly affected the reputation of Delphic Apollo. His rôle, in matters properly political, was more to provide a guaranty for the enterprises of powerful patrons than to interfere directly in affairs. When he became more closely involved in these, it was through the action of the Amphictyony, on the occasion of the Sacred Wars. Apart from these exceptional circumstances, Delphi was merely an observer, not an active participant.

Apollo, the god of all forms of knowledge, remained the highest religious and moral authority, the one that could point out effective means of putting an end to any national calamity by removing the traces of the pollution which caused it: so he did for Thasos in the matter of Theogenes, of whom we have already spoken. As well as being the sovereign upholder of religious traditions and the expert on rites of purification, the oracle also undertook to propound a certain form of wisdom. Two maxims were inscribed at the entrance to the temple: *Know thyself* and *Nothing in excess*. Counsels of practical morality? Useful reminders of the limits imposed by human weakness on the satisfaction of man's appetites and ambitions? Warnings against immoderation, the *hybris* to which so many tyrants yielded? Or was it deeper thought, advocating introspection and asceticism? It is not from the Delphian priesthood nor in the replies of the oracle that we should seek enlightenment about the real meaning of such precepts. It is sufficient for the glory of Delphian Apollo that Socrates and Plato, like Aeschylus and Pindar before them, meditated upon his maxims, by which the god showed himself to be, as he is called in Plato's *Republic* (IV, 427 c), 'the traditional spiritual director of all mankind'.

What was the manner of consulting the oracle? Our knowledge of this is still incomplete. It could only be done on certain appropriate days, which were so few that it was necessary to line up in the sanctuary. The Delphians could, in exchange for services rendered to the god or to their city, grant the privilege of *promanteia*, that is to say priority in consultation: this was a greatly appreciated favour, which the recipients readily recorded by inscriptions, such as the one which the Chians had carved in the fourth century on the altar of the great temple, whose cost they had met. Those consulting the oracle paid a sum of money, the *pelanos*, so called because it took the place of the ritual cake (which is what *pelanos* properly means) which had originally been the preliminary offering. This charge might vary in the case of different cities, according to the agreements made with the Delphians. It was considerably more when the consultation was made on behalf of a city rather than a private individual. After this a sacrifice was offered—according to Plutarch, a goat. Before being slaughtered, it was sprinkled with cold water: if it did not shiver, it was assumed that the god did not wish to answer and the consultation did not take place. Otherwise the inquirers, having handed over in writing the text of the question which they wished to put to the god, were admitted into the temple where the oracle was to be delivered.

The ruined state of the temple makes it impossible to identify the arrangement of its various parts with any precision. All we know is that, as in most of the great Greek temples, there was a vestibule and a large hall, at the far end of which was the oracular chamber, but no trace of the latter has survived on the site. It was situated on a lower level, since our texts tell us that one climbed down to it. Was there actually an underground chamber or did one merely go down some steps? There is no certain indication that enables us to decide. It seems that those consulting the oracle were not allowed to enter the innermost part, which was in fact the *adyton* (the 'place that may not be entered'), where the Pythia sat. The role of this prophetess, who was the god's instrument, is still something of a mystery. She was chosen from among the women of Delphi and lived a chaste and secluded life from the time when she was appointed as priestess. When consultations took place, she sat in the *adyton* upon a tripod, near a sacred dome-shaped stone called the 'navel' (*omphalos*), which was supposed to mark the centre of the earth. In the *adyton* there was a cleft in the rock from which, according to certain ancient authors, a kind of exhalation arose, which had the property of producing prophetic frenzy. In truth, the very reality of this exhalation is far from certain: it is probable that it never existed except in the imagination of those present, who associated it with the intervention of the god. Seated upon her tripod, the Pythia chewed bay leaves and drank water from a sacred spring, Cassotis, which rose some distance above the temple and, according to Pausanias, was believed to reappear in the *adyton* after flowing some distance underground. Then the prophetess fell into a sort of trance and mumbled indistinct words. Since most of the Delphic oracles which have been preserved are in verse, we are bound to acknowledge that the Pythia's prophecies underwent some subsequent elaboration before being transmitted to those concerned. It is assumed that the persons responsible for thus putting the oracles into shape were priestly officers who were called *prophetai*. A copy of every oracle was kept in the archives of the sanctuary.

Some of these prophecies are worded in an obscure or ambiguous manner: they justify the title *Loxias* ('crooked', 'devious') which was given to Delphian Apollo. This very obscurity, like the employment of a verse form, clearly indicates the most original feature of the oracle, namely its fundamentally verbal character. Even if many of our texts are fabrications forged *post eventum* (and this is not always easy to prove), these forgeries would have gained no credence if they had not been consistent with the usual type of oracles pronounced at Delphi. We must then acknowledge that the procedure outlined above was the normal procedure for Pythian consultations. Side by side with it, there were

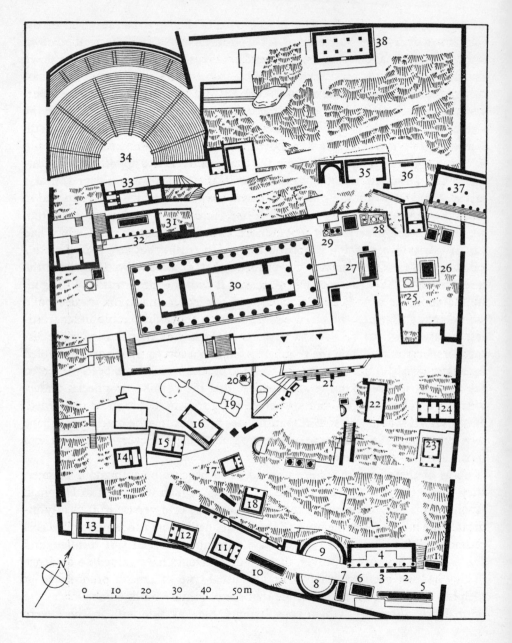

18. THE SANCTUARY OF DELPHI

(*After P. de la Coste Messelière*). This restored plan gives an idea of the over-crowding in the sanctuary in the middle of the second century B.C. In reality the offerings were much more numerous even than those whose remains are still visible on the site. In the following list, Hellenistic monuments are marked with an asterisk.

1. Bull of Corcyra.
2. Base of the Arcadians.
3.* Statue of Philopoemen(?).
4. Offering of Lysander after Aegospotami.
5. Base of Marathon, offering of the Athenians, the work of Phidias.
6. The Seven and the chariot, offering of the Argives.
7. The Trojan Horse, offering of the Argives.
8. The Epigoni, offering of the Argives.
9. The kings of Argos, offering of the Argives.
10. Horses and captive women, offering of the Tarentines.
11. Treasury of Sicyon.
12. Treasury of Siphnos.
13. Treasury of Thebes.
14. So-called Treasury of Potidaea.
15. Treasury of the Athenians.
16. Bouleuterion.
17. Treasury of Cnidus.
18. 'Anonymous Aeolic' Treasury.
19. Rock of the Sibyl.
20. Sphinx of the Naxians.
21. Portico of the Athenians.
22. Treasury of Corinth.
23. Treasury of Cyrene.
24. Prytaneum.
25. Tripod of Plataea.
26.* Chariot of the Rhodians.
27. Great Altar of Apollo, offering of Chios.
28. Tripods of Gelon, Hieron, Polyzelus, and Thrasybulus, sons of Dinomenes.
29. Palm-tree of the Eurymedon.

others, as has recently been proved from clear epigraphical evidence, which reveals a method of consultation by drawing of lots. In this case, the god chose one of two, or sometimes several, solutions written out beforehand by the inquirer. Did the Pythia also play a part in these cases? It is by no means certain.

If the secret of the Pythia remains hard to penetrate, in compensation the topography of the sanctuary is now well known. Since 1892, French excavations have opened up the ruins, previously covered by the village of Kastri, and brought to light a great number of sculptures, inscriptions, and small objects. They have also extended to the surroundings of the sanctuary and to the sanctuary of Athena, situated some distance from that of Apollo, towards the east. Thanks to the information drawn from these investigations, collated with the description given by Pausanias in Book X of his *Periegesis*, we can now identify upon the site, in spite of many uncertainties of detail, the principal buildings that surrounded the Temple of Apollo. It is an opportunity for us to form a concrete idea of a great Greek sanctuary.

A sanctuary was basically a piece of land (*temenos*) dedicated to the god and demarcated either by mere boundary marks or by an enclosing wall. At Delphi, Apollo had at his disposal a quadrilateral of 130 metres by 190, enclosed by a solid and well-bonded wall (*peribolos*), with several gates let into it. The plot of ground, which stretches to the immediate neighbourhood of the precipitous Phaedriades, is on a steep slope. Several large supporting walls made it possible to set out terraces, linked with one another by the main pathway, called the 'Sacred Way'. It traverses the sanctuary from the great gate, below to the east, to the esplanade of the temple, describing two successive hairpin bends. On each side of this road stand the 'treasuries' built by Greek cities, Sicyon, Siphnos, Thebes,

30.   Temple of Apollo.
31.   Site where the Charioteer was found.
32.* Alexander's hunt, offering of Craterus.
33.   The stage of the theatre.
34.   Orchestra and auditorium of the theatre.
35.   Offering of the Thessalian Daochus.
36.   Temenos of Neoptolemus.
37.* Portico of Attalus I.
38.   Lesche of Cnidus.

Athens, Syracuse, Cnidus, Corinth, Cyrene, and others, to which were added those of two Etruscan cities, Caere and Spina. In addition, a multitude of offerings attracted the interest of pilgrims by their sculptures and their inscriptions. We have already mentioned those which challenged one another near the entrance to the sanctuary.

The temple overlooked the slope from the height of its terrace, which was on two levels, each supported by a wall. The lower wall, called *polygonal* because of the kind of stonework employed for its facing on the outer side, dates from the second half of the sixth century. It is covered with inscriptions carved at late periods. Against its southern side leaned the Portico of the Athenians, which sheltered military and naval spoils of the fifth century. In front of this portico, the Sacred Way broadened out, forming a small and nearly circular 'piazza', named the *Halos* ('threshing-floor'): it was here that the sacred drama of the *Stepterion* was produced every eight years. By the final section of the Sacred Way, passing the tripod commemorating the Battle of Plataea, one reached the esplanade of the temple, fringed with votive offerings: the four tripods dedicated about 480–470 B.C. by Gelon and Hieron, tyrants of Syracuse, and by their brothers (they were turned into gold coinage by the Phocians during the third Sacred War), the bronze palm-tree dedicated by the Athenians after their victory at Eurymedon, the colossal Apollo called *Sitalcas*, a bronze statue more than 15 metres high, and dozens of other offerings, including the gilt statue of the courtesan Phryne by her lover Praxiteles. In front of the entrance to the temple, which was approached by a ramp, stood the altar offered by the town of Chios. The temple itself, of a type common in Greece, was surrounded by a Doric colonnade with six columns at each end and fifteen along the two sides, forming a quadrilateral of 24 metres by 60. Each column was about 11 metres high. Apart from the arrangements devised for consultation of the oracle, at the far end of the *cella*, of which we have little knowledge, the internal plan is in conformity with the usual type: an antechamber (*pronaos*) entered by a porch with two columns between the side-walls, then a great hall or *cella*, in which stood the cult statue. This room was the main part of the building, since the real function of the temple was to shelter the statue of the god. Lastly, at the back there was the *opisthodomos*, a kind of porch symmetrical with the *pronaos* but having no communication with the *cella*. Everywhere in the temple there were offerings, some of which had a history, for example the iron armchair on which Pindar sat and the bronze

160. EURIPIDES
Bust of the Roman period after a fourth-century statue, itself inspired by a genuine portrait. This type is represented by more than twenty-five surviving copies, which proves its popularity, corresponding to that of the poet after his death. By comparison with the severity of the portrait of Aeschylus and the serene nobility of that of Sophocles, Euripides' face expresses gentleness and melancholy. Ny Carlsberg Museum of Sculpture, Copenhagen.

161 & 162. HERODOTUS AND THUCYDIDES
In their admiration for Greek literature, cultured Romans often had portraits of classical authors carved for their gardens and libraries, sometimes joining the heads of two writers back to back on a single pillar. Such was the double herm of the historians Herodotus (ill. 161) and Thucydides (ill. 162), identified by means of an inscription. To judge by their characteristics of style, these two portraits seem to have been inspired by originals executed towards the end of the fifth century or early in the fourth. The features are sufficiently individualized for them to be regarded as faithful portraits. Naples Museum.

163. HIPPOCRATES
Bust of the Roman period, after an original portrait of the late fifth or early fourth century. A famous Hippocratic maxim is carved on the base which supported this bust, giving us the subject's identity. Ostia Museum.

164. SOCRATES
Bust of the Roman period. Three main types of the portrait of Socrates are known, all in keeping, though with some variations in detail, with the traditional type as described by Plato, according to whom the philosopher had the picturesque ugliness of a Silenus. The type to which the portrait belongs is the oldest and goes back to the early part of the fourth century, shortly after Socrates' death. Vatican Museum.

165. PLATO
Herm of the second century A.D. Nearly twenty replicas of this portrait are known, all probably derived from the statue which the sculptor Silanion made during Plato's lifetime, about 365 B.C. Ny Carlsberg Museum of Sculpture, Copenhagen.

166. THE PRONOMOS VASE
This famous voluted crater owes its name to the figure playing a double flute whom we see in the middle of the lower section of the picture (an inscription above his head shows that he was called Pronomos). Around him are a lyre-player and several choral dancers dressed as satyrs (one is holding his mask in his hand). In the upper section, Dionysus, with Ariadne beside him, is reclining on a couch just above Pronomos. To

161

162

163

164

167

168

169

the right there is a woman seated at the foot of the bed, holding a mask. Eros is handing her a garland. Further to the right are two actors, with their masks in their hands, representing Heracles and Silenus. A lively picture of the individuals taking part in a dramatic performance at Athens late in the fifth century or early in the fourth. Naples Museum.

167 & 169. CHORUSES FROM COMEDY
Attic black-figure goblet (early fifth century) decorated with two groups of choral dancers, one riding ostriches, the other dolphins. In front of each chorus there is a flute-player. Good examples of the fanciful imagination displayed in the costumes to prick the curiosity of the audience, even at an early period of Attic comedy. Boston Museum.

168. THE HORSEMEN
Attic black-figure amphora (third quarter of the sixth century). A chorus of horsemen, mounted on men disguised as horses, advances to the music of the double flute. In the age of Thespis it already shows the same masquerade as that of the *Knights* of Aristophanes more than a century later. Berlin Museum.

170. DEMOSTHENES
Roman copy of a famous posthumous portrait by the sculptor Polyeuctus, set up in the Agora at Athens in 280 B.C. The orator is portrayed in the costume which he habitually wore when delivering his speeches. With his hands joined, he is reflecting before beginning to speak. Ny Carlsberg Museum of Sculpture, Copenhagen.

171. AESCHINES
Roman copy of a portrait of the orator made in the second half of the fourth century. Compare the posthumous statue of Sophocles (ill. 158), which dates from the same time. The originals of these statues (and also of that of Demosthenes) were of bronze. Naples Museum.

S

statue of Homer, its pedestal inscribed with the obscure oracle supposed to have been given to the poet when he wished to know what was his native city. Moreover (and this was unusual), the *cella* contained two altars, one an altar of Poseidon (the *Earth-shaker*, as the Greeks called him, was specially honoured at Delphi, where earthquakes were frequent), the other an altar of Apollo himself.

Above the temple stretched an area which particularly suffered from the catastrophe of 373 B.C.: landslides and falling rocks, which destroyed the temple of the Alcmaeonids, had at the same time devastated all the northern part of the sanctuary. It was here, behind the supporting wall built after the catastrophe to protect the new temple, that the fragments were found of the group to which belonged the famous *Charioteer*, itself preserved almost intact by a remarkable stroke of fortune. Further up, the northwest corner of the sanctuary was occupied at the beginning of the Hellenistic Age by the theatre, which we can still see today in the form given to it by a restoration in the Roman period. On the eastern side of it there was a little *temenos* with a chapel sacred to Poseidon, in the middle of the boulders which his anger had brought crashing down from the Phaedriades, and farther still, in another *temenos* also enclosed in that of Apollo, men venerated the tomb of Achilles' son Neoptolemus, who had died in Delphi at the hands of the Delphians, as described in Euripides' *Andromache* (ll. 1085 ff.). Finally, right at the top of the sanctuary, against the northern wall, the pavilion (*lesche*) of the Cnidians sheltered famous pictures of Polygnotus, described in careful detail by Pausanias.

Such was the appearance of a great Greek sanctuary of the Classical Age, in which as a rule several other cults found shelter along with the main deity. Numerous buildings stood around the temples: altars, treasuries, shelters for pilgrims, built throughout the ages, in a disorder which reveals the absence of any unified plan. Each building was devised for itself and not as a part of the whole. Religious proprieties and practical necessities were alone taken into consideration. The care to create beauty corresponded in the first place with the desire to honour the god, and secondly with the desire to dazzle the spectator and outshine the neighbouring monuments without any concern for producing harmony with them. It was not until the Hellenistic Age, and first under the influence of the architects of Pergamum, that the principles of town planning for public buildings began to emerge: on the Acropolis at Athens, as one entered the sanctuary after passing through the Propylaea, one saw only the top of the posterior façade of the Parthenon, all the rest being concealed by lesser buildings which have now disappeared. Even the famous frieze which we can today admire at close quarters in museums was barely visible and very badly illuminated above the external wall of the *cella*, shrouded in darkness by the colonnade of the peristyle: we can realize this by looking at the frieze on the west side, which is still in its original position above the entrance to the *opisthodomos*. It had nevertheless been carved with devoted care: its purpose was to please the goddess. The same applies to the offerings which were crowded into every available space, without any consideration for systematic composition. We find it difficult to imagine the profusion of these votive offerings, mostly bronzes, of which there were hundreds; they have all been plundered by Barbarians or destroyed by Christians, and the survival of such a statue as the Charioteer is quite exceptional (his horses and chariot have almost completely disappeared). But the very detailed lists of Pausanias, though they represent only a selection of the public buildings that he saw, enable us to some degree to imagine the remarkable jumble of a sanctuary crowded with offerings, in which the eye was distracted on every side both by the brilliant gilt on the bronzes, which a systematic method of cleaning, well known from inscriptions, preserved from patina, and by the marble sculptures, painted in bright colours, which gave life to the pediments, metopes, and friezes on the main buildings. Then there was the throng of pilgrims, the peddlers' stalls, the donkeys and the mules, the beasts for sacrifice, the flocks of birds that nested under the roofs of the temples and which young Ion, at the beginning of Euripides' play, tries to drive away with his arrows. Add to this the festoons of flowers, the perfumes of incense, the smell of roasting meat, calling and shouting, and then we shall have called up to our mind's eye the appearance of these sacred precincts in which the Greek people met together, in order to find, in the presence of the god venerated by their simple faith, advice for some enterprise or comfort for their miseries.

Hope of healing has always been one of the most powerful motives for religious belief. When attacked by illness the Greeks turned naturally to their gods. The local god, whoever he might be, was their first resort. But Apollo was regarded more specially as a healer, and several of his cult titles, *Paean, Epikourios, Alexikakos* and *Akesios*, refer to this quality. Certain heroes played the same rôle: there was in Attica in the fourth century a *Heros Iatros* ('Physician') who was known only by this name. From the latter part of the fifth century, the popularity of these healers was eclipsed by Asclepios, a deity specializing in this function. An incident in the life of Sophocles illustrates the success of this new god: Sophocles was a priest of a hero healer, of whom we have little knowledge, called *Alcon*, or perhaps *Amynos*, and later he also became a devotee of the cult of Asclepios, composed a paean in honour of this god, and sheltered his statue in his own house when, in 421, the Athenians had it brought from Epidaurus to set it up in a sanctuary prepared for it close to the Theatre of Dionysus, on the southern side of the Acropolis. So at this period Asclepios had already been raised to the ranks of the gods, whereas Pindar, when he composed his third *Pythian Ode* in 474, spoke of him only as a hero, a son of Apollo, brought up in the study of the art of medicine by the Centaur Chiron and finally struck with lightning by Zeus for having broken the laws of nature by restoring a dead man to life. It was in connection with Asclepios that the Theban poet produced the admirable maxim: 'Aspire not, my soul, to immortal life, but be content to exhaust all practicable possibilities.'

Asclepios was worshipped in a sanctuary of Apollo at Epidaurus in Argolis, where he soon became the principal deity. His renown became great because of spectacular cures. This was the time (the last thirty years of the fifth century) when clinical medicine became established, thanks to Hippocrates of Cos. From Epidaurus the new cult spread through the Greek world with astonishing speed: to Athens and the Piraeus (where Aristophanes in his *Plutus*, performed in 388, represents the healing of the blind Plutus as taking place), to Delphi, Pergamum, Cyrene (where the *Asclepieion* of Balagrai was founded in the fourth century), and Cos, Hippocrates' native place, where an important school of medicine grew up. Epidaurus, the original sanctuary, remained the most famous and the most frequented: its prosperity in the fourth century is attested by a fine temple, a mysterious rotunda designed by the architect Polycletus the Younger, a theatre built by the same architect, and numerous buildings connected with the cult. The faith of the pilgrims and their hopes were strengthened by reading about the miraculous cures accomplished by the god, as recorded in the fourth-century inscriptions which Pausanias saw and some of which have been discovered: sixty-six miracles by Asclepios are thus described in detail, from the healing of a dumb girl and the delivery of a woman who had been pregnant five years to the removal of a stone or a tapeworm. We can even see the god carrying his benevolence so far as to repair by a miracle a vase that had been broken through falling! Few texts more clearly reveal the ingenuous piety of the Greeks than these edifying case-histories compiled by some unknown official drawing upon the archives of the sanctuary or commenting on ancient offerings whose meaning he does not always understand.

Polytheism. 'Multivalence' and multiplicity of the gods. Multiplication of minor divinities. Proliferation of heroes. Deification of allegories. Welcome offered to foreign gods. Daimones

This brief survey of the main acts of worship shows how close the Greeks felt to their gods during the Archaic and Classical Ages. The gods, in their almost boundless multiplicity, revealed themselves to mankind on every side, both in the forces of nature and in the life of the human community. Every deity of a place or of a group responded with remarkable adaptability to the essential needs of man and showed himself graciously disposed towards man's various petitions. This 'multivalence' of the deity is one of the features of Hellenic polytheism that rationalizing mythology, by organizing Olympus on hierarchical lines, and systematically defining the specialized functions of each deity, has most concealed from our view. Nevertheless, it remains quite visible in the case of the great national divinities that occupy the first place in individual cities. In Athens, this was Pallas; in Argos and Samos, Hera; in Sparta, Miletus, and Cyrene, Apollo; in Ephesus, Artemis; in Thasos, Heracles; in Lampsacus, Priapus. This local primacy was due to historical circumstances, but it can be observed that, through all the variety of legends and cult traditions, any major divinity almost everywhere assumed the same functions as guardian of the social group. In the Hellenistic Age this came to be expressed by personal participation on the part of the god in the administration of the city, when, in the absence of any citizen capable of meeting the expenses involved by the supreme magistracy, the god himself (with his sacred treasury) assumed this eponymous magistracy and, by virtue of this office, had his name entered for a year at the head of all official documents.

But this pre-eminence was not always to be found, and even in cases where it was evident it did not hinder the proliferation of cults. Even the calendar, which regulated the life of the several states and differed from one to another, was essentially a calendar of religious festivals, the regular celebration of which marked the return of each new season. Just as the town and the country had sanctuaries at regular intervals, so the months of the year were marked by a succession of sacred ceremonies, which were so many landmarks to indicate the passage of time. When by chance, as a result of faulty astronomical calculations, a too perceptible discrepancy between the official calendar and the sun's course arose, it caused great embarrassment, as at Athens about 430 B.C., when the astronomer and geometrician Meton reformed the calendar. 'You Athenians are not capable,' says Aristophanes in the *Clouds*, 'of observing the normal succession of days, but you turn it topsy-turvy!' (ll. 615–616). Hence Thucydides, with the precision that was second nature to him, does not date his narrative by an unreliable calendar, but merely by reference to the beginning of each season.

So, for the Greek, both the physical universe and the mental universe were completely interpenetrated with sacred influences. The variety of divine revelations enabled each man to seize upon the one that suited his temperament, his traditions, and the circumstances of his case. Side by side with the great Panhellenic gods, whose name commanded all men's veneration, but whose titles qualified them to fulfil some special function, there was the multitude of lesser gods, attached to some spot of earth, whose renown scarcely spread beyond the limits of the canton. Among these, heroes formed a numerous category, with characteristics all its own. There has long been discussion on the question whether the heroes were ancient gods fallen from their divine estate, or mortals who had been raised to divine rank. According to circumstances, either explanation may be the right one; nevertheless, during the historical period, the elevation of a mortal to heroic status is attested by many examples. The founders of colonial cities frequently received heroic honours, which were paid to them at their tomb, often situated at the city centre, in the agora. Amphipolis provides a characteristic example: when Brasidas's forces captured the city from the Athenians and Brasidas fell while victoriously defending it against an expedition led by Cleon, the Amphipolitans buried Brasidas in the main square, 'marked out a sanctuary around his tomb and paid him heroic honours, with annual games and sacrifices', regarding him thenceforth as the true founder of their city (Thucydides, V, 11). As time went on, men even began to propose such honours for the living. That is what the Thasians wished to do for Agesilaus, which, according to Plutarch, brought them an ironical reply: 'The Thasians, to whom Agesilaus had rendered great services, erected a temple in his honour and placed him among the ranks of the gods, and then sent a delegation to inform him. Agesilaus read the details of these honours, as communicated to him by the delegates, and then asked them if their country had the power to change men into gods. When they replied in the affirmative, *Well then,* said he, *change yourselves into gods! If you can manage that I am quite willing to believe that you can make a god of me too.'* (*Moralia, Lacedae-monian Apophthegms,* 210 d). The reaction of Agesilaus, a true Spartan devoted to his traditions, shows that deification of the living was repugnant to the religious conscience of the Greeks of the Classical Age. But later, in the Hellenistic Age, the practice spread widely and became toadying pure and simple.

There was yet another means of adding to the already crowded pantheon: the deification of allegories. The Greek, devoted as he was to language and with a great gift for the abstract, had a natural inclination to personify abstract ideas by converting ordinary words into proper names. In Homer we already find divine figures of this kind, such as the *Moirai* (Fates) and *Eris* (Discord). Hesiod paid special attention to this class of gods: an important place is given in his work to *Dike* (Justice) and *Mnemosyne* (Memory). The tendency to deify abstractions became greater and greater in Classical times, and temples were set up in honour of *Themis* (Divine Law) and *Nemesis* (Divine Vengeance), while altars were dedicated to *Eirene* (Peace) and her son *Ploutos* (Wealth). It is remarkable that Aristophanes, closely attached though he was by his mentality to traditional beliefs, was favourably disposed to deified allegories; Plato's behaviour on this point was in no way different. The happiest creation in this sphere was *Eros* (Love), at first imagined as a winged youth, later made younger and represented as a child; with his companions *Himeros* and *Pothos,* personifications of amorous Desire in two slightly different aspects, and *Peitho* (Persuasion), he belonged to the retinue of Aphrodite and provided both poets and artists with rich themes of inspiration.

A religious faith that offered so ready a welcome to new forms of divinity was not likely to show itself hostile to alien gods, except in so far as their introduction might threaten the foundations of the state. In fact the Greeks, throughout their long history, never ceased to welcome new gods, from the earliest times down to the establishment of Christianity. But, during the Archaic and Classical Ages, these acts of adoption implied assimilation to the customary modes of Greek religious thought. A very remarkable feature of this thought was its extraordinary ability to discover the known beneath the unknown, to recognize the familiar beneath the exotic. No one shows this tendency more clearly than the historian Herodotus when he turns his attention with sympathetic curiosity to the religious

172. TEMPLE AT BASSAE

Isolated in the mountains of Arcadia, the temple of Apollo Epicourios was erected in the second half of the fifth century on plans drawn up by Ictinus, the architect of the Parthenon. Surrounded by a Doric colonnade, it was embellished in the interior with an Ionic colonnade composed of semi-columns joined to the wall by a kind of pillar, the whole forming a series of recesses. On a level with the fifth inner side column, this colonnade turned at a right angle towards a detached central column: this column and the two adjoining semi-columns had Corinthian capitals, the oldest known. Above the inner columns thus disposed ran an Ionic sculptured frieze (Amazonomachy and Centauromachy, now in the British Museum). The temple was built of local limestone, except for the capitals of the inner colonnade, and the frieze, which were of marble.

173 & 174. TEMPLE OF APHAIA IN AEGINA

Built during the very earliest years of the fifth century, it is a perfect example of Doric architecture. The material employed was an excellent freestone. A facing of stucco gave it vividness. Part of the entablature above the outer colonnade has recently been put back in its place and also some columns of the inner two-storied colonnade (see ill. 174) which helped to support the ceiling and the framework. The two pediments were adorned with marble statues (see ill. 224), representing battles before the walls of Troy, with Athena in the centre of each pediment. The statues found are at Munich.

175 & 176. SO-CALLED TEMPLE OF NEPTUNE AT PAESTUM

One of the best preserved Greek temples. Built of local limestone, it still has its whole external colonnade with its two pediments (see ill. 215) and a part of its inner two-storied colonnade (ill. 175). In front of the main façade, towards the east, the base of the altar is still in existence (ill. 176). This temple was probably dedicated to Hera.

177. THE PARTHENON SEEN FROM THE PROPYLAEA

The building stands out against the light of the morning sun, above the rocky surface of the Acropolis. In ancient times, the buildings of the Chalkotheke partly concealed the west front of the temple, which could be seen in its entirety only after coming about half-way towards it from the Propylaea.

178. INTERIOR OF THE TEMPLE AT SEGESTA

Ever since the end of the fifth century, this temple has remained unfinished; only the outer colonnade has been set up. The columns have never been fluted, since this operation was the last to be carried out.

173

174

178

179. THE INNER PORCH OF THE PROPYLAEA SEEN FROM THE SOUTH
This side view shows the traces of incompletion on the southern face of the side wall:
the lugs which had been used for shifting and placing the blocks of marble are still
visible, the final work of re-dressing the surface never having been carried out.

180. THE PARTHENON: WEST ANGLE OF THE NORTHERN SIDE
Note the severe perfection of the fluting, made possible by the fact that it was done
after the column had been set up. The metope at the corner is the only one that was not
cut off by the Christians (they took it for an Annunciation). The mutules adorning the
lower surface of the cornice are clearly visible. The gutter has survived at the angle with
a gargoyle in the form of a lion's snout.

customs of the Barbarians. It never enters his mind that these peoples could worship other gods than those of the Hellenic pantheon: his only desire is to disclose the underlying equivalence which can be discerned in spite of differences in name and peculiarities of ritual. This is why, for example, he believes he can identify the worship of Athena among the tribes of Libya (IV, 180 and 189). Above all, it is the reason why, in Book II, he offers us such a curious picture of Egyptian religion, in which each divinity is immediately and unhesitatingly identified with a Greek god: for Herodotus, Neith is Athena, Bast Artemis, Isis Demeter, Ra Helios, Uto Leto, Osiris Dionysus, Khonsu Heracles, Hathor Aphrodite, Amun (Ammon) Zeus. It is also the reason why the Greeks had no difficulty in adopting the worship of Zeus Ammon from the fifth century onwards; this cult was a product of assimilation between the supreme god of the Egyptians, as worshipped in his oracular sanctuary at the oasis of Siwa, and the supreme god of the Greeks, as brought by the Cyrenaean colonists to their home in Libya. There was a similar development in the case of the Thracian goddess Bendis, whom Herodotus identifies with Artemis (IV, 33) and who was so soon after (429–428 B.C.) to be honoured in Athens with a cult that became brilliant and famous.

Even when no equivalence with a pre-existing Greek god could be discerned, a foreign deity could still be admitted to the Hellenic pantheon, provided that his aspect was acceptable to the visual, if not the mental, habits of his new worshippers. So it was with the Carian goddess Hecate, the keeper of gates, admitted by the Greeks as early as the Archaic Age, venerated for her magic powers and celebrated by the poets, from Hesiod to Euripides: great artists like Myron helped to fix her threefold image. The worship of the Great Mother, which included mysteries, was brought from Phrygia and introduced at Athens, not without some opposition, on the strength of certain points of resemblance to the Eleusinian cults, but she was definitely accepted by the fifth century, since the building dedicated to her was actually in the Agora and was also used as the official record-office for the city archives. It was Phidias, or perhaps his pupil Agoracritus, who was commissioned to carve the marble statue which gave the Athenian imagination a precise image of the Mother of the Gods: a draped female figure seated on a throne, with a tall cylindrical kind of headgear, holding a patera for libations in her right hand and a *tympanon* (tambourine) in the left, and flanked by two recumbent lions. When once fixed, the sculptural type provided the model for miniature votive offerings in hundreds down to the end of Antiquity. In contrast, another Phrygian cult, that of Sabazius, which also included mysteries and was akin to the worship of Dionysus, was always eyed with distrust, at least during the Classical Age: Aristophanes mocks it repeatedly and Demosthenes, in his speech *De Corona* (259 ff.), violently condemns his opponent Aeschines for having practised it in his youth.

Finally, there was yet another aspect of this polytheism whose multifarious elements we must not seek to define with an excess of rigorous logic: in addition to the traditional gods, the heroes, the personifications, and the foreign gods, the Greeks also found a place in their beliefs for what they called *daimones*. There is no more vague religious term than this. The word *daimon* can very well be applied to a god and sometimes appears, both in Homer and in later authors, merely as an equivalent of *theos*, 'god', especially when the object is to express a general or collective notion of some divinity. But its main use is to designate supernatural beings with no very individual characteristics and inferior in rank to the great traditional gods: in Hesiod the term is applied to the men of the Golden Age, elsewhere to deceased individuals who have been deified, or again to the *Agathos Daimon*, a 'demon' who watched over the family hearth and was often represented in the form of a serpent. Wide scope was thus offered to the creative imagination in the sphere of religious faith. Side by side with and underneath the traditional cults, with their solid foundations of ritual, the divine world admitted all kinds of individual beliefs, on the sole condition that they in no way threatened to weaken the foundations of society. This variety, this lack of precision, these uncertainties, contributed much to the vitality of Greek religion, which could easily renew or enrich its spiritual content while deriving advantage from the permanence of its rites: it was based upon traditions but knew no dogmas.

Critical spirit versus traditional religion. Scepticism and unbelief: Xenophanes, Anaxagoras. The trial of Socrates
One can easily imagine that, under these conditions, great intellectual boldness in religious matters was shown at an early period without causing too much scandal in so far as it kept within the limits of pure speculation. In a religion without dogma, without a priestly caste, or sacred books, great liberty was left to individual interpretation. The Greeks did not hesitate to take advantage of it. We have

already indicated the great independence of the poets with regard to the traditional myths, which they modified without hesitation at the prompting of their
imagination or their moral preferences. We have also seen how readily the terms
of extreme familiarity on which the Greeks lived with their gods encouraged
them to make fun of them without regard for the divine majesty: caricatures and
comedies give plenty of evidence of this. But speculative thought showed no less
audacity and attracted no censure except when it appeared dangerous to the
social system. As long as it confined itself to the domain of ideas, though it might
shock thinkers, it did not shock politicians. Plato, in the *Laws*, denounces ath-
eism with extreme vigour because he regards it as an intellectual error which en-
dangers the very principles of the ideal city. But the actual history of Greece
shows hardly any prosecutions of atheists except in so far as they aimed to evade
the obligations imposed on any citizen. Unbelief did not become a crime until it
turned into impiety.

This accounts for the extraordinary freedom of the criticisms of polytheism
made by some thinkers even before the Classical Age. In the sixth century,
Xenophanes of Colophon, a contemporary of Pythagoras, and, like him, resident
in Magna Graecia (where he founded, at Elea in Lucania, the so-called Eleatic
School, of which Parmenides and Zeno were shining lights), shows in some
trenchant verses that anthropomorphism is merely an ingenuous reflection of
human frailty: 'If cattle, horses, or lions had hands and could thus paint and
fashion works of art as men do, horses would paint their gods in the form of
horses, cattle in the form of cattle, each giving the gods the shape of his own
body.' Or again: 'The Ethiopians say that the gods have flat noses and black
skin, the Thracians that they have blue eyes and red hair.' And in fact Xenophanes, rejecting anthropomorphism, if not polytheism too, considers that the
multiplicity of gods, if it is a reality, is subordinate to a divine principle both
vague and eternal.

Later, in the fifth century, Anaxagoras of Clazomenae, the friend of Pericles,
was condemned at Athens for having thrown doubt on the divinity of the heavenly
bodies by teaching that the sun is a ball of fire whose light is reflected by the
moon. By these revelations he was likely to make the public less credulous with
regard to divination by atmospheric signs. So the professional soothsayers, led by
Diopithes, attacked him vehemently, after having had a decree passed by the
people authorizing the prosecution of any who did not believe in the gods or

claimed to teach the nature of celestial phenomena. Pericles' enemies took advantage of this to try to attack him through one of his intimate friends: Anaxagoras left the city in alarm. And yet many Athenians at this period, Alcibiades to begin with, did not hide the religious scepticism that the lectures of such teachers as Anaxagoras or Protagoras had instilled in them: nevertheless they were not put on trial. To arouse the anger of the state in matters of religion, there had to be either a political reason, which unbelief merely provided with a pretext, or else a positive act of sacrilege, such as the burlesque of the Eleusinian Mysteries in which Alcibiades took part, or the mutilation of the Hermae which roused the fury of the Athenians just before the departure of the Sicilian expedition. In such cases as these, Athenian justice acted with the utmost severity: thus Diagoras of Melos was prosecuted in 415 for sacrilege against the Mysteries and had a price put on his head after he left Athens. We learn from a famous speech of Lysias that severe punishment was inflicted on anyone who, even unintentionally, destroyed one of the olive-trees dedicated to the goddess Athena: Aristotle informs us that originally even the death penalty was provided for by the law. The public conscience felt that, if the profanation committed by the culprit was not punished in an examplary manner, it would arouse the wrath of the gods and the whole city would suffer for it. So it was not so much a criminal opinion as an offence against civic solidarity that was to be punished.

This also applies to the trial of Socrates in 399 B.C. The philosopher was accused, it will be remembered, of corrupting the young, of not believing in the gods of the city, and of introducing new divinities. The accusation was conducted by Meletus, a comparatively obscure young man, aided by Anytus, a politician who had played a prominent role in the democratic party during the preceding years. Socrates was found guilty by 280 votes to 220, the tribunal consisting of 500 jurymen: with thirty more votes, he would have been acquitted. Why this condemnation of a sage whom the Pythia had named as the wisest man alive? How are we to account for a verdict which, ever since the publication of Plato's and Xenophon's tracts in defence of Socrates, has been regarded as the unatonable shame of Athenian democracy? Consideration of the circumstances of the trial makes it quite easy to answer these questions.

The honest citizens of whom the court of the *Heliaea* was composed, and of whom Philocleon in Aristophanes' *Wasps* was a caricature in advance, harboured, though not without misgiving, a grievance against Socrates for having played a part by his conversations and his friendship in forming the character of some of the cold-hearted self-seekers from whom Athens had suffered so much in the previous fifteen years: Alcibiades, the promoter of the disastrous Sicilian expedition and later the too clever adviser of Lacedaemon against his own country; Critias, the greedy and cynical leader of the Thirty, who had brought death upon so many Athenians after overthrowing the democracy. The close relations between both of these and Socrates were known to everyone and the jury could not be entirely blamed for holding the master partly responsible for the wrong done by his disciples, especially as, throughout the time of their youth, Socrates' friends had done nothing to conceal tastes for which the decent people of Athens had little liking: prejudices in favour of Sparta, which they regarded as a city better governed than Athens; a philosophical curiosity and a mastery of dialectics which they had largely derived from their master's example and which endowed them with such a decisive advantage in argument that the other party to the discussion could not fail to take offence; a freedom of judgment which, combined with their youthful fieriness, led them to question the most firmly established certainties; finally—and this was not the least important thing—an avowed inclination for paederasty, the 'Dorian' form of love so much in favour in Sparta, which they were prone to discuss in their little circle, as Plato's *Symposium* shows only too clearly, and which they practised without the least embarrassment. Now the ordinary Athenian, as the reader of Aristophanes knows full well, loathed and despised this form of vice: he saw in it, and with good reason, not only mental and physical abnormality, but also the rallying-sign of an aristocratic 'fraternity', an association with political designs which the democracy had every reason to distrust. All these far too self-satisfied young men, mostly members of the richest families in Athens, hardly inspired friendly feelings in any who did not belong to their set. Socrates, upon whom they lavished a veneration not easily understood by outsiders, bore the brunt of the hostility which they aroused. Thus there seemed to be serious grounds for the accusation of corrupting the young: when we read the worthy Xenophon, and Plato who dazzles us with the radiance of his genius, we hear only one side of the case.

In addition to these circumstances, which are perhaps to be regarded as excuses rather than justifications, there was the religious aspect of the trial, which at the same time concerned the state. Here we must look the facts in the face without adopting too hastily the bitter indignation of the disciples stricken in their

admiration for a master who had succeeded in beguiling them. Did Socrates
constitute a menace to the moral and political equilibrium of Athenian democracy? One can unhesitatingly answer 'yes'. When we read the earliest dialogues
of Plato, we see Socrates, even more than in the commonplace hero-worship of
Xenophon's *Memorabilia*, as a very clever sophist, capable of getting the better
of the most wily opponents, like Protagoras or Gorgias, by the use of a superior
dialectic, itself not free from questionable methods, such as, for example,
quibbling based on the various meanings of a word. This weapon, which Socrates
wields like a master, is used to involve the other speaker in self-contradiction and
to make him feel that he is no longer sure of anything, a decidedly uncomfortable
position which is perhaps the necessary starting-point for any true philosophy,
but which, if imposed upon an insufficiently vigorous intellect, can lead to
scepticism or discouragement, or even to the abandonment of all scruples. After
having destroyed, one should rebuild, but Socrates never draws a conclusion.
He leads men into doubt, but never suggests any certainty. His noble life as a
thinker and a citizen, his honourable performance of military service and civic
duties (as in the Arginusae incident), his disinterestedness, his poverty, his
scrupulous respect for the law, and his devotion to right thinking and to truth,
even if it should cost him his life, certainly offer admirable examples on which the
generations of mankind have never ceased to ponder. But who among his contemporaries, apart from his intimates, saw him in this light? The impression that
the public retained of him was the external appearance, the picturesque figure
reminiscent of Silenus, the adroitness in contriving awkward questions, the
endless raising of doubts and the habitual lack of any positive conclusion. They
easily confused him with natural philosophers like Anaxagoras, formerly condemned for impiety, or sophists like Protagoras, who had also been banished
because of his destructive scepticism. Socrates, it is true, often alluded to the
inner voice, the 'familiar spirit' which gave him counsel in difficult circumstances
and whose intervention he regarded as the manifestation of a god. But the very
idea of this intimate and secret communion with the divine powers, unconnected
with any visible rite, was disturbing to the popular mind: it suggested some obscure threat to traditional religion, as if the ancient guardians of the city must one
day yield place to this unknown god. How could the elements that composed a
unified state, all depending on correct and whole-hearted participation in public
worship, continue to exist if the citizens of tomorrow, shaken in their conviction

by Socrates' teaching, began to doubt everything, with no other recourse but this strange secret voice which an old man claimed to hear within his heart?

I do not know if these arguments were advanced by Meletus, Anytus, and Lycon when they addressed the jury in the Heliaea. But one may regard it as probable that some of the jurymen took them into consideration during the pleading, before putting in the brazen urn, in which the votes were collected, the solid token for acquittal or the pierced one for condemnation. The fact that 220 out of the 500 members of the court preferred the solid token, thinking it better to set a just man free than to make an example apparently to the advantage of the state, does credit to Athenian democracy. As for the others, they believed, wrongly in all probability, that they were acting for the good of the city. In any case, it was certainly too late, for the spirit of free inquiry, for which Socrates did so much, had already won over too many thinkers for the old religion to survive, and with it the social order of which it was both a guarantee and a reflection.

CHAPTER VII

THE CITIZEN IN THE CITY

Definition of the city-state. Its territory. The country: agriculture and mines. The city: urban sites and plans. The house

IF the Greek of Archaic and Classical times was a soldier, it was in order to answer his city's call. If he took part in the religion of his fathers, it was with the city as the essential setting for his worship. This form of social organization was in the eyes of the Greek thinkers of the Classical Age (apart from some sophists) the distinguishing feature of civilized man. The best expression of this concept is found in the preamble to Aristotle's *Politics*, where the philosopher, in the evening of a life of which a great part had been devoted to study of the political systems of the Greek world, defines man as a 'city-dwelling creature' and shows that, 'if the city was brought into being to enable him to live, once established it enables him to live well', by providing him with the means of being independent. This is a theoretical view, no doubt, but one that aims to account for a reality which Aristotle, even more than his master Plato, knew to perfection in all its visible complexity. The idea of the city, an original and lasting creation of the Greek people, dominated all their history and all their thought. Handed on to Rome, remodelled by her and enriched for her use, it was bequeathed to Europe as a whole, which to a large extent derived from it the modern conception of the state. No more need be said to indicate its importance in the history of our civilization.

The word 'city', *polis*, has already three different senses in Homer. Sometimes

T

it means the collection of buildings constituting a city, sometimes the political unit that constitutes a state, sometimes the inhabitants considered as a citizen body—three meanings which would in Latin be expressed by the words *urbs*, *civitas*, and *cives*. In the language of Classical times this ambiguity remains, so that the word *polis* is used upon occasion by Herodotus and Xenophon even to denote Barbarian cities. Nevertheless, as soon as a Greek author is thinking in political terms, the full meaning that he attaches to the notion of *polis* is quite clear: it is the political and social unit which serves as a basis for the Hellenic world and which, along with the use of a distinctive language, marks it off from the Barbarian world. Let us attempt to analyse the content of this idea.

According to Aristotle, a city was the result of political union carried into effect between several villages. This thesis is well illustrated by some famous historical examples, such as the *synoecism* or unification of the towns in Attica to make the 'city' of Athens, an operation which the Greek chroniclers ascribed to Theseus. The normal consequence was the formation of a more important urban centre, which was the seat of the new state. For this reason the 'city' in the political sense is usually identified with the town whose name it bears. But it might well happen that no urban concentration resulted from the agreement arranged between the villages: in such cases a 'city' was, in the eyes of the Greeks, no less brought into being by the common will of the inhabitants. This emerges clearly from a passage in Pausanias (X, 4), where he mentions a wretched little place in Phocis; 'Twenty stades (about 2½ miles) from Chaeronea is the city of the Panopeans, if one can really apply the term "city" to people who possess no government buildings, no gymnasium or theatre, no main square, and no water system to supply a fountain, but who live on the edge of a ravine, in huts partly hollowed out in the soil, just like mountaineers' cabins. Nevertheless they have boundaries dividing their land from that of their neighbours and they even send delegates to the federal assembly of Phocis. They also claim that the name of their city is derived from the father of Epeus.' This Epeus, whose father's name was Panopeus, was the builder of the Trojan horse. This passage shows us what the indispensable conditions for defining a city were: a common territory with clear boundaries, a minimum of political organization recognized by the neighbouring cities, and, finally, what was not the least important thing in the eyes of the Greeks, some rudiments of a history, that is to say at least a legend concerning its foundation, with a cult connected with it. At the same time, Pausanias's very surprise at the sight of the wretched place shows that, as a rule, the conception of a 'city' implied the existence of a genuine urban centre provided with the essential amenities and services of a Greek city.

The diminutiveness of the territory of Greek cities has already been mentioned: apart from the more important states, Sparta and Athens in Greece proper, the island of Rhodes, Syracuse, and Cyrene overseas, the territory was hardly more than a little plain or valley of arable land around the actual city, with some mountain pastures or some islets off a coast. Very often the eye could take in the whole territory, or most of it, from a single viewpoint. The frontiers were clearly defined only in the areas of cultivation. In the mountains they remained vague and gave rise to frequent conflicts between shepherds. The land was cultivated either by free peasants living in villages and tilling their own farms or by slave labour on large country estates, like the one whose management is described in Xenophon's *Oeconomicus*. The agrarian system varied in different regions and in different periods. We have seen how in Attica Solon, and later Pisistratus, adopted measures favourable to the preservation of small holdings, without, however, abolishing the large estates. Men like Cimon and Pericles owned very extensive lands which brought them substantial incomes. These rich landowners usually lived in the city, though they had on their estates houses like that of Ischomachus, fairly similar to the country-houses of the Homeric lords. Having been built probably with unfired bricks, they have left no traces worth speaking of and we can only try to imagine them according to texts that are far from precise. Facing the south, the house contained several guest-rooms and a bedroom for the master and his wife, with service quarters for the kitchen and the bath; storerooms for the produce of the harvests, cereals, dried vegetables, and fruit; separate quarters for male and female slaves; and, lastly, stables, cart-houses, and toolsheds. The farm-houses of free peasants were obviously much more simple. But we know from descriptions in Aristophanes that the rough life lived in them had its own charm.

In certain regions, in which some danger of violence existed, villages and manor-houses had to be fortified: this was the case, for example, in Cyrenaica, where there was reason to fear inroads by Libyan plunderers from the inland steppes. A simple stone tower forming a fortlet might suffice to deter an aggressor: we have seen that there were many of these in the frontier regions of Greece.

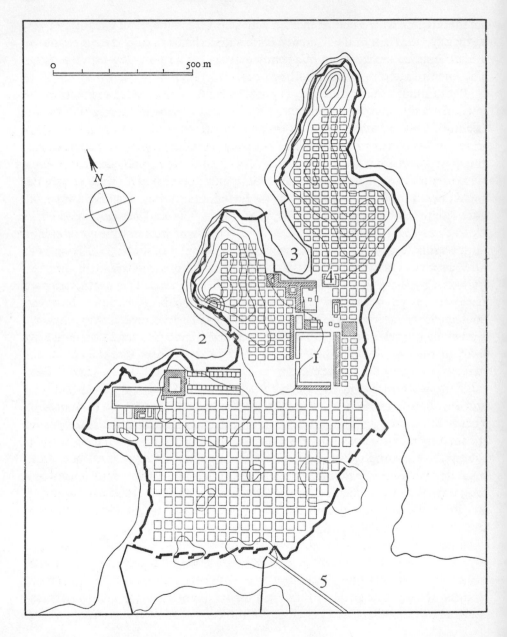

The free peasant, always subject to military obligations, kept his equipment at home and could obey mobilization orders without delay.

Cereals were grown everywhere, mainly barley, and wheat where possible. The Greek soil did not lend itself to wheat-growing, but, since the ideal of the city was economic self-sufficiency, men's foremost desire was to draw from the earth the griddle-cakes, gruel, and bread which were the staple diet. Beans, lentils, chick-peas, some green vegetables, garlic, and onions were the produce of the garden. The orchard contained fig-trees, which throve especially in Attica, quince-trees, pear-trees, and apple-trees. The olive, Athena's sacred tree, provided olives and oil in abundance, as it still does all over Greece. Aromatic herbs, thyme, cumin, basil, and marjoram, were appreciated in cookery. The vine sometimes climbed on trellis-work, sometimes stood in rows, either unsupported or supported by props about three feet high, like those which Trygaeus proposed to cut from the shafts of the spears which peace would render useless. Sheep and goats browsed in the mountains. Some cows and oxen, scarce, and so all the more strictly reserved for the great sacrifices, aided the husbandman in his task. The hives provided honey, which took the place of sugar.

There were other rustic activities directed to the exploitation of natural resources for purposes of craftsmanship, if not industry. Such were the labours of

---

19. THE CITY OF MILETUS

(*After A. von Gerkan and R. Martin*). The Milesian town-planners rebuilt the city in the fifth century on rational principles which set a fashion. The long peninsula (nearly 2 kilometres) was divided into three main districts separated by the deep indentations of the two harbours. At the junction-point of the three districts, a low-lying area (1) was set apart for public buildings and the main agora (known as the South Agora). The widest and most open harbour (2) was flanked by the theatre resting against the slopes of the hill and by the sanctuary of Athena on the south side. The other harbour, much more narrow, called the Lion Harbour, served a market near which stood the sanctuary (4) of Apollo Delphinios. The Hellenistic and Roman buildings, also marked on the accompanying plan, had no difficulty in finding their place in the setting conceived by the architects of the fifth century. The surrounding wall mostly followed an indented course. The rectilinear highway (5) which left the wall at an angle in a southeasterly direction led to the famous sanctuary of Apollo at Didyma.

the woodcutters who provided timber and the charcoal-burners who made charcoal from the copses of holm-oak. Aristophanes represents them in a lively and sympathetic manner in his play *The Acharnians*. Resin and pitch came from the forests of pine and fir, as did timber for ships, but home production was insufficient for the needs of shipbuilding and it was necessary to depend to a considerable degree on importation. Flax was grown in Elis, the only region in the peninsula moist enough for its cultivation: elsewhere linen had to be imported from Asia Minor or Egypt. As for wool, the Greek flocks provided most of what was needed: each household spun and wove clothes for everyday use, and this was the women's main occupation. It was only luxury goods that came from abroad and were handled as objects of commerce. The same applied to leather: sandals and cloaks of goatskin, rain-proof caps, leather bottles and bags were manufactured at home, except in the city, where specialized craftsmen were called upon.

The most important non-agricultural work in the country was quarrying and mining. The deposits of clay in Attica and Corinthia furnished the raw material for numerous potters' workshops. The marble quarries of Mount Pentelicus near Athens and those of Aliki in the island of Thasos were worked on the surface. Those in the island of Paros, in the Cyclades, were mostly subterranean and penetrated far into the mountain: their marble, exceptionally white and translucent, was much in demand for statuary and was the object of a thriving trade. It was called *lychnites*, from *lychnos*, 'lamp', in all probability not because it was luminous but because it was quarried by lamp-light. The various kinds of stone for building gave scope for similar quarrying activities: we are familiar with the famous quarries (*latomiai*) at Syracuse, which witnessed the agonies of the Athenian prisoners after the disaster in Sicily. Near Cyrene, in Libya, we can still see in many places the layers of conchitic limestone from which the blocks intended for the public buildings of the great African city were cut.

Little is known of the iron and copper mines. On the other hand, we are better informed about the mines of precious metals, which held the attention of ancient writers because of the covetousness they often aroused and the part they played in international politics. They brought prosperity to Thasos and won the little island of Siphnos, in the Cyclades, a reputation that did not last long, but which enabled it, in about 530 B.C., to erect a richly carved treasury at Delphi. On Mount Pangaeum, in Thrace, the gold mines of *Scapte-Hyle*, the 'Undermined

Forest', were worked by the natives, but on behalf of the Greeks: Thucydides, who owned several of them, lived there during his banishment and derived his main income from them while writing his *History*. But the most important mines were those at Laurium, at the southeastern tip of Attica. Here we can still see the low, narrow galleries in which the slave miners, bent double, worked their way along the seams of silver-bearing lead. Several thousands of slave workmen were employed in mining and processing the ore, from which were extracted on the site lead ingots and silver sufficiently refined for minting the famous Athenian coins, the 'owls of Laurium', thus named because of the emblem which ordinarily adorned their reverse side. One of the workshops for minting was installed right on the site.

Though the community drew its livelihood from the toil of the country folk, it was in the city that all important business was dealt with, both of the state and of private individuals. This is why, as early as the Archaic Age, and in spite of the very keen feeling for nature which the Greeks never lost, Greek civilization was first and foremost an urban one: it was created by men living in close groups and it put social relationships in the forefront. What did a Greek city look like in the Archaic and Classical Ages? However modest it might be, it could be seen to be the capital of a state: so it accommodated the main public services that are the *raison d'être* of the state and provided them with suitable premises and equipment. Here were sanctuaries for the public cults, fortifications to defend the citizens against attacks from without (whether an acropolis organized as a defensive redoubt, a ring of fortified walls surrounding the entire city, or both), a main square (*agora*) serving as a market-place for commercial business and a meeting-place for political assemblies, fountains for the water-supply, a necessity of life, and finally special buildings for the various administrative and legal bodies. Around these public buildings, most of which were concentrated on the acropolis or around the agora, spread a network of streets, in a disorder which, before the fifth century, revealed the complete absence of any general plan. It was not until after the Persian Wars and in imitation of the steps taken for the rebuilding of Miletus (destroyed by the Persians in 494) that an interest in town-planning first came into evidence with the employment of the orthogonal plan, also called the 'chequer-board pattern'. A decisive rôle in this development is attributed to the architect Hippodamus of Miletus, who at Themistocles' request drew up the plans for the Piraeus and took part in the foundation of

181 & 182. THE BRONZE KOUROS FROM PIRAEUS

This magnificent statue, found at Piraeus in 1959, illustrates the accomplished skill of the Greek makers of bronze statues, who, as early as the last quarter of the sixth century, showed themselves capable of casting such works as this (height, 1·9 metres). It is probably an Apollo who was holding his bow in his left hand. National Museum, Athens.

183. THE MOSCHOPHOROS

Statue of a man bringing a calf as an offering, carrying it on his shoulders; hence the name, which means the 'Calf-carrier'. As early as this period (about 570–560), Attic sculpture combines formal severity with a spontaneous feeling for life. To accentuate the polychrome effect, eyes made of opaque glass or coloured gems were inserted. Acropolis Museum, Athens.

184. A SOOTHSAYER (EAST PEDIMENT OF THE TEMPLE OF ZEUS AT OLYMPIA)

It shows the fullness of sculptural forms, well adapted to their decorative purpose in an architectural setting. The small curls of the hair and beard still smack of Archaism, but the features already possess the Classical nobility and severity. Compare the Poseidon from Artemisium (ill. 80), which belongs to the same period (about 460). The painting, no longer visible, increased the effect of realism. Olympia Museum.

185–187. METOPES FROM A BUILDING IN THE SANCTUARY OF HERA ARGEIA NEAR PAESTUM

These sandstone metopes illustrate various myths, including exploits of Heracles: his struggle with the Centaurs (ill. 185) occupies several consecutive metopes. Elsewhere he is carrying off two maleficent dwarfs, the Cercopes, fastened to a stick like game (ill. 186) or he is wrestling with the giant Antaeus (ill. 187). This last metope is unfinished and shows the first stage of the sculptor's work: only the outlines have been shaped, on parallel planes, and the forms were to be rounded off later. Paestum Museum.

188. HERMES AND A KORE

This bas-relief (early fifth century) adorned a small sanctuary of the Charites (the Graces, attendants of Aphrodite), near the agora at Thasos. Hermes, wearing a chlamys and a conical felt hat (see coloured plate III), with the caduceus in his left hand, is advancing with a sweeping gesture of welcome. Behind him there is a woman holding a garland or necklace. The carved inscription on the plinth is a cult regulation forbidding the sacrifice of a goat or a pig to the Charites. Louvre.

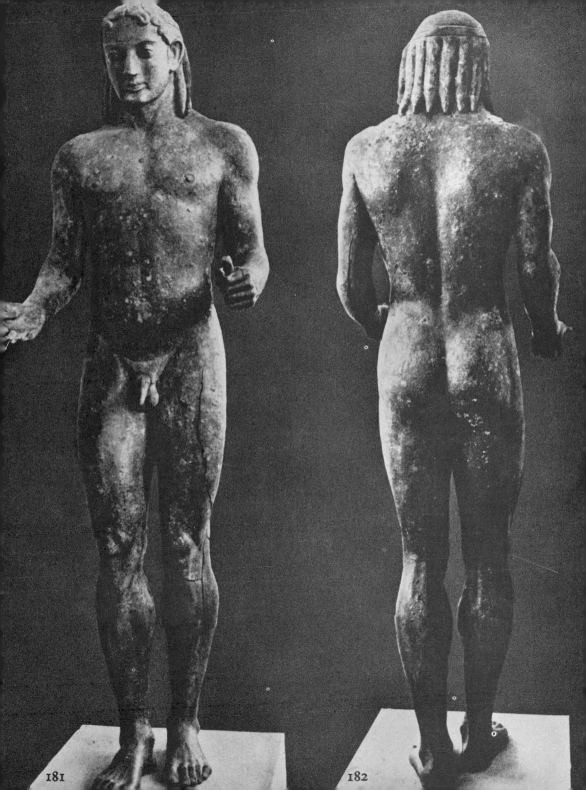

181   182

185

186

187

188

189

189. PROFILE OF THE ZEUS OF OLYMPIA

This bronze coin, minted in Elis in the reign of the Emperor Hadrian, gives the most faithful reproduction of Phidias's masterpiece. In spite of wear, we can recognize the severe majesty which so impressed the ancients. Coin-room, Berlin.

190. ZEUS

This larger than life-size head, put together from numerous fragments, belonged to a statue in the temple of Olympian Zeus at Cyrene. It dates from the time of Hadrian. The sculptor was broadly inspired by the Zeus of Phidias, but without seeking to reproduce it exactly. The marble still bears part of the original painting in colours. Cyrene Museum.

191. HEAD OF THE CHARIOTEER OF DELPHI

The statue formed part of a group representing the Chariot of Polyzelus, tyrant of Gela, brother of Gelon and Hieron of Syracuse, after his victory in the Pythian Games in 478 or 474. The head greatly recalls the works of the Attic sculptor Critius. Note the inserted eyes, with white opaque glass for the cornea and coloured stones for the iris and pupil. The lips were overlaid with a film of red copper. Delphi Museum.

Thurii in 444–443. Aristotle, in his *Politics* (1267 b), represents him as interested in political philosophy as well as architecture, and it is certain that this tendency to rationalize the designing of a city is connected with the intellectual movement, influenced by mathematical considerations, created by Thales of Miletus and carried on by Anaximander and Anaximenes, whence comes the name *Milesian School*, by which it is justifiably known. However, these innovations appeared only in new towns and did not alter the appearance of the ancient cities.

For the rest, the extreme diversity of city sites hardly lent itself at the outset to widespread adoption of a logical lay out. Cities on the plain generally grew up around or beside a height that served as an acropolis: hence arose topographical difficulties in establishing contact between the upper and the lower city. Mountain cities, like Delphi, presented marked differences of level. Few cities in Greece proper were built right upon the coast: neither Athens, nor Sparta, nor Argos, nor Thebes, nor even Corinth was a seaport. Even when the coast was near at hand, as at Corinth and Athens, the harbour was separate from the town, as if the Greeks of the Archaic Age felt some mistrust with regard to dangers approaching by sea: a recollection of the piracy of Geometric times, later transmuted in Plato's *Laws* (IV, 704 b ff.) into a condemnation in theory of coastal sites. On the other hand, most of the colonial cities, having been founded by immigrants who had come by sea, were situated on the coast. The exceptional cases of Cyrene and Barce, the two great cities in Libya, founded some distance inland, only emphasize all the more the distinctive character of the Greek settlement in this part of Africa.

Private houses were of modest size and extreme simplicity, in contrast to the usual sumptuousness of public buildings. They were rarely built of stone: their walls of unfired brick or cob, resting on a low footing of stonework, made the task of burglars ('wall-breakers') easy. We have hardly any information for the earliest period, but for the Classical Age the information derived from texts and the results of the excavations at Olynthus enable us to envisage a Greek house with some precision. Destroyed in 348 B.C. by Philip's forces, the city was never afterwards reoccupied: American archaeologists have methodically laid bare its ruins, so that the detailed plan of several districts is now known. These were new districts, planned towards the end of the fifth century. Therefore contiguous houses are not arranged in irregular groups as in earlier cities, but in rectangular

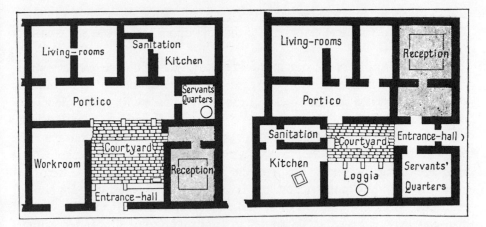

20. HOUSES AT OLYNTHUS

(*After R. Martin*). These two houses, excavated by the American archaeologists at Olynthus, belong to different blocks. On these ground-floor plans we can recognize the main parts of the dwelling: a paved courtyard reached from the street by an entrance-hall; a portico or loggia opening on this courtyard; living or reception rooms, service quarters and a block containing kitchen and bathroom.

---

units bounded by a grid of streets laid out in chequer-board pattern: here we have already the system of 'blocks', which was to become widespread in the Hellenistic Age and which the Romans later called 'islands' (*insulae*). While Athenian houses, for example, rarely had walls meeting at right angles, those at Olynthus generally form a more or less regular square, whose side averages 56 feet. In such a house, there was an enclosed courtyard behind the middle of the southern façade, which served as a passage to the ground-floor rooms surrounding it on three sides. The northern side of the courtyard was covered over by a portico (*pastas*), under which were the doors leading to the living-rooms of the private suite. A group of rooms consisting of servants' quarters, kitchen, and bathroom, and a reception room (*andron*) with its antechamber occupied the rest of the ground floor. On the northern side of the house there was often an upper storey, reached by a wooden stairway, and opening on a gallery stretching above the *pastas*. The roof was not flat, as in the cities of Greece proper, but made of round tiles on a gabled sloping roof, because of the moist climate of Chalcidice. The evidence of Classical texts implies that the upper storey was the women's quarters.

Separate houses were the rule in the Classical Age. Of course our texts mention some tenement houses, which were called *synoikia*, as opposed to an ordinary house, *oikia*. But this was the exception and the tall house with several floors was only developed later, in Rome. Some of Fortune's favourites occupied large villas with numerous rooms, large courtyards with porticos and gardens, like that of Callias, where Socrates, in Plato's dialogue, went to meet Protagoras. But even here, luxury was not obtrusive: the ground mosaics that have been uncovered at Olynthus in the richest houses, which are the oldest mosaics known, are made of black and white pebbles, with no attempt at refinement. The walls of the rooms were whitewashed or painted in colour with some simple decorations. One had to be an Alcibiades, and a rich eccentric, to have the walls of one's house adorned with frescos. The furniture consisted of chests, beds, tables, chairs and stools, to which were added carpets and tapestries, often imported from the East. Apart from common earthenware plates and dishes manufactured locally, one could see in rich houses painted pottery of high quality and vessels of metal, chiefly bronze and silver, which were the great luxury in tableware. Yet, if we read the inventory of Alcibiades' property, sold after his condemnation in the trial concerning the Mysteries, which is preserved in a contemporary inscription, we by no means get the impression of extraordinary wealth. We can well understand that Socrates, in Plato's *Alcibiades* (123 b ff.), stressed the enormous difference in resources between even the richest Greeks and the Eastern monarchs. Until the Classical Age, real ostentation was reserved for the gods.

Work. Slavery. Numerical distribution of the population
In town, as in the country, the bulk of the manual work was done by slaves. In the first place, they performed most of the domestic tasks in every house, where a minimum of slave help was regarded as indispensable: only a beggar (or, by the fourth century, a Cynic philosopher) possessed no slave. Apart from these domestic duties, it was also slaves who enabled the various trades to be carried on. We can hardly use the term 'industries' except in some very rare cases. An exceptional instance mentioned is the arms factory run by the orator Lysias and his brother Polemarchus at Athens towards the end of the fifth century. At the time

when the wealth of the two brothers was confiscated, during the rule of the Thirty Tyrants, they were employing 120 slaves and had in stock 700 shields, as Lysias himself says in his speech *Against Eratosthenes* (19). Their father, the Syracusan Cephalus, had already been considered one of the richest men in Athens, as is indicated by Plato, who introduces him in the opening scene of the *Republic*. On the other hand, in the great majority of manufacturing or trading establishments, a few slaves were enough for the work to be done. A man who, like the cripple in Lysias, practised his trade in a very small way without a single slave to help him was truly on the verge of poverty.

Moreover, a certain contempt clung to manual labour: the very term for workmen, *banausos*, carried a suggestion of disapproval; still more so did the term *kapelos*, meaning a retail trader in a small way. Anyone who followed an occupation of this kind, even if it had to do with genuine art, was not much respected in Greek society, even in the most democratic of societies like that of Athens. The only occupation really worthy of a free citizen, as we can clearly see in Plato, was to take part in public affairs: the young sons of great families who surrounded Socrates had no other ambition and the 'liberal' education which they received had no other object than to prepare them for public life—or at least it claimed to do so, which Socrates called in question. Some years earlier, Herodotus remarked that the Greeks, imitating the Egyptians, as he thought, regarded the pursuit of a manual occupation as not highly respectable (II, 167); he adds that this prejudice was strongest in Sparta and weakest in Corinth. It is true that in Athens a law of Solon enacted penalties against any idle citizen, but we do not know exactly how idleness was defined and this law does not seem to have altered the general feeling about manual work. The accepted view about this had undergone changes since the Homeric Age: the *Odyssey* on various occasions reveals Ulysses' technical skill; his endlessly resourceful spirit is as well displayed in constructing a bed as in leading an army, without the King of Ithaca seeming to lose his dignity in the eyes of the poet and his audience—far from it! Of course this was not a case of paid work, which Greek opinion in Classical times regarded with small respect, but of an independent activity. Let us, however, contrast the admiration inspired in Homer by Ulysses' raft or bed with the contempt professed by Callicles, in Plato's *Gorgias* (512 c), for the technical capacities of the engineer, and we shall see how greatly times have changed.

So in practice, contrary to what one might think, a 'democratic' city like

Athens hardly showed more respect for the work of the artisan than did aristocratic cities. To be sure, Pericles, in the famous speech put in his mouth by
Thucydides (II, 40), stresses the fact that his native city allowed skilled and un-
skilled workmen, if they were citizens, to take their part in the management of
state affairs: but this same Pericles, by introducing the practice of paying a daily
allowance (*misthos*) to all citizens performing a public service, whether magistrates, members of the Council, jurymen, or soldiers in the field, was largely
responsible for diverting his fellow-countrymen from productive work and
making them seek these duties which, though modestly remunerated, sufficed to
keep them going from day to day. So manual occupations were more and more
left to slaves and to resident aliens (*metoikoi*), of whom there was a large number:
by studying the accounts dealing with the construction of the temple called the
Erechtheion on the Acropolis, accounts known to us by inscriptions, we ascertain
that among the workmen, numbering 107, whom it has been possible to identify,
only fourteen citizens appear, the rest being metics or slaves.

From this we can see the essentially aristocratic character of a Greek city, even
when it declares itself to be a democratic state. The notions of democracy and
aristocracy were conceived by the Hellenes only in relation to the citizen body,
which in various cities played a larger or smaller part in the affairs of the state. But
this citizen body, far from embracing the major part of the population, in fact
represented a privileged minority, except perhaps in some highland city-states,
where no one was rich enough to purchase and maintain many slaves. But all the
main Greek cities present the same picture. Not only were political rights
accorded only to citizens but the chief civil rights, such as the right to own real
estate, land or houses were similarly limited. Side by side with them, the resident
aliens, the 'cohabitants' (which is the basic meaning of the word *metoikos*), enjoyed a special status providing certain guarantees: they had their share of the
financial and military obligations imposed by the state, but had no political
rights. Sparta did not authorize aliens to take up residence in its territory; Athens,
on the contrary, readily welcomed them and they played an important part in
industry, commerce, and intellectual life. As for the slave population, it was often
as numerous as the citizens and sometimes more so.

Side by side with the slaves properly so called, we find in Thessaly, Crete, and
Sparta a class of serfs bound to the soil. In the Lacedaemonian state they were
helots, descended, it seems, from peoples subdued by the Dorians on their

arrival in Laconia or during their conquest of Messenia: reduced to utter servitude, they cultivated the portions of land granted by the state to their Spartan masters. A state of war with the helots was declared each year, to keep a salutary dread alive in the victims of exploitation: the young Spartan gentry, when subjected to the test of the *crypteia*, had the right to slay any helot met out of doors during the night. These discretionary powers, upheld with savage resolution, enabled the Spartan citizens to be released from every task other than preparation for warfare. However, round the fringe of the rich cultivated lands of Laconia, reserved for the Spartiates alone and rendered productive by the helot's toil, the frontier districts of the Lacedaemonian state were occupied by inhabitants known as *perioikoi* ('Those who dwell round about'): they were not citizens, but could devote themselves freely to agricultural labour, handicrafts, or trade, in contrast with the Spartiates, subject only to the obligation to serve side by side with the latter in the Lacedaemonian army. The details of their legal position are very little known, but they seem to have enjoyed civil rights (unlike the metics in other Greek cities) and generally showed themselves loyal subjects of Sparta. The existence of perioeci is attested in other Greek states—Elis, Argolis, Crete and Cyrene—but we have very little information about these sections of the population.

The condition of slaves was in principle the same everywhere, though custom could introduce some differences in practice. According to Aristotle's expression (*Politics*, I, 3, 1253 b), which echoes the prevalent view, a slave was merely a 'living tool' at the disposal of his master. Legal texts, like deeds of emancipation, of which we have many dating from the Hellenistic Age, describe the slave by the terms 'a male body' or 'a female body', as if the slave was indeed an object, not a person. The fact is that in losing his liberty he had lost the quality of 'personality', whatsoever had been his origin, Greek or Barbarian. This is why his evidence was admitted by a court of justice only if he had been subjected to torture: the compulsion of suffering was considered essential to make him tell the truth. From the Homeric poems onwards, there is abundant evidence to show that the condition of slavery, whether due to birth or to calamity, debased a man and robbed him of all his dignity. The slave had no personal or family life. The women were used for their masters' pleasure without restraint or scruple: the captive women of Troy, Briseis, Andromache, and Cassandra, suffered this humiliation, and Aristophanes speaks with ribald zest about the sprightly Thracian servant-girl who is cheerfully tumbled in a nook in the woods. It is true that Athenian custom, perhaps more because of clearly realized economic considerations than any concern for humanity, introduced into the law some measures of protection to guard slaves against excessive acts of violence. On the other hand, certain forms of religion offered them a welcome: they could be initiated at Eleusis. On this point, and very discreetly, Eleusinian piety was opening the door to the future. But on the whole the distinction between a free man and a slave remained a fundamental distinction in Greek society. Since, by reason of the risks that war brought in its train, the threat of enslavement hung over the head of every free man (Plato himself experienced this misfortune in 388 B.C., and was delivered from it only by the generous intervention of the Cyrenaean Anniceris), human destiny, already subjected by nature to so many deadly perils, appeared in the eyes of the Greeks all the more pathetic because of it: their poets did not lose the opportunity to exploit this source of tragic pathos.

Slaves and helots, metics and perioeci, citizens with their families—we are hardly in a position to calculate the percentages of these diverse elements in the populations of the cities. As always in ancient history, statistical data are almost entirely lacking. Here however, to put the proportions in sequence, are the approximate estimates for Athens and Sparta, each envisaged at the period of its greatest prosperity. These figures are drawn from calculations recently made by V. Ehrenberg, who has himself clearly pointed out what a great margin of uncertainty they contain. Athens, at the beginning of the Peloponnesian War (about 432 B.C.) must have had about 40,000 citizens (or, including their families, nearly 150,000 persons), 10,000 to 15,000 metics (40,000 persons, including the families), and nearly 110,000 slaves, out of a total population of 300,000 souls. The Lacedaemonian state, just after the Persian Wars (about 480–470 B.C.), must have included 5,000 Spartiates (say 15,000 persons including the families), 50,000 perioeci, and 150,000 to 200,000 helots, so about 250,000 souls. Many medium-sized cities must have had a number of citizens approximating to the figure of 10,000 which Aristotle, basing his view on the data of experience, regards as the ideal. Making allowance for the fact that, among these privileged inhabitants of a city, some must have been debarred from public affairs by negligence, incapacity, or illness, we can see how restricted the compass of a Greek city must have been: among a populace composed largely of persons deprived of civil and political qualifications, all those who played a part, however exiguous it might be, must have known one another at least by sight.

Possession and conferment of citizenship. The education of the citizen. The problem of homosexuality

Let us now consider these citizens, who alone were vested with the rights which, in the eyes of the Greeks, enabled a man really to be a man. They derived their status of citizen from their birth: their father at least, sometimes their mother too (as was required at Athens by a law of Pericles), already belonged to the privileged body. So, as a general rule, citizenship was conferred by birthright; the old tradition of a 'clan' to which one belonged by birth was thus maintained in a lasting way in the framework of the city. The conferment of these rights on foreigners remained a privilege which the Greeks never showed themselves very ready to grant: it was a reward for outstanding merit or due to quite exceptional circumstances. Thus the Athenian people admitted to their ranks, in 409, the man who had killed Phrynichus, a leader of the oligarchical party who had made himself generally detested: the fact is mentioned by Lysias in his speech *Against Agoratus* (70–72), and his statement is confirmed by an inscription that has been found. A little later, in 406, to reward the metics who had served as oarsmen in the battle of Arginusae, a decree was passed conferring citizenship on them all. Finally in 405, in the confusion which followed their defeat at Aegospotami, the Athenians granted rights of citizenship to the Samians, who alone remained loyal to them in these difficult times. But these were merely exceptional cases or expedients imposed by calamity. Ordinarily, in Athens as elsewhere, the people was jealous for its civil privileges and, far from being ready to extend the enjoyment of them to new classes of residents, it made a point of avoiding such extension: that is how we should account for Pericles' law mentioned above, which restricted citizen rights to Athenians born of a father and mother themselves Athenian. Under these conditions, Themistocles, for example, whose mother was a Thracian servant-girl, would not have been a citizen! Moreover Pericles himself had later to ask for a special measure in favour of the son whom he had had by his mistress Aspasia of Miletus: the people had enough good taste not to refuse.

As for Sparta, she showed herself much more rigid still. Herodotus declares that the soothsayer Tisamenus of Elis and his brother were the only men in the world who had ever received citizenship at Sparta (IX, 35), and this was rendered possible only by the Spartans' extreme trust in the oracle of Delphi, which foretold five great victories for Tisamenus: in consideration of which, being anxious to

U

bind him to themselves, they gratified the soothsayers' demands by granting both him and his brother the exorbitant privilege that he requested.

Birth was not a sufficient qualification in itself: it was also necessary for the child to be officially recognized by its father and admitted to membership in the citizen body. Until this formality was accomplished, the child could always be exposed and abandoned. The practice was to place the infant who was being abandoned in an earthenware pot, leaving with it some objects, such as bracelets or necklaces, which could, if the occasion arose, enable it to be identified, supposing it chanced to survive: the poets of New Comedy, after Euripides, and the 'novelists' of the late period made great use of these recognitions that resulted from what our men of letters, imitating the ancients, have called 'the mother's cross'. In Sparta, the decision to let the new-born baby live did not even belong to the father, but to a council of elders of the tribe, who, after inspecting the infant, authorized it to be brought up if it seemed to them vigorous and well-formed: if not, they had it thrown into an abyss on Taygetus. In Athens, the ceremony of the *Amphidromia*, which took place on the fifth day (according to 'Suidas') or on the seventh (according to Hesychius) after the birth, marked the new-born child's official entry into the family: the women of the house, who had attended at the birth, took the child in their arms and ran carrying it around the domestic hearth. This was at one and the same time a rite of purification for the pollution caused by the confinement and a rite of admission to the family cult for the infant. A little later, on the tenth day, the child was given a name, and a banquet was held, to which the family and friends were invited. In addition to these domestic ceremonies, there was the first presentation of the child to the partly religious, partly political organization called the *phratry*, midway between the family and the tribe. Henceforth the child had a legal existence.

The education he was to receive varied entirely, according to whether he lived in Sparta or Athens (about the other cities, our information is very slight). The young Spartiate, as soon as he reached the age of seven, entered a complex system of collective education organized by the state. He passed up from one class to another, under the direction of masters and gymnastic instructors; he had to submit to regular training, to tests that were often painful, and to a rigorous discipline tending to develop physical resistance and moral strength, in order to turn the young man into a soldier. This education continued until the age of thirty: even marriage did not exempt the young Spartiate from communal life with his comrades. The place alloted to intellectual training in this system was manifestly restricted: it was limited to choir-singing, study of the national poets, Alcman, Terpander, and Tyrtaeus, and the inculcation of a harsh and narrow civic morality. Hence their mistrust of rhetoric, which surprised the other Greeks, so inclined to cultivate the art of speech, and filled them with admiration for the brief and pithy aphorisms known as Lacedaemonian apophthegms.

The young Athenian, at about six or seven years of age, escaped from the exclusive company of the women in the gynaeceum and began to go to school, accompanied by a slave called the *paidagogos*. Solon's laws made it a father's duty to see to his son's education: in the famous prosopopoeia of the laws in Plato's *Crito* (49 d), the laws claim the merit of having commanded Socrates' father to have him taught music and gymnastics. The schools were private establishments and the masters received fees from the children's parents. The *grammatistes* taught reading, writing, and arithmetic and made his pupils learn by heart the poems of Homer, Hesiod, Solon, and Simonides: Plato's dialogues show what importance was attributed to knowledge of the poets for intellectual and moral training. The music master taught his pupils to play the lyre and even the cithara, a more complicated instrument to handle, demanding a technical competence not entirely in keeping with the traditions of a 'liberal' education. The double flute (*aulos*), at one stage introduced into the schools and much esteemed by the Athenian public, was later banned, as Aristotle tells us (*Politics*, VIII, 6, 1341 a–b), because it aroused too violent emotions, which disquieted the soul instead of disciplining it. In any case, music played a primary part in the education of the young Greek. Finally, the gymnastic instructor (*paidotribes*) taught the boy the main athletic exercises in a building specially designed for this purpose (*palaistra*). From fifteen years of age, the youth frequented the public gymnasiums, at the Academy, the Lyceum, or the Cynosarges, where he had at his disposal buildings and equipment similar to those of the private palaestras, and in addition a running-track, gardens, and assembly rooms in which philosophers and sophists were pleased to meet their pupils after their physical exercises. After their two years of ephebic training, the young men would continue to visit the gymnasium, a favourite place for training, relaxation and meeting friends. Very ancient legislative enactments laid down rules for the administration of athletic establishments, fixing the opening and closing hours, curbing attempts at theft with exemplary severity, and reserving the use of these establishments for men of free birth.

We cannot avoid mentioning here a feature of morals upon which a part of Greek literature has conferred a dubious celebrity: amorous relations between young boys and grown men, referred to as paederasty. This sexual and mental perversion enjoyed a certain prestige in the Greek world because of the social position of its adepts and the talent of writers like Plato. But one would make a great mistake by thinking that such a vice was widespread in Greek society and that it gave rise to no condemnation. The sexual morality of the Greeks was certainly never very strict, except with regard to an adulterous wife and her accomplice. But if custom unreservedly sanctioned the keeping of a mistress or visits to courtesans, it was not everywhere so indulgent when it was a question of unnatural love. Here we must acknowledge differences between various states. In certain Dorian cities, at Sparta, in Crete, and also at Thebes, where youths were entrusted to adults responsible for training them to be soldiers, this 'military comradeship' had, from a very early period, lent itself to the development of 'particular' friendships which only too easily led to physical intimacies. These personal ties were sometimes encouraged in order to strengthen the moral cohesiveness of picked troops: such was the case in the Theban 'sacred band', in the time of Epaminondas. Philosophers later sought to find a utilitarian explanation of this strange practice: Aristotle, in his *Politics* (II, 10, 1272 a), imagines that it was in order to check overpopulation that homosexuality was legally authorized in Crete. But at Athens and in the rest of the Greek world this vice was the privilege of a small minority vigorously condemned by public opinion. Aristophanes misses no opportunity to belabour compatriots notorious for perversion: he would never have been so ready to do so if he had not felt sure of favourable reactions from his audience. Paederasty was rife among the aristocracy, not the people as a whole. It was to gratify this rich clientele that Attic potters, towards the end of the Archaic period, inscribed on their vases compliments to some handsome youths. It is well known that Harmodius and Aristogiton were linked by mutual attraction and that the immediate reason for their assassination of the tyrant was an offence on the sentimental plane rather than love of liberty, but this did not prevent the democracy from honouring the *Tyrannoctonoi*. At the time of the Peloponnesian War, it was in the secret societies (*hetairiai*) of the aristocracy that homosexuality enrolled its enthusiasts. Socrates' trial, as we have seen, reflects the hostility and contempt that the Athenian people felt for these young perverts. All Plato's seductiveness and his intellectual pirouettes concerning the supposed benefits of these perverted forms of love cannot conceal the natural repugnance that they inspired in most people's minds. The laws of Athens were severe towards incitement of the young to debauchery: even rape of a slave was punished in the same way as that of a freeborn child; it was the act itself that public morality condemned. When in 345 B.C. the orator Aeschines wished to discredit Demosthenes' friend Timarchus, who was preparing to bring a political charge against him, he accused him of living an immoral life and obtained his permanent degradation in the eyes of the law and of public opinion: the speech *Against Timarchus*, like the plays of Aristophanes, tells us all we need to know about the real feelings of the Athenian people in the matter of paederasty. Moreover, towards the end of his life the godlike Plato, changing from wolf to shepherd, sought to banish unnatural love from the city of his *Laws* (VIII, 836 b ff.), having at last come to realize that it is not very favourable to the acquisition of virtue.

Rights and duties of the citizen. Intermediary organizations. The tribe. The various forms of government: aristocracy, oligarchy, democracy. The constitutions of Athens and Sparta

The Greek city-state had a twofold nature, geographical and human: it corresponded at one and the same time to a well-defined territory, generally continuous, and to a group of men, the citizen body. Of these two aspects of an identical political entity, the latter was the more important: there is here a perceptible difference from the modern concept of the fatherland, which in our eyes seems closely linked with the land. The Greek city-state was, on the contrary, the totality of the men of whom is was composed. This is why the official name which it bears in our texts is not the name of a country or a city, but the name of a people—not Athens, but the Athenians, not Sparta, but the Lacedaemonians, not Corinth, but the Corinthians, and so on. This does not mean that the Greeks did not, like ourselves, feel the elementary form of patriotism that consists of attachment to the land or city of one's birth: their orators and poets gave expression to this sentiment in touching or magnificent forms which still provide us with a model. But in critical circumstances they felt that the essential thing was not the land, but the men, and they regarded the city as safe and sound, even after the loss of its territory, if the citizen body was preserved and could revive its cults and traditions elsewhere. When Harpagus, the general appointed by Cyrus to subdue Ionia, had laid siege to Phocaea, the Phocaeans, so Herodotus tells us (I, 164 ff.), seeing that resistance was impossible, 'launched their pente- conters, put their women and children on board, along with all their movable property, and also the statues of the gods from their temples and all the offerings, except bronze and stone sculptures and paintings. When all this had been put on board, they embarked and set out for Chios.' From there they proceeded to found a new city in the west, at Alalia on the eastern coast of Corsica. The people of Teos did likewise and settled in Thrace, on the site of Abdera, a former colony of Clazomenae, which the earlier settlers had had to abandon. When the Persians occupied Athens in 480 B.C., Themistocles, in the name of the Athenians who had taken refuge in Salamis, threatened the Spartiate admiral Eurybiades, who was in command of the Greek fleet, that he would abandon the allied force if Eurybiades refused to join battle: 'If you do not do what I propose, we shall immediately set off with our families for Siris in Italy, a city which has been ours for a long time and where, according to the oracles, we must found a colony.' This piece of blackmail succeeded and resulted in the victory at Salamis. But if the Athenians had put their plan into execution, they would not have felt that their civic body had been dissolved: the Athenian city-state would merely have changed its territory and its name, while the people of whom it was com- posed would have kept the dignity of citizenship of a Greek city-state on this new site.

In principle, each citizen had a share in the conduct of state business and felt himself directly bound to the state by imperative obligations. Yet it is not the case that in every instance the city and the individual had direct relations without intervening elements. In fact, the citizen was in every city a member of more restricted groups, whose function was at once religious and political, and which served as intermediate stages between the state and the individual citizen. Beyond the family, in the narrow sense of the term, there were the traditional 'clans', nobiliary in character, associated with a more or less mythical ancestor and deriving their cohesion from shared cults. There is no doubt that, in Athens at least, the development that resulted in the classical city-state had come to pass fundamentally in opposition to the formerly all-powerful authority of the heads of the 'clans': this, as we have seen, is how we should interpret Draco's legislation concerning the taking of life. The various sumptuary laws forbidding excessive expenditure on funerals were likewise designed to prevent noble families from competing with one another in display of their means in cases of bereavement. Nevertheless, the fact of belonging to an illustrious *genos* remained a reason for pride and glory in Athens during the Classical period. Pericles was, on his father's side, a member of the *genos* of the Buzygae and on the side of his mother Agariste he was connected with the 'clan' of the Alcmaeonids, which had struggled against Pisistratus during the preceding century and one of whose members, Clisthenes, had reformed the Athenian democracy. In the fourth century, the orator Lycurgus, who played the leading role in Athens during the twelve years following the Battle of Chaeronea, belonged to the *genos* of the Eteobutadae, another very ancient 'clan', which by recognized tradition possessed the priesthood of Poseidon Erechtheus (held by Lycurgus himself) and that of Athena Polias, that is to say the service of the two divinities honoured in the Erechtheum, the most venerable temple in Athens. These instances show the prestige still enjoyed at this period by the families generically designated as Eupatridae, the 'nobles'.

By no means all the citizens belonged to a *genos*. But they were all members of associations of a religious and civic character, of which we have little knowledge: 'guilds' (*hetair(e)iai*), which we find in Crete, Thera, and Cyrene, and which must not be confused with the political associations bearing the same name which played a prominent part in Athens at the time of the Peloponnesian War; 'fraternities' (*phratr(i)ai*), which were more widespread and which, as we have seen, watched over questions of citizen rights at Athens: the father had his legitimate or adopted sons enrolled in the registry of the phratry and the young husband introduced his wife to the members of this association. However, the Athenian constitution of Clisthenes, without depriving the phratries of their privileges, had created, side by side with them, a subdivision of the citizen body on a territorial basis, the *demoi*, urban or rural districts, which became the basic element of civic organization. From this time, membership in the citizen body was officially defined by enrolment in the books of a deme, which corresponded to the possession of a birth certificate. This formality was carried out when the young man reached the age of eighteen and it was ratified by a vote of the citizens of whom the deme was composed (*demotai*): after this enrolment, the young Athenian became an ephebe. His official name henceforth consisted of his personal name.

followed by his father's name in the genitive and a 'demotic' adjective indicating his deme, thus certifying his entitlement to citizenship: Pericles, son of Xanthippus, of the deme of Cholargus (in the eastern outskirts of Athens); Demosthenes, son of Demosthenes, of the deme of Paeania (now Liopesi, in Mesogeia).

Over and above the division into phratries and demes, the majority of the Greek cities retained the old division of the whole citizen population into tribes. The tribe, as its name (*phyle*) shows, had an ethnical or gentilitial origin. It often represented the ancient division of the Greek people before its arrival in the Aegean basin: thus in the Dorian cities we often find the three Dorian tribes with their traditional names, *Hylleis*, *Dymanes*, and *Pamphyloi*. Sometimes there were additional tribes, originally representing the non-Dorian population: this was, for example, the case at Sicyon, where there was a fourth tribe, the Aegialeans. Herodotus tells us (V, 68) that early in the sixth century B.C. the tyrant Clisthenes, who belonged to this tribe, changed its name to 'tribe of the leaders' (*Archelaoi*) and gave offensive names to the three Dorian tribes, formed from the two Greek words for the pig (*Hyatai* and *Choireatai*) and from that for the ass (*Oneatai*): these new names remained in use for more than sixty years after the death of the tyrant, before the former titles were resumed. In the Ionian cities, it is the four Ionian tribes that are most often found (the *Geleontes*, *Argadeis*, *Aigikoreis*, and *Hopletes*), sometimes accompanied, as at Miletus, with additional tribes. Until nearly the end of the sixth century, Athens knew only the four Ionian tribes. But after the fall of the Pisistratids, the Alcmaeonid Clisthenes, a descendant of the tyrant of Sicyon, replaced them by ten tribes based on a territorial principle, which were nothing more than groups of demes. The Delphian oracle, by naming the eponymous heroes of these new tribes, gave its sanction to a reform which was of great political significance, since it broke up the old framework and the traditional solidarities so as to fuse the Attic people as a whole in the new organization. The same procedure had already served the needs of other reformers: when in the middle of the sixth century Demonax of Mantinea had been called upon to provide laws for Cyrene, he replaced the Dorian tribes which had been established since the foundation of the colony by three new tribes, into which he divided the diverse racial elements of which the population of the great African city was then composed.

The part played by the tribe in the cities of Archaic and Classical times was, wherever this division existed, of extreme importance. Not only were the members of the tribe united by the celebration of common cults, such as that of the eponymous hero, but above all the distribution of public responsibilities, whether political, judicial, military, or fiscal, was performed within the framework of the tribe. It is at Athens that we get the clearest view of this inner organization of the state. Here the great majority of the magistracies were collegial, and each 'college' contained a number of magistrates equal to that of the tribes (ten from Clisthenes' time), or a multiple of it. The same rule applied to the membership of tribunals. The recruitment of the army had also been based, from time immemorial, on this division of the citizen body, which was carefully preserved in the units of infantry and cavalry: thus the squadron provided by each tribe was itself called a 'tribe', *phyle*, commanded by a *phylarch*. Already in Homer we can hear on the lips of Nestor advising Agamemnon to join battle: 'Separate the men by tribes and phratries [= 'by peoples and clans'], Agamemnon, so that phratry may give aid to phratry and tribe to tribe' (*Iliad*, II, 362–363). The stability of a Greek army in action appeared (except when mercenaries were employed) to depend closely on the preservation of civilian cadres in military formations. On the fiscal plane, the distribution of most of the direct obligations incumbent on individual citizens (known as *liturgies*) was organized on a tribal basis: these public expenses met by rich citizens in rotation also involved the prestige of the tribes on the occasion of a competition which set them in rivalry in the person of their gymnasiarchs or choregi. Thus in everyday life the citizen was constantly reminded of his close association with the members of his group. In this sense, the enclosure of the eponymous heroes, in the Agora, where effigies of the 'patrons' of the ten tribes stood side by side, was a symbol of the Athenian state: it was here that official summonses, both civil and military, were posted. Lastly, when the city honoured with a state funeral those who had died in battle, each tribe collected the ashes of its members in a single cypress-wood coffin and the names of those who had died for the fatherland were carved on the marble tribe by tribe.

Thus firmly embodied in intermediate organizations, the citizen had a larger or smaller share, according to the city in which he lived, in the government of the state. In the Classical Age, the old monarchy of Homeric times had almost everywhere been replaced by an aristocratic or popular form of government. National dynasties continued to exist only in less developed countries on the fringes of the Hellenic world, in Macedonia or Epirus. Such a seemingly aberrant phenomenon as the monarchy of the Battiads in Cyrene, which lasted until the middle of the fifth century, is to be explained by the tyrannical character assumed by the dynasty under the last three kings: by acting like contemporary tyrants, they prolonged by three-quarters of a century a form of government which, but for this change, would have been a complete anachronism. Everywhere else, apart from the very special case of Sparta, the memory of kingship survived only in the title held by some magistrate, such as the king–archon at Athens, whose functions were of an honorary nature and were religious rather than civic. The exercise of power was shared between the assembly of the citizens, the councils and the magistrates. These three basic elements of the Greek political system reappear in the majority of the cities, with varying prerogatives, whatever the political régime may be, aristocracy, oligarchy, or democracy. It was the methods of recruiting these bodies and the principles governing their participation in the administration of the city that determined the nature of the régime in a given state.

The assembly (*ecclesia*) in principle contained all the citizens possessed of political rights. Since it could only meet at rare intervals, a council of limited membership existed to keep an eye on affairs: it was usually known as the *boule*. When it was composed of the elders of the city (*gerontes*), it was called the *gerousia*. There might even be a *boule* and a *gerousia* in the same city. As for the magistrates, they saw to the administration of the various public services and had the decisions of the assembly and the council put into effect. As we have seen, they often constituted a 'college', or board, based on representation of the several tribes. This system in theory combined a form of direct government (decisions made by the assembly) with the rudiments of semi-representative government (action taken by the council), the magistrates being subject to constant supervision by the council and intermittent supervision by the assembly. The ancient Greek world, as has recently been pointed out, was almost entirely unacquainted with the strictly representative system, by which authorized agents delegated by the people have full power to act in its name without being obliged to render an account: only some rare federal states, such as the Boeotian Confederacy, succeeded in putting such a system into practice. But in the majority of the cities the reality of power belonged either to one or several councils of moderate size (in this case the régime is of an aristocratic or oligarchical character) or to the assembly more or less effectively guided by the *boule* (in such cases we have a democratic régime, as in Athens).

Although theorists, following Aristotle, tried as best they could to classify the different constitutions of the Greek cities, there were no constitutions that could represent one of these régimes in its unadulterated form. It is rather a question of tendency and of political philosophy which made it possible to define them amid all their infinite variety. We know that Aristotle and his pupils composed treatises on the constitutions of 158 Greek or Barbarian states. To judge from the *Constitution of Athens*, which has come down to us in a papyrus, each of these monographs contained a history of the earlier institutions followed by a description of their existing state. From this we can discern how complicated the working of institutions must have been throughout the centuries in a world so extremely partitioned as that of ancient Greece. Though we may have a fairly intimate acquaintance with the functioning of the Anthenian constitution and a less precise knowledge of the Spartan one, we should never lose sight of the fact that the constitutions of all the other cities, about most of which we have little information, had each its own original features and that each followed an evolution peculiar to itself.

It would no doubt be a mistake to seek to define a general tendency in a manner which might well be invalidated by the advance of knowledge. Let us merely say that the aristocratic kinds of constitutions restricted membership of the various councils to representatives of noble families and preferred the members of these councils to be appointed for life: such was the Council of the Areopagus at Athens before Solon's reforms. The rôle of the popular assembly was in these cases confined to more or less automatic approval of the decisions made by the councillors. Moreover, measures were taken to limit the number of the citizens who should enjoy full privileges, by excluding, for example, as was done in Thebes, any citizen who had sold goods in the market-place in the course of the preceding ten years: that is to say in practice all the small rural landowners. The oligarchical régimes differed from the aristocratic ones only in the methods employed to select the minority which, within the citizen body, reserved the main power for itself: here it was not social origin that counted, but wealth, which made possible some change in the composition of the privileged minorities. Income qualifications were laid down for admission to the Council and the magistracies and even for membership in the Assembly. According to whether the social problem was or was not presented in a sharp form, the oligarchy assumed either a violent or a moderate character and the measures restricting the number of enfranchised citizens were more or less rigorous in nature. Aristotle has described in detail the devices employed to discourage the popular element from interesting itself in public affairs: they do credit to the inventiveness of the political thinkers who devised this form of pseudo-democracy disguising what was in reality an oligarchy.

Genuine democracy might have and did in fact normally possess institutions fairly similar to those of aristocratic and oligarchical régimes, but in a democracy these institutions functioned in a very different spirit. The *ecclesia* met regularly, all the citizens were entitled to membership in it and enjoyed complete freedom of speech; it maintained a close check upon the actions of the magistrates and the council; it decided on all important questions by decrees voted upon by show of hands after public discussion; so it practised direct government, guided by the opinions of the orators who influenced its policy. This is the system to which Fénelon's remark applies: 'In Greece, everything depended on the people, and the people depended on the spoken word.' In the Athenian state, which we know best, the Assembly met, in the Classical period, four times in each *prytaneia*. A prytany was the period of thirty-five or thirty-six days during which the fifty *bouleutai* (Council members) of one tribe served as a standing committee of the Boule and held the title of *prytaneis*: since there were ten tribes, the legal year was divided into ten prytanies. So the *ecclesia* met regularly every nine or ten days, subject to feast-days or bad weather which could disturb this rhythm. Such frequency explains both the leading part taken by the Assembly in the conduct of affairs and the small proportion of citizens who could make themselves free to attend such numerous meetings. No quorum was laid down, apart from exceptional cases as in the procedure for ostracism: on these occasions 6,000 votes had to be recorded (out of about 40,000 citizens). But the attendance was generally much smaller than this. Here again we can see what a fiction ancient 'democracy' was: in spite of such expedients as the *misthos ecclesiasticos*, a fee established in the fourth century to attract citizens to the Assembly by indemnifying them for loss of working time, in spite of the action taken by the police force (Scythian archers) who headed off passers-by towards the Pnyx with a rope smeared with vermilion, and although in theory no citizen could have anything better to do than to play his part in the government of the state, nevertheless this was left to a minority of city idlers attracted either by concern for the public interests, the reputation of a particular orator, or the bait of an allowance for expenses.

However unrepresentative of the whole citizen body it really was, this minority was none the less jealous for the prerogatives granted to the people by the democratic constitution; all sovereignty and all justice resided in the people. So the former had to be exercised and the latter dispensed by the people's will.

To facilitate the assertion of this will, Clisthenes or one of his successors had contrived an institution which was employed for the first time in 487 B.C., viz. *ostracism*: each year, in the sixth prytany, the ecclesia decided whether or not there was any need to put this measure into practice. In the case of an affirmative decision, the Assembly proceeded to take a vote for which potsherds (*ostraca*) were used as 'voting papers'; hence the term *ostracism*. Each voter wrote on his potsherd the name of a politician whom he wished to proscribe. The one named by the majority was banished from Athens for ten years, thus leaving the field clear for his opponents. During the fifth century ostracism was imposed upon several political leaders who had influence but only minority support at their command, including Aristides, Themistocles, Cimon, and Thucydides the son of Melesias, whose exile in 443 left Pericles free to govern Athens according to his pleasure. More than 1,600 inscribed potsherds have been found, mainly in the excavations at the Agora, showing sixty different names, including those of all the persons known to have been ostracized. These humble documents bear witness to the intensity of political struggles in fifth-century Athens, and also to the educational level reached by the average citizen, almost all of whom were capable of writing a name correctly with brush or stylo. Ostracism fell into disuse after 417, when it became clear that party intrigues were falsifying its proper application.

The rôle of the democratic tribunals was no less important than that of the Assembly: being master of its vote in the tribunal, the people by direct consequence became the master of all political life in the city, as Aristotle justly observes in his *Constitution of Athens* (IX, 1). The general sentiment of the democrats found its most perfect expression in the shouts of the multitude during the melancholy incident of the condemnation of the strategi who had won the Battle of Arginusae: 'It is monstrous that the people should not be allowed to do whatever they wish.' The honest Xenophon here faithfully echoes the demagogues of his time (*Hellenica*, I, 7, 12). Socrates, at the time a *prytanis*, alone had the courage to maintain the authority of the law against popular fury to the very end. But it was in vain, and the Athenians were later to pay a cruel price for this outburst of uncontrolled passion, of which they repented almost immediately, but too late.

The danger of the system obviously lay in the fickleness and credulity of a crowd which skilful orators could manage as they pleased, by means of crude arguments or slapdash appeals to sentiment. A coherent and consistent policy had little chance of gaining and keeping the support of such an assembly unless it was embodied in a man capable of winning and keeping the goodwill of the multitude: Pericles' outstanding virtue was his ability to achieve this throughout nearly thirty years, during which he raised the power and prosperity of Athens to their zenith. But this miracle was not repeated and what followed was the defeat and subjection of the richest state in Greece through its inability to adopt and maintain a definite line of policy. The history of its conflict with Philip provides a melancholy illustration of the inability of the Athenian democracy, in the form it had taken in the fourth century, to face a serious foreign threat. While the Macedonian monarch pursued his plan for twenty years, employing force and cunning at different times as circumstances required, knowing how to give way on occasion or to negotiate with the intention of soon resuming his advance towards his proposed goal, the Athenian people, influenced by opposing counsels, passed from indifference to anxiety and from anxiety to despondency; it flattered itself that it could provide by half-measures against a danger in which it was only half willing to believe; for a long time it could not decide whether to accept the king's dangerous friendship or adopt open rivalry; and when, having closed its eyes for so many years to the growing threat to its interests and its independence, it at last resolved to fight, this courageous decision came too late and could only result in disaster. And yet, to judge only by the superior resources at her disposal, in her struggle with Philip as in the Peloponnesian War, Athens logically ought to have won the day, if the mechanism of her institutions had not condemned her to impotence.

Aware of the disadvantages of democracy, a number of orators and philosophers in Athens itself delighted to contrast the weakness and fickleness of their own people with the well-tried seriousness and civic spirit of the Spartans, moulded by unalterable institutions ever since, at a very remote period, perhaps about the end of the ninth century, the legendary Lycurgus had drawn up for his fellow-citizens the *rhetra* (basic legal code), defining the main features of the system. Even if, in reality, all this took place less quickly and less simply than tradition represented, the permanence of the Lacedaemonian institutions in the Classical Age is an established fact. The precise object of this constitution was to prevent any change and it did achieve its object.

The political organization of Sparta was based upon complete and exclusive domination over the perioeci and helots by a warrior caste, the so-called Spartiates. This privileged minority called itself the *Peers*: they alone were citizens and they drew their livelihood from the best land in Laconia and Messenia, farmed for them by the helots. Each Spartiate collected the income derived from the portion of land (*cleros*) allocated to him. Schooled from childhood in a rigorous collective discipline, the citizen remained subject, after attaining his majority, to strict obligations: until the age of thirty, he lived a communal life with his age-group, his married life being restricted to the minimum. After the age of thirty, he enjoyed greater freedom and possessed a home of his own, but he still had to take one meal a day with the men of his military unit and take part, as formerly, in intensive military training until he reached the age of sixty. It is understandable that such a constant maintenance of social control gave the Lacedaemonian battalions the tactical and moral cohesion which aroused universal admiration and so often brought them victory.

The Spartan constitution combined elements borrowed from the various forms of government known to the Greeks: monarchy, aristocracy, and democracy. Two hereditary kings, belonging to the two families of the Agids and Eurypontids, in principle possessed all executive power. But their authority could be freely exercised only in the military sphere, in which the army engaged in operations was usually put under the command of one of the two kings. For vital political decisions, a council of twenty-eight elders, the *Gerousia*, shared the responsibilities of power and served as a High Court of Justice. The *Gerontes* of whom it was composed were over sixty years of age and were appointed for life by the citizens meeting in the Assembly: the volume of the cheering that greeted each candidate enabled the selection board to decide which were the elected members. The Assembly of the Spartiates (*Apella*), which appointed the magistrates according to this rudimentary procedure, met regularly to hear the reports presented to it by the state authorities and to approve the decisions submitted by them: the *Apella* did not discuss, it merely declared its agreement with the leaders

192. FEMALE HEAD IN THE SEVERE STYLE
One of the masterpieces that adorned the sanctuaries of Cyrene. Though contemporary with the sculptures of Paeonius at Olympia (about 470–460), it is closer to Attic art, with its slightly cold but splendidly stylish 'calligraphy'. Cyrene Museum.

193. GOLD BOWL DEDICATED BY THE CYPSELIDS
This gadrooned bowl, a magnificent offering presented by the sons of Cypselus the tyrant of Corinth (second half of the seventh century), illustrates the accomplished skill of the Corinthian goldsmiths. An inscription in the archaic Corinthian alphabet reads as follows: 'The Corinthians dedicated [this bowl] from the spoils of Heraclea'. Heraclea was a town in the northwest of Greece, which they had conquered. Boston Museum.

194. COIN OF THE CHALCIDIANS
The Chalcidian League minted federal coins in the fourth century, with a cithara on the reverse side. Starting from the top left-hand side and reading round the three sides, we find the name of the Chalcidians (in the genitive).

193

194

who could thus in difficult circumstances avail themselves of the moral support given by the whole body of citizens.

Apart from the survival of a twofold hereditary kingship, we can recognize in the elements of the Spartan system the Council and the Assembly of the other Greek cities. It is in the application of the system that the originality of Lacedaemon appears. The *Apella* could not in practice thwart the wishes of the magistrates. Every precaution had been taken to ensure the exercise of a firm authority, which had originally rested in the hands of the two kings and was shared with them by the *Gerousia* from Lycurgus's time onwards. But in addition to these there was an annual and collegial magistracy, that of the *ephors*, which played a decisive rôle in the state. The five ephors, or 'overseers', were instituted later than Lycurgus's reforms. Elected by the *Apella* and chosen from among its members, their task was to supervise on behalf of the whole people both the actions of the kings, who had sworn in their presence to govern in accordance with the laws, and the citizens' obedience to tradition in private and public behaviour. Being responsible for the security of the state, they had full powers to ensure it by decisions that were regarded as final: instructions to the magistrates, reprimands, and various sanctions. Everyone dreaded them and did their will; they were accountable to no one but their successors in this supreme magistracy; moreover, in spite of their merciless severity, they seem for a long time to have acted in conformity with the deepest aspirations of their fellow-citizens.

This enclosed, proud, narrow, and resolutely conservative society was determined to preserve itself at all costs against contagion from without. From the middle of the sixth century it rejected all the allurements of art and architecture. Impelled by its will to survive unchanged, it proscribed trade and even the use of silver coinage. It confined its ambition to the subjection of Messenia, the granary which nourished its military caste, to the domination of the Peloponnesus at the cost of ever-repeated operations against Argos and the cities of Arcadia, and lastly to the forcible defeat of any attempt to achieve hegemony in the Greek mainland, whether by Persian invasion, Athenian imperialism, or the policy of Epaminondas, against which it wore itself out. These consistent and resolute but remarkably limited designs were for a long time crowned with success, but they brought no economic expansion or cultural prestige. Moreover, by a slow and gradual decline the very foundations of the Spartan state continued to be restricted and to rot away: the principle of equality among the citizens, based on

X

the ownership of a portion of land of equal value by each of them, was constantly undermined. The very victories of Sparta had brought an influx of unusual wealth. As Socrates reminds young Alcibiades, in Plato's dialogue which bears his name (123 a), 'one can say of the money which enters Lacedaemon what the fox said to the lion in Aesop's fable: the footsteps leading to the town are very clear, but one would look in vain for those of any money leaving it.' In spite of the strict teaching of tradition, the appetite for wealth, concealed by a seeming austerity, led many Spartans astray. At the beginning of the fifth century, the Milesian Aristagoras, anxious to obtain military support from Sparta for the Ionian rebels, tried to bribe King Cleomenes with rich gifts and the prospect of booty; it took a sign from the gods (in the form of a childish remark dropped by his daughter) to induce Cleomenes to turn the tempter out of doors. The constantly increasing desire to augment private fortunes finally brought about a concentration of landed property in ever fewer hands, at the expense of the equality laid down by the laws. A great number of Spartiates, unable to pay the required contribution towards the communal meals, sank from the caste of the Peers into that of the 'Inferiors'. The number of fully qualified citizens constantly decreased throughout the fifth and fourth centuries: from about 5,000 after the Persian Wars, it fell to fewer than 3,000 at the time of the Battle of Leuctra, in 371, according to V. Ehrenberg's calculations. This slow but steady dwindling of the citizen body was already regarded by ancient observers as the deadly malady with which Sparta was stricken, *oliganthropia*, loss of population. This deficiency could by itself have discouraged any expansive policy, even if the traditional narrowness of view of the Lacedaemonian government has allowed such a policy to be conceived.

The law. Economic regulations: money, metrology. Commerce and exchange
Whether oligarchical or democratic, the political systems of the Greek states were devised for small communities and hardly facilitated the pursuit of large designs or the formation of great states, as Greek history clearly shows. On the other hand, these régimes, for all their extreme diversity, clearly defined for the first time the relationship between the citizen and the state, thus laying the very foundations of all modern political systems. This relationship was based on law, whether written or oral, whether ascribed by tradition to divine intervention or derived from human initiative. Only the tyrants, in the meaning assumed by this

word in Classical times, governed without law: it was indeed the absence of reference to traditional laws, much more than the harshness or cruelty with which power was exercised, that characterized tyranny. On the other hand, every city that enjoyed regular government, of whatever form, aimed to put into effect the ideal of a communal life regulated by good laws: this ideal was called *eunomia*, harmony within the law, good order inspired by wisdom. The fact that the reality rarely approached this ideal perfection does not mean that the Greeks did not sincerely aim to achieve it by various means, all taking for granted a fundamental element, namely sincere acceptance by each citizen of the essential principles of the city-state. These principles found expression in the public cults and in the laws (*nomoi*), and the latter had their share of the religious veneration felt for the former. It is of course true that the juridical concepts originally regarded as sacred tended gradually to become secularized. But there always remained, in the minds of the Greeks in the Classical period, a close connection between the notion of illegality and that of impiety. We can see from the famous prosopo-poeia of the Laws, in Plato's *Crito*, how greatly inclined the most vigorous in-tellects in Athens at the beginning of the fourth century still were to revere the laws as truly divine by nature.

The object of the laws was to keep human relations free from violence and arbitrary action. They must needs make Concord (*Harmonia*) and Justice (*Dike*) reign in the city, provided that every citizen submitted himself to their authority. There were certainly sophists ready to question the very concepts of Justice and Law, to set Nature and Custom in opposition, to maintain that legality, a mere product of convention, is an obstacle to the play of natural forces, and to give a direct denial to Pindar's phrase: 'Law reigns over all beings, both mortals and Immortals.' But these subtleties, which provided the philosophers with abundant material, had little influence on the general public, and the fourth-century orators, both in their political speeches and in their legal debates, never ceased to proclaim their respect for the laws as guardians of sound morality and of the security of the citizens.

These laws varied exceedingly: the distinction between public and private law is hardly perceptible in the Archaic and Classical periods. Every action taken by a citizen could interest the city, which, in the person of its lawgivers, intervened in the most various domains. It should be added that the city was less concerned to embody principles in its laws than to provide practical measures to resolve a precise problem. Thus these measures were not always entirely coherent. That is not to say that the Greeks were unable to compile legal codes: we possess one almost complete in its original text thanks to the monumental inscription at Gortyn in Crete, carved in large letters on the enormous blocks of a bonded wall during the first half of the fifth century. Other collections are mentioned in ancient texts: we know, for example, that the Athenian codes, that of Solon's laws and the so-called code of Nicomachus (which was carved in stone at the end of the fifth century), could be consulted on inscriptions and not merely in a record office.

As a general rule, every new law was copied out on a stele. Thus the laws remained easily accessible to the public. And yet the Greeks of the Classical Age, less interested in legal studies than the Romans were after them, did not seek to unify in a systematic way the whole body of these ill-assorted texts. The professional speech-writers (*logographoi*) who composed the speeches delivered by litigants in court, the *synegoroi* who, without payment, lent their friends the aid of their eloquence, and the orators recommending a proposal in the Assembly were very clever at manipulating legal texts in support of their arguments. But they left to the philosophers the task of constructing systems which, it must be said, were very directly inspired by contemporary realities, as in the case of the *Laws* of Plato. Here again the division of the Hellenic world into so many independent political units played a decisive rôle: the legal particularism of the cities made it less necessary to bring about the unification of law which the institutions of a large state might naturally have brought to pass.

The majority of these juridical measures were concerned with the position of persons and property, thus sanctioning the privileged status of fully qualified citizens as compared with women, who were always 'minors', citizens or residents of inferior status (when, as in Sparta, these existed), foreigners and slaves. They clearly defined the rights and obligations of individuals in relation to the civic community. They fixed penalties and the procedure both for regulating lawsuits between private citizens and for punishing crimes against the state. Moreover, in addition to making these provisions of a civil, political, or judicial kind, the state also legislated in the economic sphere. It regarded the minting of money as one of its essential prerogatives: the issue of a particular coinage by each city testified to the city's independence, and the original types which it adopted served it as emblems: the term 'city's coat of arms' has actually been used in this connection. Hence comes the extreme variety of Greek numismatics.

The state also regulated metrology in all its aspects. It fixed the calendar, which varied from city to city and whose main 'guiding marks' were the solemn religious ceremonies performed by the community. The names of the months were usually derived from the names of gods or of the principal festivals. In spite of the extreme attention they paid to astronomical phenomena, the Greeks never succeeded in resolving the difficulty presented by the discrepancy between the lunar and the solar calendars: little success attended the devices to re-establish between them an agreement that was constantly subject to renewed dispute, and Aristophanes makes fun of the 'meteorologists' who, far from re-establishing order in the normal succession of the days, had left everything topsy-turvy (*Clouds*, l. 615). Things became even more complicated when an administrative calendar, like that of the prytanies at Athens, was superimposed upon the astronomical and religious calendar.

There was also great complexity in weights and measures, which civic authorities made it their business to determine for convenience of exchange and honesty in commercial dealings. Excavations have yielded up model weights and standard units for measures of capacity, often not easy to interpret. The Greeks had devised various systems of measurements, usually combining decimal and sexagesimal schemes, the latter borrowed from Oriental metrology: thus the *stade*, the normal unit for measuring long distances, measured 600 Greek feet. But the foot varied between $10\frac{3}{4}$ inches and $13\frac{3}{4}$ inches, and consequently the stade varied between 177 and 230 yards. Another unit, the *cubit*, was often used as a measure of length: it was equal to $1\frac{1}{2}$ feet. As for the foot itself, it was divided into sixteen 'fingers', or *dactyls*. One can see the difficulties of calculation with such a system, to which must also be added measures of foreign origin, like the *Persian* parasang, amounting to 30 stades (about $3\frac{3}{4}$ miles), often used by Herodotus and Xenophon. The measures of weight and capacity were no less complicated and variable from city to city. Nevertheless, the demands of commerce endowed certain systems, such as the Aeginetan system and later the Attic, with a preponderance in practice, which operated chiefly in the monetary field: whether in the case of mere units for calculation (like the *talent* or the *mina*) or of real coins (like the *drachma* and the *obol*), the names of the monetary units were those of the corresponding units of weight.

To supervise all these measures, the city employed specialized officials, such as the *metronomoi*, inspectors of weights and measures at Athens. This was, indeed, only one aspect of state intervention in economic life: from the evidence of some texts, which mention *agoranomoi*, market superintendents, *sitophylakes*, grain-inspectors, and *epimeletai* (overseers) of the port, we can appreciate the important part played by such official intervention in Athenian life. Elsewhere, isolated or fragmentary records give us glimpses of a whole system of price-fixing and protectionist measures, as at Thasos in the interests of the wine trade.

Does it follow that the Hellenic world had a genuine economy of exchange? We have no ground for thinking so. Here we must note once and for all how ill-informed we are about the economic realities of Greek antiquity. Even in specially favourable cases, such as the grain supply for the Athenian built-up areas, records are scarce, mutilated, and hard to interpret. The historian who applies himself to these deceptive researches is under constant temptation to form far-reaching conclusions from insufficient data. So it is well to be very guarded on the subject of trade relations in Archaic and Classical Greece. One point should in any case be stressed: this trade was essentially maritime. The little cargo boats at the disposal of Greek seamen were, in view of the lack of roads suitable for wheeled traffic, the only means of transport available for any considerable trading. Their tonnage was very limited: as a rule their burden varied between 80 and 250 metric tons (of 1,000 kilogrammes each). Moreover, the favourable season for navigation hardly began before April and finished by the end of October. The funerary epigrams about those lost at sea often refer to the danger of storms at the winter solstice, during the setting of the Kids, or of the spring equinox, after the vespertine rising of Arcturus. Hesiod, in the seventh century, even restricted the time when one could put out to sea to fifty days in the height of summer. The square sail of the cargo vessels, which in contrast to the trireme did not make use of oars, made manoeuvring almost impossible. There were no lighthouses until the beginning of the Hellenistic Age and the charts, which were far too lacking in detail, were of less use than the 'portolani' or *periploi* which pilots might have at their disposal.

All this accounts for the fact that the tonnage of goods transported was never very high. The cereals for the large cities came from the rich arable lands of Egypt, Cyrenaica, and southern Russia: the annual imports of Athens in the fourth century have been assessed at 500,000 hectolitres. Timber and marble and ingots of copper and lead accounted for the rest of the heavy merchandise.

But there was also merchandise with a high market value, finished products of Greek agriculture and handicraft: choice wines, like those of Chalcidice, Thasos, and Chios; oil of Attica; perfumes; textiles from Miletus, Samos, or the East; painted earthenware vases, produced by Corinthian or Attic potters and often exported with their contents; bronzes from Corinth; silphion from Cyrenaica; silver coined or in ingots; ivory; gold and silver plate. These were valuable cargoes occupying limited space. They enabled ship owners and financiers to make fortunes and they carried the fame of Greek craftsmen to distant lands. The large bronze crater found in a Hallstattian tomb at Vix, in the Côte-d'Or, came from a Greek workshop in southern Italy or the Peloponnesus, at the end of the sixth century B.C. At Kul-oba, near Kerch, in the Crimea, gold medallions have been found bearing reproductions of Phidias' masterpiece, the statue of Athena Parthenos: these are specimens of the Athenian goldsmith's art from the late fifth or early fourth century. An Attic terra-cotta in a funerary pyramid at Meroë, near the upper course of the Nile, representing an Amazon on horseback, bears witness to early contacts, via Egypt, between Greece and Nubia.

These records, curious and suggestive though they are, must not be allowed to mislead us. Such exchanges sufficed to maintain the prosperity of a certain number of merchants and seafarers; they made some favoured cities, Athens, Corinth, Tarentum, Syracuse, Cyrene, and Naucratis, the seat of transactions that were considerable for this period. But most of the Greek cities had hardly any part in these dealings and confined themselves to local trading, based on the products of the district and in keeping with the ideal of self-sufficiency which inspired the lawgivers: we are familiar with Plato's severe condemnation of cities on the coast, where the proximity of the sea, 'by maintaining trade and trafficking for profit, makes the inhabitants' characters untrustworthy and prone to swindling' (*Laws*, 705 a). In fact, the peasant tradition was stronger with the Greeks than the urge for seafaring: if they liked to behold the sea, they chiefly liked to look at it from the shore, and fearless seamen always inspired them with less admiration than hoplites. When they left dry land in the age of colonization, it was under the pressure of necessity and not through a taste for adventure: what they sought overseas was new lands rather than markets.

Outside the limits of the city-state: leagues and amphictyonies. Failure of these attempts to remedy the division of the Greek world into small units. Hellenism was above all the feeling of a shared culture.

This narrow framework of the city, in which the Greek lived, worked, exercised his civic rights and worshipped his gods, this small political entity, for which he was called upon to fight and die, perfectly suited his requirements and his tastes. Until the genius of Philip and Alexander, without actually causing the old idea of the city to disappear, imposed a different conception of the state upon the Hellenic world, the Greeks never sought to broaden their field of vision or to join several cities together in an organic and lasting union. Their rare experiments in this direction were transitory or ineffective.

Religion certainly stood for a principle of unity: it enabled some regional groups to be formed with a great sanctuary as their centre. This applies, for example, to the League of the Ionian cities, founded soon after the colonization of Asia Minor: it united several cities (at first twelve, later nine) linked in common veneration around the sanctuary of *Poseidon Heliconios*, on cape Mycale, near Miletus, naméd the *Panionion*. This league succeeded to some degree in co-ordinating the efforts of its members in the revolt of Ionia against Darius, from 499 to 494 B.C. But the organic ties that united them were not strong enough for this union to be really effective and the revolt failed, bringing about the dissolution of the league. An association of the same kind, the *Hexapolis*, had united the Dorian cities of Caria, with the temple of Triopian Apollo, in the peninsula of Cnidus, as their centre. In the Cyclades, a religious confederacy, called the *amphictyony*, united the Ionians whose centre was the sanctuary of Apollo in Delos. We have seen how Athens, after the Persian Wars, made it serve her own interests.

The most famous of these religious associations and the one whose history is best known to us is the *Amphictyony* properly so called, that of Delphi. This organization had in reality two cult centres, but of unequal renown, the sanctuary at Delphi and that at Thermopylae, known simply as *Pylae* ('gates'). Here met the delegates of twelve peoples, mostly living in central Greece: the Thessalians, Boeotians, Phocians, Locrians, and others, along with the Dorians and Ionians, sole representatives of the rest of the Greek world. Each people sent two delegates, known as *hieromnenones*, to the Amphictyonic Council, which enabled Athens to have regularly at her disposal one of the two Ionian votes, while

Sparta was represented by one of the two Dorian voters only at long intervals. This gives us an idea of the local and archaic character of the Amphictyony, which could have no claims to represent the whole Hellenic world. Its function was to manage the financial affairs of Delphian Apollo through the agency of the *hieromnemones*, to organize the Games and the traditional festivals of the sanctuary, and lastly to defend the interests of the god against any action attempted against him. This was the duty which led the Amphictyony to declare the various Sacred Wars. Save in exceptional circumstances, the Amphictyonic states were bound to one another by little more than a rather loose moral solidarity, the obligations of which were stated in the oath which they swore: they undertook not to destroy one another utterly in case of war and to chastise any who desecrated the god of Delphi. They were bound by no firm political ties, and, in the field of international politics, the Amphictyony was an instrument of individual ambitions rather than a principle of unity between the Greek states.

Efforts were, however, made in certain regions to set up local confederacies endowed with permanent political institutions creating an effective bond of union between neighbouring cities: in Thessaly and in Arcadia, for example, a Thessalian and an Arcadian League or union (*koinon*) came into existence in the fourth century, with federal assemblies and federal magistracies. In Boeotia, Thebes, which held indisputable supremacy over the other cities in the region, on two occasions (in 447 and after 379) set up a firmly organized confederacy under its own control. In Chalcidice, Olynthus founded a league of the Chalcidian cities in 432. These attempts, whose continuance and success varied, show that a certain need for unity was felt, but none of them resulted in the formation of a genuine state: the devotion of the Greek to his little fatherland always kept centrifugal sentiments alive in the cities that were members of these leagues or confederacies.

The same applied all the more when one or other of the principal states wished to form a centralized alliance under its control, or, as was said, under its hegemony. Such was the case of the Peloponnesian League, which was officially styled 'the Lacedaemonians and their allies' and which enshrined the military supremacy of Sparta in the Peloponnesus: it was scarcely more than an offensive and defensive alliance which left the member cities, each bound to Sparta by a special treaty and an oath, with complete internal autonomy. Much bolder was the Delian League, organized by Athens after the Persian Wars. The institution of tribute, the transference of the federal treasury to Athens itself, the establishment of cleruchies in allied territory, the supervision exercised in their cities by Athenian officials (*episcopoi*), and the economic measures devised to favour Attic trade, all these were actions which soon turned the league into an empire and made the Athenian yoke intolerable to the subject cities. The defections and revolts of the allies contributed greatly to the final overthrow of the imperialism conceived by Pericles. The second maritime Confederacy of Delos, established in 377, sought to avoid these disadvantages, but did not entirely succeed, since it could not prevent a war between Athens and her allies in 357–355. Thus all the efforts to give some coherence to a combination of cities bound by organic links successively failed: the firm grasp of Philip of Macedon was needed to give the League of Corinth a real federal character.

In the face of this stubborn disinclination to unite beyond the narrow limits of the city-state, we may justly wonder what, in the eyes of the Greeks themselves, entitled them to proclaim that they were one people. For this sense of unity, in spite of all domestic rivalries, was accepted by them as something evident during the great Panhellenic religious festivals or when some deadly peril from without threatened the very existence of the Greek world: this was clearly seen when Greece defended herself against Persia and against the Etruscans and Carthaginians. This feeling of solidarity was based on community of language and religion, on the legendary tradition and on the works which ensured its transmission, namely the creations of the writers and artists. The Greek people more than any other needed its literature and its art in order to achieve self-awareness. The prodigious richness of both reflects not only the supreme gifts bestowed upon the Hellenes but also the passionate interest that drew them, as if impelled by a vital need, to the works of the hand and of the mind.

CHAPTER VIII

THINKERS AND POETS

The abundant fertility of Greek literature. A written literature intended for reading aloud. The Greek book

WE know the names of about two thousand ancient Greek writers. Even in proportion to the long period of time between Homer and the triumph of Christianity, this is a remarkable number, which excellently illustrates the outstanding richness of Greek literature. The greater part of this literature has disappeared in the three great trials that befell the classical inheritance, that is, the fire that destroyed the library at Alexandria, the substitution of the parchment *codex* for the papyrus roll, and lastly the crisis of the Byzantine Empire in the age of iconoclasm, that is, in the seventh and eighth centuries A.D. Nevertheless what has survived, sometimes by chance and sometimes because of selection practised by scholars or schoolmasters, still amounts to an enormous mass of works of every kind, too often fragmentary or imperfectly preserved, but in which Western literature has never ceased to find models. The greatest among these writers or thinkers go back to the Archaic and Classical periods, whose richness was unequalled. There could be no question of outlining here a history of this literature, even a compendious one confined to the masterpieces, any more than it is possible to do so for art. But we should at least like to indicate briefly what was an important fact of civilization: the creation of the principal literary genres, which we owe to the initiative of the Greeks.

This literature was, as early as the oldest surviving classics, a written literature. We have seen this when we considered Homer: it is today admitted that the *Iliad* and the *Odyssey* could not have come into existence, in anything closely resembling the form in which we know them, without the aid of the written alphabet, which alone would have been capable of giving compositions so complex and elaborated their precise form. We must imagine the poet copying out his work on the sheepskin or goatskin parchment sheets which the Greeks called *diphtherai* and whose name they subsequently kept, as Herodotus tells us (V, 58), to denote papyrus rolls (by a misapplication of the term). It seems to have been only about the middle of the seventh century, nearly a century later than the *Iliad*, that the use of papyrus spread through the Greek world, when the first Saitic Pharaoh, Psammetichus, opened the Delta of the Nile to Greek trade. From then onwards the Greeks were to read the works of their writers in papyrus 'volumes'. The long strip of papyrus, composed of fibres of the plant glued side by side, in two layers, one with the fibres horizontal (recto), the other with the fibres vertical (verso), was wound on two wooden sticks forming handles, each fastened to one end of the strip. The text, written in majuscule, with no divisions between the words and no punctuation marks, was arranged in parallel columns at right angles to the long sides of the roll. Each roll (*tomos* in Greek) might contain about sixty columns of text, each consisting of about thirty lines. The reader unwound the width of a column and then, to proceed to the next column, wound the first on to the handle held in the left hand and unwound the second column from the rest of the roll held in the right hand. It was not until the Roman period that the *codex*, with pages inscribed on both sides and joined in sections, which were then bound into a book, took the place of the *volumen* (the Latin name usually employed to denote the papyrus roll).

Writing on papyrus, borrowed from Egypt, was certainly a great advance on the *diphtherai* of early Archaic times. Nevertheless, the use of the *volumen* presented certain disadvantages: each roll was bulky and cumbersome and the building up of large libraries was consequently impeded. Moreover, a *volumen* was awkward to handle when looking for a quotation: before finding it, one had to unroll all the preceding part of the volume. Nor was it very easy to take notes while holding the *volumen* with both hands. These practical considerations partly explain why, in ancient Greece, so much importance was attached to the training of the memory and why authors readily quoted texts from memory and without verification. There was less respect than there is nowadays for the details of expression, and variants were easily accepted so long as the general meaning was not distorted.

On the other hand we must bear in mind that among the Greeks reading as a general rule meant reading aloud. The majority of the works of literature were composed to be listened to: they were intended for recitation in a singing voice, for choral singing, for dramatic performances, or for public reading to an audience, rather than for the delight and meditation of a solitary reader. Many of the characteristics of Greek literature are to be explained by this: the great importance of poetry, and later of eloquence; the didactic form which prose works readily assumed, as if it was a case of public or private lectures: the anxiety to indicate transitions very clearly by verbal indications, in cases where modern languages are satisfied with punctuation marks; and lastly the great success met with by the genre of dialogue, an original creation of Greek genius. Served by a language extraordinarily rich both in vocabulary and in syntax, having at their disposal the resources of several dialects to vary the literary effects and the tones, resting upon a tradition which supported but did not enslave them, the writers and thinkers of those times created or developed the main literary genres while also exploring with a boldness until then unmatched the directions which logical thought might follow. They even defined clearly for the first time the process and principles of such thought. Convinced that it could be affirmed and apprehended only through the agency of words, they ceaselessly devoted themselves to the task of perfecting their admirable verbal instrument, until they made of it the most wonderfully subtle and nimble means of expression that could be imagined. Epic poetry, lyric poetry, dramatic art, history and geography, philosophy and eloquence—such are, approximately in the chronological order in which the Greeks began to cultivate them, the different fields in which they exercised their mastery. We shall now review them in succession.

Epic. The Cyclic poems. The Hesiodic tradition. The hymns

The Homeric epic, as we have seen, appears suddenly in history in its finished form and Homer's two masterpieces at once provided models which his rivals always despaired of emulating. This very perfection implies that the *Iliad* and *Odyssey* had been prepared for by many earlier poetical attempts which have completely fallen into oblivion. *The Wrath of Achilles* was only one episode in the Trojan War; the *Return of Ulysses* told of the adventures of only one single hero after the capture of the city. A long epic tradition, essentially oral, must have been built up little by little, thanks to the bards (*aoidoi*), such as Demodocus whom we meet in the *Odyssey* at the court of Alcinous, the king of the Phaeacians. Was Homer the first to fashion a part of this rich material into a long work vigorously composed, thanks to the aid of alphabetical writing? Though we cannot positively say so, the complete absence of any reference to earlier epics at least makes this hypothesis quite probable. However, imitators of Homer fairly swarmed. Though their works, no doubt justly regarded as inferior to those of Homer, have not come down to us, at least we know several titles and some names of authors, with a synopsis of the subjects treated by them.

Around the *Iliad* grew up the poems of the Trojan Cycle, commonly called the *Cycle*; they related the episodes prior to the Wrath of Achilles. The *Chrestomathia* ('summary of useful knowledge') composed by a certain Proclus, either in the second or in the fifth century A.D. (there is still uncertainty about the date), and partially preserved, provides fairly precise information concerning them: the *Cypria* recalled the events prior to the *Iliad*, from the marriage of Peleus and Thetis and the Judgment of Paris to the carrying off of Helen and the earliest episodes in the siege of Troy. The *Aethiopis*, perhaps composed at the end of the seventh century by Arctinus of Miletus, was a direct continuation of the *Iliad*; here the king of the Ethiopians, Memnon, the son of Aurora and Priam's brother Tithonus, was seen coming to his uncle's aid; he fell by the hand of Achilles, who also slew Penthesilea, the queen of the Amazons, another ally of the Trojans; Achilles perished in his turn, pierced with an arrow by the archer Paris, aided by Apollo. Another epic by Arctinus, entitled the Destruction of Troy (*Iliou Persis*) related the capture of the city. The poet Lesches composed the *Little Iliad*, also intended as a completion of Homer's *Iliad*, in which he treated the same themes as Arctinus in his own fashion. Following a course parallel to that of the *Odyssey*, Hagias of Troezen composed an epic called the *Homeward Journeys* (*Nostoi*), describing the adventures of the Achaean leaders other than Ulysses after the Trojan War. As for Ulysses himself, his tragic destiny was the subject of the *Telegonia* of Eugammon, who lived at the court of the kings of Cyrene, Battus II and Arcesilas II, about 570–560 B.C.; after his return to Ithaca, Ulysses set out again on an expedition to the mountainous land of Epirus, and then, having returned again to his island, he there met his death at the hand of a son, Telegonus, whom he had had by the witch Circe, and who, travelling in quest of his father, killed him with a spear thrust, not having recognized him.

Side by side with the Trojan Cycle, there was a Theban Cycle, devoted to the legend of Oedipus and his descendants. Cinaethon of Lacedaemon was supposed to be the author of an *Oedipodea*, which was continued in a *Thebais*, sometimes attributed to Homer himself, which related the unsuccessful siege of Thebes by the Seven Chieftains and the fratricidal duel between Eteocles and Polynices. A third epic, *The Epigoni*, dealt with the victorious expedition against the city led by the sons of the Seven, ten years later. Other poems were concerned with the various legends. Creophylus of Samos composed a *Capture of Oechalia*, describing an adventure of Heracles: as a witty epigram of Callimachus informs us, this poem was sometimes ascribed to Homer, whose contemporary and friend Creophylus was supposed to have been. Corinthian legends were told in the *Corinthiaca* of Eumelus, those of Naupactus in the *Naupactia* of Carcinus. As late as the early part of the fifth century, Panyassis of Halicarnassus, Herodotus's uncle, composed a *Heraclea* in fourteen books, which, it appears, was not devoid of merit.

Hesiod's work, like Homer's, had imitators. The *Theogony* closes with a promise to sing of the fair mortals who, as mistresses of gods, gave birth to illustrious issue. A number of poems, which the ancient world ascribed to Hesiod himself, though modern critics question the attribution, sang of these illustrious loves: they were collected in the *Catalogue of Women*, which was also called the *Ehoiai* (a name taken from two Greek words, always the same, with which each of these poems began). Many later authors, beginning with Pindar, drew from this rich legendary stock.

Homer, Hesiod, and their emulators had by their example defined the rules of the epic genre and fixed the artificial language whose use was thenceforth obligatory for any composition in this style. After them, epic in the strict sense was never to reappear in Greek literature in the form of great masterpieces: neither the *Persica* of Choerilus of Samos, towards the end of the fifth century, nor the *Thebais* of Antimachus of Colophon, in the first half of the fourth century, deserved to survive. But the so-called *Homeric Hymns*, especially those to Apollo, Hermes, and Demeter, are good specimens of religious poetry in the epic style and gave profitable inspiration to the Alexandrian poets. And through Virgil all Western literatures have inherited their conception of epic from Homer.

195. ATTIC JUG

The potter Lysias (second half of the sixth century) signed this vase on the narrow red band in the middle of the belly. He was justly proud of a perfect success in workmanship: pure and simple form, impeccable black 'varnish' covering the whole field, with no need for decoration. Louvre.

196. TORSO OF THE APHRODITE OF CNIDUS

One of the good ancient replicas (they are extremely numerous) of Praxiteles' masterpiece. The original was made about the middle of the fourth century. By representing the goddess as nude, on the point of stepping down into her bath, the sculptor was illustrating an aspect of the ritual: it was customary to bathe the cult statues of goddesses. At the same time, the complete nudity of the statue is a reminder of the fertilizing power of the deity. Lucretius's fine verses in praise of Venus at the beginning of his poem *De Rerum Natura* are inspired by the same idea. Louvre.

195

Lyric poetry. Richness and variety of Archaic lyric poetry, from Archilochus to Simonides. Pindar

Yet the greatest literary glory of the Archaic Age did not come from the immediate posterity of the Homeric poems, but from the flowering of lyricism (poetry to be sung) in the twofold form which this genre assumed in ancient times: choral song and *monody* (solo singing). These poetical compositions, of which unfortunately only insignificant traces have in many cases survived, were very popular at that time. They satisfied the keen taste that the Greeks always showed for music, regarded by them as a basic element in education. These songs were as a general rule accompanied on the lyre, a seven-stringed instrument provided with a sound-box originally consisting of a tortoise-shell; its invention was attributed to Hermes, as the Homeric *Hymn to Hermes* attests. Various modifications and improvements made it possible to increase the volume of sound: the cithara was a lyre with a wooden sound-box, larger than the resonator of shell. The flute (*aulos*) was also used—not the transverse flute, which is a modern invention, but a 'straight' flute, like a flageolet, generally double, with its two pipes joined at the mouthpiece. Singing and music were always closely associated: the poetic rhythms which we can still analyse thanks to the data provided by ancient metrists like Hephaestion (late first century—early second century A.D.) were fully effective only in terms of the accompanying music, now lost.

This lyric poetry was extremely varied. Instead of having a special language, like epic, it admitted the use of all the dialects, according to the origin of the poet or the public addressed. The themes treated satisfied the most diverse interests: liturgical hymns such as the *nomoi*, sacred songs like the *paeans* and *dithyrambs*, marching songs for processions, choral odes for dances, warlike elegies, triumphal odes (*epinicia*) celebrating victors in the Games, love-songs, lamentations for the dead, drinking-songs, civic exhortations—every human sentiment found means of expression in Greek lyric poetry. Of course, as one could expect, the majority of these sentiments concern the city and its gods. But the passions of the individual, hate or love, in the most personal forms possible, also inspired these poets: the Greeks to a certain degree gave lyric poetry the character of personal poetry which we attribute to it today.

Most of these writers have survived only in mutilated fragments. In the seventh century, Terpander of Lesbos, more famed as a musician than as a poet, distinguished himself by his virtuosity on the seven-stringed lyre and composed

Y

mainly *nomoi*. The Lydian Alcman of Sardis wrote hymns full of grace and nobility for the Spartan festivals, at which choral songs were in high favour, while Tyrtaeus put heart into the Lacedaemonian hoplites with his martial elegies. The Ionian Mimnermus of Colophon, a skilful flute-player, sang of love and the pleasures of life, in tones that were already Epicurean. Archilochus of Paros, on whose personality recent work has thrown new light, took part in the struggles of the Greek settlers in Thasos against their Greek and Barbarian adversaries: in his elegies and his other lyric poems, of great metrical polish, he yields to his passions with uninhibited violence. Plato tells us that Socrates put him on the same plane as Hesiod, if not Homer. Through the pitiful remnant of his work, the vivacity of tone still strikes us today.

A little later, before and after the end of the seventh century, Arion of Methymna, in Lesbos, frequented the court of Periander, the tyrant of Corinth: his image has been obscured by the legend which represented him as having been saved by a dolphin when cast into the sea, but he seems to have transformed and enriched the genre of dithyramb, associated with the worship of Dionysus. This was also the age of Solon, the Athenian lawgiver, who addressed elegies of lofty patriotic inspiration to his fellow-countrymen. His contemporary Stesichorus of Himera, in Sicily, developed mythological legends in his hymns, thus preparing the way for the lyricism of Pindar. It was he who, having spoken ill of Helen in one of his poems, was stricken with blindness and only recovered his sight after having made amends for his offence in a poem of recantation (*Palinode*), in which he confuted his previous allegations against the illustrious heroine. To the same generation, lastly, belong the two lyric poets of Lesbos, Alcaeus and Sappho, whose work is known to us in more extensive fragments. While the former intermingles his songs of love and feasting with political themes, such as the abuse that he levels at Pittacus, the tyrant of Mitylene, Sappho in her burning verses gives voice only to the passion inspired in her by her young female companions and her revelation of it still strikes us with all its force.

Later, in the course of the sixth century, we have the Ionian Hipponax of Ephesus, whose iambic verses were violently satirical, and the westerner Ibycus of Rhegium, in Magna Graecia, a pupil of Stesichorus, who introduced more personal concerns into the choral poetry learnt from his master. Ibycus was in contact with Polycrates, the tyrant of Samos, who also attracted to his court Anacreon of Teos, an Ionian, who was later patronized by the Pisistratids. The erotic and Baochic poems of Anacreon remained the models for gracious lyricism. In Dorian territory, at Megara, the poet Theognis, under whose name some 1,400 elegiac verses of frequently doubtful authenticity have come down to us, expressed in bitter maxims the sentiments of an aristocrat soured by partisan struggles. Simonides of Ceos, who in succession enjoyed the favours of the Pisistratids, the princely families of Thessaly, and the tyrants of Sicily and southern Italy, preceded Pindar in giving a finished form to the ode of victory, while also being regarded as a master in the art of composing epigrams, short poems written to be carved on funerary or commemorative monuments. To him are ascribed some of those that were inspired by the Persian Wars.

Of all these poets, the only one whom we can really judge by his work is Pindar, who lived in the first half of the fifth century. In spite of the loss of a great part of his work, the four books of *Epinicia* which remain sufficiently reveal the might of his genius. Writing about athletic victories in the Games (and we know how glorious these were in the eyes of the Greeks), the great Theban lyrist can bring to life in striking epitomes any myths appropriate to his theme, filling them with a lofty religious and moral significance. Never was poetical language more concentrated and brilliant than his. In spite of some obscurity, which arises more from the close texture of his thought than from syntax or choice of words, Pindar has crystallized for all time some pure and dazzling phrases, such as: 'Man is the dream of a shadow' and the pathetic entreaty that he addresses to himself: 'Aspire not, my soul, to immortality, but be content to drain the cup of possibility.'

After such pinnacles, the lyric genre was almost bound to decline. Pindar's contemporary, Bacchylides of Ceos, some of whose odes we possess, is much inferior to him. Towards the end of the fifth century Timotheus of Miletus, whose poem entitled the *Persae* has been preserved in a papyrus, resuscitated with adaptations the *nomos*, on which Terpander had conferred distinction in earlier days, while Philoxenus of Cythera composed dithyrambs. Both of them were strongly influenced by Attic drama, which was at this time the only truly living form of poetry. In the fourth century, there were few memorable names: Antimachus of Colophon, who wrote an epic entitled the *Thebais*, employed the elegiac metre in a long poem, the *Lyde*, telling stories of unhappy loves. He appears as the first in date of the 'learned' poets and he thus paved the way for the literature of the Hellenistic Age, which was divided in its estimate of his merits: if Callimachus criticized him with violence, others esteemed him highly. But nothing of his work has survived. By way of compensation, a Rhodian poetess, Erinna, who died young, brought the voice of Sappho back to life after a fashion in a hexameter poem called the *Distaff*, fragments of which have been found in a papyrus and whose inspiration, if not its form, can justly be described as lyrical.

This dry and lengthy recital was necessary in order to convey the extraordinary richness of Greek lyricism in the Archaic and Classical periods. As in the case of epic, the Greek genius fixed the rules of the genre in its most widely various aspects. Of course subsequent literature, in the Alexandrian world and in Rome, continued to enlarge the resources of personal poetry. But, while widening the field of its inspiration, it continued faithful in the main to the poetical forms created by the early poets.

Drama. Attic tragedy in the fifth century. Old Comedy
Chronologically speaking, tragedy and comedy came into existence considerably later than the other kinds of poetry. As we have seen, it was at Athens, under the tyranny of Pisistratus, that tragedy emerged from the dithyramb, and comedy from the phallic songs, within the setting of Dionysus-worship, with which dramatic performances remained closely associated. We can understand why the most brilliant tragic poets were Athenians.

The first great name in tragedy is that of Phrynichus, whose works are lost, but were still esteemed at the end of the fifth century B.C. He employed only one actor, who engaged in a dialogue with the chorus: this meant that his plays were more like oratorios than genuine dramas. He was the first to draw inspiration from contemporary history: his *Capture of Miletus* dealt with the failure of the Ionian Revolt in 494, and his *Phoenissae*, produced about 476–475, had as its theme the consequences of the Battle of Salamis. Aeschylus followed his example four years later, when he wrote the *Persae*. Nevertheless, Phrynichus usually drew his subjects from the rich repertoire of the epic legends: his successors did likewise, without ever feeling themselves bound by a mythological tradition that had no dogmatic character.

The three great Attic poets of the fifth century are for us Greek tragedy in its entirety: Aeschylus, the eldest of the three, lived in the first half of the century; Euripides, the youngest, in the second half: while Sophocles, who lived for ninety years, covered almost the whole century from the time of the Persian Wars. In their works, of which we have now only a limited selection made at a late period by grammarians from pedagogic motives, we can see the conception of tragedy developing little by little. The part played by the chorus, at first very important, becomes progressively smaller, as does at the same time the originally preponderant place given to the lyrical element. The dialogue develops and becomes more lively. Aeschylus introduces a second actor, and later, in imitation of his junior, Sophocles, a third. Since each of these actors, by a change of costume and mask, could play successive parts, the resources of production are increased and the action, originally rudimentary, takes on increasing importance. In Euripides, the part of the chorus has become little more than that of a discreet onlooker, whose interventions serve mainly as divisions between the main crises of the tragedy, occupying the *orchestra* and holding the attention of the audience during what corresponded to our intervals. On the other hand, dramatic development, striking effects, progressive portrayal of the mind and feelings of the characters, and oratorical duels between the protagonists engross the interest of the poet and his audience. The author tells us a story, stirs our emotions, arouses fear and pity in us, and now behaves like a true tragic poet: here too the Greek writers defined the rules of a genre and bequeathed them to European literature.

But there is something even more important than literary technique that modern tragedy owes to the Greek tragic poets, something that can still give it nobility and grandeur: the agonizing problem of Destiny. In Aeschylus, as in Sophocles and Euripides, what is enacted on the stage is the destiny of man, as determined by supernatural powers. Aeschylus, animated by a religious faith nurtured at the traditional springs of sacred belief, shows mortals as subject to *Nemesis*, the vengeance of the jealous gods who punish any excess, any violation of ritual law; and yet, in the final scene of the *Oresteia*, a lofty conception of justice, whose instrument the city of Athens can become through the voice of the Areopagus, appears to temper the harshness of such condemnations. Sophocles' desire is to make us care about the victims of a cruel destiny, whose unforeseen vicissitudes delude the calculations and the presumption of mankind: from this ridiculous impotence of man springs the poignant pathos of *Oedipus Rex*. But a high conception of the moral law, as in the *Antigone*, ennobles these predestined victims when they sacrifice themselves to an ideal. Euripides, the most complex

197. VOLUTED CRATER

Attic black-figure pottery (second half of the sixth century). On the neck there is a frieze of warriors (chariots, hoplites, Scythian archers, and horsemen), rhythm being contributed by seated figures. Boston Museum.

198. CYLIX-TYPE CRATER

Attic red-figure pottery (third quarter of the fifth century). Gigantomachy. Zeus and Athena are attacking the Giants, who are equipped like hoplites. In the centre is the chariot of Zeus, driven by a Victory. Ferrara Museum.

199. ATTIC CUP

A type of cup characteristic of the third quarter of the sixth century, the best period of Attic black-figure pottery. The fairly deep hollow of the cup shows a slight projection half-way up, emphasized on the outside by a black line. The high edge thus produced has caused these vases to be known as 'lip-cups'. The signature of the potter, Neandros, is inscribed on a level with the handles.

200. DRINKING MUG

Attic red-figure pottery (first quarter of the fifth century). Triptolemus, sitting in a winged chariot, flanked by serpents, is receiving in a libation-flask the wine poured out by Kore–Persephone (here designated by her other name, Phersephatta). On the left is Demeter, who has given the boy the wheat which he is going to distribute to mankind. The two goddesses of Eleusis both have burning torches in their hands. British Museum.

201. ATTIC RED-FIGURE RHYTON

A 'modelled' vase in the form of a bridled mule's head. One drank the thin stream of wine that poured out when an opening in the lower part of the vase (here the tip of the muzzle was unstoppered. The neck is decorated with a 'domestic' scene: a slightly intoxicated old man is cutting capers (first half of the fifth century). This form of vase goes back to the Mycenaean Age. Petit Palais, Paris.

202. APOLLO

Coin of Amphipolis (early fourth century). Bold foreshortening of the face seen from the front. The god is wearing a laurel wreath. Cabinet des Médailles.

203. HERMES

Coin of Aenus (early fourth century). Same boldness in foreshortening. Hermes is wearing a felt cap whose narrow rim is adorned with a row of pearls. The coin has been mutilated on the right. Cabinet des Médailles.

197

199

198

200

201

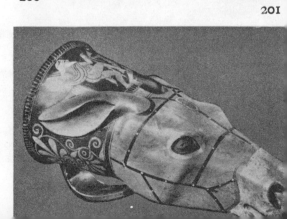

202

203

204

205

206

207

208

209

210

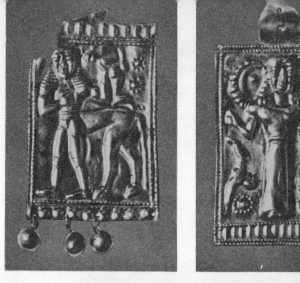

211

213

204. NYMPH OR GODDESS

Coin of Opus (early fourth century). The engraver has closely imitated the magnificent decadrachms with the head of the nymph Arethusa, signed by Euaenetus, which were minted at Syracuse towards the end of the fifth century. He has kept the garland of aquatic foliage, but made the ear-pendants richer and heavier. Cabinet des Médailles.

205. ATHENA

Corinthian coin (fourth century). The obverse side has the customary type, the reverse a 'colt' (see ill. 35). The goddess is wearing a 'Corinthian' helmet, drawn back and garlanded with laurel, with a broad, supple rear-pack of leather. The aegis, in the field, is an additional symbol establishing the identity of the issue, as is also the letter A. Cabinet des Médailles.

206. CHARGING BULL

Coin of Thurii (late fifth century). Vigorously realistic portrayal of an animal. In the space beneath there is a large fish, probably a tunny, which is caught off the coasts of southern Italy. Inscription: 'Thourion'. Cabinet des Médailles.

207. SQUATTING SILENUS

Coin of Naxus in Sicily (about 460). This type on the reverse side is accompanied by a profile of Dionysus (ill. 79) on the obverse. Bold foreshortening, characteristic of the technical audacities of the severe style. This Silenus is holding in his right hand a footless cantharus; his horse-tail can be seen beneath him. Inscription: 'Naxion'. Cabinet des Médailles.

208. PHALANTHUS ON A DOLPHIN

Coin of Tarentum (fifth century). Legend had seized upon the founder of the city and reported that after suffering shipwreck he was saved by a dolphin (Pausanias, X, 13, 10). The scallop-shell symbolizes the waves of the sea. Note his easy attitude and the realism of his hair floating in the wind and his hand pointing to the shore. Inscription: 'Tarantinon'. Cabinet des Médailles.

209. HERACLES AND THE NEMEAN LION

Coin of Heraclea (late fifth–early fourth century). This city, a colony near Thurii, has the first exploit of its patron hero Heracles represented on the reverse side of its coins. The owl between Heracles' legs symbolizes the aid of Athena. Beside him is his club. On the right is the name of the Heracleans. Cabinet des Médailles.

210. ARTEMIS DAIDALEIA

Bronze statuette (second half of the sixth century) from the neighbourhood of Olympia. Dedication from Chimaridas to Daidaleia. Artemis, in an Archaic type of peplos, without pleats and with a short lappet, is holding her bow in her left hand. Boston Museum.

211 & 212. ELECTRUM JEWELS (SEVENTH CENTURY)

A fairly large number of small plaques of gold, electrum, and silver, with repoussé work, have been found, valuable ornaments produced by the goldsmith's art. In the 'Daedalic' style, the artist has portrayed a centaur similar to the Archaic type (a man with a horse's hindquarters attached), holding a hare by both ears (ill. 211), and a winged female deity (ill. 212), of the type of the 'Mistress of the Wild Beasts', holding two animals by their hind legs. Boston Museum.

213 & 214. IMPRESSIONS FROM INTAGLIOS (SECOND HALF OF THE FIFTH CENTURY)

These two admirable animal figures, a horse and a heron, are from chalcedony seals. They are ascribed to the engraver Dexamenus of Chios, who signed several intaglios of outstanding quality. Boston Museum.

of the three poets, has a bent for phraseology and sometimes seems rather free in introducing divine powers; for all that, he multiplies dramatic changes of fortune and unexpected reversals to arouse our compassion for the misfortunes of his characters, exposed to all the blows of Destiny. Several of his tragedies end with an identical significant stanza: 'What comes to us from on high takes many forms. Changeful and deceiving is the action of the gods. What one expected comes not to pass. The divine will follows unforeseen paths. Such is the lesson of our play.' So tossed about by forces beyond their power, poor mortals suffer countless evils, for which they are sometimes to blame and above which their nobility of soul can sometimes rise. This theme has never ceased to arouse our admiration and engage our sympathy.

Classical Greek comedy is further removed from our modern conceptions. As early as the latter part of the sixth century, the Sicilian Epicharmus had composed in the Dorian dialect comedies of which we have little knowledge, but which the ancients, and Plato in the first place, valued highly because of the truth of observation revealed in them and the value of the maxims with which they were studded. It was also in Dorian territory, at Megata, not far from Athens, that the tradition of comic sketches, apparently very indelicate, was firmly established. The influence of these first attempts, combined in Attica with the very broad songs and the *lazzi* that accompanied Dionysiac processions, gave birth to what we call Old Comedy, which soon had its place side by side with tragedy in the official competitions organized at the festivals of Dionysus. There were about forty authors of 'Old' comedies, which shows the success of this typically Athenian literary genre during the fifth century. Cratinus, who began to produce about 455, and Eupolis and Aristophanes, during the last quarter of the century, were its most illustrious representatives. Aristophanes is the only one from whom we have complete plays; these give a very precise idea of what the Athenian public liked.

'Old' comedy was always a work improvised for the occasion and of a controversial character, little concerned with probability and always seeking to raise laughter by farcical inventions and constant allusions to current events. The theme was usually some fantastic or grotesque enterprise, undertaken by the principal actor in the presence of a chorus of picturesquely disguised characters: men, animals, or personified abstractions. A number of episodes show how the hero achieves his ends in spite of obstacles. Then, after an interlude in which the chorus addresses the audience, to express to it the authors' opinions on this or that subject of current interest, quite unconnected with the plot, a new series of sketches reveals the consequences of the situation thus created, until the final procession, in which the chorus leaves the theatre, singing the praises of Diony-sus. Starting from this typical plan, the poets had complete latitude to amuse the audience as their fantasy suggested: from puns to elegant literary parodies, from scatology and obscenity to the most subtle poetry, from coarse personal insult to comedy of observation and character—everything was permitted, everything was appreciated. There is extreme variety of tone in Aristophanes and the ease with which he turns from utter grossness to extreme delicacy confounds the modern reader. But if we are shocked by jokes that are too broad or confused by political allusions whose point escapes us, we are still fascinated by a zest which the lapse of centuries has in no way robbed of its flavour and by a poetical in-spiration and a feeling for nature which for us have retained all their freshness and fascination. No work puts us in more direct contact with the Athenian people in the time of Socrates, Alcibiades, and Thucydides, none to an equal degree gives us the impression of being at one and the same time a statement about the author and about the age in which he lived.

Aristophanes' latest plays, written early in the fourth century, are noticeably different from the earlier ones: with the *Ecclesiazusae* and the *Plutus*, the poet turns towards a new form of comedy, which is called Middle Comedy. The rôle of the chorus is reduced and the imagination roams less freely. Satire of indi-viduals gives place to social satire, personal attacks to portrayal of human types, farcical inventiveness to a burlesque treatment of myth. Aristophanes' succes-sors, such as Antiphanes and Alexis of Thurii, seem to have been very product-ive authors, to whom hundreds of plays were ascribed. But we know practically nothing of them, and Greek comedy, like tragedy, produced no more master-pieces in the fourth century until Menander came upon the scene; but he really belongs to the Hellenistic Age.

The birth of prose. Ionian history: Herodotus. Attic history: Thucydides, Xenophon
There is no need for surprise that, in Greek literature, the earliest prose writers were appreciably later than the earliest poets. This is a fairly common phenomen-on and the ancients themselves clearly realized it: Plutarch points it out in a famous passage of his dialogue *On the Oracles of the Pythia*. The use of prose, stripped of all the embellishments of poetic style and the aid which verse gives to

memory, indicates definite progress in the exercise of rational thought and reveals a primary concern for the investigation and communication of truth. This investigation is called *historia* in Greek; it is applied in the first instance to human events and to the natural setting in which these pursue their course. Hence comes the word 'history'; in the earliest times it included geography.

The Greeks regarded Homer as the earliest historian, and in fact originally no distinction was made between history and epic. The earliest works in which we get a glimpse of historical considerations are still epic poems, such as the *Founding of Colophon,* composed early in the sixth century by the philosopher Xenophanes. The tradition was maintained early in the following century by the poet Panyassis, Herodotus's uncle, of whom we have already spoken, who devoted his *Ionica* to an account of the founding of the earliest cities in Ionia by Codrus and Neleus, at a very remote period. Similarly the ever-lively curiosity of the Ionians was fascinated with imaginative accounts of a journey in the unknown countries north of the Black Sea, the *Poem on the Arimaspeans,* attributed to a semilegendary figure, Aristeas of Proconnesus, supposed to have lived in the middle of the seventh century.

Hecataeus of Miletus, who played an important part in politics towards the end of the sixth century and during the Ionian Revolt, broke with this tradition by composing his *Genealogies* in Ionian prose; this was a collection of legends interpreted in the light of a naïve kind of rationalism. But his chief work was a general description of the inhabited world, entitled the *Periegesis,* of which Herodotus made much use. From the fragments that survive, we can see that he had a very lively interest in ethnography and that he showed a certain critical spirit. 'Here I report,' says he, 'what I believe to be the truth, for the accounts given by the Greeks are very different and, to my mind, absurd.' He improved the use of maps, previously invented by Anaximander. He had several imitators in the fifth century, such as Acusilaus of Argos, Charon of Lampsacus, Hellanicus of Mitylene, and the Athenian Pherecydes, but none achieved the fame of Herodotus of Halicarnassus, the first prose writer whose work has survived in its entirety, the man whom Cicero justly called the 'Father of History'.

In Herodotus, this branch of literature in fact appears, in its main characteristics, as henceforth defined. Its purpose is to set forth the results of the historian's investigations in order to rescue the great deeds of men from oblivion. The work aims to give both pleasure and instruction, but these objects are implied

rather than stated, objectivity in narration being the basic law. In cases of diverg-
ence between sources or clear improbability in the tradition, the author exercises his critical faculty and makes his choice, in terms of the criteria that seem
valid to him. Of course, the criteria are not necessarily those which seem best
today, but the important thing is that in principle they are of a rational kind.
Conscientiously to establish the truth, to clarify the relationship between causes
and effects, to portray the manners of nations, to trace for all time the features of
outstanding individuals, to bring picturesque and lively scenes before the mind's
eye, to put on record great exploits worthy to be remembered, to suggest useful
lines of thought, to prick the reader's curiosity on occasion with strange or
surprising details—these were the aims of Herodotus, which he achieved with
prodigious success, thanks to the lively sympathy inspired in him by men and
nations, without prejudice of race or civilization, and thanks to the alertness of
intelligence which distrusted fables while it revered the moral laws and the
gods. The Greek and Barbarian worlds live again in his *Histories*, for our instruction and delight, by virtue of an inimitable art, sometimes prolix and sometimes elliptical, in which the story-teller, varying his effects as his interest or his
fancy dictates, falls into digressions that are sometimes rather long, expands
details that amuse him, and then airily returns to his main theme, with a non-
chalant bearing that claims the reader's cheerful indulgence. Moreover, this
earliest sample of Greek prose has still a wonderful freshness, as if in all truth,
to recall the words of a Byzantine man of learning, the 'Halicarnassian nightin-
gale' knew how to 'adorn his beautiful style with all the flowers of Ionian speech'.

Herodotus was a contemporary of Pericles, whom in fact he knew at Athens.
The Athenian Thucydides belongs to the following generation, the one which
witnessed the long course of the Peloponnesian War. After having taken his part
in it—he was a strategus at Thasos and under the walls of Amphipolis when the
city was taken by Brasidas—he found himself removed from the scene of action
after this setback and had to resign himself to being thenceforth only a spectator.
But he followed the vicissitudes of the conflict with unremitting attention and
made himself its faithful narrator. His work contrasts with that of Herodotus,
less indeed in the object which the author pursues and the method he employs to
accomplish it than in his personal temperament and the basic tendencies of his
thought. Having to record, like the 'Father of History', a major military clash
between two peoples, Thucydides allows himself no nonchalance: there are few

digressions and few anecdotes, but a rigorously chronological account, which derives its rhythm from the seasons, in default of a well-established official calendar. There is unremitting intellectual tension, with a resolute determination to understand events, to bring to light their logical connection and their causes, whether these depend upon individuals, societies, nature, or economics, a severe precision in the recital of facts, seen with the cold eye of the tactician or the strategist without any quest for picturesqueness or charm. Pathos sometimes emerges, though rarely, from this very coldness of style, as in the picture of the plague at Athens or that of the imprisonment of the Athenians after the disaster in Sicily. This lucid intelligence has at its command an elaborate and subtle style, which shuns symmetry, does not shrink from anacoluthon, and has a wonderful capacity to suggest a great deal in a few words: this earliest monument of Attic prose reveals, particularly in the speeches, what an admirable intellectual instrument the native dialect of Athens was henceforth to be.

The Athenian Xenophon, one of Sophocles' disciples, presented himself in his *Hellenica* as Thucydides' continuator by taking up the narrative of events in 411 B.C., the point at which Thucydides had left off; Xenophon's history continues down to the Battle of Mantinea in 362. However, neither in this work, useful as it is, nor in the *Anabasis*, which deals with the expedition of the Ten Thousand, in which he had taken part, nor in the historical romance (known as the *Cyropaedia*) on the upbringing of the Persian king Cyrus the Elder, can this brilliant writer stand up to comparison with his predecessors. He is certainly likeable, clear, vivid, and reasonably well informed. But his intellectual demands are obviously on a lower level: he rarely scrutinizes underlying causes, his psychology is superficial, and he is too prone to idealize characters whom he admires; in short, the history he offers us is lacking in depth and density. This enables us to see all the more clearly to what an extent the general principles implicitly laid down by Herodotus and Thucydides were definitively recognized as valid, since Xenophon, with greatly inferior gifts, undeniably deserves to be called an historian, simply because he tried to put those principles into practice.

Side by side with these three great names in Greek historiography in the fifth and fourth centuries, we know from mere references or from quotations of varying length a fairly large number of authors or works. Early in the fourth century, Ctesias of Cnidus wrote a *History of Persia*, which Dinon of Colophon completed. Theopompus of Chios, born about 377, composed an abridgment of Herodotus and a history of Philip II of Macedon. Papyri have supplied us with fragments of an anonymous work called the *Oxyrhynchus Hellenica*, apparently written in the first half of the fourth century: they deal with the events of the year 396–395. Ephorus of Cyme, who composed the greater part of his work after 350, was the first to conceive the idea of a universal history, in which he brought together the results of a vast compilation; three centuries later, Diodorus Siculus made great use of it in his *Historical Library*. Finally, several minor historians, known by the generic name of *Atthidographers*, devoted their labours to the history of Attica, as Hellanicus had done in earlier days.

Scientific and philosophical speculation: the Ionian school. The sophists and Socrates. Plato and the Academy

The birth and development of history are but one particularly favourable aspect of the beginnings of rational thought and scientific reflection, essentially the achievements of the Greeks of the Archaic and Classical periods. Concomitantly with particular research into human societies and their evolution, we find scientific inquiry and philosophy appearing in Ionia from the beginning of the sixth century. Thales of Miletus and Pythagoras of Samos (who later lived at Croton) illustrate, the former at the beginning and the latter during the second half of the sixth century, the earliest speculations in mathematics and astronomy, combined in Pythagoras's case with a kind of mystical asceticism whose influence was deep and lasting. Other Milesians, Anaximander, a contemporary of Thales, and his pupil Anaximenes, meditated similarly on nature and its real essence. Xenophanes of Colophon, at the end of the century, expounded in verse his theological doctrine of the one impersonal god and criticized anthropomorphic polytheism. Parmenides of Elea, who later moulded the thought of his disciple Zeno in his native city, and Empedocles of Agrigentum, about the same time, also employed the poetic medium, with more distinction then Xenophanes, to expound their ontological ideas. Their contemporary Heraclitus of Ephesus, who wrote in prose, declared that everything is in a state of endless conflict, movement, and coming-into-being. We can still discern the vigour and originality of these early thinkers from the fairly numerous fragments that have come down to us in quotations by other writers.

In the fifth century, Anaxagoras of Clazomenae, who was a friend of Pericles' while in Athens, held that Mind, which brought order into the primeval Chaos, is the essential principle in the universe. Further, he applied rationalist criticism to several widespread preconceptions, such as that of the divinity of the heavenly bodies, and even to certain forms of divination: this taste for free enquiry caused him to be exiled from Athens, following an accusation of impiety. Democritus of Abdera, coming shortly after Anaxagoras, conceived the idea of the atom, in which he found the explanation of all things, including the gods. Hippocrates of Cos, a member of a medical family that practised the cult of Asclepios, applied the principles of rational observation to his art: by his labours he founded clinical medicine, and he also defined the duties of doctors in the famous oath that is still their golden rule. At the same time Athens was giving an enthusiastic welcome to the teaching of the sophists, even if she was capable of prosecuting them later for impiety; they came to Athens to give lessons in eloquence and dialectics for fees paid in cash. Through some of the dialogues of Plato we can appreciate the virtuosity of sophists like Gorgias of Leontini or Protagoras of Abdera, skilful at awaking doubts by their handling of contradictory ideas.

From cosmogonic speculation to rational scepticism, such was, broadly speaking, the direction taken by Greek philosophical thought from its beginnings to the moment when, about 430 B.C., Socrates' teaching began to bear fruit. The influence which this moralist exercised by his words and his example was so decisive that all the earlier philosophers are now called pre-Socratics. 'Man,' Protagoras had said, 'is the measure of all things.' Socrates put the study of the human soul at the centre of his thinking and urged everyone to make an effort first and foremost to know himself, in keeping with the interpretation he gave of a famous Delphic maxim. Psychological observation and moral reflection were his constant preoccupations. Starting from humble instances taken from daily life, his intelligence, experienced in the verbal ingenuities of sophistic could make use of them to advance with slow but sure tread in the knowledge of truth and virtue. 'Socrates,' says Cicero in his *Tusculan Disputations* (V, 10), 'was the first to bring philosophy down from the heavens to establish it in our cities, even to admit it to our homes and compel it to concern itself with practical morality, with the problems of good and evil.' We have seen elsewhere why his outstanding merits as a citizen and a thinker could not protect him when he was accused on a capital charge. But he had already played his role as an initiator and set in motion the philosophic genius of Plato.

If Socrates wrote nothing, his disciple Plato showed wonderful fertility, and it is significant that in the great wreck of ancient literature his abundant work has survived entire. This exceptional privilege is not so much to be explained by lucky chance as by a wide-spread feeling that the works of Plato, side by side with the poems of Homer, represented the fine flower of Hellenism. His numerous dialogues, not to mention those of doubtful authenticity, have been classified chronologically by modern scholars, according to stylistic criteria that are sometimes questionable. However, this distribution must broadly correspond to reality and it enables us to follow approximately the philosopher's intellectual itinerary from the *Laches* to the *Laws*, through a long life which experienced many ups and downs. The earliest dialogues are faithful to Socrates' methods and apparently give us a true picture of his teaching. Later on, Plato's personality asserts itself and it is his own theses that he sets forth by the mouth of his master, who remains the principal speaker in his dialogues. To his primarily moral preoccupations—the defining of courage, piety, virtue, and justice—vaster and more ambitious investigations now came to be added: to understand the system of the universe (and here Plato takes up the ontological speculations of the pre-Socratic philosophers) through the theory of Ideas: to grasp the nature of the immortal soul and its relationship to the body; and lastly to formulate laws which are to govern the ideal city, since for Plato metaphysics and psychology inevitably converge on the science of politics, whose function is to translate right thought into action.

This endlessly renewed thought is inexhaustibly rich. The experience which the author derived from reading, travelling, and contact with public men, scholars, writers, and other philosophers, explains the variety of the problems he raises and also the variety of the characters he brings upon the stage to expound with wonderful force and truth in each controversy the various theses placed in opposition. The dialogue form is favourable to this pluralism, but does not prevent Plato from reaching conclusions. And his art enables him to give life to all these creations of his genius, thanks to a marvellously supple style, as well fitted for irony as for abstract speculation, for poetic description of a landscape or a myth as for parody of a sophist or an orator. The language of Plato remains an unrivalled model of Attic prose: never has a more delicate verbal instrument been put at the service of human thought.

The spread of Plato's influence was brought about both by his works and by his teaching, which he gave from 387 onwards in the gymnasium dedicated to the hero Academus, some distance northwest of the Diplyon Gate, not far from Athens: hence comes the name Academy, given to the school. It should not make us forget that other disciples of Socrates took different paths: the Athenian Antisthenes, the author of numerous dialogues or treatises now lost, founded the Cynic School, whose name is derived from the gymnasium of Cynosarges, the district of Athens in which he taught, while the Cyrenaean Aristippus, the theorist of pleasure, was paving the way for Epicureanism. As for Plato's own pupils, they were all eclipsed by the overwhelming figure of Aristotle, the lawgiver of Western thought. But, although this philosopher was an exact contemporary of Demosthenes, he cannot be separated from the team which worked under his command and whose joint labours, guided by the master's activities, belong to the Hellenistic world.

Eloquence. The earlier Attic orators. Isocrates and Demosthenes
If Plato's undertaking terminated in politics, as Aristotle's also did, it was because in the eyes of a Greek everything converged upon the city. Since one could not work upon one's fellow-citizens except by the spoken word, it is not surprising that the Greeks were the first to establish the art of oratory by laying down the rules of rhetoric. Among all the literary genres, this one, closely linked with the evolution of democracy in the assembly and in the courts, developed step by step with democracy, and was therefore the last type of composition to appear in the history of classical literature. Beyond doubt, from the latter part of the sixth century, to judge by Herodotus's testimony, the Ionians of Asia had skilful orators, such as Aristagoras of Miletus, for example. Later the partisan rivalries in the Athens of Themistocles and Pericles gave every opportunity to those who knew how to speak effectively. If the speeches that Thucydides puts in the mouth of Pericles are not strictly genuine, at least the historian declares (I, 21) that for the general sense he has kept 'as close as possible to what was actually said': the nobility of inspiration and the vigorous logic that we admire in them are, then, attributes of the orator and not an invention of the historian. But this eloquence remained more spontaneous than self-conscious: Pericles could not have received, at the time of his education, the lessons given by the sophists, who hardly appeared in Athens before the last years of his life.

Sophistic, which arose in Sicily early in the fifth century, was the science of reasoning, directed towards utilitarian ends: it quickly became the practice of specious reasoning, strengthened by all the verbal resources calculated to achieve persuasion. We have seen the part it played in philosophy. It was still more important for the development of rhetoric. Such men as Gorgias, Protagoras, and Prodicus were the first to define the requirements of speech and style with rigour and precision. In Athens they found a select audience capable of profiting by their lessons: the sophist Antiphon, who was also a political leader and died by the sentence of his fellow-citizens in 411 after the fall of the Four Hundred, has left us models of fictitious speeches for school use and some speeches for delivery in court. The metic Lysias, ruined by the exactions of the Thirty, earned his living by providing litigants, for pay, with ready-made speeches, which they had only to read in court: those which have survived sparkle with purity of language, cleverness in argument, and perfect naturalness.

The rhetor Isocrates, who died little short of one hundred years old in 338, was the one who of all these orators reflected most on his art. The weakness of his voice and the delicacy of his health prevented him from speaking himself, so, like Lysias, he composed speeches for others, but he devoted himself above all to the teaching of rhetoric, in which he was brilliantly successful, rivalling the attractiveness of Plato's Academy in the eyes of the youth of Athens. In the set speeches which he published without delivering them, like the *Panegyric* (thus named because it was intended for the *panegyris* or assembly of the Greeks on the occasion of the Olympic Games in 380), he handles with brilliance the commonplaces which he decks out with all the glamour of harmonious and rhythmical prose: the eulogy of his native Athens that he included in his *Panegyric* gained such renown that the actual title of his speech came to be synonymous with 'eulogy', in which sense we use the word today. Isocrates was, moreover, an original political thinker. Aware that Greece was wearing herself out with intestine wars, he considered that she ought to bring these quarrels to an end, put herself under a single command, and undertake the conquest of Persian-dominated Asia. When he realized that Athens was not capable of playing the part of leader which he had at first dreamt of for her, he turned his hopes towards Philip of Macedon: in a truly prophetic vision, he had conceived in advance the great project of Alexander.

No greater contrast could be imagined than that between Isocrates and Demosthenes. One was a cloistered scholar, the other a man of action. One chiselled his exquisite periods at leisure, the other gave full rein to a fiery eloquence. One believed for a long time that the King of Macedonia would save the Greek world from decline, the other opposed Philip's policy with fierce energy. Both were devoted, though in different ways, to the greatness of their native Athens. History eventually gave the professor its verdict against the statesman, and yet we are told that Isocrates died from the mental shock produced by the news of Chaeronea, while Demosthenes, steadfast in the face of defeat, was given the conspicuous honour of delivering the funeral oration in praise of those who had died in the battle. The proud and sombre herald of Athenian independence spoke in the course of the long struggle in some of the noblest strains that have ever been inspired by a man's love for his country and devotion to the common good; it little affects his glory that in the end he found himself on the losing side. When in burning words he lashed the cowardice, flabbiness, love of pleasure and blind fickleness of his fellow-citizens, he was bequeathing to future nations an example that they will always do well to ponder upon.

Beside this direct and sometimes thunderous eloquence, sustained as it is by a perfectly assimilated art, the works of the other contemporary political orators, whatever their merits, sink into insignificance. Aeschines, Demosthenes' great rival, Hyperides and Lycurgus, some of whose works we have, are on occasion skilful, fluent, lively, and even impassioned, yet none of them comes near to touching us as Demosthenes does. It is good that we should finish with him this brief review of Greek literature in the period when its greatness was bound up with the independence of the city-state: at the moment when that independence was about to be extinguished, this man, by his fight to defend it, made its fire glow and blaze for the last time.

CHAPTER IX

AN ART COMMENSURATE
WITH MAN

In ancient Greece a work of art had a meaning. The Melancholy Athena *and the* Ephebe of Marathon *as examples*

THE masterpieces of Greek literature and thought are only very imperfectly accessible to the majority of our contemporaries, because of the language barrier. In compensation, the masterpieces of art collected in museums, where they are often displayed with admirable good taste, provide direct contact with the Greek genius which imagined and fashioned them. Ever since the first transports of enthusiasm of Winckelmann and his emulators, Greek sculptures, pottery, 'medals' and jewels have never ceased to attract lovers of art in a way that is nowadays eloquently expressed by the high prices of objects that come on the market. The least important Mycenaean vase, the humblest Geometric statuette, a silver coin or an intaglio, fetch enormous prices in London, Basle, or New York. What can we say then of the major specimens, Archaic or Classical marbles and bronzes or red-figure vases painted by a known craftsman? Their value is today beyond price. Such infatuation shows how Greek art still appeals to our taste and our feelings. But we must not for all that suppose that the evidence it contributes about the civilization from which it sprang is easy to interpret. If it presents itself to us in familiar forms, this ready accessibility is really an illusion. The pure enjoyment which a Greek work of art gives to our eyes, trained to appreciate it by centuries of classical tradition, does not enable us at the same time to grasp the intelligible message which it carries. For this work of art has a meaning: it was not, as a rule, intended only for aesthetic satisfaction, but for a practical or religious purpose which it had to answer in the first place. So it is important first to grasp the artist's underlying intention; otherwise we are in danger of misinterpreting his work. Two instances, connected with well-known works of art, will suffice.

The famous bas-relief of the *Melancholy Athena*, dating from the middle of the fifth century, has caused much ink to flow since it was discovered on the Acropolis at Athens in 1888. To what various exegeses has it not given rise? The goddess, with her helmet on her head and leaning on her spear, is bending forwards toward a small rectangular pillar, which she is contemplating with slightly indifferent attention. It has been supposed that Athena was reading (as a matter of fact in a very inconvenient position) an inscribed stele, containing either reports by the treasurers of the sacred treasury or a list of soldiers killed in action; others have imagined that some object or human figure was formerly represented as reclining on the pillar, but merely painted on the smooth marble instead of being carved like the rest of the scene, and that this essential detail has been effaced in the course of time; another has thought to recognize in the supposed pillar a simplified image of the wall of the Acropolis as recently rebuilt in part by Cimon; other have regarded it as a boundary stone of Athena's sanctuary and supposed that the goddess was therefore marking with her spear the limit assigned to her sacred plot. All these explanations were erroneous, as has recently been shown by recourse to the only sure method, that of putting the monument in its place in a series of related and well-identified works. In fact numerous vase-paintings contemporary with the bas-relief make it possible to identify the pillar in question, without risk of error, as the stone in a stadium, called the *terma*, which marked the starting-place, and the finishing-place, for the foot-race. It is the *terma* which is holding the attention of Athena, in whose honour the Panathenaïc Games were held and who, according to legend, had herself practised foot-racing. So the goddess is not in the least melancholy, and the monument is nothing more nor less than a votive offering on which the victor in a race in the stadium had the patron goddess of these games represented in front of the *terma* as a symbol of the event which he had won. This quite prosaic explanation must entirely alter our mental attitude to this bas-relief, henceforth stripped of the mystery which stung our curiosity. We may no longer let our imagination roam concerning the supposed melancholy of Athena, but is it not more worth while to understand the true meaning of a work than to let oneself be deluded by some figment of the imagination?

There is another example no less striking. The famous bronze statue in the Athens Museum called the *Ephebe of Marathon* has continually aroused the interest and admiration of connoisseurs, ever since fishermen caught it in their net off the northeast coast of Attica, some years before the First World War. It shows us a boy in his early teens, unsteadily poised, with his left hand outstretched flat, the palm upwards, supporting an object now lost, and his right hand raised, with thumb and forefinger joined. Who was it, god or mortal, that was represented in this masterpiece of statuary of the fourth century, of a slightly languid elegance which already makes us think of Praxiteles? Is it a boy amusing himself by manipulating with his right hand the string of the toy made of two disks fastened together, which was known to the ancients and in modern times is called the 'yo-yo'? Is it a young victor in the games, drawing out with one hand the fillet, which was the symbol of his victory, from a casket placed on his other hand? Is he spinning with a string a top that rests on the flat of his left hand? Is he gathering fruit, or is he a cup-bearer pouring out wine? The correct solution had been proposed shortly after the discovery and has recently been confirmed by decisive arguments: he is the young Hermes, who, as stated in the Homeric Hymn in honour of him, has just found a tortoise on the road; he has placed it flat on his left hand and is cracking the fingers of his uplifted right hand, an expressive gesture which modern Greeks still spontaneously employ to express delight. Knowing that in an instant he is going to invent the lyre, whose sound-box will be provided by the shell of the tortoise, the young god yields to the naïve enthusiasm of creative imagination. This interpretation, which is made certain by many pieces of supporting evidence, enables us to interpret the statue precisely in terms of the Homeric *Hymn to Hermes*, and surrounds it anew with the poetic and sacred atmosphere in which it was conceived: the work no longer confines itself to charming our eyes; it is also a piece of evidence for the religious thought of its time.

The instances of the *Melancholy Athena* and the *Hermes of Marathon* show that Greek art, in the Archaic and Classical Ages, should not only be relished, but also understood. It is not at all a gratuitous art, an entertainment for connoisseurs, aiming merely to delight the mind and the senses. The work of art has a meaning;

it responds to precise needs and intentions. Its aesthetic quality is something additional, and we fall into a serious error of perspective if we believe that the artist's primary object was to create beauty. In fact his purpose was to create an object appropriate to the purpose for which it was intended: a temple is the god's home before it is an architectural monument; a statue is an offering before it is a work of sculpture; a cup is first and foremost a vessel to drink from, whose material and decoration merely increase its value. Stendhal expressed it well when he said: 'For the ancients beauty was only a projection of utility.' Art for art's sake is a theory foreign to Greek thought.

The artist in Greek society. Primary importance of craftsmanship. Feeling for collective work. Technical perfection

We find confirmation of this when we examine the place occupied by artists in Greek society. The fame of some of them, the most illustrious, such as Phidias, Ictinus, Zeuxis, and Praxiteles, ought not to deceive us. Let us take care not to attribute to their contemporaries a judgment which is largely that of posterity. We know the names of the great masters of classical art mainly from the works of compilers who wrote in the Roman period, like the Elder Pliny and Pausanias, whose information was itself derived from Hellenistic scholars. This art criticism—if we can so call it—reflects the attitude of an age in which the taste for works of art, nourished by a long tradition, had assumed an academic and somewhat retrospective character: it has been pointed out that, though Pausanias in his *Periegesis* or 'Journey through Greece', composed in the second century A.D., mentions so many names of artists, he does not refer to a single one later than the second century B.C. This antiquarian curiosity gives us no real information about the way in which the Greeks of the Archaic and Classical Ages regarded artists in their lifetime. It is only the rare information furnished by authors of the fifth and fourth centuries, Herodotus, Plato, and Xenophon, that enables us to reach certain firm conclusions, which at first sight may surprise us.

One thing must be said at once: in the sisterhood of the Nine Muses, who watch over the noble uses that the intellect makes of leisure, there is none in charge of architecture and the plastic arts. Such an omission is revealing: it signifies that in the eyes of the Greeks the task of the architect, painter, or sculptor does not depend upon the same kind of creative activity as that of the poet, astronomer, or musician. The artist is too dependent upon the material he works on to be placed

215. ENTABLATURE AND DORIC CAPITAL (SO-CALLED 'TEMPLE OF NEPTUNE' AT PAESTUM)

Although the travertine is badly worn, the architectural forms are quite clear: the square capital resting on the echinus shaped like the frustum of a cone (forming a cushion where it joins the abacus), the architrave, the frieze of triglyphs and metopes, separated from the architrave by the taenia (reinforced by reglets with drops just below each triglyph) and mutules (whose drops were inserted) beneath the cornice. Above is the sloping of the pediment.

216. CORINTHIAN CAPITALS (OLYMPIEUM AT ATHENS)

Although the columns of the southeast corner of the temple erected on the banks of the Ilissus only date from the Hellenistic Age (first half of the second century B.C.), their Corinthian capitals basically reproduce the type perfected by the architects of the fourth century (particularly in the Tholos at Epidaurus): but the earlier architects reserved it for interior colonnades.

217. IONIC CAPITAL OF THE PROPYLAEA (ATHENIAN ACROPOLIS)

Because of the more slender proportions of the Ionic column, Mnesicles employed it as the interior order in the Propylaea. On a cushion decorated with ovoli rest the two balusters of the capital, whose lateral volutes are connected by a broad fluting. The thin abacus has a chamfered edge. Above is the architrave with its three fascias.

218. IONIC BASE (NORTH PORTICO OF THE ERECHTHEUM)

A good example of an 'Attic' base, consisting of two tori separated by a casement (or scotia). The upper torus, with a shorter diameter, is decorated with a plaited ornament. The grooves of the fluting on the shaft of the column are separated by flat edges, whereas the Doric column has sharp edges.

219. HEAD OF THE SO-CALLED 'KORE WEARING A PEPLOS'

The sparkling brightness of the Parian marble was enhanced by the polychromy, of which some traces remain. A metal diadem encircled the hair. The famous 'Archaic' smile has here (about 530 B.C.) all its charm. This Kore has sometimes been thought to be a late work of the unknown master who made the Rampin horseman (see ill. 39). Acropolis Museum, Athens.

220. WOMAN'S FACE (TEMPLE E AT SELINUS)

Temple E, probably dedicated to Hera, was decorated with limestone metopes, in which were female heads of Parian marble, sculptured separately and then inserted (second quarter of the fifth century). This head was in a now-lost metope. It shows that the 'severe style', which has left us masterpieces in Attica and at Olympia Cyrene, and elsewhere, exercised no less influence in Sicily.

215

216

217

2

219

221

220

222

223

224

225

226

227

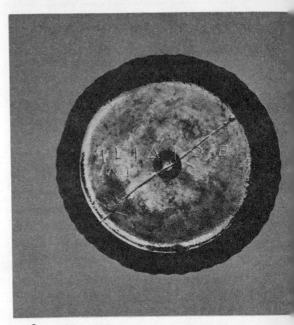

228

229

221. THE 'BARBERINI SUPPLIANT'
Whether it is an original statue, dating from the years 430–429, or a copy made in Roman times, it formed part of a group (perhaps in a pediment). It is not known what character and what scene were represented. The regularity of the features and the coldness of expression, proper to the art of this period, scarcely help us to clear up these uncertainties. Louvre.

222. WOMAN'S HEAD
This work, characterized by grace without softness, is allied to the creations of Praxiteles in the second half of the fourth century. Compare the Hermes at Olympia (ill. 226). Smyrna Museum.

223. 'CLEOBIS'
One of the two statues at Delphi in honour of Cleobis and Biton, two Argive brothers whose story is told by Herodotus. These statues, made in the early part of the sixth century, are signed by an Argive sculptor. The modelling in broad sections of relief shows vigour along with its simplicity. The man is presenting himself trustfully to his god. Delphi Museum.

224. WARRIOR OF AEGINA
The head of one of the figures of wounded men lying in the angles of the west pediment of the temple of Aphaia (early fifth century). There is no sign of suffering in this face, which still shows the 'Archaic 'smile, which has long been called 'Aeginetan' because of these sculptures. Munich Museum of Sculpture.

225. HEAD OF THE DORYPHOROS
A faithful copy in the form of a bronze herm, made by the Athenian Apollonius, son of Archias, about the time of Augustus. The slightly cold beauty of the regular features is characteristic of the works of Polycletus. National Museum, Naples.

226. THE HERMES OF PRAXITELES
Whether it is an original work of the great sculptor or an extremely careful and competent copy made in Roman times, it is the best witness we have to the slightly restless and uneasy grace for which Praxiteles was framed. On the god's left arm sat the infant Dionysus. Olympia Museum.

227. THE HERMES OF MARATHON
An original bronze of the middle of the fourth century, fished up from the sea in the Bay of Marathon. It shows the young Hermes delighted at having found a tortoise (originally on his left hand, but now lost) with which he intends to make the sound-box for a lyre. National Museum, Athens.

228. HANDWRITING OF PHIDIAS

Inscription on the bottom of a very simple little cup of Attic ware used by Phidias at the time when he was working on the Zeus at Olympia. The words are: 'I belong to Phidias'. Olympia Museum.

229. THE STRANGFORD SHIELD

A sketchy and greatly simplified marble copy of the shield of Athena Parthenos, which was decorated with an Amazonomachy in low relief. According to an ancient and perhaps legendary tradition, the bald, bare-headed figure, wearing a chlamys, who is brandishing a kind of axe (or a sculptor's hammer), a little to the left beneath the Gorgon's head, was Phidias himself. British Museum.

on the same level as those who make use of sounds and words. Whatever admiration might be felt for the products of his work, he was certainly not granted the privilege of divine inspiration accorded to the favourites of the Muses: the artist was regarded first and foremost as a craftsman.

We have another proof of this, furnished by plastic art itself. It is well known that in the Roman Age rich art-lovers, such as Cicero and the Younger Pliny, liked to surround themselves with portraits of the great philosophers, poets, and orators. Libraries and gardens were adorned with them. Accordingly, real or supposed likenesses of Homer or Plato, Socrates or Euripides, Demosthenes or Epicurus, as these likenesses had been settled upon in former days by the Greek sculptors of the fourth century or the Hellenistic Age, were copied in great numbers. Many of these portraits have been preserved, and they form a very interesting gallery of illustrious faces. But in this very numerous company we look in vain for a painter or a sculptor. The tale is told that Phidias portrayed himself on the shield of Athena Parthenos, which he adorned with reliefs, in the person of the legendary sculptor Daedalus, side by side with Theseus, to whom he gave the features of Pericles; the story goes on to say that the Athenians were scandalized by such a liberty, which they regarded as sacrilege. The anecdote is in all probability apocryphal, and the efforts that have been expended in trying to discover a genuine portrait of Phidias on the basis of copies of the famous shield have not succeeded. In fact we know nothing about the features of the great Greek artists. None of them, to our knowledge, made a recognizable portrait of himself or of any of his fellow-artists. Nobody ever thought of asking them to do so, any more than of setting up statues of them in a public place to pay them honour. The very lively admiration felt for their works did not extend to their persons.

This attitude, which may appear surprising, is on the contrary perfectly in keeping with the hierarchy of social values as conceived by the Greeks. Since in their eyes the artist was essentially a workman, or, as they said in Greek, a *banausos*, he could not claim the consideration paid to disinterested speculation. When, in Plato, Socrates speaks of Phidias, he applies to him the term *demiourgos*, which means 'artisan' or 'craftsman', and when he alludes to painters or sculptors it is to compare them with men skilled in the various forms of manual work or in techniques. Plato informs us elsewhere that the sophist Protagoras, who charged very high fees for his lectures, had earned as much money as

Phidias and ten other sculptors taken together. The sophists themselves, in spite of their great reputation, were regarded with some contempt because their activities were not pursued purely for their own sake. From this we can judge how far artists were from occupying a leading position in Greek society. And yet their modest position, far from being prejudicial to the quality of their art, was of benefit to it. If art is essentially a technique, the true artist ought to show himself an expert in his craft: he cannot conceive of any divorcement between inspiration and manual skill or see the latter as detrimental to the former. His social position thus preserves him from the allurements of slapdash improvisation or 'primitivism', with whose dangers we are nowadays only too familiar.

Attic pottery and chryselephantine sculpture as examples. The idea of a 'school'
It is no doubt to this primary importance of the craft, universally acknowledged by artists and laymen alike, that we should attribute the extraordinarily high average quality of Greek works described as belonging to the 'best period'. The Greece of this period certainly did not possess only first-class artists. Our museums include in their store of Greek art hosts of mediocre works, whether of sculpture or of pottery. But even these mediocre works are distinguished by a certain honesty of workmanship which reflects the complete sincerity of the workman and the sureness of his hand. This also explains the quality of the large groups of decorative sculpture bequeathed to us by the Greeks, which represent the greater part of the genuine works of the great period: the frieze and pediment of the Treasury of Siphnos and the metopes of the Treasury of the Athenians at Delphi, the metopes and pediments of the temple of Zeus at Olympia, the metopes, frieze, and pediments of the Parthenon, the frieze of Bassae-Phigalia, the decoration of the Mausoleum at Halicarnassus. It is quite clear that groups of such size were joint creations, in which a whole army of executants had a hand: the sculptures of the Parthenon took fifteen years to complete (447 to 432), during which ninety-two metopes, the 160 metres of the frieze (with 360 figures) and the forty colossal statues for the pediments were carved. We can imagine what problems of organization such a task presented to the overseer, whom nowadays no one any longer doubts to have been Phidias himself. There were hundreds of workmen busy in the work-yard on the Acropolis, marble-masons and stone-layers, painters and goldsmiths and silversmiths, each with his apprentices or slaves. And yet all these collaborators, no doubt of very unequal ages and talents, were

capable of submitting to a common discipline and assimilating Phidias's style so effectively that, in the frieze at least, scarcely any disparity exists, but rather an extraordinary impression of unity. Such a result, which astonishes us, was only possible if each artist abandoned all attempts at personal originality in the interests of the work as a whole. We may conjecture without much risk of error that this effort cost them few pangs: each considered that he had to perform his own task, that is to say to carry out his share of the work in obedience to the directives of the man in charge, and not to give vent to his own genius at the expense of his fellow-workers.

The same brilliant success had attended the building of the temple of Zeus at Olympia, twenty years earlier; here the unknown artist who designed the metopes and pediments knew how to keep his team working with the cohesion which alone could carry the undertaking to success: hence those prodigious compositions in marble in which echoes of Aeschylus and Pindar still reverberate and which should perhaps be ascribed to the artist who later, likewise at Olympia, carved the *Victory* dedicated by the Messenians, viz., Paeonius of Mende. The case of the Mausoleum at Halicarnassus, in the middle of the fourth century, is perhaps even more curious; according to our sources, four famous sculptors, Scopas, Leochares, Timotheus, and Bryaxis, worked together on it. Each came with the members of his studio to take his share in the decoration of the great monumental tomb. For more than a century all the sagacity of archaeologists has been trying in vain to divide the fragments found in the ruins of the building into homogeneous lots, in order to ascribe them to one or another of the four leaders in the undertaking: so well did these highly celebrated artists (each assuredly possessed of a very personal 'manner') succeed in disciplining their individual genius to the demands of the required collaboration! Team spirit in work and respect for the craft—these were the first qualities in a Greek sculptor.

Respect for craftsmanship precluded any unseasonable haste in performing the task. When it was a question of doing good work, time was not allowed to count. There are authentic documents from which we can appreciate the care taken by Greek artists in their work. We possess some parts of the accounts of the payments made to the sculptors of the frieze of the Erechtheum, on the Athenian Acropolis, towards the end of the fifth century. For one of the groups which have survived, consisting of two figures in very high relief, a young man crouching down and an older man standing, the artist received the sum of 120 drachmas, in other words, at a drachma a day, which was the average wage of a highly skilled workman, four months' salary: the group is barely three fifths of a metre high and the craftsman was supplied with the marble. From this we can judge the leisure and the minute care devoted to the work. The same attentive conscientiousness was shown in the execution of large bronze statues: detailed examination of the *Charioteer* of Delphi has revealed the extreme importance of the retouching done on the statue after the casting, to remove by hammering any surface defects due to air bubbles or scoria and to restore the high lights of the pattern by use of the cold-chisel.

In architecture we find the same solicitude for rigorous perfection: the columns of a Doric building were not fluted until after the drums had been put into position. Thus an exact correspondence was obtained between the delicate arrises of stone from top to bottom of the column. In the temple of Segesta, in Sicily, which dates from the end of the fifth century, unforeseen events interrupted the building before this phase of the work, and the columns have kept their smooth form. When a wall was particularly well finished, it was also resurfaced from top to bottom after the courses had been put into position. We are acquainted with the delicate technique employed in the construction of these walls: each block was fastened to the others by clamps of metal and the jointing surfaces were fitted without the least play, thanks to the care with which each was prepared with the chisel to fit exactly with its neighbour. This reaches such a point of perfection that in the case of a wall which has collapsed archaeologists can still assign each stone to its original place with almost complete certainty.

This conscientious attention to detail is no less apparent in the so-called minor arts, in which Greece excelled in the Archaic and Classical Ages. Engravers brought to perfection the art of intaglio-engraving, whether in hard stone for gems or in metal for coins. Their sharpness of vision and sureness of hand account for the truly monumental character of these diminutive masterpieces, which can be magnified one hundred times by photography without losing either the rightness of their proportions or the high lights of their relief, a test which few other works of art could undergo without detriment.

Recent investigations have made possible a better understanding of the complexity of a technique to which Greek art in the sixth and fifth centuries owes many of its most attractive products. German and Anglo-Saxon chemists and archaeologists, joining their efforts in a fine example of collaboration between different disciplines, have finally solved the mystery of the famous black 'varnish' which gives Attic vases their exceptional quality. In fact, there was no varnish at all: the thin black film was obtained by means of a simple colloidal solution of clay in water. This solution was prepared from extremely fine clay and it was allowed to evaporate until it had attained the consistency of a sort of thin jelly, of a dark brown colour, which was spread with a brush over the clay of the pot before firing. It was in the course of firing that this coating became black by a series of successive operations now well known. In the oven, first raised to a heat of about 800 degrees centigrade, oxidation took place with formation of ferric oxide, which gave the clay its red colour. Then began the second phase of the firing, with a chemical phenomenon of reduction: the potter partly or completely blocked up the ventilating flue and the temperature rose to about 945 degrees: under the influence of the carbon monoxide then produced in great quantities, the red ferric oxide changed into ferrous oxide or magnetic iron oxide, both black in colour; the presence of steam, produced by green wood in the fire or a bowl of liquid placed in the oven, facilitated the reaction. If the operation was arrested at this stage, the vases would be black all over, like Etruscan *bucchero*. But a third phase now began, with partial reoxidation and slight cooling from 945 degrees to about 875: the aperture of the gas outlet was opened and air was again allowed to enter the oven. Wherever the clay was porous, the ferrous oxide or magnetic oxide of iron absorbed oxygen and again became red ferric oxide, but this process did not operate for the parts of the vase covered with the coating. For this coating, because of the extreme fineness of the particles of which it was composed, had a dense consistency which did not allow the oxygen to penetrate again; so reoxidation did not take place and the coating remained black. When the firing was finished, the body of the vase was red, except in the places covered by the coating, which had retained a beautiful black lustre. Such a delicate operation, which the potters of the Ceramicus must have perfected empirically and progressively, always preserved a mysterious character in their eyes, even after they had learnt to perform it with success and with the surest touch. We can well understand that these 'artisans of fire' summoned to the aid of their labours the divine powers of Hephaestus and Athena, united by a joint cult in the temple, now wrongly called the Theseum, which overlooked their district.

It was in the art of statuary in gold and ivory, called *chryselephantine*, that the Greek taste for high technical virtuosity showed itself best. Worked out in the course of the Archaic Age, this now lost form of art reached its zenith in the colossi of Phidias: the Zeus of Olympia and the Athena Parthenos on the Acropolis. These immense statues reached a height of 12 metres. They consisted of a hollow shell braced with a timber framework. On the paved floor of the Parthenon we can still see the housing for the central beam which supported the framework of the statue of Athena Parthenos. The actual body of the statue was also of wood, resting on this frame and already sculptured in detail. The ivory and gold were then applied to this body, the ivory in thin sheets, stuck on while hot for the naked parts, the gold in leaves, decorated with repoussé work and then nailed on to the wood, for the clothes, hair, and accessories. Inlaid work of precious or semiprecious stones was used to enhance the lustre of the eyes or to enrich certain details of the attire. We can imagine what difficulties of every kind the artist met at every step in the course of such complicated work, which called for competence not only as a sculptor, but equally as a goldsmith and jeweller. In addition, once the statue was finished, it had to be maintained with extreme care to prevent the joinings from developing too much play, the various materials from coming loose or tarnishing, and rats and termites from attacking the timber. Suitable precautions were taken from the moment when the statue was set up in its place: the ground was moistened with water or oil to prevent the wood from drying. At Olympia, a family that claimed descent from Phidias was entrusted with the maintenance of the Zeus; in spite of this, restorations had to be undertaken, such as the one carried out by the sculptor Damophon in the second century B.C.

Technical prowess roused the admiration of the public in every domain: nothing won greater esteem for Greek painters than effects that tricked or deceived the eye and thus proved the skill of their brush. There was loud praise, for example, for the allegorical figure of *Drunkenness* (*Methe*), whom Pausias, in the fourth century, had represented in the form of a woman whose face showed through the large glass from which she was drinking: the rendering of this transparency filled connoisseurs with delight. It is a notable fact that at the same period the sculptors of Cyrene made a special point, in certain funerary statues, of rendering with impressive skill the appearance of a woman's face seen through a tenuous veil that half concealed it.

Thus we can see the Greek artist above all as a craftsman, a lover of beautiful work and trained by long practice in the traditions of the studio. Far from claiming to be an innovator, he was proud of having had a master and delighted in recalling him to mind: two sculptors of Argos, who, towards the end of the sixth century, inscribed their signatures in the sanctuary at Olympia, explicitly boasted of having learnt their art from their predecessors. When ancient historiographers come to mention an artist, they like to point out whose pupil he was: the notion of a school, to which modern archaeology sometimes attributes too great importance, comes partly from that. The artist's loyalty to the past reveals him as firmly rooted in his social milieu. A free worker surrounded by his fellow-citizens, a member of the middle class, that of the craftsmen and small property-owners, which was often the backbone of the city, he was eminently fitted to express the sentiments and aspirations of a society in which he found his place in the most natural way.

Art in the service of anthropomorphic religion. Idealization of the human models.
Simplification and sobriety
The first thing that this society asked of him was to meet its needs in the domain of sacred worship. An anthropomorphic religion, in which the cult was closely linked with the divine image, demanded much of the artist. His task was to give a concrete form to the mental image which his fellow-citizens formed of divine beings. He was thus led to study the human model, since the gods resemble men, and to endow it by the action of his art with the perfect beauty which alone seemed fitting for the gods. Naturalistic investigation and idealization were therefore two complementary, and not antagonistic, trends in Greek art. The former was expressed by an effort, constantly maintained from early Archaic times, to achieve anatomical truth and exactitude: in vase-painting and in sculpture we can follow with precision the progress made in drawing the eye, in rendering the surface of the belly, and in modelling the knee. But at the same time the artist shows himself anxious to fathom by an intellectual approach the secrets of the body which he is studying: he is persuaded that beauty resides in mathematical relationships, rational or irrational, whose laws our intelligence can discover. Hence comes the importance of the ideas of *rhythm* and *symmetry*, whose real content now eludes us, in default of precise definition, but classical texts assure us that these ideas served as aesthetic criteria and aroused the interest of artists themselves to the very highest degree.

With these preoccupations are connected the attempts to define a system of ideal proportions applicable to the human form. Such was the action of the sculptor Polycletus when he composed his work entitled *Canon* ('Rule') and illustrated it by making a statue in agreement with the system, a statue which was perhaps the famous *Doryphoros*, or 'Spear-bearer', copies of which survive. Athletic statuary, which Polycletus practised assiduously, offered a very favourable field for such researches. By portraying nude athletes, the sculptor was naturally led to exalt the human form in its perfection. Polycletus could express the emotion of sober admiration which the Greeks felt in the presence of manly beauty, in which physical strength and self-mastery are combined. The sculptural ideal thus defined was in harmony with the aspirations of a society for which human standards applied to all things and in whose eyes man never reached self-fulfilment better than in the intelligent discipline of the stadium. This ideal, steeped in intellectuality, always remained closely linked with reality, which it adorned and sublimated by subjecting it to the law of numbers.

Does this mean that this perfection of form entirely satisfied the Greeks? Much as they admired it, they were fully aware of its limits: the Latin rhetor Quintilian, who wrote in the first century A.D. but who was influenced by earlier Greek authors, said in this connection: 'Even if Polycletus could give the human form a supernatural beauty, he does not seem to have completely rendered divine majesty.' This judgment takes on its full sense when we compare it with the same critic's verdict on Phidias, who, according to him, 'in a sense enriched the traditional religion'. Starting from the human model, which each of these artists took as his point of departure, one of them arrived at a rigorous perfection of form, which nevertheless seems a little cold and, as it were, 'disincarnate', while the other raised man above his condition by giving him a direct apprehension of supernatural grandeur. Thus the anthropomorphic image sometimes expresses the humanistic ideal, sometimes divine transcendence. Herein lies all the richness of Hellenism.

Even though the cult statue was the sculptor's major work, as the temple was the architect's, artists were also attracted by other tasks, to which they devoted themselves with ardour and conscientiousness. The decoration of consecrated buildings, of funeral monuments and of furniture connected with cults claimed their labour and, within the limits of the programme drawn up by the responsible authority, roused their imagination. The rich treasures of ancestral mythology provided them with ample material, which they also used for secular works.

Addressing a public to which the myths were familiar, they had no need to be prolix: some characteristic features or, failing these, an inscription sufficed to denote a character. Sure of being understood by reason of this preliminary understanding with his public, the artist could go straight to the essentials. This accounts for the exclusion of everything unessential in Greek works, in which each detail counts and whose vigour of expression lies in their restraint. Two pairs of warriors suggest a battle in front of Troy, just as an apple in the hand of Heracles recalls the whole episode of the Hesperides, or a lopped tree-trunk represents a forest. This intelligent people could catch the slightest hint: it fully appreciated an art rich in allusions and symbols, which constantly demanded the active participation of the spectator, implied much with great economy of means, and made great use of metonymy and litotes. This art subsisted on daily observation, but it aspired to express what is lasting. It accepted violence, but rejected gesticulation. If it had a wonderful aptitude for story-telling, it found still more satisfaction in seizing the permanent essence of a being: nothing can better express Classical Greece than an isolated figure, sitting or standing, nude or clothed, man or woman, who meditates, or dreams or, better still, unstirred by any particular thought or action, lives for eternity a life that is calm, free from all distractions, and utterly master of itself. Without despising anecdote, of which the vase-painters were able to make excellent use, Classical Greek art usually aimed higher. It was certainly an excited and colourful art: let us not forget that all the marble statues were painted, in order to sharpen the impression of a living presence. But while arousing the senses, it addressed itself to the spirit and, over and beyond the delight given to the senses, its aim was to satisfy the spirit.

The personality of the artists. Signatures. Itinerant artists. The unity of Hellenism
In the service of an individual or a city in whose eyes 'man is the measure of all things' the Greek craftsman acquired and developed the feeling of his own individuality. Greek art was the first to throw full light upon the personality of the artist. From the very earliest times, legend clung to the fascinating name of Daedalus, the ancestor and patron of sculptors, from whom Socrates jokingly boasted that he was descended. Another legendary artist, Epeus, was supposed to have been the builder of the Trojan horse. Works of each were still displayed in Classical times. Starting from these illustrious ancestors, the line of sculptors is uninterrupted: towards the end of the seventh century, the Cretans Dipoenus

and Scyllis proclaimed themselves as 'Daedalids', as did also their pupils Tectaeus and Angelion, the creators of the colossal Apollo of Delos, seen and sung of by Callimachus. It was in Greece that sculptors adopted the habit of signing their works: their surviving signatures are so numerous that they have been gathered together in special collections, which have become an essential source for the history of art. Their evidence supplements or confirms that of Pausanias, who carefully took down the names of the famous artists whose statues were shown to him. The custom spread from the sculptors to the potters: in the course of the sixth century, Attic ceramists began to sign their finest vases, sometimes as painters, sometimes as potters. Here again the records are so numerous that they provide archaeologists with a solid foundation for chronological and stylistic classification. To define with precision what was the 'manner' of the chief artists was always the ambition of critics: the fact that this effort has proved particularly successful in painted pottery, whose painters were lowly craftsmen, shows how greatly Hellenistic society favoured the blossoming of individual talent.

Is this tantamount to saying that we are succeeding in easily identifying these talents in every sphere? Unfortunately this is not the case. Thus, in the case of sculpture, the surviving works are mostly anonymous and the signatures found usually appear on empty pedestals, while literary texts have handed down to us some pieces of information about the great masters. Every attempt is being made to put the pieces of the puzzle together, but the lacunas remain immense and the results uncertain. As for great painting, on which glory was shed in the fifth century by the names of Polygnotus and Parrhasius, and in the fourth century, before Alexander, by those of Zeuxis, Euphranor, and Pausias, it has vanished more completely still: the remote and imperfect imitations of it that we fancy we see in frescos or mosaics of Roman times make us bitterly regret that an art so brilliant, so unanimously admired by the ancients, has disappeared without leaving us a single genuine work. As compensation, chance has given us a number of intaglios and signed coins; they prove that the engravers, like the potters, were proud of their technical brilliance and sometimes desired to perpetuate the paternity of their works. In fact, Euaenetus, Cimon, and Euclidas, to whom we owe the beautiful Syracusan coins from the latter part of the fifth century and the early part of the fourth, were in no way inferior to the best sculptors of their time.

The wide reputation won by certain artists gained them commissions far beyond the limits of their native city or even of the region. This is a fact well established as early as the Archaic Age: in the sixth century Sparta enlisted the services of Theodorus, an architect from Samos, and of the sculptor Bathyclus, of Magnesia, both Ionians. A little later Miletus, itself an Ionian city, asked a Sicyonian, Canachus, to carve the cult statue for its temple of Apollo. The Dorian city of Cyrene greatly appreciated Attic art. The tyrants of Syracuse had their offerings made by the most varied artists. The Panhellenic sanctuaries, Delphi and Olympia, attracted sculptors from all over Greece in search of profitable work and fulfilled the rôle of permanent art exhibitions. The creations of the minor arts, bronzes, gold and silver work, terracottas, vases, and tapestries circulated from one end of the Greek world to the other, promoting the diffusion of styles and their influence on one another. It is understandable that under these conditions the originality of local schools is difficult to define: it was often swept away by the general evolution of style, which almost everywhere proceeded at the same pace, and by the personal influence of the great masters, which was often exerted through chance meetings. In short, it is the general interest in art that strikes us, rather than the individual tastes of this or that city. The widely spreading reputation of certain centres, especially Athens, was certainly a determining factor in the formation of common standards of taste. But it is remarkable that the diffusion of these standards was so rapid and effective: masterpieces comparable to the best works in Greece proper have been found in places as remote as Cyrene, Selinus, and Posidonia–Paestum. In the domain of art, as in that of literature, the Hellenic world had early become aware of its unity in spite of its political divisions.

CONCLUSION

I
T is to be hoped that the foregoing pages have at least given an impression of the richness and complexity of a civilization whose lineaments often tend to be excessively simplified in our recollection. Just as the Greek world cannot be reduced to the single city of Athens, so the history of Greece cannot be reduced to the Age of Pericles, an 'age' which lasted no longer than thirty years. It is a long and varied journey in time from the Mycenaean poets, Homer's predecessors, to Plato and Demosthenes, from Daedalus, the mythical ancestor of sculptors, to Praxiteles and Scopas, from the Attic potters of the thirteenth century to those of the 'Kerch style': ten centuries of effort and experiment, exploration and fighting, rivalry and emulation. During these ten centuries a small nation, at once one people and many, managed, in spite of frequent internal discord and threats from outside, patiently to create a new, original, and complete culture, in which the main aspects of human life all received their due place: religious faith and confidence in man, a sense of the mystery of the universe and a desire to understand nature, the idea of social hierarchy and that of equality, respect for the social group and interest in the individual. It is no cause for surprise that these opposing demands aroused incessant conflicts both in men's minds and in states. But these very conflicts were at times productive of progress.

Here we rediscover Heraclitus's reflection on *War, the parent of all things*. In the intellectual sphere, as in that of human relationships, the Greece of Archaic and Classical times perfectly illustrates the observation of a modern poet: 'those who live are those who strive.' In the eyes of the Greeks, the major quality of man was not, indeed, intelligence, with which they were so richly blessed, but courage, whose name in their language, *arete*, like *virtus* in Latin, came to assume the general meaning 'virtue'. Their favourite heroes were Achilles, the most valiant of men, and Ulysses, whose resourceful spirit would have been of no value without his fearless heart. In fiction as in life the Greeks put nothing above steadfastness of soul: witness Aeschylus's Prometheus and Sophocles' Antigone, Leonidas and Phocion, Socrates and Demosthenes. In this sense the Greece of Plutarch, in spite of his moralizing tone, corresponds better to historical reality than is sometimes thought. What Herodotus writes in the prologue to his *History* is something that all his contemporaries thought no less than he: 'The wonderful exploits accomplished by Greeks and Barbarians must not be allowed to vanish in oblivion.' No doubt he included the masterpieces of art or technique among these exploits. But he put a higher value on the virtues of the warrior and the political leader, who do not, like the artist, contend only with matter, but with men. So when Renan, in his *Prayer on the Acropolis*, arrogantly writes: 'Then they will go to Sparta to curse that mistress of sombre errors and insult her because she is no more', he seriously misappreciates the ancient spirit: for the Greeks of old the memory of a noble example did not need to be perpetuated in a monument in order to survive, and the renown of lofty virtue, handed down from generation to generation in the verses of Simonides or Tyrtaeus, easily defied the centuries. Athena, the Warrior-maid, had a bronze temple at Lacedaemon: she would not have understood anyone despising Sparta and her soldiers.

Let us then beware of carrying our own prejudices and imaginings into the remote past. The French scholars who, when telling the story of the Peloponnesian War, allow themselves to be carried away by their sympathy for Athens, which they mistakenly equate with modern democracies, are no less at fault than the German scholars of the Third Reich who revered Sparta as the prototype of fascism. Other times, other ways. Here Renan would justly remind us that 'genuine admiration is historical'. Nevertheless, even if societies change, man remains himself. That is why the lesson we learn from Greece is not so much a political as a moral lesson: a lesson in modesty and clear-headedness that puts man in his right place, as a creature fitted to understand much, but also wise enough to accept ignorance: loving life, but knowing how precarious it is; using his intelligence with delight, without forgetting that the future lies with the gods, those gods conceived in his image and through whom the human standard, in its ideal form, provides the universe with its supreme scale of reference. This Greek experienced human passions. He knew that nothing is obtained without struggle. But, conscious of his own weakness, he did not despise his adversary. While the monarchs of the East had themselves represented in their reliefs as crushing prostrate and trembling hordes beneath their chariots, Greek art recalls the great exploits of history or epic as combats between well-matched opponents, whether Centaurs and Lapiths, Greeks and Trojans, or Athenians and Amazons. The enemy is not always worsted, and his defeat, when it comes, does not deprive him of his claim to pity. It is no accident that the Trojans Priam, Hector, and Andromache are the most moving figures in the *Iliad*. The tale was told that Achilles became enamoured of the Amazon Penthesilea at the very moment when he was dealing her a death-blow on the battlefield. The anecdote, which is illustrated on a beautiful Attic red-figured vase, is full of meaning: the most valiant is only a plaything in the hands of Destiny.

The word *humanism* is often used to define Greek thought, and the famous chorus of the Theban elders in Sophocles' *Antigone* is very appositely quoted: 'The world is full of wonders, but there is none more wonderful than man.' Let us, however, recall that, for his humanism, man is a starting-point and a necessary standard of measurement, not a limit or an end in himself. But all speculation that is too general remains somewhat ineffectual: the legacy of Greece in the Archaic and Classical Ages is better appreciated by direct contact with the works themselves. These are rich and beautiful enough for each of us, by turning to them himself, to find in them not only the eternal features of man, but also that portion of the heritage which suits each best.

BIBLIOGRAPHY

The information given below is strictly selective. It is confined to basic works and those indicating existing problems and the present state of knowledge. For the reader's convenience, the order of the several chapters of the book is followed.

I. MYCENAEAN CIVILIZATION

The decipherment of *Linear B* was a decisive turning-point in the study of this civilization. It was brought to the attention of scholars in an article by M. Ventris and J. Chadwick, 'Evidence for Greek Dialect in the Mycenaean Archives', *Journal of Hellenic Studies*, 73, 1953, pp. 84–105. See also J. Chadwick, *The Decipherment of Linear B*, Cambridge and New York, 1958. The essential texts are collected in: M. Ventris and J. Chadwick, *Documents in Mycenaean Greek*, Cambridge, 1956. Other collections have followed and study is still in progress. As an example of research on the language, may be cited: M. Lejeune, *Mémoires de philologie mycénienne*, Paris, 1958.

Concerning the Cnossos tablets, usually ascribed to the fifteenth century, a different opinion has been maintained by L. R. Palmer, 'Mycenaeans and Minoans', London, 1963 (Second Revised edn., 1965), who places them in the twelfth century.

For the main sites, one may consult:
1. General: S. Marinatos and M. Hirmer, *Crete and Mycenae*, London, 1960 (excellently illustrated with photographs); F. Matz, *Kreta, Mykene, Troja*, Stuttgart, 1956.
2. Mycenae: A. J. B. Wace, *Mycenae*, Princeton, 1949; G. E. Mylonas, *Ancient Mycenae*, London, 1957.

3. Tiryns: G. Karo, *Führer durch Tiryns*, Athens, 1934, and the excavation reports, *Tiryns*, 4 vols., 1912 ff.

4. Pylos: Reports by C. Blegen, *American Journal of Archaeology*, 43, 1939, pp. 557 ff., and annually in this periodical since 1953.

5. Troy: C. Blegen and his collaborators, *Troy*, 4 vols., Princeton, 1950–1958.

On Mycenaean ceramics, the essential works are: A. Furumark, *The Chronology of Mycenae*, Stockholm, 1941, and *The Mycenaean Pottery: Analysis and Classification*. A special study of Attic pottery is: F. J. Stubbings, 'Mycenaean Pottery of Athens', *Annual of the British School at Athens*, 42, 1947, pp. 1 ff.

II. GEOMETRIC CIVILIZATION

Much has recently been published on the Homeric problem, brought into relation both with Geometric civilization (contemporary with the poet) and with Mycenaean civilization (with which he deals retrospectively). One may consult:

1. In English: H. L. Lorimer, *Homer and the Monuments*, London, 1950; M. I. Finley, *The World of Odysseus*, London, 1956; T. B. L. Webster, *From Homer to Mycenae*, London, 1958; D. Page, *History and the Homeric Iliad*, Berkeley, 1960; G. S. Kirk, *The Songs of Homer*, Cambridge, 1962. There is also a work by several authors, edited by A. J. B. Wace and F. J. Stubbings, *A Companion to Homer*, London, 1963 (general discussions on the various aspects of the problem, useful, but sometimes debatable).

On Geometric pottery, one may consult the general works on pottery mentioned in connection with Ch. IX, adding V. R. d'A. Desborough, *Protogeometric Pottery*, Oxford, 1952.

2. In French: A. Severyns, *Homère*, I, 'Le cadre humain'. II, 'Le poète et son oeuvre'. III, 'L'artiste', Brussels, 1943–1948; F. Robert, *Homère*, Paris, 1950.

3. In German: W. Schadewaldt, *Von Homers Welt und Werk*, 3rd edn., Stuttgart, 1959; R. Hampe, *Die Gleichnisse Homers und die Bildniskunst seiner Zeit*, Tübingen, 1952.

III & IV. THE ARCHAIC AND CLASSICAL AGES

For the history of this period, one should first turn to the text of the great Greek historians, Herodotus, Thucydides and Xenophon, and also to the 'minor' historians (for the latter, see the old, but still useful edition by C. Muller, *Fragmenta Historicorum Graecorum*, Paris, 1841–1870, with a Latin translation, and the recent edition by F. Jacoby, Berlin and subsequently Leyden, in process of publication since 1923, with a commentary in German).

General historical accounts:

1. In English: in the *Cambridge Ancient History*, one may specially consult vols. IV, V and VI, 4th edn. 1953. A recent synthetical presentation is: N. G. L. Hammond, *A History of Greece to 322 B.C.*, Oxford, 1959. Also J. B. Bury, *History of Greece*, 3rd edn., revised by R. Meiggs, London, 1952.

2. In French: F. Charpoutier and A. Aymard in P. Jouguet and collaborators, *Les premières civilisations*, Paris, 1950 (chapters relating to Greece); P. Roussel and P. Cloché, *La Grèce et l'Orient, des guerres médiques à la conquête romaine*, Paris, 1938; G. Glotz and R. Cohen, *Histoire grecque*, I. 'Des origines aux guerres médiques', II. 'La Grèce au Ve siècle', III. 'La Grèce au IVe siècle: la lutte pour l'hégémonie', Paris, 1929–1936 (a detailed but somewhat obsolete work); J. Hatzfeld, *Histoire de la Grèce ancienne*, 3rd edn. revised by A. Aymard, Paris, 1962.

3. In German: H. Bengston, *Griechische Geschichte*, Munich, 1950 (an excellent handbook, critical and remarkably well informed).

There is a useful bibliography in H. Bengston, *Einführung in die alte Geschichte*, Munich, 2nd edn., 1953, and E. Manni *Introduzione allo studio della storia greca e romana*, Palermo, 2nd edn., 1952; there are good maps in H. Bengston and V. Milojcic, *Grosser Historischer Weltatlas*, I, 'Vorgeschichte und Altertum', Munich, 1953.

On colonization, there is a general account in J. Bérard, *L'expansion et la colonisation grecques jusqu' aux guerres médiques*, Paris, 1960; see also C. Roebuck, *Ionian Trade and Colonization*, New York, 1959, and A. J. Graham, *Colony and Mother City*, Manchester, 1964. On the Archaic Age: A. R. Burn, *The Lyric Age of Greece*, London, 1960; T. J. Dunbabin, *The Greeks and their Eastern Neighbours*, London, 1957, and *The Western Greeks*, Oxford, 1948.

V. WAR

The problems of tactics and armament have hardly been treated in a general way since J. Kromayer and G. Veith, *Heerwesen und Kriegführung der Griechen und Römer*, Munich, 1928, and P. Couissin, *Les institutions militaires et navales de la Grèce*, Paris, 1932. On mercenaries: H. W. Parke, *Greek Mercenary Soldiers from the Earliest Times to the Battle of Ipsos*, Oxford, 1933. On the cavalry, see J. K. Anderson, *Ancient Greek Horsemanship*, Berkeley, 1961. On fortifications, see the bibliographical information in R. Martin, *Urbanisme*, etc., pp. 190–203, and R. E. Wycherley, *How the Greeks built Cities* (works listed under Ch. VII), and A. Aymard, 'Remarques sur la poliorcétique grecque', in 'Etudes d'archéologie classique', II, *Annales de l'Est*, mémoire no. 22, Paris, 1959, pp. 1–15. In the same collection, pp. 16–27, the same author has published a study on 'Mercenariat et histoire grecque', which has been drawn upon in the present work.

On naval forces, see L. Casson, *The Ancient Mariners*, London, 1959, and A. Koster, *Das antike Seewesen*, Berlin, 1923.

On the *Skeuotheke* of Philo, at the Piraeus, see W. B. Dinsmoor, *Architecture*, etc. (cited under Ch. IX), pp. 241 ff.

On the laws of war, see F. Kiechle, 'Zur Humanität in der Kriegführung der griechischen Staaten', in *Historia*, 7, 1958, pp. 129–156.

VI. RELIGION

The *Periegesis* of Pausanias can conveniently be consulted in two English translations: J. G. Frazer, London, 1897 ff., 6 vols. with a full commentary; W. H. S. Jones, London, 1918–1935, 5 vols. (*Loeb Classical Library*), text and translation (vol. V, by R. E. Wycherley, was re-edited with additions in 1955; it consists entirely of archaeological commentary with illustrations). There is also a German translation: E. Meyer, *Pausanias, Beschreibung Greichenlands*, Zurich, 1955 (without the historical digressions).

General accounts of Greek religion:

1. In English: J. Harrison, *Prolegomena to the Study of Greek Religion*, London, 1903 (ethnological point of view); L. R. Farnell, *Cults of the Greek States*, 5 vols., London, 1896–1909.

2. In French: E. des Places, in M. Brillant and R. Aigrain, *Histoire des religions*, III, Paris, 1955, pp. 159–291 (an account mainly based on literary sources and almost entirely concerned with the religious thought of writers and philosophers); A.-J. Festugière, in Gorce and Mortier, *Histoire générale des religions*, *Grèce-Rome*, Paris, 1944 (a subtle, profound and suggestive analysis, largely based on the witness of Pausanias and that of inscriptions and archaeological monuments); L. Gernet and A. Boulanger, *Le génie grec dans la religion*, Paris, 1932 (essentially sociological approach).

3. In German: M. P. Nilsson, *Geschichte der griechischen Religion*, I, 1941 (2nd edn. 1955); II, 1950, Munich. This is the basic handbook for any study of Greek religion. Vol. II deals with religion in the Hellenistic and Roman ages, but it also contains valuable information on the earlier period.

On mythology, one may consult P. Grimal's *Dictionnaire de la mythologie grecque et romaine*, Paris, 1951 (very handy to use: provides the main references to ancient texts); the enormous *Ausführliches Lexicon der griechischen und römischen Mythologie* by W. H. Roscher, Leipzig, 1884–1937; or H. J. Rose's *Handbook of Greek Mythology*, London, 1928 (several times re-edited, lastly in 1958). Numerous articles on mythology in the *Real-Encyclopädie der klassischen Altertumswissenschaft* (see below).

On the cults: P. Stengel, *Die griechischen Kultusaltertümer*, 3rd edn., Munich, 1920, and *Opferbraüche der Griechen*, 1910; L. R. Farnell, *Greek Hero Cults*, London, 1921.

Collections of sacred laws: I. von Prott and L. Ziehen, *Leges sacrae*, 1896–1906 ¡F. Sokolowski, *Loies sacrées de l'Asie Mineure*, Paris, 1955, and *Lois sacrées des citées grecques*, Paris, 1962.

On the cult of the dead: K. Friis Johansen, *The Attic Grave-Reliefs of the Classical Period, an Essay in Interpretation*, Copenhagen, 1951. On the Eleusinian mysteries: G. E. Mylonas, *Eleusis and the Eleusinian Mysteries*, Princeton, 1961. On Theogenes of Thasos: J. Pouilloux, *Recherches sur l'histoire et les cultes de Thasos*, I, Paris, 1954, pp. 62 ff. (with the reservations expressed in *Revue des études grecques*, 72, 1959, pp. 359–361). The Pharsalus tablet inscribed with an Orphic text was published by N. M. Verdelis, *Archaiologike Ephemeris*, 1950–1951, p. 99.

On the oracles: R. Flacelière's little volume, *Devins et oracles grecs*, Paris, 1961, provides an excellent initiation. See also M. Delcourt, *L'oracle de Delphes*, Paris, 1955; H. W. Parke and D. E. W. Wormell, *The Delphic Oracle*, 2 vols., Oxford, 1956; P. Amandry, *La mantique apollinienne à Delphes*, Paris, 1950. A general account of the sanctuary at Delphi with excellent photographs: P. de la Coste-Messclière and G. de Miré, *Delphes*, 2nd edn., Paris, 1957.

VII. THE CITY-STATE

An excellent introduction is provided by V. Ehrenberg, *The Greek State*, Oxford, 1960. G. Glotz's work, *La Cité grecque*, re-edited by P. Cloché, Paris, 1953, is both systematic and confused. There is abundant documentation on institutions in G. Busolt and H. Swoboda, *Greichische Staatskunde*, 3rd edn., 2 vols., Munich, 1920–1926 An introduction to the epigraphic sources can be found in A. G. Woodhead, *The Study of Greek Inscriptions*, Cambridge, 1959; G. Klaffenbach, *Griechische Epigraphik*, Göttingen, 1957; J. Pouilloux, *Choix d'inscriptions grecques*, Paris, 1960; L. Robert, L'épigraphie', in *Encyclopédie de la Pléiade, L'histoire et ses méthodes*, pp. 453–497, Paris, 1961.

Character of the Greek city: E. Kirsten, *Die griechische Polis als historisch-geographisches Problem des Mittelmeerraumes*, Bonn, 1956; C. B. Welles, 'The Greek City', in *Studi in onore di A. Calderini e R. Paribeni*, I, Milan, 1956, pp. 81–99.

On the economy of the Greek world: F. M. Heichelheim, *Wirtschaftsgeschichte des Altertums*, 2 vols., Leyden, 1938. The first volume (to the middle of the sixth century) has been re-edited in an English translation: *An Ancient Economic History*, I, Leyden, 1958, with bibliographical additions.

On slavery: W. L. Westermann, *The Slave Systems of Greek and Roman Antiquity*, Philadelphia, 1955.

On town planning: R. E. Wycherley, *How the Greeks built Cities*, 2nd edn., London, 1962; R. Martin, *L'urbanisme dans la Grèce antique*, Paris, 1956.

On education: H. I. Marrou, *History of Education in Antiquity* (translated by G. Lamb), London, 1956; W. Jaeger, *Paideia, the Ideals of Greek Culture*, Oxford, I, 1936; II, 1944; III, 1945. On everyday life: R. Flacelière, *La vie quotidienne en Grèce au siècle de Périclès*, Paris, 1959; Ch. Picard, *La vie privée dans la Grèce classique*, Paris, 1930.

On Greek coins: C. Seltman, *Greek Coins*, 2nd edn., London, 1955; B. V. Head, *Historia Numorum*, 2nd edn., Oxford, 1911.

On the size of cargo vessels: L. Casson, in *Studi in onore di A. Calderini e R. Paribeni*, I, Milan, 1956, pp. 231–238.

On the relations between city-states: V. Martin, *La vie internationale dans la Grèce des cités* (sixth-fourth centuries), Geneva, 1940.

On athletics: H. A. Harris, *Greek Athletics and Athletes*, London, 1964.

VIII. PHILOSOPHY AND LITERATURE

Introduction to Greek literature: H. J. Rose, *Handbook of Greek Literature*, 4th edn., London, 1950; R. Flacelière, *Histoire littéraire de la Grèce*, Paris, 1962. The best informed recent handbook is A. Lesky's *Geschichte der griechischen Literatur*, Berne, 1958 (an English edition is in course of preparation). For additional bibliographical information, one may consult M. Platnauer (and collaborators), *Fifty Years of Classical Scholarship*, Oxford, 1954. On the portraits of Greek writers and philosophers: K. Schefold, *Die Bildnisse der antiken Dichter, Redner und Denker*, Basle, 1943.

For philosophical thought, in addition to Jaeger's work referred to under Ch. VII, the following may be consulted: C. J. de Vogel, *Greek Philosophy, a Collection of Texts Selected and Supplied with some Notes and Explanations*, I, 'Thales to Plato', 1963; W. K. C. Guthrie, *A History of Greek Philosophy*, I, 'The earlier Presocratics and the Pythagoreans', Cambridge, 1962; A. Rivaud, *Histoire de la Philosophie*, I, 'Des origines à la Scholastique', Paris, 1948; P. M. Schuhl, *Essai sur la formation de la pensée grecque*, 2nd edn., Paris, 1949.

On the sciences, see P. H. Michel and J. Beaujeu, in R. Taton, *Histoire générale des sciences*, I, 'La science antique et médiévale', Paris, 1957, and M. Clagett, *Greek Science in Antiquity*, London, 1957.

IX. ART

There is a brief synthetical account of Greek art from the sixth to the fourth centuries by the author of the present work in R. Huyghe, *L'art et l'homme*, I, Paris, 1957, pp. 251–298. On the 'Mourning Athena', see *Bulletin de correspondance hellénique*, 81, 1957, pp. 141–159. On the 'Hermes of Marathon', see *Etudes d'archéologie classique*, II, *Annales de l'Est, mémoire no. 22*, Paris, 1959, pp. 38 ff. On the technique of Attic

Ceramics, see C. P. T. Naudé, *Acta classica*, II, Capetown, 1959, pp. 106–116 and J. V. Noble, *American Journal of Archaeology*, 64, 1960, pp. 307–318. Also M. Bimson, 'The Technique of Greek Black and *Terra Sigillata* Red', *Antiquaries Journal*, 36, 1956, pp. 200–204.

General works on Greek art are innumerable. A useful initiation to the subject can be found in G. M. A. Richter, *A Handbook of Greek Art*, London, 1959. A recent and brilliant synthesis: G. Hafner, *Geschichte der griechischen Kunst*, Zurich, 1961. On Archaic art: G. M. A. Richter *Archaic Greek Art*, New York, 1949. On the great period of classical art: P. Devambez, *L'art au siècle de Périclès*, Lausanne, 1955.

On architecture, the basic handbooks are: D. S. Robertson, *A Handbook of Greek and Roman Architecture*, 2nd edn., Cambridge, 1945; W. B. Dinsmoor, *The Architecture of Ancient Greece*, London, 1950; A. W. Lawrence, *Greek Architecture*, London, 1957.

On sculpture: Ch. Picard, *Manuel d' archéologie grecque: la sculpture*, 7 vols., Paris, 1935–1963 (a very detailed treatise, from the beginning down to the fourth century); G. Lippold, 'Die griechische Plastik' (in *Handbuch der Archäologie*), Munich, 1950; G. M. A. Richter, *The Sculpture and Sculptors of the Greeks*, 3rd edn., Yale, 1950. The books by J. Charbonneaux, *La sculpture grecque archaïque* and *La sculpture grecque classique*, 3 vols., Paris, 1945–1946, provide very suggestive reading.

On painting and ceramics: M. Robertson, *Greek Painting*, Geneva, 1959. There is an excellent introduction to ceramics in F. Villard, *Les vases grecs*, Paris, 1956. The basic manual is A. Rumpf, 'Malerei und Zeichnung' (in *Handbuch der Archäologie*), Munich, 1953. See also R. M. Cook, *Greek Painted Pottery*, London, 1960. On numismatics, one may refer to the work of C. Seltman quoted under Ch. VII. For glyptics, consult G. M. A. Richter, *Metropolitan Museum of Art, New York, Catalogue of Engraved Gems, Greek, Etruscan and Roman*, Rome, 1956, pp. xv ff.; also, *A Guide to the Principal Coins of the Greeks*, (British Museum), London, 1932.

X. GENERAL WORKS

Readers anxious to acquire somewhat more detailed knowledge of the main Greek sites will find introductory guidance in: M. Cary, *The Geographic Background of Greek and Roman History*, Oxford, 1949; P. Lévèque, *Nous partons pour la Grèce*, Paris, 1961; Guides to Greece, in various languages; Guides to American and other excavations; E. Kirsten and W. Kraiker, *Griechenlandkunde*, Heidelberg, 1956. There are also many useful and enjoyable illustrated books in English for the general reader, e.g. *Introducing Greece*, edited by Francis King, London, 1956; *Greece*, by J. and G. Roux, translated by L. and M. Kochan, London, 1958; *Athens*, by A. Procopiou (with fine photographs by E. Smith), London, 1964.

Special mention should be made of two recent general discussions of Greek civilization: A. J. Toynbee, *Hellenism, the History of a Civilization*, London, 1959, and A. Aymard, in *Histoire générale des civilisations*, I, 'L'Orient et la Grèce antique', Paris, 1953, pp. 256–283 (chapters on Archaic and Classical Greece).

There are two great encyclopaedias which provide an inexhaustible mine of information on classical antiquity: C. Daremberg, E. Saglio and E. Pottier, *Dictionnaire des antiquités grecques et romaines*, 5 vols. and index in 10 vols., Paris, 1877–1919 (for institutions and for terms relating to private and public life, it provides a very full documentation, deeply based on the study of literary texts); *Real-Encyclopädie der klassichen Altertumswissenschaft*, by Pauly, Wissowa, Kroll and collaborators, Stuttgart, in progress since 1893 (about 70 vols. vastly rich in information; certain articles are long dissertations; equally informative on persons, historical facts and monuments). English readers will find a much less ambitious work, in one volume, very useful: *The Oxford Classical Dictionary*, Oxford, 1949. Plans are in hand for a revised edition.

INDEX